A Modernist in Exile
The International Reception of H. G. Adler (1910-1988)

LEGENDA

LEGENDA is the Modern Humanities Research Association's book imprint for new research in the Humanities. Founded in 1995 by Malcolm Bowie and others within the University of Oxford, Legenda has always been a collaborative publishing enterprise, directly governed by scholars. The Modern Humanities Research Association (MHRA) joined this collaboration in 1998, became half-owner in 2004, in partnership with Maney Publishing and then Routledge, and has since 2016 been sole owner. Titles range from medieval texts to contemporary cinema and form a widely comparative view of the modern humanities, including works on Arabic, Catalan, English, French, German, Greek, Italian, Portuguese, Russian, Spanish, and Yiddish literature. Editorial boards and committees of more than 60 leading academic specialists work in collaboration with bodies such as the Society for French Studies, the British Comparative Literature Association and the Association of Hispanists of Great Britain & Ireland.

The MHRA encourages and promotes advanced study and research in the field of the modern humanities, especially modern European languages and literature, including English, and also cinema. It aims to break down the barriers between scholars working in different disciplines and to maintain the unity of humanistic scholarship. The Association fulfils this purpose through the publication of journals, bibliographies, monographs, critical editions, and the MHRA Style Guide, and by making grants in support of research. Membership is open to all who work in the Humanities, whether independent or in a University post, and the participation of younger colleagues entering the field is especially welcomed.

STUDIES IN COMPARATIVE LITERATURE

Studies in Comparative Literature are produced in close collaboration with the British Comparative Literature Association, and range widely across comparative and theoretical topics in literary and translation studies, accommodating research at the interface between different artistic media and between the humanities and the sciences.

ALSO PUBLISHED IN THIS SERIES

A Modernist in Exile

The International Reception of
H. G. Adler (1910-1988)

❖

EDITED BY LYNN L. WOLFF

l

LEGENDA

Studies in Comparative Literature 42
Modern Humanities Research Association
2019

Published by Legenda
an imprint of the Modern Humanities Research Association
Salisbury House, Station Road, Cambridge CB1 2LA

ISBN 978-1-78188-871-1 (HB)
ISBN 978-1-78188-872-8 (PB)

First published 2019
Paperback edition 2021

Copy-Editor: Dr Birgit Mikus

CONTENTS

❖

NOTES ON THE CONTRIBUTORS

❖

Jeremy Adler is Emeritus Professor and Senior Research Fellow of King's College London. Before being granted the established chair in German at King's College, he was a lecturer in German at Westfield College of the University of London and was awarded a personal chair at Queen Mary and Westfield College. He has written books on Goethe and Kafka and edited the works of August Stramm, Franz Baermann Steiner, and Elias Canetti. In addition to the publications *Literatur und Anthropologie: H. G. Adler, Elias Canetti und Franz Baermann Steiner in London* (with Gesa Dane; Wallstein, 2014), and *Das bittere Brot: H. G. Adler, Elias Canetti und Franz Baermann Steiner im Londoner Exil* (Wallstein, 2015), he has edited some seven books by H. G. Adler. He is a member of the German Academy of Language and Literature.

Christopher R. Browning is Frank Porter Graham Professor Emeritus of History at the University of North Carolina, Chapel Hill. His research focuses on Nazi Germany and the Holocaust. He has written extensively about three issues: first, Nazi decision- and policy-making in regard to the origins of the Final Solution; second, the behaviour and motives of various middle- and lower-echelon personnel involved in implementing Nazi Jewish policy; and thirdly, the use of survivor testimony to explore Jewish responses and survival strategies. His major publications include *Remembering Survival: Inside a Nazi Slave Labor Camp* (W. W. Norton & Co., 2010), *The Origins of the Final Solution: The Evolution of Nazi Jewish Policy, September 1939–March 1942* (University of Nebraska Press, 2004), *Nazi Policy, Jewish Workers, German Killers* (Cambridge University Press, 2000), *Ordinary Men: Reserve Police Battalion 101 and the Final Solution in Poland* (HarperCollins, 1992), *The Final Solution and the German Foreign Office* (Holmes & Meier, 1978).

Julia Creet is Professor of English, York University, Toronto. On the cusp of history and literature, she teaches memory studies, literary nonfiction and satire. She is the co-editor (with Andreas Kitzmann) of *Memory and Migration–Multi-disciplinary Approaches to Memory Studies* (University of Toronto Press, 2011) and co-editor (with Sara Horowitz and Amira Dan) of *H. G. Adler: Life, Literature, Legacy* (Northwestern University Press, 2016), winner of the Jewish Thought and Culture Award from the Canadian Jewish Literary Awards. She is also the director and producer of 'MUM: A Story of Silence' (38 min, 2008), a documentary about a Holocaust survivor who tried to forget and 'Data Mining the Deceased' (56 min, 2017), a documentary about the industry of family history. *The Genealogical Sublime*, a book about the development of contemporary genealogy, will be published by the University of Massachusetts Press in 2019.

Peter Filkins is the translator of three novels by H. G. Adler, *Panorama, The Journey,* and *The Wall*, all of which are available from Random House. Filkins is also the author of the authorized biography *H. G. Adler: A Life in Many Worlds* (Oxford University Press, 2019). He is the recipient of fellowships from the American Academy in Berlin, the Leon Levy Center for Biography, and the National Endowment for the Humanities. He is Richard B. Fisher Professor of Literature at Bard College.

Anthony Grenville is a leading figure in British exile studies. He was Lecturer in German at the Universities of Reading, Bristol and Westminster, 1971–1996. He is currently Editor of *AJR Journal*, the monthly publication of the Association of Jewish Refugees, and Chair of the Research Centre for German and Austrian Exile Studies, University of London. His publications include *Jewish Refugees from Germany and Austria in Britain, 1933–1970: Their Image in 'AJR Information'* (Vallentine Mitchell, 2010) and *Encounters with Albion: Britain and the British in Texts by Jewish Refugees from Nazism* (Legenda, 2018).

Kirstin Gwyer is Departmental Lecturer in German at Oxford University. She is the author of *Encrypting the Past: The German-Jewish Holocaust Novel of the First Generation* (OUP, 2014) and has also published on H. G. Adler, Günter Grass and W. G. Sebald, on recent American and German-language Jewish literature, and on the German family novel. She is currently working on contemporary Jewish post-Holocaust literature in its intersections with postcolonial and transnational studies, post-terrorism studies, and dementia studies.

Olivier Jouanjan is Professor at the University Panthéon-Assas (Paris 2) and Associate Professor at the Albert Ludwigs University, Freiburg in Breisgau. He is the recipient of a Research Prize from the Alexander-von-Humboldt Foundation and was a Junior Fellow at the Institut universitaire de France and a Fellow at the Wissenschaftskolleg (Institute for Advanced Study) Berlin. His books include: *Une histoire de la pensée juridique en Allemagne 1800–1918* (Presses universitaires de France, 2005), *Avant Dire Droit* (Presses universitaires de Laval, 2007), *Hans Kelsen: Forme du droit et politique de l'autonomie* (Presses universitaires de France, 2010), *Hermann Heller: Crise de l'État, crise de la théorie* (Dalloz, 2012), *Le 'Moment 1900': Critique sociale, critique sociologique du droit en Europe et aux Etats-Unis* (Éditions Panthéon-Assas, 2015), and *Justifier l'injustifiable: L'ordre du discours juridique nazi* (Presses universitaires de France, 2017).

Katrin Kohl is Professor of German at the University of Oxford and Fellow of Jesus College. She is the author of *Rhetoric, the Bible, and the Origins of Free Verse: The Early 'Hymns' of Friedrich Gottlieb Klopstock* (De Gruyter, 1990), *Friedrich Gottlieb Klopstock* (Metzler, 2000), *Metapher* (Metzler, 2007), and *Poetologische Metaphern* (De Gruyter, 2007). Rainer Maria Rilke–Erika Mitterer, *Besitzlose Liebe: Die poetische Briefwechsel* (Insel, 2018) provides the first comprehensive editions of this poetic correspondence, with commentary. She has published several articles on H. G. Adler and together with Franz Hocheneder, brought out the first complete edition of his poetry: *Andere Wege: Gesammelte Gedichte* (Drava, 2010). She is currently directing an interdisciplinary research project on 'Creative Multilingualism'.

Julia Menzel is a doctoral candidate and instructor at the Institute of History and Literary Cultures at Leuphana University of Lüneburg. Her dissertation project investigates the representations of time in H. G. Adler's scholarly and literary writings. Her publications include '"Von jetzt an also ist keine Zeit": Zeitordnungen und Zeitbrüche in H. G. Adlers wissenschaftlicher und literarischer Auseinandersetzung mit der Shoah', in *Der Holocaust: Neue Studien zu Tathergängen, Reaktionen und Aufarbeitungen*, ed. by Jörg Osterloh and Katharina Rauschenberger on behalf of the Fritz Bauer Institut (Campus, 2017); 'Between "Nothing" and "Something": Narratives of Survival in H. G. Adler's Scholarly and Literary Analysis of the Shoah', *Leo Baeck Institute Year Book* LXI (2016); 'Gespenster, Masken und "spukhafte Wirbel" in H. G. Adlers Studie *Theresienstadt 1941–1945* und dem Roman *Eine Reise*', in *Ordnungen des Unheimlichen: Kultur — Literatur — Medien*, ed. by Florian Lehmann. (Königshausen & Neumann, 2016).

Peter Pulzer was Gladstone Professor of Government and Public Administration and is Emeritus Fellow of All Soul's College, Oxford. He has received various honours, including the German Federal Cross of Merit (2004) and the Grand Silver Medal of Honour for Meritorious Service to the Republic of Austria (2008). His books include: *The Rise of Political Anti-Semitism in Germany and Austria* (Wiley, 1964), *Germany 1870–1945: Politics, State Formation, and War* (Oxford University Press, 1997), and with Wolfgang Benz and Arnold Paucker, *Jüdisches Leben in der Weimarer Republik* (Mohr Siebeck, 1998).

Michael Schaich is Deputy Director of the German Historical Institute London. In addition, he teaches modern history at the Ludwig Maximilian University Munich. His research focuses, among other topics, on the cultural and political history of Anglo-German relations from the seventeenth to the twentieth century. Currently he is researching, with Ines Schlenker, a book on the German exile community in London during the 1930s and 1940s for a wider public.

Martin Swales is Emeritus Professor of German at University College London. He studied at the Universities of Cambridge and Birmingham, and before UCL, he taught German at Birmingham, Toronto and King's College London. He has published extensively on German literature from the eighteenth century to the present, with particular emphasis on prose narrative. His monographs include: *Studies of German Prose Fiction in the Age of European Realism* (E. Mellen Press, 1995), *The German 'Novelle'* (Princeton University Press, 1977) and *The German 'Bildungsroman' from Wieland to Hesse* (Princeton University Press, 1978).

Ruth Vogel-Klein is emerita of the École Normale Supérieure in Paris. Her research specializes on the representation of the Holocaust, and she has published many articles on Ilse Aichinger, Heinrich Böll, Max Frisch, Ruth Klüger and W. G. Sebald. Publications on H. G. Adler include: 'Bilder der Shoah in Gedichten von H. G. Adler und Franz Baermann Steiner', in *Literatur und Anthropologie*, ed. by Jeremy Adler and Gesa Dane (Wallstein, 2014); 'History, Emotions, Literature: The Representation of Theresienstadt in H. G. Adlers *Theresienstadt 1941–1945: Das Antlitz einer Zwangsgemeinschaft* and W. G. Sebald's *Austerlitz*', in *Witnessing, Memory,*

Poetics: H. G. Adler and W. G. Sebald, ed. by Helen Finch and Lynn L. Wolff (Camden House, 2014); 'H. G. Adler: Zeugenschaft als Engagement', in *Monatshefte*, Special Issue *H. G. Adler: Dichter, Gelehrter, Zeuge*, ed. by Klaus Berghahn and Rüdiger Görner, vol. 103 (2011); '"Keine Anklage?" Der Deportationsroman *Eine Reise* (1951/1962) von H. G. Adler. Publikation und Rezeption', in *Die ersten Stimmen: Deutschsprachige Texte zur Shoah 1945–1963* (Königshausen & Neumann, 2010), which she also edited.

John J. White was Emeritus Professor of King's College London before his death in 2015. A scholar of literary modernism, his work was not limited to German Studies but rather comparative in nature. His major scholarly contributions include *Mythology in the Modern Novel: A Study of Prefigurative Techniques* (Princeton University Press, 1971, second edition 1973), *Literary Futurism: Aspects of the First Avant-Garde* (Clarendon Press, 1990), *Bertolt Brecht's Dramatic Theory* (Camden House, 2004), and *Bertolt Brecht's 'Furcht und Elend des Dritten Reiches': A German Exile Drama in the Struggle against Fascism* (Camden House, 2010), which he co-authored with his wife Ann White. Together with Ronald Speirs, White edited and commented H. G. Adler's correspondence with Hermann Broch (2004). During his career, he edited several volumes, and he served as editor of both the journal *German Life and Letters* and the Bithell Series of Dissertations.

Lynn L. Wolff is Assistant Professor of German in the Department of Linguistics & Germanic, Slavic, Asian, and African Languages at Michigan State University. Her research deals with the intersections of literature and historiography, the relationship between text and image, and theories of translation and world literature. She is the author of *W. G. Sebald's Hybrid Poetics: Literature as Historiography* (De Gruyter, 2014, paperback 2016). With Helen Finch she edited *Witnessing, Memory, Poetics: H. G. Adler and W. G. Sebald* (Camden House, 2014), and with Hans Adler she edited *Aisthesis und Noesis: Zwei Erkenntnisformen vom 18. Jahrhundert bis zur Gegenwart* (Fink, 2013). She is currently co-PI of the Graphic Narratives Network, an interdisciplinary research initiative, and working on a book project that explores different modes of abstraction employed in visualizing Holocaust testimony.

ACKNOWLEDGEMENTS

❖

For their kind and steady support of this volume, I would like to thank the following: the contributors for their insights into H. G. Adler's life and works and their dedication to this project; Ann White for the generous offer to publish her late husband's manuscript here; Elinor Shaffer (Fellow of the British Academy; Cambridge University) for organizing the conference on H. G. Adler that served as the starting point for this publication and the Institute of Modern Languages Research in London for hosting the event. For archival and image permissions and for answers to queries and sustained support over the years, I would like to express special thanks to Jeremy Adler. For additional images and permissions and for sharing his memories of H. G. Adler with me, I thank Manfred Sundermann. My thanks and appreciation go to Naomi Segal and Susannah Ellis for their translations of the contributions by Olivier Jouanjan and Ruth Vogel-Klein, and to Daniel Nemeth for his assistance in compiling the indexes. For productive discussions of literature and exile in general and H. G. Adler in particular, I would like to extend heartfelt thanks to Andrea Albrecht and the members of her research colloquia at the universities in Stuttgart and Heidelberg.

This volume has benefitted greatly from the materials available in the Deutsches Literaturarchiv in Marbach, Germany and the Foyle Special Collections of King's College London. It was not merely the availability of these sources but the resourceful and knowledgeable staff that made my research stays so productive. At King's College, I thank Katie Sambrook, Head of Special Collections, as well as the many helpful assistants in the archive. At the DLA in Marbach, I thank Susanna Brogi (now Germanisches Nationalmuseum, Nuremberg), Heidrun Fink, Caroline Jessen, Thomas Kemme, Rosemarie Kutschis, Julia Maas, Susanne Rößler, and last, but certainly not least, Katharina von Wilucki. One of my research stays in Marbach was generously funded by a C. H. Beck Fellowship, and for their support and assistance, I thank Marcel Lepper (now Akademie der Künste, Berlin), Anna Kinder, Gerhild Kölling, and Birgit Wollgarten.

It has been a pleasure to work with Legenda on this publication. Graham Nelson has been an efficient and encouraging editor every step of the way. I thank him as well as Emily Finer and Wen-Chin Ouyang, editors of *Studies in Comparative Literature*, and an anonymous reader for accepting this volume in the series.

I am grateful to Michigan State University for its generous research support: a grant from the Humanities and Arts Research Program helped fund the production of this volume, the College Fund for International Travel supported my travel to London, and a Summer Faculty Fellowship from the College of Arts and Letters provided further support for archival research in London and Marbach.

L.L.W., Lansing, December 2018

FOREWORD

❖

Opening Address to the H. G. Adler Conference
20 May 2016

Jeremy Adler

FIG. 1. 96 Dalgarno Gardens, home of H. G., Bettina, and Jeremy Adler
from July 1947 to February 1959, taken by Manfred Sundermann.
Copyright © the Estate of H. G. Adler.

This conference is something like a homecoming for my late father, H. G. Adler, who lived the greater part of his life in London. He actually started out a stone's throw from here, in Gower Street. For the most part, however, he lived in West London, light years away from Hampstead Exile Land, making him an exile even among exiles. First, he lived in the lower half of a miserable semi in Notting Hill, the area that Dickens calls 'a plague spot', 'scarcely equalled in insalubrity by any other part of London.' This was the district that had the distinction of seeing the first race riots — but also the first settlers from Windrush. Here, he observed the gradual emergence of modern Britain, and, as has yet to be recognized, the experience filtered into his work. These were the years of penury, anxiety, and ceaseless toil. Here he wrote *Theresienstadt 1941–1945*, the first systematic study of any concentration camp, anywhere, and also his novel, *Eine Reise [The Journey]* — two masterpieces, whose sombre matter echoes the dismal war-torn mood of the metropolis. He belongs with Primo Levi, David Rousset, and Eugen Kogon as one of the first witnesses. Then, when affluence beckoned, he moved to Notting Hill Gate, the area that Chesterton depicts in *The Napoleon of Notting Hill*, a few streets away from Harold Pinter and Lady Antonia Fraser. This was a desirable residence, formerly occupied by the Jazz Saxophonist Alexis Korner. These were the years of renown, when he hobnobbed with scholars, generals and high court judges. Here, he compiled *Auschwitz: Zeugnisse und Berichte [Auschwitz: Testimony and Reports]* with the resistance fighter, Hermann Langbein, the first significant book on Auschwitz in any language. Here, too, as an acquaintance of Peter Benenson, he became a founder member of Amnesty International. He was now a well-known voice in the Federal Republic. But, when our landlady began to lose her marbles, he decamped to Earls Court, then known as Kangaroo Valley, and rented a spacious apartment in Earls Court Square. Patrick Hamilton famously describes the area in his novel *Hangover Square*: smoke-filled rooms and seedy watering holes. Here, Adler created a replica of Central Europe — furniture, pictures, cuisine: the whole shebang. Truly a home in exile. Here he completed his scholarly magnum opus, *Der verwaltete Mensch [Administered Man]*, the first book that showed the complicity of ordinary Germans in the Final Solution. And here, too, he completed his testimony, published shortly before his death, *Vorschule für eine Experimentaltheologie [A Prolegomena for an Experimental Theology]*. The house lay opposite the Poetry Society, where W. H. Auden and John Ashbery came to read, and just a short walk from the Kensington of T. S. Eliot and Ezra Pound. My father also regularly wandered in the nearby Brompton Cemetery. This was where Beatrix Potter used to walk, and where she came across the grave of a Mr Nutkin — the true original of The Squirrel Nutkin. My father preferred the grave of his fellow exile, the Austrian tenor Richard Tauber, which served model for his own tomb. Here, then, in Earl's Court, close to its massage parlours and pubs and shady hotels and the cafe where Bob Dylan gave his London debut, he experienced his years of fulfilment, when anxieties and despair alternated with festivities and heroic inspiration. Poems from these years like 'The Saints of the Tender Conscience' with their sarcasm and sardonic wit have a distinct affinity with the poet of 'Desolation Row', rooted in a shared sense of political outrage and a love of Dylan Thomas.

My father's literary life scarcely intersected with English writers, except via the books on his shelves — W. B. Yeats, T. S. Eliot, Ezra Pound, George Eliot, and Henry James: his reading was voracious. Among the English novelists, he knew only a handful personally — Iris Murdoch, E. M. Forster, and Angus Wilson. It was a different crowd who came to call: Elias Canetti and Erich Fried, Heinrich Böll and Ilse Aichinger, Günter Eich and Peter Tramin, Walter Mehring and Ernst Jandl, Joseph Roth's housemate Hermann Kesten, and Kafka's young friend Johannes Urzidil, who had visited Café Edison with Kafka — not to mention the confirmed exiles, Grete Fischer, Robert Neumann, and Gabriele Tergit. Then there were fellow poets such as Michael Hamburger, Franz Steiner, and Franz Wurm, with whom he debated into the small hours. It was in his home, too, that Michael and he examined the newly discovered manuscript of Hölderlin's *Friedensfeier*, to authenticate the handwriting, and thereby played a small part in textual scholarship. All these figures, then, and many more, descended on his atmospheric study. Émigrés rubbed shoulders with Europeans, as editors and critics, painters and composers, architects and lawyers came and went. At times, they could be quite a nuisance, as when one German luminary borrowed a fiver off my penniless father and spent it on a bottle of bubbly — which he presented to my mother. For the most part, visitors were benign, inspiring, and productive. The household was constantly in a state of high alert, as new acquaintances appeared — such as Ligeti, Stockhausen, and Gisèle Celan — and gave cause for fresh excitement. If this was exile, and it certainly was, it was an exile buzzing with life.

Life however was a constant battle — for recovery from the war, for survival, for employment, for publication, for recognition, and for recompense from his persecutors. The terrors of the past survived not just as recollection, but as a constant presence, a permanent *angst*. At a time when the name Auschwitz was hardly spoken, and when the term Holocaust had yet to gain currency, H. G. Adler slaved up to eighteen hours a day to commemorate the dead. But not just that. To record. To analyse. To criticize. To explain. To admonish. To warn. To safeguard the future. This mission, first formulated in the camps, directed his life. It was to bear witness to a truth too terrible to bear. Yet despite his knowing scholars like Leonard Ashley Willoughby and Mary Wilkinson, or William Rose, Eithne Wilkins, and J. P. Stern, during his forty years of English life, he was only once invited to speak at an English university. His sole publication for a wider audience was a letter to *The Guardian*, calling for the resignation of the gaffe-prone Labour Foreign Secretary, George Brown. The establishment treated émigrés as if they were surrounded by the odour of shame. Moreover, his writings contained an excess of truth, and the truth, being painfully exacting, cauterizes the heart, and cannot by its nature be popular. His final tax return recorded nil earnings. No royalties. Exile was bitter, to the end.

Only now, years on, can we grasp his achievement. It has taken a succession of events. I recall the occasions in London, Oxford, Paris, Prague, Berlin, Vienna, Toronto, Vancouver, New York, and Marbach. Then there are the works by and about him appearing in a steady stream — every year brings new titles. Mention

FIG. 2. 35A Linden Gardens, home of H. G., Bettina, and Jeremy Adler from February 1959 to November 1963, view of the mews taken by H. G. Adler on 3 June 1962. Copyright © the Estate of H. G. Adler.
FIG. 3. Linden Gardens, view of H. G. Adler's study, taken by him on 17 October 1963. Copyright © the Estate of H. G. Adler.

FIG. 4. Linden Gardens, view of H. G. Adler's study from outside, taken by him on 3 November 1963. Copyright © the Estate of H. G. Adler.
FIG. 5. H. G. and Bettina Adler in Lauterbrunnental, Switzerland, late August 1977, taken by Manfred Sundermann. Copyright © Manfred Sundermann.

should here be made of Franz Hocheneder, who catalogued H. G. Adler's archive, wrote the first full biography, and is now editing the complete stories in four volumes.

I would like to single out several people and institutions who have played a part, chiefly behind the scenes. Firstly, Father Willehad Paul Eckert, Pastor Eberhard Bethge, and Wilhelm Unger, who together founded *The Society of Friends of H. G. Adler* in 1975, based on the model of the Robert Musil Society, to further Adler's works and support his writing. Eckert was a Dominican monk, who worked for Jewish-Christian reconciliation; Bethge was the nephew and biographer of Dietrich Bonhoeffer; and Unger was a fellow émigré, who collaborated with my father in 1949 to found a Goethe Library for Anglo-German reconciliation. Their volume, *Buch der Freunde* [*The Book of Friends*], of 1975, collected testimonies by Hermann Broch, Heinrich Böll, Heimito von Doderer, Walter Jens, and others and so laid the basis for all later scholarship and all subsequent publicity. Secondly, the philosopher Derek Bolton, a student of Wittgenstein's editor, Elizabeth Anscombe, who is with us today, and whose weekly tutorials with H. G. A. encouraged him to finish his philosophical masterpiece. Thirdly, *Stern* journalist Jürgen Serke, whose lavishly illustrated book *Böhmische Dörfer* [*Bohemian Villages*] of 1987 launched the wider discovery of H. G. Adler as a writer. Fourthly, Dr. Inge Belke of the German Literary Archives in Marbach, who recognized the value of the Adler papers, and secured them for the chief literary archive in Germany. This led directly to the 1998 exhibition: 'Ortlose Botschaft' ['Message without a Place'], which was shown in four towns in three countries and became critical in launching Adler's literary afterlife internationally. Fifthly, the Beinecke Library at Yale, which acquired an important collection, and thereby began the North American reception. This was mediated by Wendy Cruise, then of Bernard Quaritch. Sixthly, the much-lamented Henning Ritter of the *Frankfurter Allgemeine Zeitung*, who founded its celebrated Humanities Page. As an opinion-former, Henning Ritter heralded the acceptance of H. G. Adler in the press. He was ever on hand to proffer help and advice. Seventhly, Michael Krüger — poet, publisher, and friend, who first met my father in a Soho pub. Krüger, the internationally connected and unchallenged king of German independent publishing, was the vital force in publicizing Adler worldwide, which enabled the translations into Czech, French, Italian, Spanish, and Hebrew, not to mention English. Eighthly, Elizabeth Winter, formerly of *The Times Literary Supplement*, who commissioned the first article in the English press, still a live reference, which stimulated international interest. Ninthly, let me name the sorely missed Heinz Ludwig Arnold, editor of *Text + Kritik*, whose special number in 2004 brought H. G. Adler to the attention of subscribers and libraries around the world. Tenthly, the publisher Thedel von Wallmoden, who brought out several titles, chiefly a re-edition of *Theresienstadt 1941–1945*, which for the first time introduced the book to a wider public. Eleventh, Barry Ife, Vice Principal, as well as Katie Sambrook, Head of the Special Collections at King's College London, and Patricia Methven, Director of the Archives, who saw the importance of the private papers, and offered to create an Adler Archive at King's. Twelfth, I think of Peter

Fig. 6. H. G. and Bettina Adler in Lauterbrunnental, Switzerland, late August 1977, taken by Manfred Sundermann. Copyright © Manfred Sundermann.

Filkins, the tireless and enterprising translator, who performed the incalculable service of introducing H. G. Adler to an English-speaking readership, who publicized him in North America, and is now writing the authorized biography.★ Finally, and with a deep sense of loss, mention must be made of the curious mixture of homage and plagiarism by Max Sebald in *Austerlitz* in 2001. Max borrows far more than he acknowledges, as for instance his much-praised ten-page sentence, which is largely borrowed from my father's *Theresienstadt* book — it wouldn't get by a University Exam Board — , but on the positive side he gave a stupendous boost to my father's reputation. If one were to pick out just one or two key moments, it would have to be the Marbach exhibition 'Message without a Place', and the subsequent reprinting of *Eine Reise* by Michael Krüger, with its phenomenal echo in the press. These events formed the nodal points in the international reception. Everything else followed directly from these initiatives. They created the impetus for the American reception, but also for the Czech, in the author's homeland, which thanks to the urging of the writer, dissident, and finally ambassador, Jiří Gruša, and the plucky Moravian publisher Barrister & Principal, became the most successful reception anywhere, with a total of seven titles. From all this, it can be seen that bringing H. G. Adler to the world has involved a grand array: fellow writers and poets, scholars, young admirers, politicians, diplomats, university staff, museum directors, curators, archivists, literary societies, academies, doctoral students and their supervisors, editors, publishers, broadcasters, journalists, reviewers, free-lancers, translators, booksellers, CD-makers, and grant-giving agencies.

This conference is unique in its breadth — from history and law to criticism, text editing, reception studies, and exile writing. By this, it aims to capture the writer's paradoxical diversity: a wholly central-European intellectual, who was both deeply distanced and yet thoroughly enmeshed with his host country. It will likely be typified by the ferment upon which my father thrived.

★ Peter Filkins, *H. G. Adler: A Life in Many Worlds* (New York: Oxford University Press, 2019).

PART I

H. G. Adler within the Context of the Holocaust and Holocaust Studies

CHAPTER 1

❖

Framing H. G. Adler:
A Survivor, Scholar, and Author
in the Wake of the Shoah

Lynn L. Wolff

Exile and Modernism: The Reception of H. G. Adler in Profile

In the foreword to this volume, Jeremy Adler paints a vivid picture of his father's life in exile, relating both literary encounters and cultural intersections. This new life in London was not without great hardship and bitterness, however. H. G. Adler's first place of residence in London made him, in Jeremy Adler's words, 'an exile even among exiles'. This status was not only determined by geographical location, but could also be applied to the reception of Adler's work.[1] In *Das bittere Brot: H. G. Adler, Elias Canetti und Franz Baermann Steiner im Londoner Exil*, Jeremy Adler presents a more detailed and moving portrayal of this part of his father's life.[2] Drawing compelling connections between modernity and exile — 'Die Moderne ist das Zeitalter des Exils' [modernity is the age of exile], Jeremy Adler highlights Marx, Einstein, and Freud as the founders of this new world of homelessness, in which revolution, relativity, and the unconscious replace security and certainty.[3] H. G. Adler's work, both his scholarship and his literary texts written during his years in exile, are marked by the concerns of modernity and the forms of modernism. The present volume sets out to explore the connection between exile and modernism for H. G. Adler and more broadly the inextricable link between the reception of his work and our understanding of him.

H. G. Adler (2 July 1910, Prague–21 August 1988, London) survived forced labour in Prague as well as imprisonment in Theresienstadt, Auschwitz, and two satellite camps of Buchenwald — Niederorschel and Langenstein-Zwieberge. These experiences were determining factors in Adler's life, and they have in turn greatly influenced the reception of his works. Although Adler did not want to be strictly defined by his experiences in the camps, he became a pioneer in the now well-established field of Holocaust studies.[4] What sets Adler apart from fellow survivors, who also bore witness through documentation and scholarship,[5] is the unique double perspective of his work. He took both a scholarly and creative approach, documenting the National Socialist concentration camp system as a historian and writing through the camp experience in fictional poetry and prose.[6] During his lifetime, Adler became famous for his historical, sociological, and psychological study of Theresienstadt, which was and, to some degree, is still known as a 'ghetto', but which functioned as a concentration camp, as his book clearly demonstrates. This first definitive account of a single camp and Adler's first major scholarly publication, *Theresienstadt 1941–1945: Das Antlitz einer Zwangsgemeinschaft* appeared in 1955, went to second edition in a revised form in 1960, and was reprinted in 2005.[7] In 2017, the work appeared in English translation as *Theresienstadt 1941–1945: The Face of a Coerced Community*, with Cambridge University Press and with the support of the United States Holocaust Memorial Museum and the Terezin Publishing Project.[8] This major publication, certain shortcomings notwithstanding, along with the English translations of Adler's literary works outlined below, will open the door for more scholars in the Anglophone context to engage with Adler's multifaceted body of work.[9] A further phase of reception is yet to be undertaken.

In contrast to the recognition Adler received for his socio-historical scholarship, he encountered particular hardships in his attempts to convince publishers of his novels, short stories, and poetry. As Ruth Vogel-Klein and Kirstin Gwyer have shown in their work, such 'first voices' and members of the 'first generation', like Adler, often went without an immediate echo, although their works had an effect on subsequent memory discourses in Germany.[10] In her important study of Holocaust novels written in the German language by members of the first generation of Jewish survivors, Gwyer accounts for the difficult reception of such works. She writes, 'For one thing, the authors in question were writing Holocaust fiction not just before such a category had been designated, and before debates over the fundamental representability of the Holocaust were under way, but before the events themselves had even entered public consciousness and parlance as "the Holocaust".'[11] While Adler may have been a representative 'first voice' and member of the 'first-generation', he emphasized repeatedly that he did not want to gain literary currency through writing literature of the camps.[12]

To a certain degree, Adler's scholarly reputation impeded his literary career. As Franz Hocheneder asserts in his 2009 biography, Adler simply could not succeed as a poet within the German context.[13] While the reception of Adler's literary works during his lifetime was relatively modest, the tables have turned in recent years. The English translations of his published novels (*The Journey*, 2009, *Panorama*, 2011, and *The Wall*, 2014) have appeared to wide acclaim, and a volume of his collected poetry has been published (*Andere Wege*, 2010). A further project to publish Adler's collected short stories will draw more attention to his literary achievements as well.[14] In the foreword to the inaugural publication of the four-volume, chronologically ordered collection, Jeremy Adler speaks to the reception history, highlighting the importance of the rediscovery of the novels but explaining how this unfortunately covered up an important area of Adler's literary production that drew particular interest during his lifetime, namely the works of short prose.[15] In an effort to highlight Adler's essayistic work, Peter Filkins, the translator of

Adler's novels into English, has edited two volumes of essays on history, sociology, literature, Judaism, and politics.[16] Filkins has also written the first authorized English-language biography of Adler, which will create further avenues for the international reception of Adler.[17]

While Adler's work has seen a degree of renewed attention, there is still much to be done, especially when one considers the vast amount of unpublished materials in his estate.[18] Adler avidly corresponded with countless authors and scholars, and, as Sven Kramer has noted, the thousands of letters in the Adler estate deserve serious consideration as an essential part of his œuvre and for the valuable post-war narrative of the Shoah that they contain.[19] Adler was also active as an amateur photographer and published a small collection of his photographs alongside an essay in the volume *Kontraste und Variationen*.[20] His more than 8,000 images held in the archive were completely ignored until the Hungarian author Péter Nádas drew attention to them in an exhibit at the Museum of Modern Literature in Marbach, Germany in 2014.[21] The majority of these images were taken by Adler, but his archive also contains compelling images of Adler, surrounded by his books, hiking in the Swiss Alps, and in discussion with other authors, family, and friends.

These thousands of photographs, many of which are unknown and thus invisible to the public, call us to take a closer look at H. G. Adler. This volume offers a response, seeking to present a more detailed image of H. G. Adler and to provide certain frames through which to view this important figure of the twentieth century and his varied artistic and scholarly achievements. These frames include considerations of the form Adler's literary modernism takes within the context of his exile in London, individual investigations of his works and the interdisciplinary contexts in which to examine them, as well as the developments in his international reception. To provide an overarching framework for this volume, the following will highlight the multiple dual roles that Adler played, in particular as both a survivor and scholar of the Shoah. The volume as a whole elucidates Adler's complex reception history and is the first comprehensive scholarly publication that responds to the new international acclaim that Adler is receiving. In addition to offering innovative perspectives on his individual works, the major intervention that this volume aims to make is in the examination and contextualization of Adler's significant contributions to literary modernism and scholarly investigations of persecution and genocide under National Socialism.

A Vigilant Survivor and Documentarian: H. G. Adler's Contribution to Holocaust Studies

The photograph of H. G. Adler that adorns the cover of this volume is an intimate portrait — one taken by his son Jeremy on a hiking trip in Fex, near Sils Maria, Switzerland in 1965. It is also an evocative image — one in which Adler does not face the camera, but rather looks through a telescope into the distance. This view of Adler, on the lookout, as it were, quite literally illustrates his position as a 'sentry', calling to mind the description that Jeremy Adler formulates in his afterword to the *Theresienstadt* book.[22] He characterizes both his father's position as a survivor and his scholarly ethos as a particular 'combination of grief and optimism'.[23] With reference to Adler's immediate post-war correspondence with Franz Baermann Steiner, Jeremy Adler points to his father's 'inner strength, a sense of superiority toward all those who want to look away, forget, repress, or even deny [...]', and thus how, 'Being on sentry duty "at the edge" would always remain Adler's vantage point'.[24] In addition to the notion of vigilance, this photograph of Adler also embodies his prescience. The fact that Adler did pioneering work in the scholarly study of persecution and genocide at a time 'when the Holocaust did not yet have a name',[25] is a testament to the presence of mind he had, not only during his years of imprisonment in the camps, but already at the moment of deportation. On several occasions after the war, Adler formulated his decision and dedication to represent the experiences of persecution in two ways, both scholarly and artistically:

> Als es zu den Deportationen kam, habe ich mir gesagt: das überlebe ich nicht. Aber wenn ich es überlebe, dann will ich es darstellen, und zwar auf zweierlei Weise: ich will es *wissenschaftlich* erforschen und in dieser Gestaltung vollkommen von mir als Individuum loslösen, und ich will es *dichterisch* in irgendeiner Weise darstellen.[26]

> [When it came to the deportations, I told myself: I won't survive this. But if I do survive, I want to represent it, and in two different ways: I want to explore it in a scholarly manner and so separate it from myself completely, and I want to portray it in a literary manner.[27]]

Furthermore, Adler recalls how the decision to write about Theresienstadt helped him overcome the numbness he felt upon arrival in the camp. This decision to write his *Theresienstadt* book had a positive and convalescent effect upon him ['Seltsam, dieser Entschluß verlieh mir eine heilsame Kraft.'], and it helped him regain a certain mental and emotional balance, or his 'seelisches Gleichgewicht', as he described it.[28] In addition to writing hundreds of poems while imprisoned in the camps, Adler turned to literature after the war as well.[29] Writing literature, like his work on the scholarly documentation of Theresienstadt, provided not only a source of strength but also a 'survival strategy'[30] for H. G. Adler.

The decision to write a book about Theresienstadt was, however, not yet a decision about *how* to write it or what form such a book would take. Adler recounts that he did not keep a diary or take notes while in Theresienstadt, but that he kept his senses together ['hielt [s]eine Sinne beisammen'][31] and collected materials and documents, which he entrusted to Rabbi Leo Baeck before being deported to Auschwitz.[32] Adler describes how he trained himself in a form of cool observation ['kühle[] Betrachtung'],[33] looking to ethnological field research as a model for his own approach.[34] He also recounts how he had to make a concerted effort to remain free of prejudice and sober ['vorurteilsfrei und nüchtern'] in his observations. This intentionality contributes to shaping the *Theresienstadt* book into a work that goes beyond existing forms of both testimony and scholarship. Also indicative of Adler's intentionality is his formulation of a neologism — *Zwangsgemeinschaft* [coerced community] — to encapsulate the world of Theresienstadt. Jeremy Adler draws out the implications of this in his afterword, stating, 'The author accepts neither the vocabulary of the Nazis nor the traditional concepts of social science. He wants to rethink modernity'.[35] The idea that *l'univers concentrationnaire*, to use David Rousset's term,[36] can be seen as the world of modernity itself clearly resonated with other scholars and was even appropriated by some.[37]

The historical import of Adler's documentary work was recognized immediately, and *Theresienstadt 1941–1945* was often compared to or reviewed alongside Eugen Kogon's foundational study of the concentration camp system, *Der SS-Staat: Das System der deutschen Konzentrationslager* (1946) [*The Theory and Practice of Hell: The German Concentration Camps and the Theory Behind Them* (1950)].[38] In addition to the historical, sociological, and psychological pillars of Adler's study, contemporary reviews also highlighted both philosophical and religious dimensions of the work. Acknowledging the absence of explicit personal testimony, several reviewers point to Adler's individual experiences that were necessary for the creation of such a work, but which he ultimately suppressed in his writing. In a review for the *Jewish Quarterly*, Michael Hamburger writes,

> Dr. Adler's account is different because he has achieved a detachment admirable in one who suffered the 'enforced community' of Theresienstadt for 32 months — a fact mentioned in the bibliography. He was also qualified to appreciate the difference between Theresienstadt and other concentration camps, for he came to Theresienstadt from a Jewish labor camp in Czechoslovakia and was subsequently removed to Auschwitz — where his wife and mother-in-law were immediately put to death — thence to two other camps attached to Büchenwald [sic]. The vast body of factual information provided in this book [...] would be incomplete without the author's first-hand experience of his subject: but the work would be less impressive and less authoritative if he had not made a point of excluding all reference to himself.[39]

Though some reviewers, like Hamburger, praise this extraction of the personal, others hint at the potential risk in such an approach. J. Petersen, for example, describes Adler's 'fast gefährliche Objektivität' [almost dangerous objectivity].[40] In the over twenty reviews of *Theresienstadt 1941–1945* — most of which are in German and English, but there are also others in Danish, Dutch, French, Hebrew, and Italian — it was practically unanimously projected that the work would remain a standard reference.[41] Hermann Broch, already in 1948, wrote a statement in support of the volume, calling it a 'Standardwerk' for both present and future generations, not only highlighting the 'kühle Methodik' that was Adler's intended approach but expressing his awe that such an approach was possible under the constant risk of death.[42]

Underlining this positive contemporary reception of the work, Jeremy Adler writes, 'It was immensely successful when it first came out in the 1950's — attracting the attention of leading figures in the Jewish community such as Martin Buber and Gershom Scholem, or key German writers such as Heinrich Böll and Walter Jens — but it was subsequently overtaken by more recent literature, and had to wait some years after Adler's death to be reprinted in an affordable format'.[43] That this work could be overtaken is also an indication of shifting notions of what is deemed historically valid scholarship. Wolfgang Benz's 2013 study, for example, which strives to revise the longstanding view of Theresienstadt as a privileged 'Altersghetto',[44] acknowledges Adler's pioneering work — 'Sein Buch ist das bedeutendste historiografische Werk über Theresienstadt.'[45] [His book is the most significant historiographical work on Theresienstadt.] — but at the same time Benz takes issue with Adler's presentation of the 'ghetto' as a 'Zwangsgemeinschaft' and his designation of it as a 'Lager'.[46] Benz moreover views Adler's *Theresienstadt* critically for its emotional and moralizing tone,[47] while also admitting that — due to both Adler's own temperament and character ['Temperament und Charakter'] and the fact that the work was written in the immediate post-war years — it was not and could not be written without such emotion.[48] Criticisms, such as Benz's, give rise to disciplinary questions that are rooted in the epistemological claims of historiography: that is, how to write a history of those events that one directly experienced.[49] A more differentiated analysis of historiographic approaches, such as that outlined by Dominick LaCapra in *Writing History, Writing Trauma* (2001), offers further insight into the problem of writing history that is fundamentally rooted in individual experience. LaCapra carves out a space for empathy in historiographical work, emphasizing that 'knowledge involves not only the processing of information but also affect, empathy, and questions of value'.[50]

Beyond the work's major documentary contribution to early Holocaust historiography, *Theresienstadt 1941–1945* remains unique in the way that Adler structures his study in three separate sections — history, sociology, and psychology.[51] In the work, moreover, he utilizes different styles and tones and purposefully interlaces multiple genres to create a work that resists categorization in one established scholarly field, demonstrating Adler's 'interdisciplinary intellectual orientation'.[52] Ultimately, the unique boundary breaking form of this work reveals how the experiences of the Holocaust demand a new form of representation,[53] and its tripartite structure anticipates the development of Holocaust studies as an inherently interdisciplinary field.

Beyond his major publications — *Theresienstadt 1941–1945* (1955), *Die verheimlichte Wahrheit: Theresienstädter Dokumente* (1958), and *Der verwaltete Mensch: Studien zur Deportation der Juden aus Deutschland* (1974) — Adler helped lay the groundwork for the development of the international and interdisciplinary field of Holocaust studies through his involvement with the International Auschwitz Committee and his collaboration with Hermann Langbein and Ella Lingens-Reiner on the volume *Auschwitz: Zeugnisse und Berichte* (1962).[54] His collaborative work can also be seen in the significant contributions he made in the form of radio essays and reports, lectures, and conference presentations.[55] He made a further mark on the field through his reviews of scholarly works. His estate in Marbach contains over 68 reviews written from the 1950s through the 1970s on volumes having to do with National Socialism in particular, history, politics, and sociology more generally.[56] These reviews are all the more significant for the reflections on historiography that they contain, such as his review of *Persecution and Resistance under the Nazis* (1960) that points to the emergence of Holocaust studies as a field.[57] While acknowledging the important place that the documentation of personal experiences has for this field, he asserts the need for scholarly studies that deal with the 'Phänomen Auschwitz' [phenomenon of Auschwitz]. In an article for the *Wiener Library Bulletin* entitled 'The Scholar and the Catastrophe', in which Adler reviews Jacob Robinson and Philip Friedman's *Guide to Jewish History under Nazi Impact* (1960), he reflects on the particular problems posed to historians of the emerging field of 'Contemporary History'.[58] In discussing the volume, Adler never directly names the subject matter — what today is covered by the terms Holocaust or Shoah — but writes instead of 'the terrible events', 'the Catastrophe', and 'the subject'.[59] In formulating an understanding of historical research vis-à-vis other forms of writing, he advises that critical distance is necessary for any historical research that deals with the 'latest Jewish tragedy'. This necessity of distance is specific to historical research as opposed to the various other text types that have been created in response to the events, such as 'the memoirs of those involved' as well as 'their reports, letters, records, stories and poetry'.[60] However, this distance is not yet attainable, according to Adler, due to the highly emotional nature of responses to the events. He states, 'Nevertheless it seems extremely early today, sixteen years after the fall of Nazidom, to cover the distance required by the scholar for due assessment of historical matter. Where the life of contemporaries is affected, in some cases painfully, in others shamefully, the past recedes but slowly and with laborious effort.'[61] Demonstrating how much he valued the efforts to enlighten a broader public, Adler also highlights the importance of this historical research guide, not only for other historians but for 'indeed any educated man or woman'.[62] Adler remained convinced of the collective responsibility toward humanity — both to current society and future generations — not only to obtain knowledge but also to develop a critical understanding of what happened during the years of National Socialism and how deportation, persecution, and genocide became possible.

In addition to giving contour to the development of Holocaust studies and Holocaust literature as an emerging discipline and genre, Adler's unpublished works and correspondence with other authors and scholars as well as with publishers shed light on the implication of the survivor's personal experiences in such scholarly and literary endeavours. In the section that follows, I will examine one such exemplary unpublished essay. Adler's correspondence moreover reveals how he engaged — in a semi-private medium — with the ethical, aesthetic, and epistemological challenges inherent to writing after and out of the trauma of the Holocaust. In his correspondence with other survivors in particular, he draws on their similar experiences and explicitly formulates the therapeutic function that scholarship can have. Adler asserts how one's personal experiences and emotions directly inform research. Likewise, according to Adler, intellectual engagement will ultimately help in overcoming the traumatic experiences of persecution, not as a way of forgetting them but rather as a way to learn to live with this past.[63] As a way to connect these aspects to the image of Adler's vigilance and prescience described above, I would like to conclude this section with a statement Adler makes in a letter to a fellow survivor, Jehuda Bacon. Adler cared for and mentored Bacon, who was only an adolescent at the end of the war, and Adler continued to support him in his efforts to study art at the Bezalel Academy of Arts and Design in Jerusalem, after Bacon immigrated to Palestine in 1946. Evoking the same sentiment that he communicated to Franz Baermann Steiner, Adler expresses in this letter to Bacon in 1953 both his sorrow over what happened during the 'years of the evil past' and his conviction that his life has nevertheless been enriched by the experience. He writes,

> Ich bin sehr glücklich darüber, wie Du Dich zu den Jahren der bösen Vergangenheit einstellst. Wer sich davon etwas zu nehmen verstand, wird davon für sein Leben bereichert bleiben, und ich denke genauso wie Du, dass wir Gott für diese Erfahrungen zu danken haben. Ich sage mir immer: ich bedaure alles, was geschehen ist, aber wenn es schon geschehen musste, bin ich froh, dabei gewesen zu sein.[64]

> [I am very happy about your attitude toward the years of the evil past. He who was able to take something away from that time will remain enriched for the rest of his life, and I think just like you do that we have God to thank for these experiences. I always say to myself: I lament everything that happened, but if it had to happen, then I am glad to have been there.]

Scholar versus Learned Person: Between 'Sprachkritik' and Autobiography

To elucidate the complexity of Adler's œuvre beyond the duality of scholarship and literature,[65] and to further frame his contribution to the field of Holocaust studies, I now turn to one of his unpublished essays from 1962.[66] Entitling the essay with the question 'Wissenschaftler oder Gelehrter?' [Scholar or Learned Person?], Adler draws a distinction that can shed light on both the particularity of his historiographical work and his particular subject position as a survivor and independent scholar. The majority of this eight-page manuscript details the various connotations and values ascribed to each of these terms, which can be understood as the suggestion of an opposition between the two. In addition to considering the formation of each word alongside its etymology, Adler devotes some attention to the umbrella term ['Sammelbegriff'] of 'Wissenschaft', that is, science or scholarship, as well as the plural form of 'Wissenschaften', referring to entire systems of knowledge. He then draws further differentiations between the natural sciences ['Naturwissenschaften'] and the humanities ['Geisteswissenschaften'], which he sees as rooted in the difference between nature/natural phenomena as something given and products of human creation. Adler holds 'Wissenschaft' in high esteem, as something sublime ['etwas Hohes'], but he deplores the fact that this human achievement can be destroyed when scholars, through their conceit, hold themselves apart from society. The word for such behaviour, he says, is scholarly arrogance ['Gelehrtendünkel'] (2), which, Adler laments further, has led to a general devaluing of the term for a learned person ['Gelehrten']. He goes on to describe how the term has practically fallen out of common usage and, if it is used, then with an all but strange, if not contemptuous overtone ['einen beinahe leicht komischen, wenn schon nicht verächtlichen Beiklang'] (3). The result, he states, is that the scholar/scientist has ousted the learned one ['Der Wissenschaftler hat den Gelehrten verdrängt'] (3).

There is a clear value judgement tied to this shift in usage when he goes on to say that the linguistically better word ['das sprachlich besser gelungene Wort'] — *learned person* — has had to give way to the less human ['weniger menschlichen'] word of *scholar/scientist*. Hearkening back to his essays on language, written for the journal *Muttersprache* in the 1950s, the comments Adler makes in his short unpublished essay underline further his investment in language in addition to his understanding of the power of the written and spoken word, both of which directly influence his high standards of linguistic propriety.[67] Perhaps most important, however, is the connection between language and humanity that we find formulated here. The unpublished essay, like his aforementioned publications on language, are not mere considerations of etymology, semantic fields, or the value words have within a linguistic system, but they also explore pragmatics: the relationship between signs and their users. Adler makes clear how language can have far-reaching consequences for what it means to be human, and by extension, how language can be instrumentalized in both humane and inhumane ways. Words themselves, then, depending on how they are used, contain a degree of humanity as well as the flipside of inhumanity, which explains the inherent value judgements Adler makes when identifying 'good' versus 'bad' words. Examples of this follow in his further elaborations on the difference between the scientist/scholar and the learned person.

Despite the fact that scholarship is by nature abstract ['die Wissenschaft ist ihrem Charakter nach abstrakt'] (3), the word for an erudite person ['Gelehrter'], which is derived from the verb *to teach*, implies a human element. Adler thus establishes the grounds for his higher estimation of the term *Gelehrter* by identifying a more intimate and deeper relationship between the learned person and the scientific subject. He states,

> So steckt in der Gelehrtheit die Lehre, das Lernen und die Erfahrung, die Kenntnis, kurzum ein geistiger Prozess persönlicher Anteilnahme an einem Wissen. Die Verbindung mit Bildung und Erziehung wird offenbar. Darum ist das Verhältnis des Gelehrten zur Wissenschaft unvergleichlich *inniger*, wenn schon nicht *tiefer* als das Verhältnis des Wissenschaftlers zur Wissenschaft, den man sich eher als jemanden vorstellt, der sie nur *betreibt* oder der, *von ihr erfüllt*, sie *dispensiert*. Der Wissenschaftler erscheint uns als *unbeteiligt*, *neutral*, als *unpersönlich*' (5, my emphasis).

> [Within the term learnedness are the terms for teaching and learning, as well as experience and cognition, in short, a mental process of personal participation in knowledge. The connection between formation and education becomes obvious. Therefore, the relationship of the educated one to scholarship is comparably more *intimate*, if not even *deeper* than the relationship of the scholar toward science whom we imagine as someone who only *pursues* science or, when *filled by science*, *disposes* of it. The scientist/scholar appears then as *uninvolved*, *neutral*, *impersonal*.]

The conclusion to this essay makes clear what the stakes of this semantic parsing are, and one can understand these reflections with regard to the particular form of history Adler carries out: one that is born out of personal experiences. Adler

points to the larger problem indicated by the linguistic shift from 'Gelehrter' to
'Wissenschaftler' — a problem that he raises repeatedly in his essays on language —
namely the drastic and devastating effects of linguistic amnesia and ignorance. To
drive home his point about the 'Wissenschaftler', the more abstract and disconnected
and thus less human figure, versus the 'Gelehrter', or the learned human being who
is more connected to that which he has learned and teaches; Adler concludes his
essay with an analogy from the recent past, and more specifically, from *his* recent
past. The linguistic shift he identifies is analogous to a comparable descent in social
welfare ['einen von ferne vergleichbaren Abstieg in der öffentlichen Wohlfahrt']
(7–8), which is encapsulated in the shift in usage from the word 'Fürsorge' [care,
welfare] to 'Betreuung' [assistance, supervision], a term that was used by the Nazis
to euphemistically refer to and thereby cover up the murder of the Jews (8). Adler
expands upon the maleficent use of this term in greater detail elsewhere, notably in
the glossary of his *Theresienstadt* book, where he elucidates the verbal and nominal
forms (*betreuen, Betreuer, Betreuung*) as being euphemisms for murder and the act of
murdering,[68] and in his essay on 'Die Sprache der Gewalt und ihre Wörter' [The
Language of Violence and its Words].[69] He mobilizes this comparison to insist upon
the importance of a healthy form of linguistic criticism ['Sprachkritik'], calling for
a critical and reflected use of language and ending with a plea that *Wissenschaft*, via
the *Gelehrter*, forge a deeper connection with life.

Though it is possible to take issue with the etymological distinctions Adler
draws between the scholar and the learned person, the significance of his essay lies
in the implicit autobiographical underpinnings and implications. Through critical
etymological considerations, Adler finds a way to first describe and then assert
his own subject position as a *Gelehrter*. To make such an assertion had existential
ramifications for him. An academic position should certainly not be the sole
determining factor for scholarly achievement, but the risk of being ignored or
overlooked was an acutely felt reality for this German-speaking independent scholar
of bohemian Jewish origins, living in exile in London during the post-war years.
Considering this autobiographical dimension, the essay underscores the notion
that scholarship can be an essential way for survivors to establish the coordinates
of their own past in an attempt to understand the causes that determined their life
experiences. The scholar should look to the learned one, and not remain distanced
[*unbeteiligt*] from his subject matter, for the scholarly enterprise ultimately makes it
possible for individuals to regain control of their own identity.

Overview of this Volume and Individual Contributions

The starting point for this volume was an international and interdisciplinary
conference held at the Institute of Modern Languages Research (IMLR) in London
and co-sponsored by the Wiener Library, the Austrian Cultural Forum, and the
Research Centre for German and Austrian Exile Studies, featuring invited speakers
from Canada, France, Germany, Great Britain, and the United States.[70] The
conference found immediate resonance in the German press, signaling both the

interest and relevance of H. G. Adler's work. An article in the *Frankfurter Allgemeine Zeitung* reported positively on the conference, emphasizing the diversity of aspects covered in the talks and that the question of Adler's reception sheds new light on how Germany has dealt with its past.[71] A lecture by historian Nikolaus Wachsmann at the Austrian Cultural Forum opened the conference and presented his major study *KL: A History of the Nazi Concentration Camps*.[72] Both Wachsmann's lecture and the introduction by Ben Barkow, director of the Wiener Library, an institution which provided important sources for Adler's *Theresienstadt 1941–1945*, underlined the significance of Adler's method and line of inquiry in his scholarship as well as the considerable challenges he faced in obtaining the attention he deserved. Both scholars provided a detailed context to the development of Holocaust historiography: Wachsmann described how most German historians 'made a wide berth around the Holocaust', leaving the writing of this history and the documentation of testimony to the survivors.[73] Barkow sketched out the 'scandalous publishing history' of foundational works, like Adler's *Theresienstadt 1941–1945* and *Der verwaltete Mensch*, and asserted not only their profundity but also the role they played for the founding generation of Holocaust scholars. Wachsmann also described Holocaust historiography as a 'collective endeavour', which is certainly true when one thinks of the volume *Auschwitz: Zeugnisse und Berichte* that was the collective effort of H. G. Adler, Hermann Langbein, and Ella Lingen-Reiners, or the efforts of the International Auschwitz Committee. It is important to point out, however, that much of H. G. Adler's work was done to a large degree in isolation.

This volume aims to put into perspective aspects of the international reception of Adler's works while also showing the international scope of his concerns, central to which are the broader issues of exile and modernism. Within the context of Adler's reception, it should be emphasized that the volume builds on the renewed attention Adler has been receiving since the centenary of his birth in the form of translations, conferences, and publications. The present volume continues the discussions of Adler within an international context by bringing together the work of both European and North American scholars from different academic areas, and the fifteen chapters offer a methodologically diverse array of investigations. In the opening section on *H. G. Adler within the Context of the Holocaust and Holocaust Studies*, Christopher Browning and Peter Pulzer expand upon the ideas outlined here and set the stage for the specific analyses that follow. Browning offers a panoramic overview of Adler's 'Shoah Trilogy', and Pulzer incisively compares Primo Levi and Adler with regard to memoirs of the camps. Browning further elucidates the uniqueness of Adler among other Holocaust scholars, suggesting that the fact of Adler's exile in England was 'doubly isolating' for him, since he remained intellectually and linguistically in a continental context by continuing to write and publish in German.

Section two on *Modernism in/and Exile* deals with the productive and problematic impact of exile on Adler's modernism. Opening this section is Anthony Grenville's close reading of Adler's depiction of Britain, captured in the still unpublished manuscript *England: Eindrücke eines Ahnungslosen* [*England: Impressions of an Innocent Abroad*], started by Adler upon arrival in London in 1947 and completed in 1949.

Complementing Browning's consideration of Adler alongside other 'survivor scholars', Grenville places Adler in the context of other Jewish writers; and, like Browning, Grenville sees Adler as an 'exception' among those who settled in Britain after 1933. Following Grenville's chapter, which highlights Adler's 'dialectical method of analysis', Peter Filkins explores how Adler understood his writing not only within the context of literary but also musical modernism. Filkins shows how Adler upholds both the ideal of a transcendental dimension of creative writing and the nexus of aesthetics and ethics to the extent that literature has the 'potential to transform the artistic act into an ethical act affecting others'. Kirstin Gwyer's contribution delves deeper into considerations of Adler's modernist representative modes, drawing connections between his *Theresienstadt* book and his three 'Holocaust novels' to ultimately challenge the distinction between the 'literary and the non-literary' — thereby serving as a bridge from the focus on modernist techniques to the focus of the next section on his individual literary works.

Essays in section three examine previously underexplored aspects of Adler's three major published novels and his poetry, including irony, humour, and the function of letters and letter writing. Building on the discussions of the previous section — the dialectical tension between reflecting on Britain and the British in the German language — Katrin Kohl's chapter shows how poetry was the genre most characterized by the exile condition, for '[Adler's] poetry was [...] at odds with the language and poetic tradition of his environment'. Already preceding exile, the poetry Adler wrote in the camps can be seen as both 'a form of resistance and a means to create an identity'. In fact, Adler reflected upon this in his 1980 essay 'Dichtung in der Gefangenschaft als inneres Exil' [Literature during Captivity as Inner Exile]. The modernist quality of Adler's poetry resists easy consumption and interpretation. The same can be said for Adler's novels and short stories, and this is shown in detail with regard to his prose piece *Eine Reise* [*The Journey*], which he categorized as a ballad. John J. White's chapter examines the role of irony and black humour in *Eine Reise* and how these techniques challenge our understanding of the work.[74] Martin Swales reads Adler's *Panorama* as a novel in its own right, and more precisely within the tradition of the *Bildungsroman*, intentionally avoiding any judgements about the autobiographical dimension of the work, which has been the common mode of interpretation since Adler's own characterization of it as steeped in autobiography ['einen mit Autobiographischem getränkten Roman'].[75] Concluding this section is Julia Menzel's in-depth analysis of the role of epistolary elements — the letter as leitmotif and 'The Letter Writers', the story within the story — in Adler's *Die unsichtbare Wand* [*The Wall*]. More than a close reading of the novel, Menzel underlines how letters served an existential function during Adler's exile in London and how writing more broadly was an act of self-constitution.

Section four brings into focus the interdisciplinary contexts in which to view Adler's work, including politics, philosophy, religious and legal studies. Illuminating a heretofore unexplored dimension of Adler's contribution to scholarship, Olivier Jouanjan elucidates Adler's understanding and representation of the legal system in *Theresienstadt 1941–1945*. Jouanjan's examination of legal discourse under National

Socialism helps reveal the fiction of law itself, that is, the 'Rechtskomödie', in Theresienstadt. Jeremy Adler sheds new light on H. G. Adler as a public intellectual by critically examining his debate with Hannah Arendt and Jean Améry. This analysis, which includes a discussion of the role the *Theresienstadt* volume played in the Eichmann trial, provides a further contextualization of both the work and its reception. Michael Schaich builds upon the notion of Adler as a public intellectual by examining his role as public historian and the work he did for the West German broadcast system in the post-war years. Schaich also provides the first analysis of *Die Juden in Deutschland* [*The Jews in Germany*], arguably one of Adler's most popular publications and the only major work of his to be translated into English during his lifetime.

The examination of two major phases of Adler's reception concludes this final section of the volume. Two pieces, written by scholars who themselves represent aspects of the development in Adler studies, highlight the reception of his works in the West German and North American contexts. Ruth Vogel-Klein focuses on *Eine Reise* [*The Journey*], outlining three stages of reception between 1951 and 2003 while demonstrating the significant role of paratextual elements on the response to the work in post-war West German society. Julia Creet's account of the North American reception of Adler closely overlaps in chronology with Vogel-Klein but is carried through to the present day and focuses on the English translations of Adler's works. Like Vogel-Klein, Creet outlines three phases of reception, but these reveal important differences between literary critical and academic reception.

The contributions gathered here offer new perspectives on Adler's individual works and draw attention for the first time to unpublished essays, radio manuscripts, and letters held in the Archive of German Literature in Marbach, Germany and in the Archive of King's College London. While the interdisciplinary approaches shed light on the encyclopaedic reach of Adler's work, the volume as a whole, like most of the existing literature on H. G. Adler to date, focuses on his work from the time in the camps until his death. So as not to restrict Adler within the different frames sketched out here, it is important to mention the poetry and prose as well as his dissertation in musicology on Klopstock, that were all written during the rise of National Socialism, that historical turn of events that led to the Jewish tragedy ['jüdische Tragödie'], as Adler often referred to it. The frames of analysis with which to examine these pre-war works are yet to be drawn by scholars.

Notes to Chapter 1

1. H. G. Adler was among the authors discussed at a symposium co-organized by the Society for Exile Literature [*Gesellschaft für Exilliteratur*]. See Otto F. Best, 'Panorama und Topographie: Anmerkungen zu Alfred Döblin, Peter Weiss, H. G. Adler und anderen', *Deutsche Exilliteratur, Literatur der Nachkriegszeit: Akten des III. Exilliteratur-Symposiums der University of South Carolina*, ed. by Wolfgang Elfe, James Hardin, and Günther Holst (Bern: Peter Lang, 1981), pp. 96–102. Although H. G. Adler had a place in these early discussions of exile literature and was a member of the PEN-Zentrum for German-speaking authors in 1953, serving as its president from 1973–1985, it is worth noting that he is not included in the *Handbuch der deutschsprachigen Exilliteratur*, ed. by Bettina Bannasch and Gerhild Rochus (Berlin: De Gruyter, 2013). In her new history of

German-language literature, Sandra Richter discusses Adler in terms of his scholarly and literary work that bore witness to the Shoah. See Sandra Richter, *Eine Weltgeschichte der deutschsprachigen Literatur* (Munich: Bertelsmann, 2017), p. 310.

2. Jeremy Adler, *Das bittere Brot: H. G. Adler, Elias Canetti und Franz Baermann Steiner im Londoner Exil* (Göttingen: Wallstein, 2015). Here, Jeremy Adler also provides a more complete understanding of exile from religious and classical perspectives, by also considering notions of banishment [*Verbannung*], discrimination [*Abgrenzung*], and expulsion [*Vertreibung, Austreibung, Ausweisung*], p. 7.

3. See Adler, *Das bittere Brot*, pp. 9–10.

4. The 2004 *Text + Kritik* volume dedicated to H. G. Adler frames him as one of the founders of the scholarly study of the Shoah: 'H. G. Adler gilt als Mitbegründer der Wissenschaft von der Shoah'. See back cover of *H. G. Adler (Text + Kritik 163)*, ed. by Heinz-Ludwig Arnold (Munich: text+kritik, 2004).

5. Laura Jockusch has termed this significant group of individuals 'survivor documentarians'. Jockusch writes, 'These survivor documentarians also recorded the individual stories of other survivors in thousands of testimonies and questionnaires. In a war-torn Europe short of even such basic materials as pencils and paper, they often recorded these stories on unused stationary — emblazoned with Nazi emblems — abandoned by departing German military personnel and bureaucrats. [...] The survivors' use of this paper symbolized the act of "turning the page" to a new era in which the survivors of genocide took revenge on their tormenters by registering the details of their crimes.' Laura Jockusch, *Collect and Record! Jewish Holocaust Documentation in Early Postwar Europe* (New York: Oxford University Press, 2012), p. 4.

6. For a more detailed analysis of this dual approach, see Lynn L. Wolff, 'H. G. Adler and W. G. Sebald: From History and Literature to Literary Historiography', in Special Issue: H. G. Adler, ed. by Rüdiger Görner and Klaus L. Berghahn, *Monatshefte*, 103.2 (2011), 257–75.

7. The publication was made possible in part thanks to the financial help of Theodor W. Adorno. See Marcel Atze, *'Ortlose Botschaft': Der Freundeskreis H. G. Adler, Elias Canetti und Franz Baermann Steiner im englischen Exil* (Marbach am Neckar: Deutsche Schillergesellschaft, 1998), p. 137. A more detailed discussion of Adler's *Theresienstadt 1941–1945* follows below.

8. Offering an excellent overview of the uniqueness of the Theresienstadt book as well as putting the volume's reception into context, Ben Barkow quite rightly takes issue with several aspects of this new translated edition: the deletion of the glossary, the drastic reduction of the original three indexes to one of limited scope, and the translation itself. See Ben Barkow, 'A Heroic Work of Extraordinary Scholarship: On the New Translated Edition of H. G. Adler's *Theresienstadt* of 1960', *German Historical Institute London Bulletin*, 40.1 (2018), 86–98 (pp. 92–98).

9. Both reflecting and contributing to this phase of reception history are the volumes: *Witnessing, Memory, Poetics: H. G. Adler and W. G. Sebald*, ed. by Helen Finch and Lynn L. Wolff (Rochester, NY: Camden House, 2014) and *H. G. Adler: Life, Literature, Legacy*, ed. by Julia Creet, Sara R. Horowitz, and Amira Bojadzija-Dan (Evanston, IL: Northwestern University Press, 2016).

10. Ruth Vogel-Klein, introduction to *Die ersten Stimmen: Deutschsprachige Texte zur Shoah 1945–1963 / Les premières voix: Écrits sur la Shoah en langue allemande 1945–1963*, ed. by Ruth Vogel-Klein (Würzburg: Königshausen & Neumann, 2010), pp. 7–30. Kirstin Gwyer, *Encrypting the Past: The German-Jewish Holocaust Novel of the First Generation* (Oxford: Oxford University Press, 2014).

11. Gwyer, *Encrypting the Past*, p. 50.

12. On Adler's reluctance to be seen as a 'Holocaust author', see Helen Finch and Lynn L. Wolff, 'Introduction: The Adler-Sebald Intertextual Relationship as Paradigm for Intergenerational Literary Testimony', in *Witnessing, Memory, Poetics: H. G. Adler and W. G. Sebald*, ed. by Helen Finch and Lynn L. Wolff (Rochester, NY: Camden House, 2014), pp. 1–21 (pp. 7–8).

13. Hocheneder is referring to Adler's volumes of poetry *Vier Jahreszeiten* (1975), *Blicke: Gedichte 1947–1951* (1979), and *Stimme und Zuruf* (1980). See Franz Hocheneder, *H. G. Adler (1910–1988): Privatgelehrter und freier Schriftsteller* (Vienna: Böhlau, 2009), pp. 206–07. It is interesting to note that, outside of the German context, *Stimme und Zuruf* was received positively. See Jerry Glenn, review of: H. G. Adler, *Stimme und Zuruf* [Hamburg: Knaus, 1980, 94 pages], *World Literature Today: A Literary Quarterly of the University of Oklahoma*, 55 (1981), 464–65.

14. Volume four of the collection (*Schuldig und Unschuldig: Symphonische Miniaturen*) appeared in 2016, and the publisher's website describes how Adler worked on these stories between 1953 and 1967, the years during which he also wrote his epic novel *Die unsichtbare Wand*. See <http://www.loecker-verlag.at> [accessed 1 April 2018]

15. Jeremy Adler writes, 'Durch die Wiederentdeckung der Romane, auch und gerade in den USA, ist jedoch der Blick auf ein Feld verdeckt worden, das gerade zu Lebzeiten des Autors auf besonderes Interesse stieß: die Kurzprosa.' Jeremy Adler, 'Vorwort', H. G. Adler, *Schuldig und Unschuldig: Symphonische Miniaturen*, ed. by Franz Hocheneder, *Gesammelte Erzählungen* Vol. 4. (Vienna: Löcker, 2016), pp. 9–10 (p. 9).

16. See H. G. Adler, *Nach der Befreiung: Ausgewählte Essays zur Geschichte und Soziologie*, ed. by Peter Filkins with Jeremy Adler (Konstanz: Konstanz University Press, 2013) and H. G. Adler, *Orthodoxie des Herzens: Ausgewählte Essays zu Literatur, Judentum und Politik*, ed. by Peter Filkins with Jeremy Adler (Konstanz: Konstanz University Press, 2014).

17. Peter Filkins, *H. G. Adler: A Life in Many Worlds* (New York: Oxford University Press, 2019).

18. H. G. Adler's estate, with its 320 archive boxes, is one of the largest in the holdings of the Archive of German Literature (Deutsches Literaturarchiv, DLA) in Marbach, Germany. The Foyle Special Collections Library at King's College, London, UK also holds significant materials. The 'H. G. Adler Collection' at King's College comprises over 1,000 books, pamphlets, and journals from Adler's reference library that were fundamental to the research for his book on Theresienstadt. The Beinecke Library at Yale University also holds works and papers by H. G. Adler. The documents he collected from Theresienstadt are held in the Netherlands, in the Institute for War Documentation, which has merged with the Center for Holocaust and Genocide Studies to form the NIOD Institute for War, Holocaust and Genocide Studies (NIOD Instituut voor Oorlogs-, Holocaust- en Genocidestudies).

19. Sven Kramer has argued that there is a valuable post-war narrative of the Shoah to be found in H. G. Adler's letters. See Sven Kramer, ' "Über diesem Abgrund wölben wir unsere Liebe": Die Gegenwart der Toten und der Glücksanspruch der Überlebenden in H. G. Adlers Briefwechsel mit Bettina Gross 1945–1946', in *Literatur und Anthropologie: H. G. Adler, Elias Canetti und Franz Baermann Steiner in London*, ed. by Jeremy Adler and Gesa Dane (Göttingen: Wallstein, 2014), pp. 138–57, and 'Shaping Survival through Writing: H. G. Adler's Correspondence with Bettina Gross, 1945–1947', in *H. G. Adler: Life, Literature, Legacy*, ed. by Julia Creet, Sara R. Horowitz, and Amira Bojadzija-Dan (Evanston, IL: Northwestern University Press, 2016), pp. 69–85.

20. H. G. Adler, *Kontraste und Variationen* (Würzburg: Echter, 1969).

21. See *Düsteres Idyll: Trost der deutschen Romantik*, Fotografien von H. G. Adler mit einem Essay von Péter Nádas (Marbach am Neckar: Deutsche Schillergesellschaft, 2015 [Marbacher Magazin 149].) A small selection of Adler's travel photographs were also included in the 2014 exhibit 'Reisen: Fotos von unterwegs' at the Literatur Museum der Moderne in Marbach. See *Reisen: Fotos von unterwegs*, ed. by Heike Gfrereis (Marbach am Neckar: Deutsche Schillergesellschaft, 2014 [Marbacher Katalog 67]), pp. 288–89, 302–03, 305.

22. Jeremy Adler, 'Afterword', in H. G. Adler, *Theresienstadt 1941–1945: The Face of a Coerced Community*, trans. by Belinda Cooper (New York: Cambridge University Press, 2017), pp. 803–28 (p. 811). This text is translated by Jeremiah Riemer and is a slightly revised version of Jeremy Adler, 'Nachwort', in H. G. Adler, *Theresienstadt 1941–1945: Das Antlitz einer Zwangsgemeinschaft* (Göttingen: Wallstein, 2005), pp. 895–926.

23. Jeremy Adler, 'Afterword', p. 811.

24. Jeremy Adler, 'Afterword', p. 811.

25. *Als der Holocaust noch keinen Namen hatte — Before the Holocaust Had Its Name*, ed. by Regina Fritz, Éva Kovács, and Béla Rásky (Vienna: New Academic Press, 2016). In their introduction, 'Der NS-Massenmord an den Juden: Perspektiven und Fragen der frühen Aufarbeitung', the editors refer to Dan Michman's Simon Wiesenthal Lecture given at the Vienna Wiesenthal Institute for Holocaust Studies, which provides a detailed historical overview of terminology for this paradigmatic atrocity of the twentieth century (p. 19). See Dan Michman, 'Shoah, Churbn, Cataclysm, Judeocide, Holocaust, Genocide (and more): On Terminology and Interpretation', 23 October 2014 <https://www.youtube.com/watch?v=vfScF7cxjCs> [accessed 1 April 2018].

26. Quoted in Jeremy Adler, 'H. G. Adler: A Prague Writer in London', in *Keine Klage über England? Deutsche und österreichische Exilerfahrungen in Großbritannien 1933–1945*, ed. by Charmian Brinson (Munich: Iudicium, 1998), pp. 13–30 (p. 15, my emphasis). Original quotation in 'H. G. Adler im Gespräch mit Hans Christoph Knebusch', *Zeugen des Jahrhunderts*, ZDF 11.11.1986. Interview also transcribed as 'H. G. Adler im Gespräch mit Hans Christoph Knebusch: Aufzeichnung der Gespräche im Januar 1986. Erstsendung 11.11.1986', in *Jüdische Lebenswege — Nahum Goldmann, Simon Wiesenthal, H. G. Adler*, ed. by Karl B. Schnelting (Frankfurt a/M: Fischer, 1987), pp. 157–86 (p. 170).

27. See Jeremy Adler, 'The World of My Father's Memory Writing: The *Gesamtkunstwerk* of H. G. Adler', in *H. G. Adler: Life, Literature, Legacy*, ed. by Julia Creet, Sara R. Horowitz, and Amira Bojadzija-Dan (Evanston, IL: Northwestern University Press, 2016), pp. 23–46 (p. 25).

28. H. G. Adler, 'Warum habe ich mein Buch *Theresienstadt 1941–1945* geschrieben?' in *H. G. Adler — Der Wahrheit verpflichtet: Interviews, Gedichte, Essays*, ed. by Jeremy Adler (Gerlingen: Bleicher Verlag, 1998), pp. 111–14 (p. 112). Adler wrote this essay in 1956, but it was published for the first time in the 1998 volume. See H. G. Adler, 'Warum habe ich mein Buch "Theresienstadt 1941–1945" geschrieben?', Typescript 5pp., 12.4.1956, A: H. G. Adler, Deutsches Literaturarchiv Marbach, A II 26: Folder 'Theresienstadt / Kleine Arbeiten' [Theresienstadt / Shorter Works]. Unless otherwise noted, all translations from unpublished texts are my own.

29. The poems that Adler wrote in the camps between the years 1942 and 1945 are comprised in section III 'Gedichte aus der Lagerzeit (1942–1945)' of his collected poems *Andere Wege: Gesammelte Gedichte*, ed. by Katrin Kohl and Franz Hocheneder, with the collaboration of Jeremy Adler and with an afterword by Michael Krüger (Klagenfurt: Drava, 2010), pp. 157–288.

30. See Jeremy Adler, 'Good Against Evil? H. G. Adler, T. W. Adorno and the Representation of the Holocaust', in *The German-Jewish Dilemma: From the Enlightenment to the Shoah*, ed. by Edward Timms and Andrea Hammel (Lewiston, NY: Mellen, 1999), pp. 255–89 (p. 259).

31. H. G. Adler, 'Warum habe ich mein Buch *Theresienstadt 1941–1945* geschrieben?', p. 113.

32. After liberation in April 1945, Adler returned to Prague, and at the end of June, he made the trip to Theresienstadt to meet Baeck, who had been able to keep the notes safe. See Gesa Dane, 'Einleitung', *Literatur und Anthropologie: H. G. Adler, Elias Canetti und Franz Baermann Steiner in London*, ed. by Jeremy Adler and Gesa Dane (Göttingen: Wallstein, 2014), pp. 7–15 (p. 8).

33. Adler, 'Warum habe ich mein Buch *Theresienstadt 1941–1945* geschrieben?', p. 113.

34. For further details on the various influences on Adler with respect to ethnology, in particular the influence of Bronislaw Malinowski's method of participant observation, which he learned about before the war from his friend Franz Baermann Steiner, see the following contributions: Peter Filkins, 'Both Sides of the Wall: Theresienstadt in H. G. Adler's Scholarship and Fiction' and Erhard Schüttpelz, 'Der Auszug aus Ägypten: Zum Vergleich der sozialtheoretischen Schriften von H. G. Adler, Elias Canetti und Franz Baermann Steiner', in *Literatur und Anthropologie: H. G. Adler, Elias Canetti und Franz Baermann Steiner in London*, ed. by Jeremy Adler and Gesa Dane (Göttingen: Wallstein, 2014), pp. 82–96 and pp. 158–75, respectively.

35. Jeremy Adler, 'Afterword', p. 804.

36. David Rousset, a French survivor, coined the term 'l'univers concentrationnaire' [concentrationary universe] in *La Revue international*, December 1945, January and February 1946.

37. Jeremy Adler notes, 'The continuity between modernity and the world of the camps, as explained in *Theresienstadt 1941–1945* using the theory of mechanical materialism, is something *Der verwaltete Mensch* locates concretely in the theory and practice of administration. This theory was borrowed by Zygmunt Baumann in his book *Modernity and the Holocaust*, as Baumann has since tacitly acknowledged.' See Adler, 'Afterword', p. 826. See also Zygmunt Baumann, *Modernity and the Holocaust* (Ithaca, NY: Cornell University Press, 2000).

38. Just as Adler reviewed Kogon's work, Kogon reviewed Adler's. See Eugen Kogon's 'Radio-Essay' for Süddeutscher Rundfunk, broadcast on 11 September 1956. The eight-page manuscript, 'Ein Buch und eine Meinung: Eugen Kogon spricht über das Buch *Theresienstadt* von H. G. Adler', is held in the Deutsches Literaturarchiv Marbach, A: H. G. Adler, A II 64.

39. Michael Hamburger, 'The Face of Force', *The Jewish Quarterly* 4.3, (1956/1957), 42. Hamburger's review of Adler's work follows directly after Adler's review of Léon Poliakov's *Harvest of Hate*

[Translated by Albert J. George from the French *Bréviaire de la Haine*] (London: Elek Books, 1956). H. G. Adler, 'The Great Tragedy', *The Jewish Quarterly* 4.3, (1956/1957), 41–42.

40. See J. Petersen's contribution to *Das Buch der Woche*, Hessischer Rundfunk, Frankfurt am Main, 'H. G. Adler: Theresienstadt'. The program aired 25 March 1956, and the ten-page manuscript is held in the Deutsches Literaturarchiv Marbach, A: H. G. Adler, A II 64, here p. 9.

41. See the collection of reviews and newspaper clippings in the Deutsches Literaturarchiv Marbach, A: H. G. Adler, A II 47.

42. Paul Michael Lützeler notes that Broch wrote this report in support of the *Theresienstadt* manuscript at the request of Veza Canetti, who wrote him on 6 May 1948 from London. Hermann Broch, 'H. G. Adler: Theresienstadt' (1949) in Hermann Broch, *Schriften zur Literatur I: Kritik*, Kommentierte Werkausgabe 9/1, ed. by Paul Michael Lützeler (Frankfurt a/M: Suhrkamp, 1976), pp. 404–05 (p. 405).

43. Jeremy Adler, 'The World of My Father's Memory Writing', p. 28.

44. See Wolfgang Benz, *Theresienstadt: Eine Geschichte von Täuschung und Vernichtung* (Munich: C. H. Beck, 2013).

45. Benz, *Theresienstadt*, p. 8.

46. In his introduction, Benz focuses his attention on the problem of how to understand and thus name Theresienstadt ('Ghetto' vs. '(Konzentrations)Lager'). Adler also considered the importance of this distinction, deciding, however, for the other term — 'Lager' — which he elucidates in both the glossary of the *Theresienstadt* book (pp. xxxix, xliv) and in *Der verwaltete Mensch* (p. 187). See also Jeremy Adler's commentary in his essay, 'The World of My Father's Memory Writing', footnote on p. 42.

47. For example, Benz notes Adler's 'persönlichen und moralischen Wertungen' [personal and moral judgements] of Dr. Paul Eppstein, who was a member of the Theresienstadt Judenrat. See Benz, *Theresienstadt*, p. 52.

48. Benz, *Theresienstadt*, p. 8. Ben Barkow productively contextualizes early accounts, like Adler's *Theresienstadt*, highlighting the social and political conditions under which these works were written and the role of emotion in them. See Barkow, 'A Heroic Work of Extraordinary Scholarship', pp. 89–90.

49. Dominick LaCapra raises similar questions, asking for example, 'How is experience related to truth claims and to critical value judgments?' See Dominick LaCapra, *Writing History, Writing Trauma* (Baltimore: The Johns Hopkins University Press, 2001), p. 37.

50. LaCapra, *Writing History, Writing Trauma*, p. 35.

51. Michael Schaich has noted that the publisher Kösel suggested a separate publication of the 'psychology' section of the *Theresienstadt*-book, but Adler preferred to overhaul the entire book, so this plan never came to fruition. See Michael Schaich's contribution to this volume.

52. Jeremy Adler, 'Afterword', p. 807. For an excellent analysis of Adler's methodology and assessment of the book's formal innovations, see François Ottmann, 'H. G. Adlers *Theresienstadt 1941–1945: Das Antlitz einer Zwangsgemeinschaft*: Ein gattungsübergreifendes Manifest für den Menschen', in *Die ersten Stimmen: Deutschsprachige Texte zur Shoah 1945–1963 / Les premières voix: Écrits sur la Shoah en langue allemande 1945–1963*, ed. by Ruth Vogel-Klein (Würzburg: Königshausen & Neumann, 2010), pp. 113–26.

53. Julia Menzel makes a similar observation with regard to Adler's literary works, 'For Adler, the extraordinary nature of the events of the Shoah made modernist methods of narrative representation imperative, methods that clearly differ from the documentary realism that characterizes the majority of early examples of Holocaust literature.' Julia Menzel, 'Between "Nothing" and "Something": Narratives of Survival in H. G. Adler's Scholarly and Literary Analysis of the Shoah', *Leo Baeck Institute Year Book*, 61.1 (2016), 119–34 (p. 121).

54. *Auschwitz: Zeugnisse und Berichte*, ed. by H. G. Adler, Hermann Langbein, and Ella Lingens-Reiner, with an introduction to the 6th edn by Katharina Stengel (Hamburg: Europäische Verlagsanstalt, 2014).

55. See for example the excerpts from a roundtable discussion between Adler, Fritz Bauer, Horst Krüger, Hans Schwerte, Dietrich Strothmann, and Ernst Weymar on the topic 'Was hat Auschwitz mit dem "Deutschen Menschen" zu tun?' included in the volume *Das Nürnberger*

Gespräch: Haltungen und Fehlhaltungen in Deutschland: Ein Tagungsbericht ed. by Hermann Glaser (Freiburg: Rombach, 1965), pp. 107–19.

56. Deutsches Literaturarchiv Marbach, A: H. G. Adler, A II 30: Buchbesprechungen.

57. See H. G. Adler, review of *Persecution and Resistance under the Nazis*, ed. by Ilse R. Wolff (London: Vallentine Mitchell, 1960) in *Neue politische Literatur*, 5.12 (1960), columns 1113–16 (column 1115).

58. H. G. Adler, 'The Scholar and the Catastrophe: A Guide to Research', in *The Wiener Library Bulletin*, 15.2 (1961), 23.

59. Adler, 'The Scholar and the Catastrophe', p. 23. On the challenges to and implications of naming this paradigmatic atrocity of the twentieth century, see Dan Michman's Simon Wiesenthal Lecture referenced above.

60. Adler, 'The Scholar and the Catastrophe', p. 23.

61. Adler, 'The Scholar and the Catastrophe', p. 23.

62. Adler, 'The Scholar and the Catastrophe', p. 23. Further evidence of this ideal can be found in Adler's many contributions to West German radio in the form of reports and essays. In one radio manuscript, for example, Adler recounts several stories of humanitarian acts within the concentration camps and thereby testifies to his unwavering faith in humankind. See H. G. Adler, 'Nicht mit den Wölfen heulen: Menschlichkeit gegen Unmenschlichkeit' [Not Howling with the Wolves: Humanity versus Inhumanity], WDR (Hauptabteilung Politik), program of 20 August 1961. Deutsches Literaturarchiv Marbach, A: H. G. Adler.

63. This is formulated explicitly in his correspondence with Hans Winterfeldt, a young scholar writing his dissertation on the language of the Nazis. Adler states, 'Gerade durch Ihre Beschäftigung mit diesem Thema werden Sie das Emotionelle überwinden, was Ihnen auch gesundheitlich und allgemein menschlich helfen wird. Wir alle müssen es lernen, <u>mit</u> unserer Vergangenheit zu leben, und das gelingt nur durch angespannt mutige Arbeit. Sie haben das Zeug dazu und werden es schaffen'. Letter from H. G. Adler to Hans Winterfeldt, 22 October 1964, Deutsches Literaturarchiv Marbach, A: H. G. Adler, A I 63.

64. See H. G. Adler letter to Jehuda Bacon on 15 February 1953, in *Jehuda Bacon: Malerei und Grafik*, ed. by Michael Koller and Jürgen Lenssen, trans. by Sarah Polewski and Jens Oertel (Würzburg: Stiftung Kunstsammlung der Diözese Würzburg, 2015), p. 62.

65. The subtitle of Franz Hocheneder's 2009 biography of Adler — *Privatgelehrter und freier Schriftsteller* — underscores this dual role.

66. H. G. Adler, 'Wissenschaftler oder Gelehrter?', Typescript 8pp., 9.2.1962. Deutsches Literaturarchiv Marbach, A: H. G. Adler, A II 25. All references to this manuscript will be cited parenthetically in the text. All translations are my own.

67. See Lynn L. Wolff, '"Die Grenzen des Sagbaren": Toward a Political Philology in H. G. Adler's Reflections on Language', in *H. G. Adler: Life, Literature, Legacy*, ed. by Julia Creet, Sara R. Horowitz, and Amira Bojadzija-Dan (Evanston, IL: Northwestern University Press, 2016), pp. 273–301.

68. In the glossary of his *Theresienstadt* book, Adler writes, 'Die für die Nazisprache typische Entwertung von Begriffen und Wörtern wurde auch in T verspürt; "Betreuung" näherte sich oft bedenklich dem Betrug'. [The devaluation of concepts and words, which was typical for Nazi language, was also felt in T; 'assistance/supervision' came ominously close to deceit.] See H. G. Adler, 'Wörterverzeichnis', in *Theresienstadt 1941–1945: Das Antlitz einer Zwangsgemeinschaft* (Göttingen: Wallstein, 2005), pp. xxix–lix (p. xxxiv). As mentioned above, the glossary was unfortunately not included in the translated edition.

69. H. G. Adler, 'Die Sprache der Gewalt und ihre Wörter', in *Abhandlungen aus der Pädagogischen Hochschule Berlin*, vol. 7, of *Spätlese aus Forschung und Lehre einer aufgelösten Hochschule*, ed. Walter Heistermann (Berlin: Colloquium Verlag / Otto H. Hess, 1980), p. 202. In his considerations of 'SS-Sprache', or SS language, as he terms it, Adler explores how originally innocuous words became terms of violence under National Socialism. The Nazis frequently used military expressions in everyday contexts and employed various forms of euphemisms to cover up murder and mass murder, including the manipulation of bureaucratic language to conceal criminality. In addition to *betreuen* [to take care of], *Sonderbehandlung* [special treatment] is Adler's key example. See Wolff, '"Die Grenzen des Sagbaren"', p. 286.

70. Prior to the conference, a roundtable event held at Oxford University's Taylor Institution introduced several of the topics that were then discussed in greater detail at the IMLR.

71. See Gina Thomas, 'Zeuge des Grauens', in *Frankfurter Allgemeine Zeitung*, Nr. 131 (8 June 2016), N3.

72. It is worth noting Wachsmann's choice of the indefinite article in his title. The volume, despite its nearly 900 pages, is conscious of its status as one of many histories of the camps. Nikolaus Wachsmann, *KL: A History of the Nazi Concentration Camps* (New York: Farrar, Straus and Giroux, 2015). With direct reference to Adler's concept of the 'Zwangsgemeinschaft', Wachsmann titles one section of his study of the Nazi concentration camps 'Coerced Communities' (pp. 499–512). See discussion of the implications of this neologism above.

73. For additional context on the development of early Holocaust historiography, see Nicolas Berg, *Der Holocaust und die westdeutschen Historiker: Erforschung und Erinnerung* (Göttingen: Wallstein, 2004) and Aleida Assmann, *Der lange Schatten der Vergangenheit: Erinnerungskulturen und Geschichtspolitik* (Munich: C. H. Beck, 2006). Ruth Vogel-Klein emphasizes why historians in exile and from persecuted families played such an important role, explaining, 'Der Grund war vor allem die Tatsache, dass sie spezifische Informationen und Einsichten besaßen und dass an den deutschen Universitäten viele Professoren mit dem NS-Regime verstrickt waren oder für dieses Thema keinerlei Interesse zeigten'. [The reason was above all the fact that they possessed specific information and insights and that many professors at German universities were implicated in the National Socialist regime or showed no interest in this topic.] Vogel-Klein, introduction to *Die ersten Stimmen*, p. 14. A further publication that examines the work of survivors in the post-war period is *Opfer als Akteure: Interventionen ehemaliger NS-Verfolgter in der Nachkriegszeit*, ed. on behalf of the Fritz Bauer Institute by Katharina Stengel and Werner Konitzer (Frankfurt a/M: Campus Verlag, 2008).

74. My sincere thanks to Ann White for making this contribution available for publication. John J. White presented his essay at the H. G. Adler conference in Toronto, organized by Julia Creet, Sara R. Horowitz, and Amira Bojadzija-Dan, but was no longer able to rework it for publication in the volume *H. G. Adler: Life, Literature, Legacy* (2016). White's previous research on *Eine Reise* points not only to his continued engagement with Adler's work but also to the reception of Adler's work more broadly. White's article ' "Zum Humoristen geboren": Irony and Black Humour in H. G. Adler's Novel *Eine Reise*' was published in a volume dedicated to the Austrian Germanist Joseph Strelka, who was long interested in Adler as a writer and scholar. In that article, White highlights Strelka's 'pioneering essay on Adler's concentration camp poetry', which was published in *Zu Hause im Exil: Zu Werk und Person H. G. Adlers*, ed. by Heinrich Hubmann and Alfred O. Lanz (Stuttgart: Steiner, 1987), pp. 3–9. See *Mnemosyne Träume: Festschrift zum 80. Geburtstag von Joseph P. Strelka*, ed. by Ilona Slawinski (Tübingen: Francke, 2007), pp. 511–27.

75. H. G. Adler, 'Sonderinterview von Alfred Joachim Fischer', in *Zu Hause im Exil*, ed. by Heinrich Hubmann and Alfred O. Lanz (Stuttgart: Steiner, 1987), pp. 191–201 (p. 192).

CHAPTER 2

❖

H. G. Adler's
Shoah Trilogy

Christopher R. Browning

In this contribution, I would like to place H. G. Adler within a wider historiographical context. Among Holocaust scholars, Adler is unusual in two additional ways beyond his prolific fiction writing. First, there were a number of survivors, who experienced the Holocaust years while in their teens or early twenties, subsequently obtained a university education, and became professional scholars who devoted themselves to the study of National Socialism and the Holocaust. But Adler belongs to a smaller group of somewhat older men born in the first decade of the twentieth century, who were educated in the interwar period. This provided an analytical lens through which this older cohort experienced the Holocaust years. Immediately after liberation, they set about collecting documentation to underpin their subsequent academic studies of the event. Alongside Adler (1910–1988), I am thinking here in particular of Philip Friedman (1901–1960) and Isaiah Trunk (1905–1981). Friedman collected documents on behalf of the Central Jewish Historical Commission in Poland and, after leaving Poland, for YIVO in New York; he wrote many seminal articles before his untimely death in 1960. Trunk also left Poland and collected documentation on behalf of the Ghetto Fighters' Kibbutz in Israel and YIVO. A resident of Lodz in the interwar period, he published a major work on the Lodz ghetto in Yiddish in 1962 and a masterful study of the Jewish councils of Eastern Europe in 1972. In some ways his scholarly post-war career remarkably paralleled Adler's, who collected documents on behalf of the Jewish Museum in Prague, fled to England, wrote a major study of the Theresienstadt ghetto and the massive study of the German bureaucracy of deportation, *Der Verwaltete Mensch*, in 1974.

Second, among historians of the Holocaust, Prague Jews are heavily represented. Most — for example Yehuda Bauer, Saul Friedländer, and Dov Otto Kulka — moved to Israel and wrote primarily in Hebrew, English, and French, but not German. Adler was the exception in moving to England rather than Israel and writing and publishing his scholarly works in German.

As I read the three Adler novels that have been translated into English, I was intrigued by several questions. First, why did Adler not become as central or prominent in Holocaust historiography as many other survivor-scholars despite his two weighty contributions? Second, insofar as his novels are at least partially autobiographical, how are the obstacles to an academic career represented or portrayed in them? Concerning the first question, I suspect that Adler's living in England and publishing in German was doubly isolating. In England, he could not interact easily with either Israeli or American-Jewish scholars. His 700-page study *Theresienstadt 1941–1945*, published in Germany in 1955, appeared in a country then at the height of its post-war wallowing in self-pity and alleged victimization, while internationally memories of Nazi atrocities and post-war trials were being eclipsed by the urgencies of the Cold War. Academically, Holocaust scholarship as a legitimate field of study simply did not yet exist.

If *Theresienstadt* was premature, ironically *Der Verwaltete Mensch* appeared too late. By then Raul Hilberg's thesis that the Final Solution should be seen as a vast administrative-bureaucratic process was accepted by many, and Adler's detailed and massive Germanic tome, studying one small aspect of the 'machinery of destruction' that deported a very small percentage of all Holocaust victims to their death, was too overwhelming in its concentrated detail. Moreover, scholars were building on but also moving beyond the bureaucratic template by asking questions about the political dynamics of decision-making. So-called 'functionalist' scholars were now exploring the implications of a polycratic model of Nazi governance (as opposed to the older totalitarian model) and plotting the evolution of policy within the context of changing circumstances, while opposing hard-line 'so-called' intentionalists, like Lucy Dawidowicz, adamantly insisted on the centrality of Hitler's and Germany's antisemitism. Adler's approach was deemed too static for the former, and too structural and universalistic for the latter, and thus was invoked and cited by neither faction.

If we accept that *Die unsichtbare Wand* (*The Wall*) is at least partially autobiographical, how did Adler understand the fate of his own scholarly career at that stage of his life? The novel can be understood as an exploration of a four-fold alienation: as a survivor alienated from those who died; as a returnee unable to resume a normal life among those who had not been deported; as a stranger living in exile; and as an aspiring academic alienated from all the peers and contacts upon whom such an academic career would depend. As an academic novel of sorts, *The Wall* begins with the Kafkaesque nightmare of the protagonist Arthur Landau's teacher Prenzel inviting him to return and then denouncing him, and ends more in the spirit of Kingsley Amis and David Lodge, with the ardent Resi Knispel throwing herself at Arthur and the conference of the International Society of Sociologists taking place as a fair, with his academic nemeses appearing as various circus characters.

Adler's portrayal of differing reactions to Arthur's *The Sociology of the Oppressed* presumably reflects some of the reactions he experienced in the 1950s concerning *Theresienstadt*. Three reactions are particularly revealing. The first is that, as a person who had survived a terrible ordeal, Arthur was viewed with 'amazement' and 'astonishment', but that did not translate into any sustained interest in actually hearing much less thinking about his work or the subject in general.[1] Arthur notes that 'publishers had turned up their noses at so much sadness and didn't want anything to do with it, no one having ever shown any interest in sinking himself into my thoughts [...]' (*WE* 124). ['die Verleger rümpften ihre Nasen, wenn sie so viel Trauer rochen, und wollten das nicht haben, niemand hatte je den Wunsch gezeigt, sich in meine Gedanken zu vertiefen [...]' (*W* 133)]. The character So-and-So warns Arthur to give up the project entirely, since 'horror was in fashion for a moment, but already in serious circles interest has essentially waned' (*WE* 214) ['die Greuel einen Augenblick lang in Mode waren, aber gerade in ernsten Kreisen lässt das Interesse schon wesentlich nach' (*W* 226)].

Second and third, Professor Kratzenstein gives him two contradictory critiques. On the one hand, he wants only the facts without getting 'bogged down' in the 'nonsense' of 'ethical matters'. 'If I were you', Kratzenstein advises, 'I would just write a short, clear account about [...] what you experienced and observed. [...] Reflections about it all should be left out. They will only muddle your account, making it too emotional, such that no one will take it seriously' (*WE* 98). ['An Ihrer Stelle würde ich einen kurzen klaren Bericht verfassen, [...] was Sie erlebt und beobachtet haben. [...] Reflexionen darüber sind zu unterlassen. Sie verdunkeln nur den Bericht, verfärben ihn emotionell und interessieren keinen ernsten Menschen' (*W* 105–06)]. On the other, he insists upon a rigid ideological framework: 'all suffering [...] was the result of economic conditions' and the concentration camps were a 'specific kind of exploitation', he proclaims (*WE* 336) ['alles Leid [...] auf ökonomische Faktoren zurückzuführen ist. [...] eine[] spezifische[] Ausbeutung' (*W* 350)].

Fortunately, Adler's *Theresienstadt*, unlike *The Sociology of the Oppressed*, was published, and it was highly regarded both then and now. In some ways, it anticipates by decades the current demand for 'integrated' histories of the Holocaust, which combine the previously separated studies of perpetrators and victims. As was the case eventually with Adler's novels, *Theresienstadt 1941–1945: The Face of a Coerced Community* was finally published in English translation in 2017. But the various reactions Adler portrays in his novel *The Wall* ring true, and the writing and publishing of *Theresienstadt* must have been as nearly a lonely and frustrated enterprise as the writing and publishing of his fiction.

Note

1. H. G. Adler, *Die unsichtbare Wand* (Vienna: Paul Zsolnay Verlag, 1989). H. G. Adler, *The Wall*, trans. by Peter Filkins (New York: Random House, 2014). References to the German original and English translation will be made in parentheses in the text, hereafter abbreviated as *W* and *WE* respectively.

CHAPTER 3

❖

Two Memoirs of the Camps: Primo Levi and H. G. Adler

Peter Pulzer

Es ist keiner so herausgekommen, wie er hineingegangen ist.
No-one came out as he went in.[1]

Few events of the twentieth century have been covered more voluminously and, in many respects repetitively, than the National Socialist project of camps whose purpose was to segregate, isolate, exploit, degrade and ultimately murder the prisoners. A fair proportion of this literature verges on the worthless; some of it appeals in an offensive way to a sado-masochistic readership. It is therefore all the more remarkable that there is an impressive number of works that have stood the test of time. These works examine the thinking behind what David Rousset called *L'univers concentrationnaire*,[2] i.e. the purpose and organization of the camps, the conditions of life in them and the effect that the camp experience had in the inmates. They stand out as monuments to the heart of darkness that marked the middle decades of the twentieth century. Some of the earlier attempts at a scholarly analysis that over-emphasised the destructive effect of camp life, for instance those of Elie Cohen[3] and of Bruno Bettelheim, who observed a 'childlike dependency on the guards' and a 'regression into infantile behaviour [as] a mass phenomenon',[4] have been superseded by more nuanced studies. The earliest of the memoirs, that of the German Catholic academic and publicist Eugen Kogon, a prisoner for six years in Buchenwald, remains 'das grundlegende und unübertroffene Werk zum Thema' [the foundational and unsurpassed work on the subject], according to Adler,[5] for its attempt at calm balance. But if one were asked to select the two most impressive of the many hundreds of memoirs, the choice would surely land on those of Primo Levi and H. G. Adler.[6]

For both Levi and Adler, as for countless others, the camp experience was a learning process that affected and formed the rest of their lives, yet their learning processes displayed marked differences as well as obvious similarities. To start with there was the difference in their backgrounds. True, they both came from the educated bourgeoisie of central Europe. But Adler, nine years older than Levi, had completed his training in literature and the social sciences with a PhD from the Charles University in Prague by the time of his deportation, while Levi had studied chemistry at Turin, completing his doctorate just as the severity of the

Fascist régime's anti-Jewish laws were beginning to bite. Before his deportation
Adler had been able to observe the escalation of the National Socialist régime's
measures first in Germany itself, then in Austria and finally in the 'Protectorate' of
Bohemia-Moravia. He therefore arrived in Theresienstadt with some awareness of
the kind of fate that awaited him and of the type of institution into which he had
been condemned. As he recorded after his liberation, it did not take him long to
formulate an intellectual agenda:

> Als es zu den Deportationen kam, habe ich mir gesagt: Das überlebe ich
> nicht. Aber wenn ich es überlebe, dann will ich es darstellen, und zwar
> auf zweierlei Weise: ich will es wissenschaftlich erforschen und in dieser
> Gestaltung vollkommen von mir als Individuum loslösen [...]. Die besondere
> Gesellschaftsform, der Alltag eines Lagers, seine konkreten Lebensbedingungen
> müssen erfaßt und erschöpft werden. Immer wieder ist die Frage zu stellen:
> was folgt und erfolgt auf Grund aller Anordnungen und Verbote? Wie setzt
> sich die Gemeinschaft und das Individuum mit der gegebenen Zwangslage
> auseinander?
>
> [When it came to the deportations, I said to myself: I won't survive this. But
> if I do survive this, then I want to depict it, in fact in two ways: I want to
> investigate it in a scholarly way, detaching myself completely (in this particular
> configuration) from myself as an individual [...]. The particular social system,
> daily life in the camp, its concrete manifestation need to be noted and explored.
> The question needs to be asked over and over again: what follows from, and
> happens by virtue of, orders and proscriptions? How does the community, and
> how does the individual, deal with the predicament at hand?[7]]

The younger Levi could not have embarked on his ordeal in a more contrasted
way. Aged 24, he had, as he himself records, 'little wisdom, no experience and a
decided tendency [...] to live in an unrealistic world of my own.'[8] He was not a
born writer.

> If I had not lived the Auschwitz experience, I probably would never have
> written anything. I would not have had the motivation, the incentive, to write
> [...]. It was the experience of the camp and the long journey home that forced
> me to write.[9]

Unquestionably a quick learner, he had nevertheless to start from scratch. Not that
he was apolitical: he was, after all, a founder member of a partisan group, who had
experienced Fascism at first hand. Like Adler, he avoids any attempt to explain or
analyze the ideological premise on which the Nazi persecutions rested. Though
Adler devotes two chapters to summarizing Nazi policies in Bohemia-Moravia
after the creation of the 'Protectorate' and the origins of the Theresienstadt ghetto
he does not ask why any of this happened. He simply knows, from observation and
experience, the high priority that 'the solution of the Jewish Question' occupied
in Nazi policy-making. Levi, if anything, goes further. In an often-quoted passage
he insists

> Perhaps one cannot, what is more one must not, understand what happened,
> because to understand is almost to justify. Let me explain: 'understanding' a
> proposal or human behaviour means to 'contain' it, contain its author, put

oneself in his place, identify with him. Now no human being will ever be able to identify with Hitler, Himmler, Goebbels, Eichmann, and endless others. This dismays us, and at the same time gives us a sense of relief, because perhaps it is desirable that their words (and also, unfortunately, their deeds) cannot be comprehensible to us. They are non-human words and deeds, really counter-human, without historical precedents, with difficulty comparable to the cruellest events of the struggle for existence.[10]

His learning process begins shortly after his arrival in Auschwitz. He tries to slake his thirst from an icicle, which is then broken off by a guard. When he asks 'Why?', he is told 'here there is no why' (*Hier ist kein warum*). 'The explanation is repugnant but simple', he concludes. 'In this place everything is forbidden. Not for hidden reasons, but because the camp has been created for that purpose.'[11] The five words of this exchange have become universal property. They are emblematic of the mind-set of those on whom the world's totalitarian institutions depend. They could as easily have been uttered in a *gulag*, a 're-education centre' of the Khmer Rouge or of Mao Zedong's Red Guards, or by the myrmidons of Generals Franco and Pinochet.

Both Adler and Levi, like Kogon before them, reflect on the impact that the 'enforced community' (*Zwangsgemeinschaft*) had, not only on its victims, but also on their captors. The purpose of all types of Nazi camps, and for that matter analogous institutions like the *gulag*, was to humiliate and dehumanise the inmates, to ensure that they abandoned whatever elements of bourgeois decency they brought with them, to sow universal distrust and envy in an economy of enforced scarcity and a society based on maliciously invented hierarchies. Adler cites from a survivor's account, 'Das haben die Deutschen an uns verbrochen, das, daß sie uns zu Verbrechern machen, daß sie uns dazu zwingen, zu stehlen, zu rauben, zu plündern' (*T* 675). [That is what the Germans have done to us — they have made us into criminals, they have forced us to steal, to rob, to plunder. (*TE* 593)] From another account, he quotes,

> Es wurde hier eine künstliche, kranke, in Angst und Elend lebende Gemeinschaft gegründet, in der Menschen, die man stets als unbescholtene Persönlichkeiten angesehen hatte, moralisch zugrunde gingen. Bedingt durch die eigentliche Haftpsychose, durch Entbehrungen, Hunger etc. gelangte der Großteil, insbesondere die Jugend, zu einem moralischen Tiefstand. Der Unterschied zwischen 'mein' und 'dein' war vielfach vollkommen verwischt [...]. (*T* 675)

> [Here, living in fear and misery was established an artificial, sick community in which people whom one always had seen as respectable figures decayed morally. Conditioned by an actual prison psychosis, by deprivation, hunger, etc., the majority, especially the young people, reached a moral nadir. The difference between 'mine' and 'yours' often was completely erased [...]. (*TE* 593)]

Adler, and presumably not only he, was particularly concerned about the effect of these pressures on the young:

> Einem Kinde konnte kaum beigebracht werden, daß im Alltag des Lagerlebens die Lüge nicht nur notwendig, sondern auch, in dieser entwerteten Welt,

sittlich verantwortbar wäre, obwohl sie, unbedingt genommen, verwerflich sein sollte. Es war die ärgste Folge des Regimes, daß es alles Gute schlecht und alles Schlechte gut werden ließ. Im Lager war eine unbedingte Sittlichkeit rein vital unmöglich. Eine bedingte Sittlichkeit zu rechtfertigen, vermag nur einer regen Gewissensforschung gelingen, die eine Lüge stets als Lüge ansieht und in allen sittlichen Konsequenzen beurteilen kann. Das konnte nur eine geringe Minderheit, während die überwältigende Mehrheit im Dickicht einer doppelten Moral strauchelte. (*T* 641)

[It was almost impossible to teach a child that lying was not only necessary in the everyday life of the camp but also morally justified in the camp's morally devalued world, although, unconditionally speaking, it was reprehensible. The worst consequence of the regime was that it turned everything good into bad and everything bad into good. In the camp, unconditional morality was impossible from a purely vital standpoint. A justification of conditional morality can be achieved only through active probing of the conscience, in which one always sees a lie as a lie and can judge all its moral consequences. Only a small minority were capable of this, whereas the vast majority foundered in the thickets of double standards. (*TE* 567)]

Mutatis mutandis the policy of those in power, whether in a ghetto like Theresienstadt or a concentration camp like Buchenwald or a death camp like Auschwitz, was to reduce the inmates to the dog-eat-dog level of existence (*diese Krümelwelt der Gier* — this world of crumbs and greed)[12] so graphically illustrated in the film *Son of Saul*. Kogon anticipates this depiction by citing the saying 'The prisoner is the prisoner's worst enemy'.[13] Predictably the more degraded the prisoners became, the more they were despised by their captors. Levi recounts this graphically,

They see us reduced to ignoble slavery, without hair, without honour and without names, beaten every day, more abject every day, and they never see in our eyes a light of rebellion, or of peace, or of faith [...]. This naturally did not stop many of them throwing us a piece of bread or a potato now and again [...]. They do it to get rid of some importunate starved look, or through a momentary impulse of humanity, or through simple curiosity to see us running from all sides to fight each other for the scrap, bestially and without restraint, until the strongest gobbles it up.[14]

In all the descriptions of the Dante-like universe in which they tried to exist and survive, Adler and Levi do not forget the exceptions to the apathetic, fatalistic or degraded mass of the inmates. Towards the end of the war, a consignment of prisoners infected with typhoid fever arrived in Theresienstadt and some of the local prisoners volunteered to care for them, in some cases at the cost of their own lives (*T* 212 / *TE* 171–72). Two of Adler's thirteen types of inmate are the 'Helfer' [helpers] and 'Gütige' [kindhearted people] — minorities, but all the more to be honoured for that (*T* 674 / *TE* 592–93). Levi probably owed his life to an Italian civilian labourer who passed him food without any expectation of reward or reciprocity: 'Thanks to Lorenzo I managed not to forget that I myself was a man'.[15] Adler devotes only one chapter to the counterpoint of the demoralization and dehumanisation of Theresienstadt: the phenomenon that is probably its best-known aspect among the laity, its incredibly impressive cultural life — the continuing programme of lectures, the prose and poetry, the artistic creations, including those by the child inmates, and above all the music, which has made Pavel Haas, Hans Krása and Viktor Ullmann household names in the post-war world. Perhaps the most moving episodes of all were the performances of the Verdi *Requiem* with its dual message, the *Libera Me* for the performers and the *Dies Irae* for their oppressors.

A final question that needs to be answered is this: What conclusions did Adler and Levi take with them into their post-liberation lives on the basis of the learning process that they had undergone? Was Kogon right in asserting that anyone who survived the camps was irrevocably changed by the experience? Both of them became significant writers. This is less surprising in the case of Adler, who was already well equipped intellectually at the beginning of the Second World War, than for Levi who, as we have seen, turned to writing only on the basis of his Auschwitz experience. Adler asserts that his devotion to Enlightenment principles was untouched by his experiences, 'Verändert habe ich mich nicht. Meine Grundsätze sind die gleichen geblieben, nur noch gefestigter, intensiver und vielleicht gereifter' (*T* 905) [I haven't changed, my principles remain the same, only more firm, more intense, and perhaps more mature (*TE* 811)], he wrote to Franz Baermann Steiner in 1947. It is the qualification that is significant. After Theresienstadt it was much clearer to him than before what the nature of oppression is, how it robs the individual of his unique humanity, how it turns him from a living being into a thing. 'Menschen dürfen nicht verwaltet werden, nur Sachen sind zu verwalten' (*T* 924), he wrote in *Der verwaltete Mensch* [Human beings may not be administered, something reserved only for things (*TE* 826)]. Levi, too, developed notions that were already there before his deportation, though almost certainly less consciously, less explicitly articulated, more instinctively assumed. He is happy, even eager, to share with others what he learned not only at Auschwitz, but also from living in the decades of the European dictatorships:

> It is therefore necessary to be suspicious of those who seek to convince us by means other than reason, and of charismatic leaders. We must be cautious about delegating to others our judgment and our will. Since it is difficult to distinguish true prophets from false, it is well to regard all prophets with suspicion. It is better to renounce revealed truths, even if they exalt us with their splendour, or if we find them convenient because we can acquire them gratis. It is better to content oneself with more modest and less exciting truths, those one acquires painfully, little by little and without shortcuts.[16]

Thus, both Adler and Levi remained true to their Enlightenment heritage, but interpreted and adapted in their own way. Both wrote works that only tangentially reflected their camp experiences. The humanist scepticism of Levi, contained in the passage quoted above, had its roots in his belief in science and scientific knowledge as guides to life and in his schoolboy admiration for Lucretius's *De Rerum Natura*. 'There is nothing more vivifying than a hypothesis' he was to write later in *The Periodic Table*.[17] Adler cast his net even more widely. In addition to his scholarly works on deportation and ghettoization he wrote literary criticism, fiction and, significantly, poetry; significantly, that is, as a challenge to Theodore Adorno's much-debated assertion that 'to write a poem after Auschwitz is a barbarism'.[18]

From what we now know about the cultural life of Theresienstadt or the boost to morale that the members of the women's orchestras of Auschwitz and Bergen-Belsen gained from their playing, the arts are the greatest imaginable antidote to barbarism. Let me therefore end with the works of three poets of the twentieth century, who have respectively anticipated, recorded and looked back on the mid-century *Zivilisationsbruch* — the rupture in civilization.[19]

My first choice is Rudyard Kipling, whose *Storm Cone*, written in late 1932, anticipates the looming *Zivilisationsbruch*:

> This is the midnight — let no star
> Delude us — dawn is very far.
> This is the tempest long foretold —
> Slow to make head but sure to hold ...
>
> If we have cleared the expectant reef
> Let no man look for his relief.
> Only the darkness hides the shape
> Of further peril to escape ...
>
> She moves, with all save purpose lost,
> To make her offing from the coast,
> But, till she fetches open sea,
> Let no man deem that he is free!

My second is W. H. Auden, whose career exactly spanned the *Zivilisationsbruch*. In *September 1, 1939*, he casts a cold eye on 'the windiest militant trash Important Persons shout':

> Exiled Thucydides knew
> All that a speech can say about democracy, and what dictators do.
> The elderly rubbish that they talk
> To an apathetic grave [...]
> The enlightenment driven away.

And in *Musée des Beaux Arts* he dissects the unwitting accomplice of oppression, the ordinary person who looks the other way when something terrible happens:

> In Breughel's *Icarus*, for instance, how everything turns away
> Quite leisurely from the disaster; the ploughman may
> Have heard the splash, the forsaken cry
> But for him it was not an important failure [...]

My third is a survivor of the *Zivilisationsbruch*, Paul Celan, whose *Todesfuge* shows his mastery in recalling the irreparable personal tragedies of the 1930s and 1940s:

> der Tod ist ein Meister aus Deutschland sein Auge ist blau
> er trifft dich mit bleierner Kugel er trifft dich genau
> ein Mann wohnt im Haus dein goldenes Haar Margarete
> es hetzt seine Rüden auf uns er schenkt uns ein Grab in der Luft
> er spielt mit den Schlangen und träumet der Tod ist ein Meister aus
> Deutschland
>
> [death is a master from Germany his eyes are blue
> he strikes you with leaden bullets his aim is true

a man lives in the house your golden hair Margarete
he sets his pack on us he grants a grave in the air
he plays with the serpents and daydreams death is a master from Germany]

What unites all my writers, not to mention Anna Akhmatova or Alexander Solzhenitsyn, or the growing number of Chinese memorialists,[20] is the hope, and the
intention to ensure, that the world will not forget. 'Das Wissen', György Konrád
said at the opening of the Berlin Holocaust Exhibition, 'ist eine Schutzimpfung'
[Knowledge is an inoculation].[21] Experience has shown that this a necessary
condition for guarding against infection. It is not a sufficient one.

Notes to Chapter 3

1. Eugen Kogon, *Der SS-Staat. Das System der deutschen Konzentrationslager* (Munich: Alber, 1946),
   p. 301; Kogon, *The Theory and Practice of Hell. The German Concentration Camps and the Theory
   behind them* (London: Secker and Warburg, 1950), p. 272.
2. David Rousset, *L'Univers Concentrationnaire* (Paris: Éditions de Pavois, 1946); Rousset, *A World
   Apart*, trans. by Yvonne Moyse and Roger Senhouse (London: Secker and Warburg, 1951).
3. Elie Cohen, *Human Behaviour in the Concentration Camp* (London: Cape, 1954).
4. Bruno Bettelheim, 'Individual and Mass Behavior in Extreme Situations' in *Readings in Social
   Psychology*, ed. by Theodore M. Newcomb, and Eugene C. Hartley (New York: Holt, Rinehart
   & Winston, Inc., 1958), pp. 300–10 (p. 308).
5. H. G. Adler, *Theresienstadt 1941–1945: Das Antlitz einer Zwangsgemeinschaft* (Göttingen: Wallstein,
   2005), p. 763. H. G. Adler, *Theresienstadt 1941–1945: The Face of a Coerced Community*, trans. by
   Belinda Cooper (New York: Cambridge University Press, 2017), p. 696.
6. Primo Levi, *If this is a Man*, trans. by Stuart Woolf (London: Abacus, 1979).
7. H. G. Adler, cited in Jeremy Adler's afterword to the *Theresienstadt* volume, pp. 899, 906; in
   the English edition, Jeremy Adler's afterword is translated by Jeremiah Riemer, pp. 806, 812.
   Further references to these editions, abbreviated hereafter as *T* and *TE* respectively, will be
   made in parentheses in the text.
8. Levi. op, cit., p. 19.
9. Ibid., p. 397.
10. Ibid., p. 395.
11. Ibid., p. 35.
12. As Adler formulates it in unpublished story 'Der Hungernde' (1942).
13. Kogon, op. cit., p. 311.
14. Levi, op cit., p. 127.
15. Levi, op. cit., p. 128.
16. Levi, op. cit., p. 396.
17. Primo Levi, 'Nickel', in Primo Levi, *The Periodic Table* (London: Abacus, 1985), p. 76.
18. Theodor W. Adorno, 'Cultural Criticism and Society' [1951] in idem. *Prisms*, trans. by Samuel
    and Shierry Weber (Cambridge, MA: The MIT Press, 1983), pp. 17–34 (p. 34).
19. See *Zivilisationsbruch. Denken nach Auschwitz*, ed. by Dan Diner and trans. by Susanne
    Hoppmann-Löwenthal (Frankfurt a/M: Fischer, 1988).
20. E.g., Jun Chang, *Wild Swans: Three Daughters of China* (New York: Simon & Schuster, 1991); Dai
    Sije, *Balzac and the Little Chinese Seamstress* (London: Vintage, 2002).
21. György Konrád, 'A Speech at the Opening of the Holocaust Exhibition in Berlin's Historisches
    Museum', *Kultur Chronik*, 20/2 (2002), 19–21 (p. 21).

PART II

❖

Modernism in/and Exile

CHAPTER 4

❖

H. G. Adler's
England: Eindrücke eines Ahnungslosen in the Context of Exile Writing

Anthony Grenville

H. G. Adler is an exception among the Jewish writers who settled in Britain as exiles in the years after 1933. The great majority of those writers were refugees from Nazism who had escaped to Britain before the outbreak of war and had spent the wartime years in Britain, whereas Adler, unable to leave Czechoslovakia in time, was first incarcerated by the Nazis in Theresienstadt (Terezín), then deported to Auschwitz, before being sent to satellite camps of Buchenwald; he was liberated at Langenstein in April 1945. It was as a camp survivor that he fled to Britain in February 1947, to escape the looming Communist takeover in Prague. Adler's experiences thus differed very significantly from those of his fellow writers from Germany and central Europe who had arrived in pre-war Britain. Britain played host to a considerable number of writers who had fled before the outbreak of war: well-known names included Stefan Zweig, Alfred Kerr, Gabriele Tergit, Elisabeth Castonier, Elias Canetti, Robert Neumann, and, among the younger generation, Erich Fried, Judith Kerr, Eva Figes, and Lore Segal. But the number of victims of Nazi persecution who came to Britain after 1945 was far smaller, and among them were hardly any writers.[1] H. G. Adler was almost the only major literary figure among the later wave of exiles, and even he was hardly recognized in Britain during his lifetime.

The Britain with which Adler was confronted in the late 1940s differed greatly from the Britain to which the earlier wave of refugee writers had fled; the bomb-damaged country of the post-war austerity era was no longer the proud imperial power of pre-war days, whose wealth and standing had so impressed itself on the earlier arrivals.[2] Jeremy Adler has left a vivid picture of the shabby-genteel poverty of post-war Britain in his novel *The Magus of Portobello Road*,[3] where a family that closely resembles the Adlers lives in the forlorn hinterland west of Ladbroke Grove in London, where North Kensington shades over into Wormwood Scrubs; they move largely among other deracinated intellectuals from German-speaking central Europe, almost all of them pre-war refugees. The earlier refugees had experienced the war in Britain; they had seen at first hand the spirit of resistance to Nazi Germany that inspired most sections of British society in 1940 and the dogged courage with which the British civilian population in cities like London (where the refugees were concentrated) faced the suffering and hardships caused by the German bombing onslaught. This had a profound influence on their entire relationship with the British people; the more so as they felt that they had participated in the war effort on equal terms with their British counterparts, in marked contrast to the discrimination and persecution that they had suffered in their native countries.[4] Adler had not undergone that experience, and though he wrote admiringly of Britain's stance during the war, it was at second hand. His depiction of Britain should be understood in the light of these considerations.

Adler's *England: Eindrücke eines Ahnungslosen* is a remarkable document that surprises the reader at every turn; it deserves to be far more widely known than it is, languishing as an unpublished typescript in the archives.[5] For a start, its title is deceptive; it is also difficult to translate, like much of the text.[6] One might render it as *England: Impressions of an Ignoramus* or, more idiomatically, as *England: Impressions of an Innocent Abroad*. Adler's description of himself as 'ahnungslos', meaning 'clueless' or 'ignorant', is far from the truth. He displays a knowledge of England that is both broad and deep, and his analysis of English society is intellectually highly sophisticated. 'Eindrücke' translates as 'impressions', arousing expectations of a somewhat superficial, humorously impressionistic survey of English society from the point of view of a recently arrived refugee from Central Europe, in the style of George Mikes's popular bestseller *How to Be an Alien* (1946). It suggests images of tall, taciturn Englishmen in tweeds gazing with incomprehension and barely concealed dismay at short, rotund Continentals clad in bow ties and gesturing volubly in broken English, and of jokes about English food, heating, and emotional desiccation.

Adler's analysis, however, is profound, systematic, and rigorously academic. It is a multi-disciplinary study, relying primarily on social anthropology. Adler employs a technique of detached, objective observation combined with close-up, detailed analysis, reminiscent of Bronislaw Malinowski's participant observation; he was to deploy this technique in his celebrated analysis of the ghetto-cum-concentration camp at Theresienstadt, where he had himself been incarcerated. The study also shows the influence of the sister disciplines of sociology and social psychology, while some sections of it are art history, devoted to analysis of the visual arts — painting, architecture and, especially relevant to England, landscape gardening — and other sections consist of musicological analysis, the field in which Adler had earned his doctorate. The study consists of a brief foreword and seven sections, some 150 pages in length in all. Adler calls it a 'Versuch', in academic parlance the term for a scientific experiment; I refer to it as a study. It is elegantly written, with a clarity and immediacy that belie the complexity and subtlety of the ideas conveyed.

The circumstances of its genesis were also remarkable. Adler had arrived in Britain from Czechoslovakia on 11 February 1947; after surviving the Nazi camps, he had been forced to flee the land of his birth by the looming threat of a Communist takeover. By October 1949, two and a half years later, he had, according to the date on the typescript, completed *England: Eindrücke eines Ahnungslosen*. One can only marvel at the breadth of the knowledge of English society that he had acquired in so short a time and at the quality of his insights into it, especially given the terrible nature of his experiences in the years preceding his flight to England. The first section, which shares the title 'Eindrücke eines Ahnungslosen', begins with a frank admission of his bafflement at England: 'Stets ist es das Gefühl der Ahnungslosigkeit, das mich überkommt, wenn ich mich mit dem Erlebnis Englands auseinandersetze' (3) [Ignorance is always the feeling that comes over me when I seek to confront the experience of England]. That sense of bewildered disorientation does not, however, stem from the curious customs of the English, but rather from Adler's delighted admiration for what he sees as England's best qualities. He had, he writes, arrived in England 'wie ein Schiffbrüchiger' (3) [like a shipwrecked man]: 'Ich kam auch in einem Zustand, in dem ich mit meiner Vergangenheit abgeschlossen hatte. Ich brauchte keine Brücken hinter mir abzubrechen, denn sie bestanden nicht. Hinter mir lag nur Dunkel und Unsicherheit, Grauen und Zerstörung' [I also arrived in a condition in which I had broken with my past. I had no need to burn my bridges behind me, since they no longer existed. Behind me lay only darkness and insecurity, horror and destruction]. These were memories not suitable as the foundations for a new life.

Adler flew into Croydon Airport through an impenetrable fog, but met with a reception that brought light back into his life. To his astonishment, the customs and immigration officers were friendly, treating him in a professional manner that respected his human dignity; they carefully repacked his suitcase after searching it, behaviour that stood in striking contrast to his experience of officialdom in the years after 1939. Describing himself as a refugee who had survived the void, 'ein Flüchtling vor dem überstandenen Nichts' (4), Adler claims that he would never have escaped from that void in his former country of residence, especially given the nature of his convictions and his love of freedom. He continues with a remarkable tribute to his new homeland: 'Nun, diese Freiheit habe ich hier gefunden. Sie war der erste Eindruck und ist zum dauernden Erlebnis geworden. Ich habe in diesem Lande meinen inneren Frieden gefunden. Ich bin, wenn dies gesagt sein darf, glücklich geworden und segne jeden Tag, den ich hier leben darf' (4) [Well, I have found that freedom here. It was my first impression and it has become a lasting experience. I have found my inner peace in this country. I have, if I may say this, become happy and I bless every day that I can live here]. He then makes a remarkable declaration of affection for England: 'So wird man auch verstehen, daß ich meinen Ankunftstag in England als den Tag meiner endgültigen Befreiung feiere und nicht den Tag im April 1945, an dem ich aus der Gewalt Hitler-Deutschlands gerettet wurde' (4) [So one will understand that I celebrate the day of my arrival in England as the day of my definitive liberation and not the day in April 1945 when I was freed from the power of Hitler's Germany].

Adler celebrates freedom as the greatest good that he has encountered in Britain. But his analysis of that freedom is not limited, as in many accounts of English life in the 1930s and 1940s by refugees from Nazism, to casual, empirical observations about the freedom to walk on the grass in public parks, about the unrestrained freedom of speech at Speakers' Corner, or about the helpfulness of policemen, elsewhere the curtailers of freedom. Adler's starting point is the great degree of freedom enjoyed by the citizen in England from the agencies of the state and from arbitrary interventions by officialdom, which he had already noted during his arrival at Croydon Airport. For him, the survivor and analyst of the Nazi camps, the state's respect for the humanity of the individual was of paramount importance, contrasting as it did with his experiences in Theresienstadt, which he saw as the *nec plus ultra* in the dehumanization of the citizen and the stripping away of his individuality by a modern, inhumanly rationalized bureaucratic machine. 'Welch glückliches Land, das den Menschen noch über seelenlose Funktionen stellt!' (39) [What a fortunate land that still ranks human beings above soulless functions!], he exclaims.

Adler's method of analysis, I would argue, can be described as dialectical, notwithstanding his at times difficult relationship with Theodor W. Adorno, then generally regarded as the leading practitioner of dialectics.[7] Adler's analysis of English individualism is dialectically interlinked with his analysis of English conformity and uniformity; in similar dialectical combinations of opposites, he sees freedom in England as guaranteed by and inseparably linked to voluntary submission to the rule of law, the sacrosanct realm of the private sphere as indissolubly intertwined with the public sphere, and the living present of English life as interpenetrated by traditions and customs from the past. An example of this dialectical approach brings the first section of the study to a ringing conclusion:

> Der Mensch wird als Herr respektiert, aber seine freiwillige Unterordnung ist eine Selbstverständlichkeit, die zum gesellschaftlichen Zwang, zur unverletzlichen Konvention wird. Dieser Eindruck haftet, bevor man noch etwas anderes von diesem Lande weiß. Nur jener Fremde wird sich in England einordnen und wohlfühlen können, der gewillt ist, die gebotene Freiheit anzunehmen, dafür aber auch bereit ist, seine Schuldigkeit gegenüber den Mitmenschen zu erfüllen. Wer sich mehr oder weniger erwartet, wird sich kaum eingewöhnen können oder zumindest ein Außenseiter bleiben, der nur durch die ungemeine Toleranz des Landes ein abgesondertes Dasein fristen kann. Er wird sich unbehaglich fühlen, dabei überall Anstoß erregen, und dieses so fremdartige, rätselhafte Land wird sich ihm nie erschließen. (25–26)

> [The individual human being is respected as his own master, but his voluntary subordination is taken for granted, becoming a social constraint, an inviolable convention. This impression sticks in one's mind even before one has come to know anything else about this country. Only the foreigner who is willing to accept the freedom that he is offered, but is also prepared in return to fulfil his obligations towards his fellow citizens, will be able to take his place and feel happy in England. Whoever expects more or less for himself will scarcely be able to settle down or will at the very least remain an outsider, enabled to eke out a life in isolation only by the unusual tolerance of this country. He will feel ill at ease, thereby causing offence everywhere, and this country, strange and enigmatic as it is, will never disclose itself to him.]

Adler's first major experience in England was, he writes, his discovery of a social order under which freedom and individual dignity could flourish intact: 'Das Glücksgefühl einer primitivsten, in vielen kontinentalen Ländern leider jedoch nicht mehr selbstverständlichen Ordnung, in der Freiheit und Vertrauen bestehen dürfen, war mein erstes großes Erlebnis in England' (5) [The feeling of happiness at a most basic order, where freedom and trust can exist, but which is unfortunately no longer to be taken for granted in many continental countries, was my first great experience in England]. He has come, he says, to see the agents of the state, policemen and officials, as the representatives of a legally sanctioned order, of the rule of law, and therefore as guarantors of freedom not of terror. That freedom and that sense of trust between human beings are closely linked to the individuality that Adler discerns in England, which, however, is in turn dialectically related to the homogeneity of English society, to a conformity and uniformity that transcends barriers of social caste — Adler considers the term 'class' unsuited to English conditions — and, though giving an impression of monotony and conventionality, binds the people together.

At the end of his second section, devoted to English daily newspapers, Adler expresses this dialectical union of opposites clearly:

> Diese Zeitung ist für ein Volk bestimmt, das bei höchster Einschätzung seines individuellen Privatlebens und seiner persönlichen Freiheit in sich gleichartig zu sein begehrt. Wie es bei mir bestellt ist, so soll es auch bei allen meinen Mitmenschen sein, zumindest im Prinzip [...] Bei allem Individualismus in diesem Lande sind die Menschen so typisiert und relativ individuell unausgeprägt, wie es ihre Hausfassaden und schließlich auch ihre Zeitungen sind. (43–44)

> [This newspaper is designed for a people which, though it places the highest value on its individual private life and its personal freedom, desires to be uniform within itself [...] For all the individualism in this country, the people are as standardized and as relatively undeveloped as individuals as the facades of their houses and also their newspapers.]

Elsewhere, he comments similarly on the uniform appearance of English men and women in the streets. Adler was influenced in his broadly positive view of this uniformity by the solidarity displayed by the English during the war, when their voluntary self-subordination to the requirements of total war led to a degree of mobilization that far outdid the forced mobilization imposed by a totalitarian regime. England, says Adler, was never invaded and did not fall into the abyss of moral corruption that affected both oppressors and oppressed in continental countries. During the war, individuals in those countries were thrown back on themselves in deciding whether or not to try and mount a resistance to evil, whereas the English could concentrate on confronting an external foe from a position of internal unity: 'Das englische Volk hatte in Gesamtheit zu bestehen. Dieses Volk von Individualisten hatte sich in der Abwehr zu einem Kollektivum umzubilden' (7) [The entire English people had to stand together as a unit. In defending itself, this nation of individualists had to transform itself into a collective].

To judge by their newspapers, claims Adler, the pragmatic and empirical English lack an interest in abstractions as well as a highly developed faculty of imagination; instead, they want what is vivid, immediate, images that make a strong visual impact or reports of words spoken that appear to record 'reality' or 'the truth' directly. He also notes that newspaper reports are often personalized, focussing on the individual actors in the story rather than on its wider context and general significance. This emphasis on the personal leads on to one of Adler's central themes, the important function played by the concepts 'private' and 'public' or 'common' in English life: 'Die Dinge, die geschehen und berichtet werden, sind zwar häufig allgemein, aber die Personen, die mit ihnen zu tun haben, sind persönlich, sind wichtig. Dem liegt ein besonderer Mechanismus zugrunde, der den englischen Realismus charakterisiert — die Öffentlichkeit ist individualisiert, der Privatbereich ist anonym — annähernd umgekehrt wie in kontinentalen Ländern' (33) [The things that occur and are reported are frequently general, but the persons involved in them are personal, are important. Underlying that is a particular mechanism that characterizes English realism — the public sphere is individualized, the private sphere is anonymous — approximately the reverse of continental countries].

This resolute preservation of privacy leads, in Adler's view, to the stylization and conventionalization that is so marked a feature of English life and social intercourse. He notes especially the way in which conversation in England consists in considerable measure of polite formulae, of exchanges about such subjects as the weather and of semi-meaningless words like 'lovely' or 'wonderful'. English small talk, which can never be mastered by someone who has not grown up and been educated in England, may make the English appear dry, arrogant, unapproachable, even stupid or emotionally impaired. But Adler believes English small talk to be the art of relaxing one's privacy to that minimum degree required to engage with another, an act of courtesy that deploys the private individual into the public sphere, in an effort to make contact with another individual without trespassing excessively on that person's privacy. The conventions that rule English life have admittedly resulted in a hollowing out of certain aspects. Adler notes for example that English first names have lost their original biblical or Christian significance: English people were astonished that a foreign Jew should hit on the idea of giving his son the allegedly quintessentially English name Jeremy (as Adler himself had done).

Adler uses the English word 'privacy' to denote the private sphere and the quality of 'privateness' that the English prize so highly, speaking for example of the private, upstairs rooms in the family home as 'den erhöhten und intimsten Bereich der Privacy, die sich mit Reserve nach unten hin zur Publicity öffnet' (62) [the raised and most intimate sphere of privacy, which with a certain reserve opens itself out below [i.e. downstairs] to the public sphere]. He invents a new meaning for the English word 'publicity' to denote the public sphere and the quality of 'publicness'. The family home plays an essential role in English life, where everyone aspires to home ownership, to the secure and intact space inside one's own four walls or inside the fenced off grounds of one's property. Living in rented accommodation is regarded as inferior, argues Adler, citing the fact that in comparison to the German word 'Wohnung' and the French 'logis' the English word 'flat' is completely colourless. (71) 'Das englische Heim', he writes, 'ist vor allem und wirklich ein Heim in einem Lande des unbedingten und von niemandem gestörten Privatlebens' (64) [The English home is above all a real home in the land of the absolute right to a private life undisturbed by others]. The Englishman's home is not so much his castle as the private kingdom of his family life:

> In ihrem, sei es noch so bescheidenen Rahmen ist die englische Wohnung wirklich das Reich einer Familie, in dem sie es sich nach eigenem Gutdünken einrichten kann. Niemanden geht es etwas an, wie sie das tut, denn es liegt in hohem Maße nur an ihr, daß sie nach ihren Neigungen innerhalb ihrer respektierten Wände das größtmögliche Maß an Zufriedenheit erreicht. (65)

> [In its setting, however modest, the English dwelling really is the kingdom of a family, where it can make its own domestic arrangements as it sees fit. How it does so is no one else's business, for it is to a high degree up to the family alone to achieve the greatest possible measure of happiness within the respected walls of its home in accordance with its own inclinations.]

Privacy in England is sacrosanct, it must be preserved against any intrusion — the mere appearance of a sign marked 'private' ensures this — and it frequently overlaps into public life, giving such institutions as public houses their peculiar character. The three sections of the pub of that time correspond, at least symbolically, to the three classes: the public bar is for the lower middle class, the private bar for the middle class, and the saloon bar for the upper middle class. The saloon bar implies by its very name, deriving from the French 'salon', something exclusive, a sphere that is not private, yet not part of normal everyday life, promising access to a realm beyond the usual run of bourgeois life. The private bar stresses the private sphere, recreating the bourgeois domesticity dear to the hearts of the middle classes; though the latter are perfectly well aware that they are in a pub, not a private house, they nevertheless recognize 'daß auch das Pseudo-Private von vornehmerem Range ist als der Raum, der sich unverhüllt als öffentlich erklärt' (78) [that even the pseudo-private is of nobler rank than the space that openly declares itself to be public], i.e. the lower-class public bar. Elsewhere Adler argues that privacy, not Christianity, is the religion of the English: 'Der Sinn für das Transzendente ist bei diesem Volke umgebildet in den Sinn für die Privacy' (103) [The sense of the transcendental has in the case of this people been transformed into the sense of privacy]. 'In England ist PRIVATE ein Bereich, dem eine fast kultische Funktion zukommt; private ist heilig, private ist unantastbar, private ist das Ziel. Private wird von jedem respektiert und bedingungslos anerkannt.' (103) [In England PRIVATE is a realm that is accorded an almost cultic function; private is holy, private is sacrosanct, private is the ultimate goal. Private is respected by everyone and accepted unconditionally].

The enviable range of Adler's observations and the dazzling nature of his insights become clear in one of his examples illustrating the superior status accorded in England to the private, domestic, and familial sphere over the public sphere. He argues that in English houses the bedroom, the most private area, is situated on the upper floor, whereas the lower floor leads out into the public sphere; therefore, the servants live downstairs and their masters upstairs. But he takes this division further, to the heart of English public and constitutional life. In England, he states, people and things only exist insofar as they belong to a person or can at least be brought into a perceptible relation to a person and conceived of in that way. All institutions, even the state, are individualized, since England is, in sociological terms, 'familiär geordnet' (34), structured along family lines, with the royal family taking the role of parents. The royal family, he notes, make their public appearances on the balcony of Buckingham Palace — most famously on V-E Day together with wartime Prime Minister Winston Churchill — emerging from their private rooms at the top of the building into the public sphere: 'Wer sich das vergegenwärtigt, weiß, was die Monarchie und die Konstitution in diesem Lande bedeuten. In dieser Ordnung sehe ich die Größe der englischen Zivilisation, gar in einer Zeit, die kollektive Bindungen ohne schwerste Verletzungen der individuellen Würde und persönlichen Freiheit weder zu bilden noch zu erhalten fähig ist' (34) [Anyone who can visualize this knows what the monarchy and the constitution mean in this country. In this order I see the greatness of English civilization, especially in a time which is incapable of forming or preserving collective ties without the gravest violations of individual dignity and personal freedom].

For that reason, the monarchy cannot be democratized; as England is a representative democracy, the monarch must 'represent', a symbolic function that he can only exercise within the framework of his royal household, remote from the populace and therefore unquestioned in his paternal authority. It is not the least of this text's many surprises to find a central European social scientist singing the praises of English constitutional monarchy in such terms:

> Der Begriff des Landesvaters und der Landeskinder ist im übrigen Abendland kaum je so tief erlebt worden und längst ungültig geworden. Die Wohltat einer solchen Gesellschaftsordnung, mag sie auch ihre Schwächen haben, weiß man besonders zu schätzen, wenn man erkennt, welchen natürlichen Schutz sie gegen das Aufkommen von Diktaturen gewährt, wie sie auf dem Kontinent herrschen. (34)

> [The concept of the sovereign as father of the people and the citizens as his children has hardly ever been so deeply experienced elsewhere in the West, where it has long lost its validity. Though it may have its weaknesses, one especially appreciates the blessings of such a social order when one recognizes what a natural defence it affords against the rise of the dictatorships that hold sway on the continent.]

In a section with the seemingly unpromising title 'Angleichung von Stadt und Land', focusing on the blurring of the differentiation between town and country in England, Adler continues to elaborate his conception of the uniformity of the English, building on his analysis of English architecture as an amalgam of city and country; in the absence of a distinct peasant class in England, the differences between the urban and rural environments were indeed relatively small even in the 1940s. The English, observes Adler, are far more uniform ('einheitlich') than any continental people: everywhere one sees the same double-decker buses, the same houses and shops, the same hedges and fences, the same inns and hotels, one encounters the same food and the same lack of night life and coffee houses; 'überall finden wir den Engländer mit dem gleichen Auftreten und mit der gleichen

Kleidung, den einheitlichen Engländer, der kein richtiger Stadtbewohner ist und auch auf dem Dorfe so viele städtische Züge aufweist' (85) [everywhere we find the Englishman with the same appearance and the same dress, the uniform Englishman who is not a real town-dweller and who even in the country displays so many urban traits]. But this unitary community has the inestimable advantage of having developed over the centuries a self-confident nationalism, encapsulated in the phrase 'my country right or wrong' (78–79), and so deeply rooted that it is resistant to the inflammatory rabble-rousing of continental demagogues. The division of English society into long established social castes rather than along class lines has weakened the impetus towards class conflict and towards a violent reordering of society by revolutionary means; England has experienced nothing of that kind since the mid-seventeenth century.

In England, social change occurs within the framework of the existing order. Adler acknowledges such disadvantages as the barriers to social mobility created by the English educational system and other institutions that perpetuate the privileges of elite groups; but he mounts a determined defence even of the entrenched position of the aristocracy, arguing that it is balanced by the Honours List, which provides for the granting of knighthoods and peerages to commoners, 'so daß Verdienst und angeborenes Recht einander angeglichen werden und so für eine mit Leben erfüllte Gesellschaftsordnung sorgen' (81) [so that merit and hereditary rights are brought into harmony and provide for a social order that is filled with life]. That coexistence of tradition and reform is a central feature of Adler's understanding of British constitutional life: 'Darin sehe ich eine besondere Stärke Großbritanniens, wo die Beibehaltung der ältesten Einrichtungen sich mit der Einführung der verschiedensten Reformen vereinbaren läßt, so daß sich beide fast immer zum Vorteil des Landes assimilieren' (81) [In this I see a particular strength of Great Britain, where the retention of the most ancient institutions can be compatible with the introduction of all kinds of reforms, so that almost always both can be integrated to the benefit of the country]. The parliamentary system, an independent judicial system, and the crown as the acknowledged symbol of national unity combine to ensure that change can be secured by legal means and without attacking, let alone overthrowing, the existing order; at the same time, the large measure of freedom allowed to individuals defuses any desire for revolution.

Writing from the perspective of one who has observed the failures of both fascist and socialist programmes of reform at close hand and who would wish to preserve Britain from such calamities, Adler summarizes the virtues of the British system:

> Die Herrschaft gewährt dem Volke in reichem Maße die Möglichkeit einer freien Entfaltung von Wille und Tat, sie gewährt ihm demokratische Rechte, Schutz vor Übergriffen. Sie gewährt ihm, was ich als Gast in diesem Lande am höchsten bewerten möchte, die Freiheit vor Angst. Vielleicht kann man in England unter Umständen genau so verelenden und verhungern wie in allen anderen Ländern, aber man kann es zumindest in Freiheit, ungequält von staatlichen und sonstigen öffentlichen Übergriffen, und es ist kein Funken Ironie dabei, wenn ich diese bittere Tatsache noch als unvergleichliches Verdienst der Ordnung dieses Lands hervorhebe. (82)

[This system of government grants the people in rich measure the possibility of a free development in will and in action, it grants them democratic rights, protection from excesses. It grants them, which I as a guest in this country would value most highly, freedom from fear. It is perhaps possible that one can become destitute and starve in England just as one can in all other countries, but at least one can do so in freedom, not tormented by the excesses of the state or other public institutions, and it is without the least hint of irony that I highlight even this bitter fact as an incomparable merit of the order of this country.]

This argument reaches its culmination in the section simply but eloquently entitled 'Mensch unter Menschen' [A Human Being among Human Beings]. England, Adler states, reached maturity socially and culturally earlier than other European countries and was thus able to preserve more of what had given society strength in earlier centuries; it had, as he puts it, been able to crystallize or at least to stylize feudal, ecclesiastical, aristocratic, and bourgeois forms and values before they were devalued and destroyed by the development of modern mass society.[8] On this firm basis, innovations could be considered critically for acceptance or rejection, abrupt upheavals were avoided, 'und so wurde England zum Lande der vorsichtigen Evolution' (110) [and so England became the land of cautious evolution]. The English system is not soulless and mechanized, a scheme based on abstract rationalization, since government and parliament are subject to the people, the public, in a way that Adler defines as follows: 'Die Öffentlichkeit ist eine organische Größe, sie heißt England und Großbritannien, sie ist die Familie aus allen Familien, die aus privaten Menschen bestehen. Darum ist der Mensch in diesem Lande ein Mensch unter Menschen' (111) [The public is an organic quantity, it is called England and Great Britain, it is the family of all families that consist of private people. Therefore each human being in this country is a human being among human beings].

That order is a lived and living order:

> weil ihre Grundlage das Volk ist, der Inbegriff einer in allen Mitgliedern anerkannten menschlichen Gemeinschaft, einer Summe von durch Gesetze und Sitten geschützten Individuen, aber keine unbeseelte 'Masse', keine mechanische und abstrakte Größe, in welcher der Mensch nicht als freies und verantwortliches Subjekt bestehen darf, sondern zum verwalteten Objekt erniedrigt wird. (111)

> [because its foundation is the people, the essence of a human community recognized in all its members, a sum of individuals protected by laws and customs, but not a soulless 'mass', not a mechanical or abstract quantity in which the human being may not exist as a free and responsible subject, but is reduced to the level of an administered object.]

Human beings as an anonymous, soulless mass, human beings as 'administered objects' is what Adler had experienced in the camps; the phrase gives its title to his Holocaust study *Der verwaltete Mensch: Studien zur Deportation der Juden aus Deutschland*.[9] But in England one is free, even as a foreigner, provided only that one submits to the limitations on one's freedom imposed by respect for the freedoms of others, as Adler proclaims in a ringing, almost rhetorical conclusion:

Wo aber in Europa darf man noch seinen Wert behalten? In England! Und dieser
Wert ist größer und heiliger als alle Werte, die man finden kann. Dieser Wert
ist die Duldsamkeit des Menschen für seine Mitmenschen. [...] Hier handelt
es sich um keine theoretische, nur auf dem Papier zugesicherte Toleranz, es
handelt sich wirklich um Freiheit in sonst kaum gekannten, weitgesteckten
Grenzen. Wo gibt es eine Polizei in Europa ohne Schußwaffen? In England!
Wo darf man, auch als Fremder, sagen, was man denkt? In England! Wo tun,
was das Gewissen bietet? In England! (112)

[Where in Europe can one still preserve one's value? In England! And that value
is greater and more sacred than all the values that one can find. That value is
the tolerance of one human being for his fellow human beings. [...] Here it is
not a matter of a theoretical tolerance that is promised only on paper, it really
is a matter of freedom within bounds set so wide as to be scarcely known
elsewhere. Where in Europe is there an unarmed police force? In England!
Where may one, even as a foreigner, say what one thinks? In England! Where
may one do what conscience dictates? In England.]

Adler's vision of England as the land where an organic constitution in tune with
the customs, conventions, and mentality of the people had arisen through a process
of gradual evolution over time and within the framework of a representative
parliamentary system was rare among his fellow refugees from Central Europe. It
is very different from the perceptions of England to be found in the writings of
the two refugee intellectuals who were personally closest to him, the novelist Elias
Canetti and the social scientist Franz Baermann Steiner. One of the few texts to
come close to it is Elisabeth Castonier's autobiographical prose work *Mill Farm*, an
almost lyrical celebration of the English countryside and the people (and animals)
who live in it, linked to it organically by timeless traditions and a way of life that has
evolved over the centuries.[10] In his vision of the British constitution as an organic
unit developing through a process of evolutionary change, not by revolution, and
in accordance with the intricate complexities of human society, not from a spirit
of arid, rationalizing abstraction, Adler seems to me to come close to one of the
great figures of British parliamentary conservatism of the late eighteenth century,
Edmund Burke. As Burke reacted in his *Reflections on the Revolution in France* to the
revolutionary upheavals that had beset that country since 1789, so Adler reacted to
the very different upheavals that had laid waste to Europe in the years after 1933.
The American conservative political analyst Yuval Levin comments on Burke's
concept of 'the great law of change' in terms that could well be applied, *mutatis
mutandis*, to Adler's thinking about Britain:

The solution is not to liberate individual reason, but on the contrary to seek
proof of what political institutions and practices will work by considering those
that have passed the test of time; to govern with the aid of what Burke calls
'prescription': the collective wisdom of the ages as expressed in the form of
long-standing precedents, institutions and patterns of practice.

Prescription does not mean that nothing can change in political life. On the
contrary, Burke describes prescription as a kind of principle of change. But it is
gradual change, in line with the preexisting patterns of a society's life — change

that is justified against existing precedents, and so strengthens society, rather than undermining its foundations. Throughout his career, Burke was a reformer of British institutions, not a defender of the status quo at all costs. But he always sought to make clear that change should be carried out for the purpose of preservation, or of perfection in line with the best of the nation's political traditions.

'We must all obey the great law of change,' Burke writes: 'It is the most powerful law of nature, and the means perhaps of its conservation. All we can do, and that human wisdom can do, is to provide that the change shall proceed by insensible degrees. This has all the benefits which may be in change, without any of the inconveniences of mutation.'[11]

By concentrating on the core of Adler's ideas, this essay may have made *England: Eindrücke eines Ahnungslosen* appear drier, more abstract, and less infused with vivid observations from daily life than it in fact is. The study is full of the details of English life in the later 1940s. Adler praises some of its features, such as the provision of public parks, the honesty that allows bottles of milk to be left on doorsteps, and the humour of the advertisements in public places, while condemning others, like the vagaries of London buses, the difficulty of locating street names and house numbers, and the bad behaviour of children and young people. I would point to the final section of the study, 'Abenteuerliches England' [Adventurous England], where Adler compares England's geographical position, jutting out from Europe into the Atlantic, to the spirit of adventure that led to its worldwide, imperial project. He goes on to argue, with characteristic originality, that the English love the sea, the wild, unpredictable, adventurous element, as they love their open fires, but that they also love the serenity of the landscape that they have created, a landscape that reflects their love of convention and stability, as the open fire has been transformed into a symbol of domesticity. As the pirates of the early days of empire made way for the later traders and merchants, so adventurousness came to be balanced by a measured adherence to convention. As always, the riddle that is England can for Adler be resolved, insofar as that is possible, by understanding it as a delicately dialectical synthesis of opposites.

Notes to Chapter 4

1. The number of refugees who came to Britain before the war can be estimated at over 60,000. The Jewish victims of Nazi persecution who were admitted to Britain after the war consisted mainly of children — a group of several hundred young people known as 'The Boys', who arrived in a flight from Czechoslovakia, being the best known — and those admitted under the Distressed Persons scheme, mostly people who had relatives in Britain, as well as some women who married British servicemen; in all a far smaller number.
2. On the arrival and early years of the refugees in Britain, see the opening chapters of Anthony Grenville, *Jewish Refugees from Germany and Austria in Britain, 1933–1970: Their Image in 'AJR Information'* (London: Vallentine Mitchell, 2010).
3. Jeremy Adler, *The Magus of Portobello Road* (London: Alphabox Press, 2015).
4. On the evolution of refugee perceptions of British society, see Anthony Grenville, *Encounters with Albion: Britain and the British in Texts by Jewish Refugees from Nazism* (Cambridge: Legenda, 2018).
5. The typescript of *England: Eindrücke eines Ahnungslosen* is in the King's College London Archives. I am grateful to the staff at the Archives for their help in making this typescript available to

me, and to Professor Jeremy Adler for drawing my attention to it. That there is a copy in the Deutsches Literaturarchiv Marbach as well: A II 2, Mappe 5, which also includes an English translation. All references to the manuscript will be made in parentheses in the text.

6. The English translations that follow the German quotations in the text are all mine.

7. On Adler's relations with Adorno, see Jeremy Adler, *Das bittere Brot: H. G. Adler, Elias Canetti und Franz Baermann Steiner im Londoner Exil* (Göttingen: Wallstein, 2015), pp. 96–107.

8. For a fuller discussion of Adler's concept of the mass, see Jeremy Adler, *Das bittere Brot*, pp. 31–38.

9. H. G. Adler, *Der verwaltete Mensch: Studien zur Deportation der Juden aus Deutschland* (Tübingen: Mohr (Paul Siebeck), 1974).

10. Elisabeth Castonier, *Mill Farm und ihre zwei- und vierbeinigen Originale* (Munich: Heimeran, 1959).

11. Yuval Levin, 'Burke, Paine and the Great Law of Change', <https://thepointmag.com/2011/politics/burke-paine-and-the-great-law-of-change> [accessed on 8 March 2016].

CHAPTER 5

❖

The Displaced Modernist

Peter Filkins

In an unpublished statement titled 'Literarische Selbsteinsicht' [What My Writing Means] written in November 1968, H. G. Adler says that it is easy to talk about his own writing, given that he is bound to 'no aesthetic nor any extra-literary agenda' ['keinem ästhetischen und keinem außerliterarischen Programm'], and that really the only thing he can say about his literary work is that it 'means exactly what it means' ['Genau das bedeutet, was sie bedeutet']. Recognizing that this might sound arrogant, he nevertheless holds to his point by observing, 'This sentence, even when expressed differently, is not a statement of my own making, but is by now a classic assertion of contemporary modernism' ['Dieser Satz, wenn auch anderes geprägt, stammt nicht von mir, er ist eine bereits klassische Erklärung der heutigen Moderne']. Adler, however, does not name any specific modernist writer as a model or influence. Instead, he elaborates on what he wishes to suggest in saying that his literary work 'means exactly what it means' by explaining, 'within the "meaning" there are references to that which is denoted, whether it be the content, related elements or other linguistic expressions, but what transcends the literary expression is the sound and above all the distinctive features of the language itself, even when the object of the meaning is not something extra-linguistic, but is itself meant to be expressed in words' ['Im "Bedeuten" steckt der Hinweis auf Bezeichnetes, mag das nun Inhalt, ein Verhältnis oder ein anderes sprachlich Ausdrückbares sein, was den Schall und alle übrigen zur Sprachgestalt gehörigen Merkmale der literarischen Aussage transzendiert, auch wenn der Gegenstand des Bedeutens nicht etwas Außersprachliches, sondern Sprachliches selbst ist']. In other words, and as Adler concludes, 'Everything that is said, so long as it does not say what it means in itself, transcends the language' ['Alles Sprachliche, soweit es nicht nur sich selbst bedeutet, transzendiert die Sprache'].[1]

Adler's statement not only invokes the tension between the spoken and the unspoken found in post-war writers like Paul Celan and Samuel Beckett, his valuation of a text's ability to say something beyond what the text says itself harkens back to the aesthetic aims of early modernism forged by James Joyce, Virginia Woolf, and Gertrud Stein. However, a bit further in his statement Adler raises, in glancing fashion, particular consequences for his own work when he makes clear that what he is saying applies to 'creative writing' ['von schöpferischer Literatur'] and not to other forms of writing, though he concedes that some non-literary writing 'also transcends what we generally refer to as 'meaning' through its expression' ['auch allgemein als "bedeutende" Aussage das Sprachliche transzendiert']. While he does not make clear exactly what kind of non-literary writing he has in mind, clearly philosophy, memoir, or even the writing of history can aspire to the expression of a 'truth' that supersedes what is spelled out in the text itself. Adler was well aware of this, having himself aimed for the same in *Theresienstadt 1914–1945: The Face of a Coerced Community*, a work seated squarely in its facts, but which he also intended to be 'readable, lively, a Kafka novel with reversed signification' ['lesbar, lebendig, ein Kafka-Roman mit umgekehrten Vorzeichen'].[2] Meanwhile, in regards to literary writing, Adler insists upon a finer distinction, namely that of the 'artistry' ['das Künstlerische'] of any given literary expression and how 'in a linguistic work it "means" also "*something*"' (Adler's emphasis), and 'that is something special in its own right' ['in einer sprachlichen Leistung "bedeutet" auch "*etwas*", und das ist ein Besonderes'].

Adler thus makes a distinction between what a work actually says and the artistry with which it is said, though this distinction in no way cancels out what is expressed *within* a text, but values as well what is evoked *by* or *through* a literary text. Adler reiterates, 'Literary expression means a work of art that achieves linguistic transcendence as literature, as a literary work' ['Die dichterische Aussage bedeutet als Kunstwerk sprachlich Transzendierendes als Literatur, als dichterische Leistung'], and goes on to say that this is also what he 'has in mind when I offer up my works to the critic' ['Das habe ich im Sinn, wenn ich meine literarisch schöpferischen Versuche einer Krtitik anbiete'], who should appreciate that 'each of my respective works first of all means exactly what it means' ['jede meiner einschlägigen Arbeiten zunächst genau das bedeutet, was sie bedeutet']. A final implication of this is spelled out in the statement's last sentence when Adler concludes, 'In my work I seek to maintain the ability to convey to my listeners and readers transcendental meaning through what I express' ['In meinem Schaffen möchte ich ein Können bewähren, bei dem meinen Höreren und Lesern das transzendental Bedeutete sich durch meine Aussage vermittelt']. This raises the stakes of what he is aiming for by not only avowing what a literary work can or should do in itself, but also the effect it will have upon its audience. And if that effect is indeed 'transcendental', then it holds the potential to transform the artistic act into an ethical act affecting others, a work's aesthetic approach thereby entailing a moral project for the writer and reader alike.

Jeremy Adler has made the most thorough and convincing case for the ethical dimension of his father's literary and scholarly works and how they counter Adorno's famous dictum about the 'barbarism' of writing poetry after Auschwitz.[3] In subverting what he calls the 'fallacy of negativism' so often found in critical theory, he contends that 'H. G. Adler's work seeks to argue the opposite position, ultimately grounded in his Jewish faith, that a system of beliefs, ethical values and the basic political concepts of human rights and democracy do make sense' and remain viable in the post-Holocaust world.[4] Adler's literary works, however, offer a particular challenge in their effort to 'mediate the unimaginable', the result being that the 'disaster experienced by others thereby becomes ontologically problematic for the reader'.[5] A major part of the reason why is because 'the novels reject normal literary consolation, the illusion of identification'.[6] Instead the reader 'falls victim to a double-bind: to experience the guilt of ignorance, or that of knowledge', which in turn demands the need for the reader 'to engage in active memory and respond to the texts not just aesthetically, but ethically'.[7]

Kirstin Gwyer, while agreeing with Jeremy Adler on the double-bind faced by the reader of Adler's novels, looks at the problem from an opposite standpoint in arguing that it is 'essential that we not only respond to the texts ethically, but engage with their aesthetic', for only then can we see how the novels reveal 'an adjustment of narrative towards the postmodernist' and thereby do what 'encompassing, explanatory, or descriptive representations of the Holocaust cannot,... [namely] pursue the challenge to meta-narratives to its conclusion: by enacting their breakdown at a structural level and denying the reader a spectator's vantage point'.[8] In quoting Steven M. Rosen's *Dimensions of Apeiron*, Gwyer makes clear that this breakdown amounts to 'the disruption [...] of all the "points of reference used by individuals and groups in the past to plot their life courses"', thus pointing to 'a total unraveling of centuries of progress in human affairs'.[9] Noting Adler's invocation of *apeiron* in the final chapter of his Theresienstadt monograph as the disorder or disharmony that 'precludes objectivizing consciousness', she illustrates how it is manifested even more profoundly in the ability of Adler's novels to approach and confront the manner in which 'in the unlimited and unquantifiable abyss that is the world after the return of *apeiron*, chronological time has been subverted, and along with it any notion of causation, coherent space, and independently cognizant subjectivity'.[10]

In focusing on the aesthetic of the novels, Gwyer does not so much counter the general view first forwarded by Jeremy Adler about the necessity of reading Adler's scholarship and literary works in tandem in order to understand fully his two-fold project as a witness; instead she challenges us to think specifically about 'what the literary [allowed] Adler to do that the non-literary did not'.[11] Yet despite the reader's ethical 'double-bind' or the way the novels illustrate the 'impossibility of integrating the traumatic event into a continuous life story of a single stable self', what are we to make of Adler's insistence that '[e]verything that is said' in the novels transcends 'the distinctive features of the language itself', and at the same time each novel 'means exactly what it means'? For if Adler felt it necessary that 'a literary work [...] "means" also *something*, and that is something special in its own right', this would seem to beg two questions: what is that *something* special and how are we to square it with the constant undermining of integration, cohesion, and continuity in the novels themselves? In asking this I wish to explore not *what* the novels mean, but *how* they mean, and more importantly not only for the reader, but for Adler himself. For in considering the gulf between what the literary did for Adler and what it does for the reader, it may be possible to arrive at a reassessment that encompasses just what Adler took from modernism and what he displaced within it in order to remake it on his own terms, to aspire to a 'system of beliefs, ethical values and the basic political concepts of human rights and democracy',[12] and to simultaneously acknowledge the disruption of the same.

Adler's 'Literarische Selbsteinsicht' on the meaning of his work was never published, nor does he define elsewhere exactly what he intends as the 'transcendental meaning' he seeks to convey to his readers. However, in his 'Einladung zu meinem *Panorama*' [Invitation to My *Panorama*], which also was written in 1968 and appeared in the catalogue of the novel's publisher, Walter Verlag, Adler does touch on what he sees as that novel's artistry.[13] There he speaks generally of the 'Panorama-Situation of humankind' ['Panorama-Situation des Menschen'], likening it to the technical forerunner of the cinema, the panorama that displayed wonders of the world to the viewer, whereby 'each stands on his own, and yet at the same time in a way — even as an observer — is connected to the outer world' ['jeder auf sich selbst angewiesen ist, jedoch trotzdem auf diese eine Weise — eben als Betrachter — mit der Außenwelt in Verbindung steht']. This being the book's 'central symbol' ['Grundsymbol'], Adler sees the novel as a 'new kind of attempt... at the coming-of-age-novel, but with unexhausted means that also allow it to be done in a new way' ['ein neuartiger Versuch des... Entwicklungsromans, doch mit unverbrauchten Mitteln, die ihn auch neu rechtfertigen'], for here the protagonist is not 'developed from the outside' ['nicht von außen entwickelt'] but instead 'illustrated from within' ['von innen her gezeigt'].

In addition to this inner life, thirty years of contemporary history shaped by the lead-up to and experience of the Holocaust is also covered, the result being that, according to Adler, while the novel is 'generated within the stadia of its time, it is also just as much set above its time, as if describing no history at all' ['aus den Stadien seiner Zeit; er ist also ebensowenig über die Zeit gesetzt, wie er keine Gechichte beschreibt']. Ultimately this lends it 'the character of a rhapsody, an epic work of art, and not just a novel composed of novelistic events' ['den Charakter einer Rhapsodie, eines epischen Kunstwerkes und nicht nur gerade des Romans mit seinem dazugehörigen romanhaften Geschehen']. In language that echoes that which he used in his 'Literarische Selbsteinsicht', Adler goes on to argue, 'This particular claim is supported by the nature of the [novel's] linguistic form' ['Dieser besondere Anspruch ist durch die sprachliche Gestaltung zu rechtfertigen']. Besides the development of its narrative, exposition, and description, *Panorama* utilizes what he describes as a 'structured syntax, one repeated deliberately with constantly fresh intonations throughout the entire work, while at the same time introducing surprising motifs in broad strokes and in particulars, there being — perhaps the chief linguistic distinction — a hidden rhythmical form to the entire text which has its own and (I think) unique cadence' ['der reihende Satzbau, die erwogene, durch das ganze Werk sich immer wieder frischen Ansätzen wiederholende, doch zugleich auch überraschende Motivik in großen Zügen wie in Einzelheiten, und da ist — vielleicht als sprachliches Hauptmerkmal — eine versteckte rhythmische Durchgestaltung des gesamten Textes mit ihren eigenen und (wie ich denke) unverwechselbaren Kadenzen'].

In emphasizing the cinematic and musical qualities of *Panorama*, Adler touches upon the two artistic forms that, arguably, were the most important influences on modernism. While certainly literature and visual art achieved new forms of expression in the early decades of the twentieth century, film was not only a child of the times, it would go on to affect powerfully the way stories are now told, written, and most of all understood and consumed by the vast majority of contemporary audiences. And while music has transformed itself constantly across centuries and cultures, Arnold Schoenberg's invention of the twelve-tone scale elevated dissonance, disruption, and asymmetry to viable tools of artistic expression which were then utilized by literary artists to render both subtle degrees of interaction between human beings and cataclysmic changes in the human condition. Only the turn toward abstraction in visual art would appear to have had as profound an effect on the way we appreciate art in general, but even then one need only consider the predominance of film and video in contemporary art to appreciate cinematic dominance, while the dissemination of recorded music, be it classical, jazz, or popular, also has created a 'Panorama-Situation' in which 'each stands on his own' yet simultaneously 'is connected with the rest of the world' through technical media. Thus, music and film, the two art forms whose *raison d'être* is most inherently tied to shared mass consumption, are also the forms that have most profoundly affected the way the individual sees and hears. In like fashion, Adler's *Panorama* is a novel that in essence is not only about what the protagonist Josef Kramer sees and hears, but also the fact that he sees life as a cinema of unfolding, yet disconnected scenes, the rhythms of his thoughts, memory, and consciousness being the music that links them all together.

Adler was of course a novelist, not a filmmaker, nor was he at all a moviegoer. However, the techniques of mise-en-scène and montage that literary modernism borrowed from film and photography are central to his novels. Less visible, but no less important, is the role of music. Adler held a doctorate in musicology, and as a young man he even composed a piano sonata, two suites, a fantasy, and several songs, though he later claimed that he was 'superbly ungifted' as a composer.[14] Nevertheless, music lies at the core of his artistic sensibility, its ability to say without saying, and thus transcend its own content, again speaking to the 'artistry' that he valued above all in his literary work. Although Adler's dissertation 'Klopstock und die Musik' revealed his admiration for poetic intricacy that would later inform the poems he wrote in the camps, Wilhelm Unger also recalled the muted sound of Schoenberg and Anton Webern coming from the radio in Adler's London flat after the war, while letters to Franz Baermann Steiner from this same period make reference to his enthusiasm for the music of Zoltán Kodály, Belá Bartók, and again Schoenberg.[15]

Schoenberg in fact remained one of Adler's great artistic heroes, and his 1976 essay, 'Arnold Schoenberg: Eine Botschaft an die Nachwelt' [Arnold Schoenberg: A Message to the After-World], is as much a statement of his own artistic values as it is a consideration of Schoenberg's career.[16] In this essay, Adler celebrates three essential components to Schoenberg's work and career, and interestingly each speaks to key elements in his own artistic approach to his novels. The first is Schoenberg's unique and modernist approach to words and music. Schoenberg specifically claims that he feels first a musical inspiration and idea take shape within him, and that only secondly does he seek a poetic text to use to express it, and that text is only one *component* of the expression, rather than the music being there to illustrate or interpret the words. Adler describes this practice as 'Textdichtung', rather than the more common notion of 'Tondichtung', and he pointedly values Schoenberg as much as a literary/poetic artist as a composer of music.

This relates to Adler's own artistic practice in *Panorama*, for in a 1974 letter to Theodor Sapper, Adler describes *Panorama* as 'ten "musical movements", each of which contains an abundance of correlative links and correspondences, and in total formulate an — again "musical" — totality that approximates the structure of the classical sonata, though of course on a much larger scale' ['zehn "musikalischen Sätzen", die untereinander eine Fülle von korrelativen Beziehungen und Entsprechungen aufweisen, und insgesamt auch eine — wiederum "musikalische" — Groß-form bilden, die im Aufbau dem klassischen Sonatensatz, allerdings in mächtiger Ausweitung, nahekommt'].[17] Adler even says the novel's fifth chapter, in which Josef Kramer reflects on the resonance released by the sound of Johannes Tvrdil's gong, ends ' "on the dominant" ' [' "auf der Dominante" ']. There Josef contemplates the sense of the note's finality as he realizes that

>...his memory will die with him, no one recalling it, both the true and the false teachings meaningless, for Josef is meaningless, Herr Koppelter is meaningless, Thomas as well, even Johannes is meaningless, soon it will not be memory but rather just the sound of the gong reverberating among the shadows, spreading throughout the world from the tower room like wafts of smoke, as Johannes opens the window during the night and plays much louder until it is no longer just chamber music but now a blaring temple music, though this music has the quality of being heard by only a few, even though its incredible sound vibrates over all, spreading out in unearthly, trembling waves and pressing to the furthest reaches of space, and now tumbling into and setting this room aglow as an almost unbearably strong voice calls, "And so one must penetrate to the truth, to the one and only, which is God himself". Thus one should forsake duality, it splits everything that is not a single entity, as the sound waves press the skin, already reverberating through the body and at last reaching the heart's loneliness until it responds to the universe, Johannes now nothing more than a memory, he being already forgotten, the drumstick having fallen soundlessly to the floor, the gong swaying quietly back and forth, as if it were a beating heart that does not beat in any recognizable manner, the heart beating like a gong, and then there is peace, the empty night, oneness, sleep, and deep endless sleep.

>[So wird das Gedächtnis mit Josef dahinsterben, keiner entsinnt sich, die wahre und die falsche Lehre ist müßig, Josef ist müßig, Herr Koppelter müßig, Thomas auch, sogar Johannes ist müßig und bald nicht einmal mehr Erinnerung, nur die Klänge des Gongs hallen noch immer im Schatten, aus dem Turmzimmer dringt es jetzt als verwehender Rauch in die Welt, denn Johannes hat die Fenster in die Nacht geöffnet und spielt viel lauter als bisher, jetzt ist es keine Kammermusik, jetzt ist es schmetternde Tempelmusik, aber dies Musik hat die

Eigenschaft, daß nur wenige sie vernehmen, obwohl sie mit übermächtigem Schall erbebt, sie verbreitet sich in überirdisch zuckenden Strahlen und dringt durch die Weiten des Weltraums, jetzt taumelt sie glühend in die Stube herein und ruft mit fast unvernehmlich gewaltiger Stimme: "Darnach soll man vordringen in die Wahrheit, zu der bloßen Einheit, die Gott selber ist". Und man soll die Zweiheit aufgeben, weil sie alles zerteilt, was nicht in Einheit ist, und da dringen die tönenden Strahlen bis an die Haut, schon durchfluten sie den Leib und erreichen in seiner letzten Einsamkeit das Herz, bis es dem Weltall antwortet; doch Johannes hockt noch immer an seinem Gong, nur hat er jetzt den Schlegel fallen lassen, Johannes ist bloß Erinnerung und Gedächtnis, er ist schon vergessen, lautlos ist der Schlegel zu Boden gesunken, das Gong schaukelt noch leise hin und her, als wäre es ein pochendes Herz, das in keiner bestimmten Tonart schlägt, es schlägt das Herz wie ein Gong, und nun ist Friede, einsame Nacht, Einheit, Schlaf und tiefer endloser Schlaf.][18]

Here we see a direct linkage between Josef's writing, his thoughts, and music that is played out across the movement from journal to memory to music. Josef feels his writing to be 'a vain game of fragile words,... he wanting to just sleep and wake up and sleep again' ['ein eitles Spiel mit brüchigen Worten,... er wird einschlafen und aufwachen und wieder einschlafen'], during which time, 'as soon as one image freezes for a moment it is ripped away, though another replaces it, the previous image now irretrievable and unable to be extracted from memory to see the light of day, memory's riches remaining dubious, even when one memorializes them in a journal, for soon they seem strange, strange, and unattainable' ['das eine Bild verharrt einen Augenblick, bald wird es fortgerissen, doch dann mag etwas Neues auftauchen, aber das vergangene Bild ist unwiederbringlich fort und wird von der Erinnerung nie wieder mehr an den Tag gefördert, Schätze des Gedächtnisses sind fragwürdig, auch wenn man sie als Denkmal in ein Tagebuch aufzeichnet, fremd sind sie bald geworden, fremd und unerreichbar'].[19]

Here the notion of images being yanked away and replaced by other images of course invokes the novel's central motif of the panorama, while the striking of the gong also echoes the little bell that sounds each time a new picture appears in the actual panorama Josef visits at the beginning of the novel. Josef's urge to fall asleep similarly mirrors his falling asleep at the end of each chapter, the lengthy sentence quoted above functioning as a clear example of Adler's 'Textdichtung', the lulling cadence of clause following upon clause. These elements are the kind of 'correlative links and correspondences' that Adler conceived of as the book's musical score, which he further described to Sapper as a 'ten-movement suite, which could be better understood as a "partita"' ['zehnsätzige Suite, genauer als "Partita" aufzufassen'], each scene referring at least once to the 'basic "panoramic" situation (or is made manifest): the sight of things which cannot be grasped' ['die "panoramatische" Grundsituation erscheint (oder verwirklicht wird): das Sehen der Dinge, zu denen man nicht gelangen kann'].[20]

In regards to the panorama, such a failure to grasp what is seen leads to a perceptual and a cognitive aphasia, for Josef cannot see or understand 'the universe', though the music reverberates through his body. The reader, however, can fathom 'the universe' of the novel by linking the motifs of the panorama, sleeping and waking, and the gong across chapters. Josef may be depicted 'from the inside out', but it is we who see him that way, Adler's musical structure allowing us to knit together the micro and the macro into a vision of reality *beyond* him. This, I would argue, is the extra-linguistic 'something special' that Adler claims for his work in his 'Literarische Selbsteinsicht'. Even though Adler said of *Panorama* that it was 'steeped in autobiography' ['ein mit Autobiographischem getränkter Roman'], it was the music of its rendering that mattered most to him.[21] His statement about having said to himself in Theresienstadt that, if he survived it, he would render his experience 'in both scholarly and artistic fashion' is often cited as the rationale for the program that he set for himself.[22] In fact, the degree to which he was committed to not foregrounding his own experience in either his scholarly or literary works is the same degree to which he was concerned with finding formal solutions that would allow their depiction to transcend mere reportage or the indulgence of memoir.[23]

Nowhere is this more intensely evident than in *The Journey*, a novel whose aim Adler said was to capture 'the scope and unity of an entire world' ['der Umfang und die Einheit einer ganzen Welt'].[24] Given that from start to finish the 'world' depicted is no less than *L'Univers concentrationnaire*, its constant shifting of voices and perspectives, as well as its sudden metaphorical transformations testify to Adler's clear rejection of realistic reportage in favor of a kind of magic realism that aspires to a mythic plane of regard. Meanwhile, in his essay Adler also cites Schoenberg's unrelenting pursuit of artistic truth without devolving into false effects or mere musical technique, as the second element that he treasures most about the composer, and which he thought defined his integrity as an artist and person. Schoenberg knew his ideas were often misunderstood, which in turn prevented him from enjoying greater success, but what Adler finds important is that Schoenberg never courted controversy for the sake of controversy, but instead simply wrote the music that he felt within, and that despite his important breakthroughs in atonal or pantonal music, he followed no specific theory or project. Instead, it was the musical ideas themselves that mattered most to him, just as Adler's compositional ideas for his novels, and the 'participant observer' approach he brought to his scholarship were what he refused to compromise on, even though this often came at the price of his work not gaining an audience and reception at the time.[25]

Thus Adler's epic stance in *The Journey* is never in service to sensationalism or mere literary effects, nor a naturalistic rendering of extreme suffering. Instead, as he says in the letter to Sapper,

> The horror is not so much... neutralized as it is transcended. I believe I have developed a narrative method hitherto unknown in world literature (or at least in western literature) which I would call Lyrical Irony.... Irony, because of course what is said cannot be, for that would make it a mockery. Lyrical, because the text at its greatest extreme is a poem, indeed an epic poem, but whose details are suffused with a lyrical transformation throughout (as well as a lyrical abstraction). Lyricism, when it is really of consequence, disdains irony; and vice versa, irony is also not lyricism. However I have transcended irony as well as lyricism, and this is exactly what I call Lyrical Irony, which results in yet another kind of transcendence: the ongoing transformation of reality, or in other words: the other-worldly depiction of reality.

[Grauen wird auf diese Weise weniger... neutralisiert als transzendiert. Ich glaube, ich habe hier eine vorher in der Weltliteratur (wenigstens der abendländischen Literatur) Erzählmethode entwickelt, die ich lyrische Ironie nenne.... Ironie, weil es ja so, wie es gesagt ist, nicht sein kann, das wäre nur Hohn. Lyrisch, weil der Text auf die weitesten Strecken hin Gedicht ist, episches Gedicht zwar, aber im Detail fast durchwegs in der lyrischen Transformation (auch in der lyrischen Abstraktion). Lyrik, wenn sie wirklich konsequent ist, schließt nun Ironie aus; umgekehrt ist Ironie nicht lyrisch. Ich habe aber die Ironie und noch einmal die Lyrik transzendiert und so (wie, genau, weiß ich freilich nicht) eine Darstellungsebene gewonnen: genau dies ist aber die lyrische Ironie, in die — da ich es gerade bedenke — noch eine andere Transzendierung eingemündet ist: die fortschreitende Verwandlung der Wirklichkeit, anders gesagt: die übernatürliche Betrachtung der Realität.][26]

Jeremy Adler argues such a transformation does not involve escapism, but rather that 'Adler insists on restoring the very subjectivity that Adorno problematizes and with that restores enlightenment and hope in an affected but unfractured form'.[27]

Adler himself says earlier in the letter to Sapper, 'Whoever is present in the novel also is given his own psychology, his own imagined world (or so-called soul space)' ['Wer immer vorangestellt wird, ist zugleich auch mit seiner Psychologie, seiner eigenen Vorstellungswelt (seinem Seeleninnenraum sozusagen) dargeboten'].[28] Hence, the pursuit of lyrical irony is not for the sake of mere invention, but instead to release the characters from what Jeremy Adler describes as a memory that 'condemns the victims to everlasting subjugation',[29] thereby allowing them to insist 'our eyes are open, and suffering is not all we experience' ['weil wir die Augen offen halten und nicht nur leiden'],[30] though as H. G. Adler also notes to Sapper, 'one realizes what is especially tragic: There are the dead who remain entirely outside of this novel who should not have died so prematurely (so inopportunely!)' ['Es gibt Tote, die, außerhalb dieser Ballade verblieben, nicht vorzeitig (unzeitgemäß!) sterben müßten'].[31]

The fact that Adler distinguishes between those who are given life in *The Journey* and the dead lost to the history outside of it also points to a potentially neutral space between Jeremy Adler's view of how the novels rescue 'the victims from their tormentors and [answer] the unfathomable crimes with an essentially Jewish affirmation of humanity',[32] and Gwyer's position that they confront us with 'the unlimited and unquantifiable abyss that is the world after the return of *apeiron*, [in which] chronological time has been subverted, and along with it any notion of causation, coherent space, and independently cognizant subjectivity'.[33] Adler's conscious distinction between the living and the lost also links to the third aspect of Schoenberg's career and character that he highly valued, namely the importance of the composer's role as a teacher. As we know, Schoenberg's influence as a teacher on both sides of the Atlantic was tremendous, whether it be his mentoring of Alban Berg or Anton Webern in Berlin and Vienna, or his influence on John Cage, Lou Harrison, or Leon Kirchner in the United States. Indeed, Adler sees this as Schoenberg's greatest gift and most important message to posterity, even going so far as to speculate that the composer's 'unswaying commitment to teaching was — one might say (at least I may say) — the central gift of his Jewish heritage, namely the value of teaching as the highest of all arts' ['mit unwiderstehlicher Leidenschaft für den Unterricht, die hier — und das mag vielleicht (vielleicht sage ich) die Hauptgabe seines jüdischen Erbes sein, das Lehrerschaft als höchste Kunst begreift'].[34] This above all connects Adler's essay on Schoenberg back to his own essay 'Nach der Befreiung: Ein Wort an die Mitwelt' of 1945. There he underscores the need to convey 'not what we have suffered, but what we experienced, and how that must be heard and understood'. This reveals Adler to be at heart a teacher, rather than merely a memoirist constructing monuments to himself.[35] Like Schoenberg, he pursued the music that he heard amid the calamity of experience, and that pursuit was in service to the truth he saw and knew, and for the sake of those who would later have the opportunity to understand it more fully, even if they did not.

Quite similarly, at the end of *The Wall*, Arthur Landau addresses his children, Michael and Eva, and hopes that 'everything I have written here, may it help you find a right awareness. Your father's work, especially this book about the wall, all of these efforts, should make the experience and achievements of a tested and fragile and yet, amid his ultimate despair, an honest and hardworking person at least a little comprehensible and credible, if indeed not endearing and beloved' ['alles, was ich hier aufgeschrieben habe, möge euch zu rechter Erkenntnis fruchten. Die Werke eures Vaters, besonders aber dieses Buch von der Wand, alle diese Versuche sollen euch als Erfahrung und Leistung eines geprüften und schwachen, doch noch in seiner letzten Verzeiflung meist rechtschaffen bemühten Menschen wenigstens verständlich und achtbar, wenn schon nicht lieb und teuer werden'].[36] From here, in the last three paragraphs, he goes on to urge his children 'to visit the site of your childhood' ['die Stätte eurer Kindheit aufzusuchen'] while speculating that, when they do, 'Perhaps across the street at a window two women will appear and look down at you, between them a cat strutting along the sill. On the street there might be a ragman like old Ron there now, pulling his cart and knocking on doors, asking for old clothes and rags' ['Vielleicht werden gegenüber an einem Fenster zwei Frauen erscheinen und auf euch herabschauen, zwischen ihnen eine Katze, die auf dem Sims herumstolziert. Auf der Straße mag, wie jetzt der alternde Ron, ein Trödler mit seinem Karren ziehen, an die Türen klopfen und alte Kleider und lumpen begehren'].[37] This of course is precisely the scene with which the novel opens, and it, too, includes 'the heavy smoke from the squat chimney [that] faintly drift[s] smoky and dark over the streets' ['die schwere Rauchfahne aus dem niedrigen Schornstein wird kaum mehr qualmig und dunkel über die Straßen ziehen'] in much the same way that the smoke of the crematorium continues irreparably to blacken the air of the post-Holocaust world. However, beyond Arthur's spiritual and pedagogical hope that his blessing may help his children 'to set your sons and daughters on the right path' ['Söhne wie Töchter auf dem rechten Wege zu unterweisen'], the simultaneity of the novel's end and its beginning also implies a tantalizing possibility, namely that the entire narrative has taken place inside of Arthur's head on a single day, if not even within a single instant. As impossible as this might seem, given the book's six-hundred page journey through the labyrinth of Arthur's past, present, and often hallucinatory psychology, it does imply the possibility of an 'independently cognizant subjectivity' on the part of Landau, and most of all in the reader as well. For characters are not human beings, no matter how vividly they may manifest themselves within our imagination; instead, readers are the beings who imagine and digest them, carrying them away as part of our own memory.

Landau arrives at this very same realization in quite another way in confronting the problematic nature of his work in a museum full of artifacts left behind by the dead. Though he is deeply troubled by the portraits of the dead gathering dust in the museum's basement, he nonetheless thinks of them as 'patients', whom he must care for, and defends his approach by saying:

> We are remnant survivors, who are there for all who are not. That's true in general; the living are there for the dead, for their predecessors, and thus we also represent the history of the dead. How difficult it is, then, to exist as oneself when we are also history, so much history! But we are particularly there for all those dragged away by force and annihilated. You know what I mean, those of whom not a trace... We are the history of the exterminated, the history of the shadow that consumed them. And we collect what was stolen from them, what we can store up of their remains. But that is indeed alive and really not history. It amounts to neither memory nor keepsakes; it is commemoration.

> [Wir sind Überbliebene, sind für alle da, die nicht sind. Das gilt allgemein; die Lebenden sind für die Toten da, für die Vorfahren, wir sind also die Geschichte der Toten. Wie schwer ist es dann, auch noch selbst zu sein, wenn wir Geschichte sind, so viel Geschichte! Besonders sind wir aber für alle da, die man mit Gewalt fortgeschafft und zertrümmert hat. Sie wissen schon, spurlos... Wir sind die Geschichte der Vernichteten, die Geschichte der Schatten. Und wir sammeln, was man ihnen gestohlen hat, was wir von ihrem Nachlaß stapeln können. Das ist aber wieder lebendig und eigentlich nicht Geschichte. Es ist weder Erinnerung noch Andenken, es ist Gedächtnis.][38]

Though Landau continues to think of himself as 'something that is split into pieces' ['versteh ich bei mir etwas Aufgespaltenes'][39] the act of commemoration, at least temporarily or even metaphysically, suggests the possibility of a tenuous, if not fragile unity between the living and the dead. Indeed, Landau emphasizes, 'It amounts to neither memory nor keepsakes', thus escaping a descent into the ontological error of imprisoning the victims in their own subjugation or opting for empty sentimentality. Instead it is commemoration, an act meant to shape, honor, and both silently and saliently point to that which is not there, knowing that it is not there, and yet by insistence forging the consciousness that it is. Although memory, like pain, can never be truly shared, we continue to feel a powerful urge to point to it and assume that it passes between us and speaks our shared relation. How it does is of course deeply tied to the nature and purpose of story, for without story there can be no commemoration, an act jointly forged by writer and reader alike which results in different but related outcomes. For Adler the novels function as a memorial to the lost, as does his scholarship, but the novels carry the extra burden of rendering as well the suffering of the Josef Kramers, the Paul Lustigs, and the Arthur Landaus who survived. For the reader, there is the respect we pay to the dead and the living by parsing the signs and noting the correspondences of the text in order to manifest both the writer's consciousness and our own. Though Gwyer argues that the 'primary subject matter [of the novels] becomes the breakdown of their own structures',[40] both writer and reader participate in the awareness of that breakdown, thus creating a rupture in both the creation of the text and our reading of it that functions simultaneously as a commemoration of what can be understood and what cannot, the hope being that a transcendent shared relation is maintained somewhere within the breach.[41]

And as with commemoration, so too with teaching, for when conducted on the highest plane, neither succeeds through bombast or blunt instruction, but rather through careful modelling, subtle delineation, and understated, shared moments of revelation. Adler's valuation of Schoenberg's teaching as 'the highest of all arts' is at heart an affirmation of the commemoration of the value of values, knowledge, and knowing that must pass down through generations in order to hold out the last hope that Landau has for his children, namely that 'Perhaps then your life will seem to you an enormous treasure' ['Vielleicht wird euer Dasein euch dann zu einem gewaltigen Fund'].[42] In similar fashion, great novels do not instruct us, but instead reveal the enormous treasure that life offers us, even when that same treasure is all too often wasted, persecuted, oppressed, or tragically obliterated. We may not understand, and perhaps we cannot understand, but in the hands of a gifted novelist, even one who is a 'survivor, condemned to cling to a signpost in the deadly snowstorm of misery',[43] there is in our submission to the need to engage the imagination an act of commemoration of that which cannot be remembered, but must be thought through, again and again, if we are indeed to miraculously experience that '*something* very special' — a glimmer, a consciousness, a hope.

Notes to Chapter 5

1. H. G. Adler, 'Literarische Selbsteinsicht', Adler Archive, DLA-Marbach. While there is no clear indication of what this statement was intended for, or if it was ever submitted for publication or delivered, the fact that it is dated November 1968 would argue that it was written as potential promotional material for the publication of Adler's novel *Panorama*. Hence my translation of 'Literarische Selbsteinsicht' as 'What My Writing Means', rather than the more cumbersome 'Literary Self-Understanding' or 'Literary Self-Definition', neither of which would suit a publishing catalog or publicity venue.

2. H. G. Adler, Letter to Wolfgang Burghart, October 17, 1947. Adler Archive, DLA-Marbach.

3. See Jeremy Adler, '"Die Macht des Guten im Rachen des Bösen": H. G. Adler, T. W. Adorno und die Darstellung der Shoah', *Merkur* (June 2000), 475–86. See also Jeremy Adler, 'Good against Evil?: H. G. Adler, T. W. Adorno and the Representation of the Holocaust', in *Studies in Social and Political Thought* ed. by Robert Fine and Charles Turner, 2: *Social Theory after the Holocaust* (Liverpool: Liverpool University Press, 2000), pp. 71–100, and Jeremy Adler, *Das bittere Brot: H. G. Adler, Elias Canetti und Franz Baermann Steiner im Londoner Exil* (Göttingen: Wallstein, 2015), pp. 98–107.

4. Jeremy Adler, 'Good against Evil', p. 73.

5. Ibid., 83.

6. Ibid., 88.

7. Ibid., 90.

8. Kirstin Gwyer, *Encrypting the Past: The German-Jewish Holocaust Novel of the First Generation* (Oxford: Oxford University Press, 2014), pp. 80, 69, 81, respectively.

9. Ibid., p. 69.

10. Ibid., pp. 70 and 74, respectively.

11. Ibid., p. 60. See also Jeremy Adler, 'Nachwort', in H. G. Adler, *Theresienstadt 1941–1945: Das Antlitz einer Zwangsgemeinschaft* (Göttingen: Wallstein, 2005), p. 922.

12. Jeremy Adler, 'Good against Evil', p. 73.

13. H. G. Adler, 'Einladung zu meinem *Panorama*. H. G. Adler über seinen neuen Roman', *Literarium* 16 (Olten: Walter Verlag, 1968), p. 3.

14. See H. G. Adler, Letter to Wilhelm Unger, May 10, 1950, Adler Archive, DLA-Marbach.

15. See Wilhelm Unger, 'Das andere Deutschland', in *H. G. Adler: Buch der Freunde*, ed. by Willehad P. Eckert and Wilhelm Unger (Cologne: Wienand Verlag, 1975), pp. 14–18 (p. 17). See also Carol Tully, ed. *Zeugen der Vergangheit: H. G. Adler — Franz Baermann Steiner, Briefwechsel 1936–1952* (Munich: Iudicium, 2011).

16. H. G. Adler, 'Arnold Schönberg: Eine Botschaft an die Nachwelt', *Literatur und Kritik* 103 (1976), 129–39. For further discussion of Adler's essay on Schoenberg and its relation to Adler's writing, see my biography, *H. G. Adler: A Life in Many Worlds* (New York: Oxford University Press, 2019), pp. 323–28.

17. H. G. Adler, Letter to Theodor Sapper, January 21, 1974. Adler Archive, DLA-Marbach.

18. H. G. Adler, *Panorama* (Olten: Walter Verlag, 1968), p. 293. For the translation see H. G. Adler, *Panorama*, trans. by Peter Filkins (New York: Random, 2011), pp. 218–19.

19. Ibid., pp. 292 and 218, respectively.

20. H. G. Adler, Letter to Theodor Sapper, January 21, 1974. Adler Archive, DLA-Marbach.

21. H. G. Adler, 'Sonderinterview von Alfred Joachim Fischer', in *Zu Hause im Exil*, ed. by Heinrich Hubmann and Alfred O. Lanz (Stuttgart: Steiner, 1987), pp. 191–201 (p. 192).

22. H. G. Adler, '"Es gäbe viel Merkwürdiges zu berichten": Interview mit Hans Christoph Knebusch', in *H. G. Adler — Der Wahrheit verpflichtet: Interviews, Gedichte, Essays*, ed. by Jeremy Adler (Gerlingen: Bleicher, 1998), pp. 32–55 (p. 45).

23. Thomas Krämer sees Adler's novels as an effort to step beyond the early efforts of witness literature and argues that they should be read as Adler's 'expression of a conscious effort to forge an identity' ('Ausdruck bewusster Identitätsarbeit zu lesen'), though he also observes of *Panorama* that 'the rhythmical, lyrical language which distinguishes the novel as a whole' coheres with 'Adler's apt acknowledgement that his novels should be understood as poetry' ('rhythmisierten, lyrikgleichen Sprache, die den Roman ganz allgemeinkennzeichnet, aufschlussreich ist diesbezüglich Adlers Aussage, seine Romane seien als Gedichte zu verstehen [...]'). See Krämer, *Die Poetik des Gedenkens: Zu den autobiographischen Romanen H. G. Adlers* (Würzburg: Königshausen & Neumann, 2012), pp. 90 and 158, respectively.

24. H. G. Adler, Letter to Theodor Sapper, January 21, 1974, Adler Archive, DLA-Marbach.

25. For a discussion of Adler's use of Bronislaw Malinowski's practice of 'participant observation', see Jeremy Adler, 'Nachwort', in H. G. Adler, *Thereseienstadt 1941–1945: Das Antlitz einer Zwangsgemeinschaft* (Göttingen: Wallstein Verlag, 2005) pp. 898–99.

26. H. G. Adler, Letter to Theodor Sapper.

27. Jeremy Adler, 'Good against Evil', p. 95.

28. H. G. Adler. Letter to Theodor Sapper.

29. Adler, 'Good against Evil', p. 77.

30. H. G. Adler, *Eine Reise* (Vienna: Paul Zsolnay Verlag, 1999), p. 8, and *The Journey*, trans. by Peter Filkins (New York: Random House, 2008), p. 6.

31. H. G. Adler, Letter to Theodor Sapper.

32. Jeremy Adler, 'Good against Evil', p. 85.

33. Gwyer, *Encrypting the Past*.

34. H. G. Adler, 'Arnold Schönberg: Eine Botschaft an die Nachwelt', p. 139.

35. Lynn Wolff, in discussing Adler's philosophy of language, also sees a 'broader pedagogical approach' in Adler's scholarly work and notes, 'One of the themes that runs through both his scholarly and radio essays is the effort to enlighten society and educate future world citizens of the atrocities of National Socialism'. See Lynn L. Wolff, '"Die Grenzen des Sagbaren": Toward a Political Philology in H. G. Adler's Reflections on Language', in *H. G. Adler: Life, Literature, Legacy*, ed. by Julia Creet, Sara R. Horowitz, and Amira Bojadzija-Dan (Evanston, IL: Northwestern University Press, 2016), pp. 273–301 (p. 292).

36. H. G. Adler. *Die unsichtbare Wand* (Vienna: Paul Zsolnay Verlag, 1989) p. 644, and *The Wall*, trans. Peter Filkins (New York: Random House, 2014), p. 618.

37. Ibid.

38. Adler, *The Wall*, p. 401 and Adler, *Die unsichtbare Wand*, p. 385.

39. Adler, *The Wall*, p. 470 and Adler, *Die unsichtbare Wand*, p. 451.

40. Gwyer, *Encrypting the Past*, p. 81.

41. Thomas Krämer argues, 'The goal of *remembrance* [in Adler's novels] is to open the closed space of the past, making it fruitful in the effort to "master" the present' ('Das Ziel des *Gedenkens* ist es, den geschlossenen Raum des Vergangenen zu öffnen, um das Gewesene für die "Meisterung" der Gegenwart fruchtbar zu machen').

42. Adler, *The Wall*, p. 644 and Adler, *Die unsichtbare Wand*, p. 618.

43. Ibid., p. 640 and p. 615.

CHAPTER 6

❖

H. G. Adler's 'Grenzgängertum': Trans-Border Travel between Enlightenment Epistemology and Modernist Representation

Kirstin Gwyer

With the belated critical recognition that H. G. Adler's work has been receiving has come a fuller appreciation of the encyclopaedic reach into different disciplines and across genre boundaries that characterizes the ambition and achievement of his 'Gesamtkunstwerk'.[1] This fuller appreciation has been accompanied by a heightened awareness of the importance of responding comprehensively to such a comprehensive enterprise. Thomas Krämer, in his perceptive study of Adler's novels, for instance, speaks of a 'komplementäre Beziehung', a complementary relationship, between in particular the *Theresienstadt* study and the trilogy of Holocaust novels, arguing for an overarching reception that treats them as two facets of a single 'autobiographisches Projekt'[2] [autobiographical project].

Yet while now being regarded as related, and considered side by side, the academic and the literary in Adler's undertaking continue to be thought of as very much quantitatively and qualitatively distinct. As Lawrence Langer has said in respect of Adler's 'dual vocation as a chronicler of Theresienstadt and as a poet and fiction writer', Adler was 'keenly aware from the start of the differences between the scholarly and the literary approach to what we now call the Holocaust experience', with the former reflecting, according to Langer, 'his determination to capture the objective reality' and the latter 'his equally firm resolve to explore the personal dimensions of German oppression'.[3]

Thus the distinction between the literary and the non-literary in Adler's work continues to be assumed to be fairly clearly demarcated and predominantly one of degrees of objectivity. And this is felt to manifest itself at every level of the texts: conceptually, thematically and stylistically. As Krämer has argued, the two approaches draw on a 'bipolare Methodik' [bi-polar methodology] to reflect their two different 'Modi der Erinnerung' [modes of recollection / remembrance]. In the academic mode, where Adler 'describes how individuals become part of the phenomenon called "mass men" (*Massenmenschen*)', the historian's 'main task', as Langer puts it, 'is not to enter the consciousness of individual victims condemned to death'.[4] It is 'in the guise of novelist', Langer suggests, that Adler gains access here and is able to 'rescue individual identity from the stifling intrusion of the depersonalized mass that threatens to efface it'.[5] Krämer sums up this 'bi-polar' reading of Adler's work by proposing that only the academic writing should be read as testimony ['unter dem Aspekt des Zeugnisses'] while the novels should primarily be understood as the subjective products of personal trauma processing, bearing 'den Charakter therapeutischer Identitätsarbeit, die der Neuverortung des Selbst dient' [the characteristics of therapeutic identity work aimed at repositioning the self].[6] In stylistic terms, each approach, according to Langer, sees Adler 'inhabit a different world of discourse', and in each, his 'prose rhythm is totally different', with the distinction coming down 'to the way the author uses language in each kind of writing'.[7]

Though it is in many contexts valid and useful to distinguish between Adler's modes of recollection and representation in this way, there are certain risks inherent in assessing his work exclusively in such polarizing terms. On the one hand, we risk reducing his literary œuvre to the product of a purely personal attempt to come to terms with his traumatic past, or even to a conciliatory counterpoint to what Jeremy Adler has aptly called the 'unbearable objectivity' of his scientific project.[8] On the other hand, we risk underestimating the self-consciousness of his scholarly work, which, on closer inspection, seems to stand in a more nuanced relationship to its epistemological origins and testimonial objective than one might suspect. And finally, we also risk overlooking broader questions raised precisely by the points of contact, and entanglement, between Adler's scholarly and his literary testimony, questions that suggest that far from them representing two methodologically and formally distinct poles, their 'bi-polar' approach in fact exists on a sliding scale, and a closer-range investigation of them as a 'unified whole' reveals the boundary between them to be more fluid and permeable than we may have been assuming.[9]

The aim of this chapter will be to foreground the fluidity of this boundary by reading some of Adler's non-literary writing not simply alongside but against, and through the lens of, his literary work. To aid me in outlining the parameters of my non-polar reading, I am gratefully drawing and building on a term originally employed by Richard Sheppard to describe Adler's position, in a literary review in which Sheppard, too, apparently situates Adler between two poles — between the 'classical idealism' of his training, mind-set, and scholarly objectives, and the formal 'modernism' characteristic of some of his non-academic style — and so, in Sheppard's words, in a state of 'Grenzgängertum'.[10] However, Sheppard seems not to be stressing polarity here so much as the point that any modernist features in Adler's literary work must be understood to 'exist in tension with' what Sheppard calls his 'rootedness in the mind-set and epistemology of the Enlightenment', with the words tension and 'Grenzgängertum' both suggesting less a rigid and static and more a mobile, even negotiatory position between conflicting modes.[11] 'Grenzgängertum' is a difficult term to translate into English, as a 'Grenzgänger' can be someone who criss-crosses a border or someone who follows along it, but also someone who pushes at boundaries, with the suffix '-tum', more or less equivalent to the English '-dom', denoting a state or condition, as well as a domain. Though Sheppard himself does not spell this out, it is therefore a term that beautifully captures a reading in which Adler the author and scholar is operating in a border zone and stress field, rather than traversing a line of demarcation, constantly negotiating, rather than abruptly switching, between different modes in his writing. It is on this reading of Sheppard's 'Grenzgängertum', in contradistinction to a dichotomizing 'bi-polar' assessment of Adler's œuvre, that the following points will be based. Within this framework, I shall examine a select number of passages drawn from the *Theresienstadt* monograph on the one hand, and from the three Holocaust novels on the other, with the contention that such close reading will bring to light the extent to which Adler's fiction and his non-fiction are not just complementary but can be read as entwined strands, rather than separate poles, of a single encompassing effort. And I shall suggest that reading them in this way shows how not the least of Adler's achievements was the way in which he managed to problematize and render productive the tensions inherent in his 'Grenzgängertum'.

I shall start with, and at the end return to, *Theresienstadt*, in order to show how these tensions — between objective and subjective, academic and literary, Enlightenment epistemology and modernist representation — play out not just across the 'boundary' between Adler's fiction and non-fiction but within the scholarly text itself, informing and, occasionally, unsettling Adler's study at both a thematic and a formal level, in a way that makes it appear in certain respects less as a counter-point to, and more as a proto-text for, the fictional works, and which therefore serves to highlight the limitations of drawing any overly rigid distinctions between Adler's Enlightenment epistemology and his modernist forms, or indeed between his scholarly and his literary practice.[12]

* * * * *

The *Theresienstadt* monograph faces a fundamental challenge: by its author's own assertion, and by the nature of its undertaking, it is conceptually and methodologically 'rooted', as Sheppard has said, in an Enlightenment 'mind-set and epistemology'.[13] Yet at a thematic level it also reflects on the failure of the Enlightenment project, a failure that saw the very individual the Enlightenment meant to emancipate and liberate disempowered and extinguished. In his original foreword, as well as the further preface written for the second edition, Adler stresses the breadth, depth, and comprehensiveness to which his 'weit ausholende Monographie' [almost all-encompassing monograph] aspires (XIV, xv). On the first page of the second preface alone, Adler's use of terms such as 'Materialsammlung', 'Übersicht', 'Darstellung', 'geklärt', 'beleuchtet', or 'Dokumentation' [list of resources, overview, account, clarify, shed light, documentation] (XI, xiii) clearly gestures towards the potential ideal of an encyclopaedic account in which the 'innere Geschichte des Lagers' will become 'noch viel lückenloser in fast mikroskopischer Betrachtung vieler Einzelheiten darstellbar' [an account which will 'depict the camp's internal history much more (literally: even more — KG) comprehensively and in near microscopic detail'] (XIII, xiv). His goal, as Jeremy Adler has summarized it in his afterword to the English translation, is 'the precise depiction of historical reality' (812), and it is a depiction geared towards 'Durchleuchtung' (XIV, xv): towards scrutinizing, intellectually penetrating, shedding light on — and shining a light in — this darkest of periods in human history. The volume in its entirety is dedicated to 'Menschenwürde', to human dignity, and it concludes with a call to 'Humanität' [humanity] as our most important value, even if we have lost sight of it (685, 601).

Yet the text's final chapter also presents us with Adler's theory of mechanical materialism, in the context of which the camps, as the terrible culmination of an 'ungezügelter Rationalismus' [unbridled rationalism] (643, 569), embody the 'Tragödie des Zeitalters', the tragedy of the modern age (658, 580). Moreover, Adler is quite clear that the demise of the Hitler regime does not spell the end of the tragedy. On the contrary, Theresienstadt should be understood as a 'Menetekel', as the writing on the wall (684, 600), leaving Adler to conclude, only at first glance contradictorily, as his account of his time in the camps draws to a close: 'Wir haben eine Welt durchwandert [...]. Wir stehen mitten in dieser Welt darin [...]' [We have explored (literally: traversed — KG) a world [...]. We stand in the midst of this world [...]] (682, 599).

Where these two aspects — his rational 'Durchleuchtung' and the irrational darkness it is up against — collide for Adler, in the present time of reflecting and in the reflected past, is also where the 'distanzierte Objektivität seiner Darstellung' [the detached objectivity of his account], as the back-cover blurb of the German edition terms it, gives way, and the scholarly and the literary, the objective and the personal, converge in his writing.

Where this seems to occur most strikingly in the study is whenever Adler's account attempts to convey existence inside the 'unwirkliche Wirklichkeit' [unreal reality] of Theresienstadt — as the experience of the loss of autonomous subjectivity and all its attendant points of reference — not just as an individual psychological but as a comprehensive epistemological breakdown (667, 587).

Adler proposes that when immersed in the 'Wahnwelt' [illusory world] of the concentrationary universe, the individual is likely to display trauma symptoms or even quasi-psychotic behaviour, not because they are experiencing a break *with* reality but as a reaction to a break *in* reality (666, 586):

> Im wahren Wortsinn war die Wirklichkeit ver-rückt. Nichts deckte sich in ihr mit dem, was gemeinhin Wirklichkeit gewesen war [...]. [...] So erfuhr man sie als Trug, Schein, Traum, Ausgeburt kranker Phantasie. [...]
> Utitz spricht mit gutem Grund von der Schizophrenisierung der Menschen, aber überdies muß erkannt werden, daß sich die Psychose nicht bloß subjektiv im Bewußtsein abgespielt hat, wie es auch keine echte klinische Psychose war, sondern ein das Bewußtsein aufspaltender Reizzustand im Bereich der unentrinnbaren psychischen Affektion, wo der Mensch, verwirrt und zerworfen, sich gleichsam schizoid betragen mußte, um die elementaren Zerwürfnisse im angeborenen und anerzogenen Weltbild mit dem unablässigen Flackern irritierender Erscheinungen mühsam auszugleichen. Es ist gewagt,

trifft aber besser die Verhältnisse, wenn wir sagen, daß die Psychose in der Außenwelt feststand, denn die Wirklichkeit selbst war schizophren gespalten und zerfallen. [...] Jeder Wert, jedes Merkmal, jede Eigenschaft hat seine ursprünglich gültigen Bedeutungen eingebüßt oder verändert. (665–66)

[Reality was dis-placed (*ver-rückt*, a play on the words *verrückt* [crazy] and *ver-rückt* [displaced]) in the truest sense. There was nothing in it that conformed to what was commonly seen as reality [...]. [...] Thus it was experienced as deceptive, bogus, a dream, the spawn of sick fantasies. [...]

Dr Emil Utitz [author of *Psychology of Life in the Terezín Concentration Camp* (Prague, 1947) — KG] speaks, with good reason, of people's schizophrenization, but in addition it must be recognized that this psychosis did not just play out subjectively in people's consciousness, and that it was not a genuine clinical psychosis but an irritable condition that split consciousness in the area of inescapable psychological disorder, where the human being, confused and divided, had to behave in a schizoid manner, as it were, in order painfully to balance the elementary discords in his innate and learned worldview with the ceaseless flicker of irritating phenomena. It may seem bold but it better reflects the circumstances to say that the psychosis was established in the outside world, for reality itself was schizophrenically divided and decayed. [...] Every value, every characteristic, and every trait had lost or changed its original meaning.] (586–87)

In his effort to capture aspects of this 'Ver-rücktheit' of reality and collapse of a 'Weltbild' [worldview], Adler establishes a complex network of imagery in *Theresienstadt*. Drawn from philosophy, psychology, religion, sociology, and natural science, these images include 'das Nichts' [nothing], which appears more than a dozen times over the course of the text, the abyss, chaos, and tohu va bohu, centripetal versus centrifugal forces, the 'verwaltete Masse' [administered mass], or the uncanny. What all of these have in common is their association with a state of pre- or deindividuation: a state before or beyond individuality and autonomous subjectivity. A further such image, and perhaps the most revealing among them for our purposes, is that of 'das Apeiron'.

As a concept, *apeiron* originates in ancient Greek philosophy, with Anaximander identifying it as the origin or principle of all things. *Apeiron*, meaning that which has no *perata*, or boundaries, denotes an indeterminate state of pre-differentiation. As that which is before and beyond all distinctions, *apeiron* is unbounded in both space and time. It is neither perceptible nor intelligible, for, in preceding individuation, it precludes objectivizing consciousness. As philosopher Steven Rosen has said, it was the 'drive toward differentiated being or individuality, toward individuation' that allowed Western culture to be 'forged from the struggle of human reason with the irrational forces of nature', vanquishing '*apeiron*'s chaos in favour of perfected order and unadulterated rationality'.[14] By thus 'stabilizing his position in relation to a stabilized world, "man", the detached subject' put himself in a position to 'exert his influence over nature; [...] treat it as an object; [...] measure it with ever greater precision'.[15]

In denoting a state in which subject and object are indistinguishable, *apeiron* in Adler's use of the term evokes the abrogation of individuality to which the interned were subjected in the concentration camps. At the same time, this more personal association is embedded in a bigger Enlightenment critique. In the broader context of an 'allgemeine abendländische Kulturkrise' [general Occidental crisis of culture], the 'concentrationary universe', as the negative apex of Enlightenment modernity, marks the return of *apeiron* (634, 562). As Adler puts it:

> Man hat die Welt vergeblich um einen nicht mehr ersetzbaren Preis aufgeklärt, indem man das Unheimliche, das Abgründige, das Apeiron aus der Welt geschafft hat — nun ist es wieder erschienen. (667)

> [The world had been enlightened, in vain, at a no-longer-recoverable cost, by eliminating the uncanny, the unfathomable, and the apeiron; now this uncanniness had reappeared.] (587)

The conjunction of the subjective and objective, the personally experienced and the abstract, is underscored by Adler's equation of *apeiron* with the uncanny, 'das Unheimliche', as a mark of both traumatic re-experience at an individual level and of the elimination of *apeiron* by the Enlightenment as a process of repression. 'Objective reality' and the 'personal dimensions' are more inextricably intertwined across Adler's œuvre than a conception of it as relying on a strictly 'bi-polar' methodology is likely to reveal. Moreover, as we shall see, this is true not just at a thematic but above all also at a formal level.

★   ★   ★   ★   ★

It has become a fairly well-established argument that the attempt to convey the 'concentrationary universe' saw Adler draw on a modernist aesthetic in his works of fiction, that the recourse to modernist techniques of representation in his novels seems to have arisen almost organically out of their subject matter.[16] The experience of being immersed in, and the concomitant impossibility of conceptualizing, the *apeiron* of the camps — regarded as both a lived reality and as evidence of the ultimate distortion of Enlightenment ideals — has given rise, in the Holocaust novel trilogy, to three texts that, each in its own way, problematize autonomous subjectivity and stable perspective, as well as all of modernity's founding assumptions regarding time, space and the self related to these. This is expressed not just thematically but above all by means of the disruption of linear, chronological structure and an unsettling of narrative perspective.

Indeed, if we read the three novels purely with a view to what happens to narrative perspective in them, it becomes possible to identify a logical progression from one work to the next. *Panorama* begins the process by destabilizing the notion of a detached, autonomous subject observing a distinct panorama from a stable viewing position. This is especially notable in the 'Lager Langenstein' chapter, where the dehumanizing treatment to which the prisoners are subjected in the camp, the erosion of their individuality, and the abrogation of their right to a point of view are expressed formally through personal pronouns, by means of a second-person address that objectivizes the prisoners and illustrates their loss of selfhood:

Du sollst nicht entrinnen, geh nur hinein, geh mit den anderen, wie Tausende und Tausende gegangen sind und nachfolgen werden, geh, es ist so leicht zu gehen; [...] geh und warte, bis der Schrein gefüllt ist, daß man ihn sicher schließen kann; dann verlöschen die Lichter, dann wird dein Sterbliches erstickt, es dauert nicht lange, bald ist die Läuterung gewonnen, man lüftet den Schrein, dann kommt ein Sonderkommando von Verlorenen [...], sie holen das Sterbliche aus dem Schrein, das mit blutigen Augen und Nasen und Mündern seinen Boden bedeckt, verschmutzt in dicke Klumpen geballt [...].

[You shouldn't run away [Thou shalt not escape — KG], just go on in, go with the others, just as thousands and thousands have gone before you and will follow you, go, it's so easy, just go. [...] go and wait until the shrine is full so that one can seal it for good. Then the lights will go out, then your mortal being will be consumed, it won't take long, soon salvation [salvation / purification — KG] will follow, the shrine is opened, then a special command of lost ones [...] haul the mortals [the mortal remains — KG] from the shrine who cover its ground with their bloody eyes and noses and mouths, filthy and piled up in clumps so thick that the bodies often cannot be separated [...].][17]

Here, in an extraordinary replication and subversion of biblical language and religious imagery that distorts the ten commandments and sees the gas chamber referred to as the holy shrine, an unspecified 'du' is exhorted to enter into the shrine to achieve 'Läuterung' and be 'purged' into the *apeironic* 'Klumpen' of mortal remains of the final line. From this, as the 'du' is told at the outset, 'Thou shalt not escape'. It is technically ambiguous who is focalizing whom in this direct address, if it is the camp guards addressing the prisoners or the prisoners reminding themselves or one another. What is more, the absence of a stable perspective and detached vantage point is extended beyond the text to the reader. The ability to tell these perspectives apart would allow us to remain detached observers. Because of the sentence's direct address, we feel personally implicated. If we assume an exoperceptive focus on events, it is aligned with the perspective of the perpetrators, which forces us into an uncomfortable complicity with them. But if we identify with the 'du' of the address, we become part of the collective object of their destructive gaze, part of the de-individuated 'Klumpen', in a narrative move that succeeds in gesturing towards the otherwise (for us) inconceivable horror of being denied a sense of selfhood, autonomy, or consciousness. The text manoeuvres us into a position where we are, impossibly and *apeironically*, at once complicit subjects and implicated objects.

An extended and more complex version of this kind of pronominal play also lies at the heart of *Eine Reise*, as Julia Creet has compellingly explored.[18] More extensively than in *Panorama*, the loss of autonomous subjectivity and self-determination, expressed as the absence of a detached perspective on the unquantifiable abyss of *apeiron*, here also goes hand in hand with the undermining of associated other conventions and constructs vital to modern Western culture. This becomes apparent in the following quotations, excerpted from a passage that sees Paul trying to reflect on his situation while he is being marched through Leitenberg with his fellow prisoners. Paul wonders what it would be like if the procession of which he is a part were forced to walk blindfolded, shuffling along as a single, senseless unit:

Es *würde* genügen, die Augen der ersten Reihe unverbunden zu lassen, die dann nichts anderes zu tun *hätte*, als auf den Weg zu achten und vorsichtig die Füße auf den Boden zu setzen. Die anderen *schlichen* hintendrein, die Hände auf den Schultern ihrer Vordermänner, die stumme Geisterbahn, die keine Geleise *braucht*, immer vorwärts durch den unbestimmten Hauch, mag es Tag sein oder Nacht, jedes Glied des Zuges nichts als unverwandtes Schreiten [...], durch die Entfernung aller freundschaftlichen Nachbarschaft ins unmitteilsam Abgründige vertieft [...].

[It would be sufficient to leave the eyes of the front row uncovered, who would then simply have to watch the path and place their feet carefully on the ground. The others would just shuffle along behind, their hands on the shoulders of those in front of them, a mute ghost train [...] that just keeps plodding along through the indeterminate haze, unaware of whether it is day or night, each member of the train nothing but an unrelenting / unrelated ['unverwandt' plays untranslatably on both meanings] marching, with the withdrawal of all friendly relations plunging them into the incommunicable abyss [...]. [my paraphrase — KG]][19]

Paul is attempting here to speculate on what it would be like to be 'ins unmitteilsam Abgründige vertieft', but though he and his fellow ghosts are not literally blindfolded, they have in fact already been deprived of a sense of individuality and autonomy, of an awareness of their surroundings and the passing of time, and of a sense of direction and emotional connection. Paul's attempt fails as soon as it turns out that he is already immersed in the very thing on which he is trying to reflect, an immersion that precludes him from gaining the kind of detached vantage point that would make such reflection even conceivable. The slide from the perspectival to the aperspectival is signalled by a shift in tense and mood, from the conditional of hypothesis in the 'würde' and 'hätte' of the first sentence, to the ambiguous 'schlichen', which can be read as either subjunctive or indicative, to the present-tense indicative of 'braucht' when it is revealed that *apeiron* is already and inescapably all around.

As in the passage from *Panorama*, cited above, the only way in which Paul is theoretically able to achieve a vantage point is exoperceptively, by sharing the perpetrators' perspective. As soon as he attempts to focalize isoperceptively, he finds himself already in the abyss, and the adoption of a perspective is revealed to be impossible:

Dann könnte die Zeit auslöschen; nur eine Richtung hätte die Reise, aber kein Ziel; sie würde währen und ginge doch nicht weiter. Unsinnig würde die Frage werden, wann einer geboren ist, weil sein Tod viel weiter zurückliegen könnte als der Tag seiner Erschaffung. Habt ihr es noch nie empfunden, wie in einer ausgestochenen Zeit alles durcheinandergeriet? Was ihr heute zu halten vermeint, wäre entfernt, euer verlogener Traum von Sicherheit würde sich endlich von euch abwenden, denn Ersparnisse werden müßig, es gäbe keine Zinsen und Zinseszinsen, weil man auch nichts von einem Kalender wüßte, nichts von einem Datum, nur trübe rollte man durch trübe Masse hin, alles wäre gleichzeitig und in eins verbacken [...], aufgehoben der Grund, aufgehoben die Wirkung. [...]

> Von jetzt an also ist keine Zeit. Doch von jetzt an? Sinnlose Rede. Wenn keine Zeit ist, war sie auch nicht und wird nicht sein, die Sprache zertrümmert ohne das Zeitwort, alles huscht durcheinander, verdorbene Reise. (108)

> [Were this to happen, time would be erased. The journey would have only a direction, but no destination. It would continue and yet lead nowhere. Senseless would be the question about when you were born, for the day of your death could come long before the day of your conception. Have you never noticed how in a turbulent time everything falls apart [how in an excised chunk of time everything turns topsy-turvy — KG]? What you take for granted today can suddenly disappear, each of your false dreams no longer a certainty, savings now being a necessity [now otiose — KG] since there would be no interest or compounded interest, since you would know nothing of calendars, nothing of dates, yourself having to roll along among the dreary masses, everything the same and fitting a single mold [rolling along in a turbid mass, everything simultaneous, everything clumped together as one — KG] [...], both cause and effect made meaningless.

> From this point onward there is no such thing as time. And yet what exists from this point onward? [But what does that even mean, from now on? — KG] Senseless talk. When there is no time, there can be no talk nor will there be, for without verbs ['tense-words' — KG] language is destroyed, everything scurrying along higgledy-piggledy on the wretched journey.] (99–100)

Beyond the disruption of individual life stories, the text suggests that the entire way in which Enlightenment modernity views and thinks about the world has been dealt a blow: being denied the privilege of perspective — of a stable, detached vantage point from which to survey, and make oneself the measure of, what one beholds — calls into question the very possibility of existing as an autonomous, self-determined subject, and in the absence of being able to individuate and situate ourselves in relation to the world, both our faith in the possibility of reliably quantifying and negotiating time or space, and our reliance on common transactional media such as language or money to help us do so, are also undermined. The faltering of these touchstones suggests the return of the original uncanny repressed by the Enlightenment project: the return of *apeiron*.

Apeiron, here invoked in the image of a 'trübe Masse', a turbid mass, appears as a spatialized conception of time without direction and delineation, origin or aim, cause and effect. In this indistinct mass, the conventional view of chronological time as a line or arrow is superseded, and notions of life as a journey, with a clear beginning and end, are supplanted by images of eternal aimless wandering. This unmappable chronotope can no longer be travelled in any straightforward sense. As the passage concludes: it is a 'verdorbene Reise', a corrupted, tainted, perverted journey.

Finally, in *Die unsichtbare Wand*, Artur Landau has emerged from the camps able to say 'ich', I, again. In a sense, he therefore picks up where Paul in *Eine Reise* left off.[20] There is a sense of the future again, even if it is a future for others and hard to imagine with himself in it. However, the novel suggests that while Landau has survived, *apeiron* has not been fully overcome, and the description of his 'post'-Holocaust existence, especially in the famous snowstorm passage, reads not unlike

Paul's failed attempt to conceputalize *apeiron* from within it: as a chaotic chronotope without the possibility of signification, and without hope of orientation or true escape:

> Ein überlebter Mensch, an einer Wegmarke in tödlichem Schneesturm vom Unheil verschmäht; als der Sturm verzogen war, lagen alle Gefährten erfroren, die Wegmarke ist zersplittert, auf ihren Spänen sind keine Ziele mehr zu entziffern [...]. [...] jeder Wandel eines Vergessenen führt überall in die Irre. Keine Richtung verheißt einen verläßlichen Sinn, auch die Strecken der Zeit werden in stockender Verwirrung immer undeutlicher [...]. Schon gibt es keine Stunde mehr, die Reiche der Vergangenheit und der Zukunft sind zerschellt [...]. Aller Ablauf ist zerschüttelt und verbogen [...]. (640–41)

> [A survivor [a man survived — KG], condemned to cling to a signpost in the deadly snowstorm of misery [spurned by disaster at a signpost in the deadly snowstorm — KG], and when the snowstorm had cleared all the others were frozen, the signpost split [in splinters — KG]. On the post [on its fragments — KG], no destinations were legible any longer [...]. [...] every transformation of the forgotten leads to error [reading 'der Wandel' as 'das Wandeln': any progression by a man forgotten is doomed to lead him astray — KG]. No direction provides a reliable sense of things to come, and the roads of time continue to become lost in confusion [...]. Then there are no more hours, the realms of past and future are shattered [...]. The run of things is twisted and destroyed [...].] (615)

The main consequence of this approach for the form of the texts is that content and discourse in them converge. The novels come as close to reflecting the abyss from within as is possible, by evoking the experience of *apeiron* through the enactment of a failure to gain epistemological purchase. In an important sense, their subject matter becomes the breakdown of their own structures. This approach results in a great deal of the imagery we encounter in the text doubling up as a blueprint of its form, with the structures of the outside world after the return of *apeiron* mirroring those of the traumatized mind attempting in vain to navigate that world, and the two between them providing a model for and of the textual structures.

★   ★   ★   ★   ★

On this evidence, we could be forgiven for thinking that the academic and the literary in Adler's work do indeed adopt polar-opposite methodologies, inhabit different discourses, and use language in clearly distinct ways. Pursuing a challenge to metanarratives to its conclusion by enacting their breakdown both formally and structurally, and denying the reader an observer's vantage point, is not generally an option available to academic studies, which by their nature tend towards the encompassing, explanatory, and descriptive, and especially not to a study with the scope and express objectives of the *Theresienstadt* monograph.

And yet, there are sections of *Theresienstadt* that are in fact strikingly close in both intention and effect to what we encounter in Adler's literary writing.

Stylistically, as has already become apparent above from Adler's choice of imagery to evoke the *apeironic*, the passages communicating what happens 'wenn eine Welt aus den Fugen gerät' [when a world is turned upside down [comes out of joint — KG]] mark a departure from the neutral, matter-of-fact tone that characterizes the greater part of the study, and they see Adler resort to a more literary idiom (674, 593). However, the sense of an out-of-joint reality causing not only individuals but an entire world view to founder apparently cannot be captured through straightforward description alone. This becomes especially evident where Adler speaks of the final weeks of Theresienstadt in April of 1945. As he discusses in the last chapter of the section detailing the camp's history, a chapter titled 'Verfall und Auflösung' [Decline and Dissolution], the influx of survivors being marched from extermination camps all over Europe, and a raging typhoid epidemic, dissolved any semblance of order in the ghetto. As Adler attempts to convey the dissolution of all structures and points of reference that ensues when the 'Weltbild', the worldview, and the reality experienced are hopelessly beyond reconciliation, his account slides, over the space of two paragraphs, from scholarly report to literary evocation:

> Am 24. April wurde unter den Neulingen zum ersten Male Flecktyphus festgestellt. Bald wurden hunderte Fälle erkannt, schließlich weit über zweitausend, und die Einheimischen wurden nicht verschont. Etwa 400 Tote haben die Elendstransporte bereits ins Lager mitgebracht, wo sich das Sterben an Erschöpfung und Krankheit fortsetzte, vor allem an Flecktyphus, obwohl es gelang, die Sterblichkeit bei dieser Infektion unter 25% hinunterzudrücken. Viele freiwillige Helfer steckten sich an, manche konnten nicht gerettet werden (s. 16. Kap.).
>
> Jetzt galt keine Ordnung mehr, nicht einmal eine Lagerordnung; dazu waren die Entwürdigten nicht mehr bereit. [...] Wo der Mensch an jenem Ende steht, das ihn als ein unversöhnlicher Abgrund umringt [...] — wer will da noch ein Mindestmaß von Zucht und Ordnung beschwören [...]? Wie kindisch und aussichtslos mußte sich dieses Unterfangen ausnehmen! Diese Menschen glaubten nicht mehr, sie glaubten nichts und niemandem. Sie glaubten nicht mehr an sich selbst. Alles war ausgelöscht, alles entwertet. [...] Es war das Ende — Ende als Untergang, als Weltgericht — als *Nichts*. Und es gab keinen Bestand mehr. Wer diese Vernichtung nicht an sich selbst erfahren hat, weiß es nicht, wird es nie wissen. Er hat zu schweigen. Er hat anzuhören [...]. Wer aber durch diese letzte Verzweiflung, durch die Nacht der Nächte, durch den namenlosen Untergang geschritten ist, ihn überdauert hat [...], der soll seine Stimme erheben und sagen, wie es wirklich war. Er soll die Wirklichkeit verkünden [...], jenseits von allem theatralischen Grauen noch lebender Verwesung und toter Knochenberge, die nichts von der inneren Wahrheit enthüllen, da sie nur Schandmäler sind, aber nicht die Wahrheit selbst. Nein, die Wirklichkeit gilt es zu nennen [...], die Wirklichkeit des *Nichts*, die weder denkbar noch nachfühlbar ist, denn nicht zu denken und nicht zu fühlen ist das Nichts, nur ungeschaffen ist es [...] zu leiden [...]. [...]
>
> Wie man in jenen wüsten Tagen die Verlorenen in Theresienstadt ansah, verdeutlichen die Worte einer Augenzeugin: [...]. (212–13, original emphasis)

[On April 24, typhoid fever was found for the first time among the newcomers. Soon hundreds of cases were diagnosed; the number ultimately grew to well over two thousand, and the natives were not spared. The transports of misery had already brought 400 dead to the camp, where death from exhaustion and disease continued, above all from typhoid fever, although it was possible to keep the death rate from this infection under 25%. Many volunteer helpers were infected, and some could not be saved (see Chapter 16).

No regime mattered now, not even a camp regime; the degraded ones were no longer willing to accept it. [...] When a human being stands at an end that surrounds him like an implacable abyss [...] — who would still conjure there a minimum of discipline and order [...]? How childish and futile must this endeavor have seemed! These people no longer believed; they believed nothing and no one. They no longer believed in themselves. Everything was obliterated, everything devalued. [...] It was the end: the end as doom, as Armageddon — as *nothing*. And there was no more substance. If one did not experience this annihilation oneself, one cannot know, will never know, what it was like. One must be silent. One must listen [...]. But anyone who went through this final despair, this night of nights, this nameless doom [...] he should raise his voice and say what it was really like. He should proclaim the reality, [...] beyond all the theatrical horror of living decay and dead mountains of bones, which reveal none of the inner truth, for they are merely stigmas, not the truth itself. No, it is necessary to name the reality [...] — the reality of *nothingness*, which is neither imaginable nor comprehensible, for not thinking and not feeling is nothingness [for nothingness cannot be thought or felt empathetically, it can only be experienced as raw, uncrafted suffering — KG] [...]. [...]

How the lost ones in Theresienstadt were seen in those desolate days is made clear by the words of an eyewitness: [...].] (172, original emphasis)

The passage is marked by a contention between narrative voices.[21] There is the voice of the historian, who arranges events into a sequential, chronological narrative, observing and quantifying them from the detached vantage point of the present time of narration. Vying with this voice, however, is a second one, which, resorting to more literary language, undermines chronology by suggesting that the past will never be past. Between them, the vying voices give the impression of inhabiting two worlds at once: a life *after* the abyss, and one in which the 'Abgrund' is still all around. The net result of their contention is a calling-into-question of any certainty regarding the coherence and stability of time, space, and autonomous subjectivity, expressed at the level of structure.

The first paragraph is still largely anchored in the scholarly mode and apparently born of the conviction of being able to document objectively and quantitatively. This narrator is detached and strives for objectivity. He favours impersonal constructions and separates himself both from the 'Neulinge' arriving in the camps and from the 'Einheimische' already present there. He cites dates, figures, percentages. And he imposes order and structure: on the text's subject matter, and on its form, for example through intratextual cross-referencing to other chapters as in the final sentence of the first paragraph. We do note one interesting slippage — in the sentence beginning 'Etwa 400 Tote' — in the use of the perfect tense, rather than, as perhaps expected, the pluperfect, a slippage which, through its blurring of diegetic levels, with the past seemingly enduring into the present of narration, may hint at a brief loss of objective distance and detachment. This remains relatively unobtrusive though and at most momentarily unsettles the narrative's measured tone and chronological current.

However, as the narrator goes on to evoke the disruption and dissolution of all structures, culminating in 'Unbestand', in the abyss of *apeiron* or, here, of the 'Nichts', the voice of the historian is supplemented with, and increasingly supplanted by, that of the poet, and a breakdown of narrative chronology, structure, and perspective ensues to mirror the 'Ver-rücktheit' of the world that is being evoked.

The slight temporal slippage from the first paragraph carries over into the second one, which is introduced with 'Jetzt', rather than, say, 'Von da an'. At the same time, the bird's-eye view of the objective chronicler gives way to a position of empathetic involvement with the 'Entwürdigten' and 'Unglücklichen', as well as, increasingly, to suggestions of personal familiarity with 'jenem Ende'. Formally speaking, this initiates a sequence of perspectival oscillation. Empathetic but still exoperceptive statements such as 'Wie kindisch und aussichtslos mußte sich dieses Unterfangen ausnehmen!' alternate with statements that are formally indistinguishable from isoperception, for instance in: 'Alles war ausgelöscht, alles entwertet', and 'Es war das Ende — Ende als Untergang, als Weltgericht — als *Nichts*. Und es gab keinen Bestand mehr'.

The introduction of the term 'Nichts' marks the complete suspension of narrative flow and disruption of its structures. The past tense of historical documentary cedes to a present tense of address and exhortation and finally culminates in the timeless insurmountable persistence of the 'Nichts'. The impersonal 'wer', which up to this point had afforded the narrator a vantage point of non-involvement, from which to separate himself both from the 'Entwürdigten' and from those with no personal experience of 'Vernichtung', now subsumes him in the collective of those who have known the abyss. And it is from this experience that the narrative voice emerges split: with one part testifying to the possibility of traversing the 'Untergang' and coming out the other side to give an account of its 'Wirklichkeit', and the other, still and always inside the abyss, dismissing this as a possibility by invoking the essentially unknowable formless void of the 'Nichts' whose 'innere Wahrheit' cannot be communicated, conceptualized, or empathetically accessed for 'nicht zu denken und nicht zu fühlen ist das Nichts, nur ungeschaffen ist es [...] zu leiden'.

Because of this vying of voices, what started out at as an apparently linear, chronological account breaks down as the narrator, in a *mise en abyme* perhaps of the thought processes and tensions informing the work as a whole, impossibly, both calls for, and so projects into the future, the creation of the very enterprise in which he himself already appears, and at the same time rejects, and places under erasure, the very existence of that self-same enterprise.

In this process of narrative self-deconstruction, the narrating subject itself breaks down as well. The stable perspective and posture of detached analysis from a transcendent vantage point maintained by the seemingly autonomous and indivisible narrator from the beginning of the passage is called into question. The subject first splits, with the narrator-as-chronicler observing, and addressing, possibly himself in the third person, possibly a third party in an analogous position, possibly an impersonal collective, as someone who is subject to an ethical imperative, starting from the sentence: 'Er soll die Wirklichkeit verkünden'. However, as the narrative founders on the ambiguity inherent in the term 'Wirklichkeit', between communicable factual accuracy and incommunicable 'innere Wahrheit', the focalization appears to be reversed, and in the process breaks down completely. In the sentence starting with 'Nein, die Wirklichkeit gilt es zu nennen', which reads like a rebuttal to 'Er soll die Wirklichkeit verkünden', the objectivizing subject appears itself objectivized, as the voice that does not have the distance from the 'Nichts' to conceptualize it but can only suffer it 'ungeschaffen' seems to turn the tables on the first speaker. However, with no more personal pronouns to guide us and no clear clues as to the point of origin of any focalization, the boundary between narrating subject and narrated object appears to have dissolved, leaving us, too, for just a moment, with no perspective at all: immersed in the 'Nichts', right along with the text, as it briefly hovers on the brink of disappearing down its own abyss. It does not do this, of course, but draws back. After the end of the passage just cited, the narrator extracts himself (though in the process temporarily eclipsing himself) by handing over the narrative, in the form of citation, to a third-party eye-witness account, before then resuming the neutral, detached third-person stance from the beginning of the passage.

This destructuring mode of writing that testifies to the experience of *apeiron* and the challenge it poses to attempts to come to epistemological terms with the Holocaust is undeniably more familiar to us from Adler's novels. However, though on balance subdued, it has evidently also informed, and left traces on, his academic writing. While this does of course bring to light a tension between an Enlightenment mind-set and a modernist style, or perhaps between an all-encompassing project and an anti-totalizing approach, the tension is a productive one. It seems born of the (almost proto-*post*modern?) realization that bearing witness to the *experience* as well as the facts of *apeiron* would have to involve a rethinking of reference and problematizing of metanarratives, and that the shortfalls of linear, chronological, descriptive writing when it comes to evoking the 'inner truth' of the abyss, might be compensated for (though never completely overcome) by drawing attention to them and enacting their collapse at a structural level. In other words, it is a tension that, in reintroducing an element of split consciousness and self-reflexivity into an Enlightenment mind-set, has allowed Adler to recuperate his epistemology, to draw it back from the brink, while at the same time using it to shed some light on — and shine a light into — the abyss. Not just in a thematic, but also in a formal sense, this suggests that, as Lynn Wolff has already persuasively argued in a different context, we might constructively think of him as an ' "enlightener" of the modern age'.[22] And it is this 'Grenzgängertum', on the edge of the abyss, using the breakdown of forms to give shape, and the (temporary) collapse of language to signify, to acknowledge meaninglessness and wrest back meaning from it, that has made it possible for Adler to give us a remarkably encompassing, encyclopaedic, detailed, factually accurate report of the 'Wirklichkeit' of the 'concentrationary universe' while at the same time staying true to the inconceivable, incommunicable 'innere Wahrheit' of the 'Nichts' that is 'nur ungeschaffen [...] zu leiden'.

Notes to Chapter 6

1. The much-cited term 'Gesamtkunstwerk' to emphasize the complexity of Adler's œuvre was introduced by his first biographer, Jürgen Serke, in Serke, *Böhmische Dörfer: Wanderungen durch eine verlassene literarische Landschaft* (Vienna: Zsolnay, 1987), p. 327. See also Jeremy Adler, 'The World of My Father's Memory Writing: The *Gesamtkunstwerk* of H. G. Adler', in *H. G. Adler: Life, Literature, Legacy*, ed. by Julia Creet, Sara R. Horowitz, and Amira Bojadzija-Dan (Evanston, IL: Northwestern University Press, 2016), pp. 23–46.

2. Thomas Krämer, *Die Poetik des Gedenkens: Zu den autobiographischen Romanen H. G. Adlers* (Würzburg: Königshausen & Neumann, 2012), p. 10.

3. Lawrence Langer, 'Holocaust Fact and Holocaust Fiction: The Dual Vision of H. G. Adler', in *H. G. Adler: Life, Literature, Legacy*, ed. by Creet, Horowitz, and Bojadzija-Dan, pp. 139–59 (pp. 142, 146, 147).

4. Langer, 'Holocaust Fact and Holocaust Fiction', pp. 145, 144.

5. Langer, 'Holocaust Fact and Holocaust Fiction', pp. 144, 146.

6. Krämer, *Die Poetik des Gedenkens*, p. 257.

7. Langer, 'Holocaust Fact and Holocaust Fiction', pp. 147, 145, 146.

8. Jeremy Adler, 'Good against Evil? H. G. Adler, T. W. Adorno and the Representation of the Holocaust', in *The German-Jewish Dilemma: From the Enlightenment to the Shoah*, ed. by Edward Timms and Andrea Hammel (Lewiston, NY: Mellen, 1999), pp. 255–89 (p. 263).

9. Jeremy Adler, 'Afterword', in H. G. Adler, *Theresienstadt 1941–1945: The Face of a Coerced Community*, trans. by Belinda Cooper (New York: Cambridge University Press, 2017), pp. 803–28 (p. 806).

10. Richard Sheppard, 'Book Review: Helen Finch and Lynn L. Wolff (eds), *Witnessing, Memory, Poetics: H. G. Adler and W. G. Sebald*', *Journal of European Studies*, 45 (2015), 275–77 (p. 277).

11. Sheppard, 'Book Review', p. 277.

12. H. G. Adler, *Theresienstadt 1941–1945: Das Antlitz einer Zwangsgemeinschaft* (Göttingen: Wallstein, 2005); *Theresienstadt 1941–1945: The Face of a Coerced Community*, trans. by Belinda Cooper (New York: Cambridge University Press, 2017). Further references to both editions will be included in parentheses in the text. On the few occasions where I have included a paraphrase or more literal rendering alongside Cooper's excellent translation, this serves purely to clarify my argument.

13. Sheppard, 'Book Review', p. 277.

14. Steven M. Rosen, *Dimensions of Apeiron: A Topological Phenomenology of Space, Time, and Individuation* (Amsterdam: Rodopi, 2004), p. 3.

15. Rosen, *Dimensions of Apeiron*, p. 3.

16. See especially *Witnessing, Memory, Poetics: H. G. Adler and W. G. Sebald*, ed. by Helen Finch and Lynn Wolff (Rochester, NY: Camden House, 2014), and *H. G. Adler: Life, Literature, Legacy*, ed. by Creet, Horowitz, and Bojadzija-Dan, where the contributors addressing themselves to Adler's prose fiction between them have foregrounded a number of different ways in which Adler's experiments with narrative voice and perspective, language, structure, and tense speak to his 'dedication to [a] modernist aesthetic' in his novels (Creet, Horowitz, Bojadzija-Dan, 'Introduction: Encountering H. G. Adler', in *H. G. Adler: Life, Literature, Legacy*, p. 16). Here, as in the chapter on Adler's fiction writing in Gwyer, *Encrypting the Past: The German-Jewish Holocaust Novel of the First Generation* (Oxford: Oxford University Press, 2014), there appears to be a broad consensus with Lawrence Langer that these features and strategies arose out of the effort of finding 'a language that might convey [...] the unconveyable, [...] to help readers imagine the unimaginable' (Langer, 'Holocaust Fact and Holocaust Fiction: The Dual Vision of H. G. Adler', in *H. G. Adler: Life, Literature, Legacy*, ed. by Creet, Horowitz, and Bojadzija-Dan, p. 141).

17. H. G. Adler, *Panorama: Roman in zehn Bildern* (Munich: Piper, 1988), pp. 482–83; H. G. Adler, *Panorama: A Novel*, trans. by Peter Filkins (New York: Modern Library, 2012), p. 365. Where, on occasion, I have added to Filkins's translations, or supplied a clumsier, more literal version in place of his elegant one, this was done purely in the interest of clarifying my argument.

18. Julia Greet, 'A Dialectic of the Deictic: Pronouns and Persons in H. G. Adler's *The Journey*', in *H. G. Adler: Life, Literature, Legacy*, ed. by Creet, Horowitz, and Bojadzija-Dan, pp. 205–27.

19. H. G. Adler, *Eine Reise* (Vienna: Zsolnay, 1999), p. 107–08, my emphasis; H. G. Adler, *The Journey*, trans. by Peter Filkins (New York: Modern Library, 2009), p. 99. Further references to both editions will be included in parentheses in the text.

20. H. G. Adler, *Die unsichtbare Wand* (Vienna: Zsolnay, 1989); H. G. Adler, *The Wall: A Novel*, trans. by Peter Filkins (New York: Random House, 2015). Further references to both editions will be made in parentheses in the text.

21. I am gratefully borrowing the concept of contending or vying narrative voices from Lawrence Langer, who has identified the contention between a voice of continuity — which seeks to embed what has happened in a sequence of cause and effect — and a voice of disruption — which undermines any chronology and causality and disputes all rhyme or reason — as an important recurring characteristic of oral Holocaust witness testimonies, but which is a feature that may affect any attempt in any genre to give a chronological, factual account of the events and effects of the Holocaust. See for instance Langer, *Holocaust Testimonies: The Ruins of Memory* (New Haven: Yale University Press, 1991).

22. Lynn Wolff, '"Die Grenzen des Sagbaren": Toward a Political Philology in H. G. Adler's Reflections on Language', in *H. G. Adler: Life, Literature, Legacy*, ed. by Creet, Horowitz, and Bojadzija-Dan, pp. 273–301 (p. 292).

PART III

❖

Individual Studies of Adler's Literary Works

CHAPTER 7

❖

Poetry in Exile — H. G. Adler's Dialogue with Past and Present

Katrin Kohl

H. G. Adler wrote poetry throughout his life — during his early years in Prague, during his internment in concentration and death camps, and during his many decades in London from the late 1940s until his death in 1988. The diversity of the poems with respect to their geographical and cultural origin interacts with a consistency of linguistic choice for his verse: his poetic medium is always German. He occasionally toyed with writing in English, and in 1981 he composed a cycle entitled 'České vzpomínky' [Czech Reminiscences] in a language that had surrounded him in his youth, but this group of ten poems marks the only foray into a language other than German in the collected edition of poems he designated as his poetic legacy.[1] Moreover, while he was widely read, and worked with English verse by poets such as T. S. Eliot and Dylan Thomas, the poetic tradition that above all sustained and inspired him was poetry in German — by Luther and Gryphius, Klopstock and Goethe, Hölderlin and Eichendorff, Alfred Mombert and Georg Trakl. During his life in exile, his poetry was consequently at odds with the language and poetic tradition of his environment. This tension precluded wide-spread reception in Britain, and there was also a tension with poetic developments in Germany and Austria, where audiences in the post-war decades were not attuned to the deep sense of tradition that underpinned Adler's use of language and form, or to the allegiances within the German poetic tradition which he had established in Prague. Even more than his work in other genres, Adler's poetry is thus characterized by the exile condition. Yet his poetry does not exist in a vacuum, and it does not seek hermetic inwardness. Rather, it is suffused with a spirit of dialogue that challenges the confines of spatial, temporal and cultural context.

Adler strove not for an international medium but rather exploited the specific features of the German language and poetic tradition to withstand the regime that sought to appropriate German culture for a momentous crime against the Jewish people and humanity itself. The purpose of this essay is to explore the significance of Adler's inventive engagement with the voice of the German language for an understanding of his verse. His work with his linguistic medium and its communicative strength affords an insight into the deeply meaningful ways in which he deploys the interaction between language, poetic tradition and cultural context to respond to the cataclysmic historical moment he experienced first-hand. Writing poetry in German became the most direct means of resisting the powers that exploited a shared human medium for murderous purposes. More than that, it became a means of forging an independent identity that would outlast the regime, and a voice that would bear witness to the crimes that had been committed.

In an interview in 1981, Adler defined himself as a 'deutscher Schriftsteller jüdischer Nation, der aus der Tschechoslowakei kommt, dem österreichischen Kulturkreis angehört und loyaler britischer Staatsbürger ist' [a German writer with Jewish nationality who comes from Czechoslovakia, belongs to the Austrian cultural area, and is a loyal British citizen].[2] He thereby highlights the complexity of his roots in the Austro-Hungarian Empire with its many cultural groups and wealth of identities, and connects his identity with the country in which he then made his home. National identity is ironically acknowledged only for his Jewishness, while Czech, Austrian and British elements are associated in each case with a specific cultural or political allegiance. German is strictly confined to, and reserved for, his authorial identity. Writing in German was not a choice for Adler but a necessity — it was his native language, and when political circumstances divested him of the opportunity to make his career as a scholar and writer in Prague, he devoted himself to forging German into an expressive instrument that could articulate a response to the Holocaust. From the start, however, the language he grew up with was part of a culturally complex environment in which it was the medium of the German-Jewish community, shared with other parts of the cultural elite, accorded high status owing to its administrative role and connection with the language of Vienna and Berlin, but part of a linguistic mix in which Czech was the language spoken by the majority. During the years of internment in Theresienstadt, Niederorschel, and Langenstein, German was the language used by the Nazi regime, and Adler looked to poetic tradition and the morphological and syntactic possibilities deeply embedded in the German language to forge an idiom that would act as a counterforce. This spirit of writing against the grain remained a characteristic of his poetry in the exile years.

Adler would regularly visit Austria and Germany to keep in touch with the living German language while remaining firmly committed to living outside the German-speaking territories. Conversely, he never changed the language of his verse as he made a new life in Britain and engaged with English poets. In an essay entitled 'Zu Hause im Exil' [At Home in Exile] published in 1981, he comments on his initial intention to start writing in English, a project he quickly recognized as impossible to implement. In this context, he stresses that the single exception was to be his poetry: 'meine Lyrik [... sollte] unbedingt deutsch bleiben' [my poetry was definitely to remain German].[3] His reflections take account of constraints arising from lacking familiarity with the English language but the central criterion arises from the fundamental interdependence between language and innermost personal identity:

Sicher bietet auch das Englische sehr viel, was mich sprachlich außerordentlich fesselt, mir lieb und angenehm ist, sowie anderes, was mich abstößt, aber im Innersten geht es mich doch nur wenig an, und nun finde ich Zeit und mit ihr Muße und Abstand, um mich, wenn ich so sagen darf, mit *meinem* Deutsch auseinanderzusetzen und es nach *meiner* Art zu pflegen.[4]

[Undoubtedly English also offers much that truly grips me linguistically, much that I like and find pleasurable, as well as other aspects I find repulsive, but in my innermost being it does not greatly concern me. Now I am finding the time, and with it the leisure and distance, to engage with *my* German, if I might put it like that, and to foster it in *my* way.]

Adler's metaphor of interiority indicates how closely the choice of language is bound up with other dimensions of his œuvre. Language is fundamental to the intellectual ambition of his work, its spiritual dimension, and its ethical mission. In this statement he negotiates the tension between collectivity and individuality that is inherent in language: he is using a collectively established language that has evolved over time in the daily discourse of the people and peoples whose cultural identities it continues to define. For every individual who uses that language, it is both an internal and an external medium. Adler's sense of language as an inner resource gains depth over a lifetime of seeing language, and languages, being used and abused. Nurturing his very own German in all its facets is an expression of Adler's fierce spirit of independence forged in the face of catastrophic adversity. Developing German as an individual, personal medium gives the individual voice a supple strength that becomes a powerful means of resisting political and cultural pressures that seek to functionalise and subjugate the individual.

During his early years in Prague, Adler was beginning to establish himself as part of a literary circle that drew inspiration from the illustrious tradition of poets which he was later to portray in his essay 'Die Dichtung der Prager Schule' [The Literature of the Prague School].[5] The Prague School's identity was founded on the medium of 'Prague German' — characterised both by its proximity to Austrian German and by its role as a lingua franca that transcended the dialects and languages of the eastern part of the erstwhile Austro–Hungarian Empire. Prague German was the language of a cultural elite, noted for its stylistic refinement and clarity, and it was a medium shared by writers from different cultural groups such as Rilke, born into a Catholic family, and Kafka, a member of the German-Jewish community. German speakers in Prague valued their philological and literary heritage, and writers nurtured its expressive range and strength. Adler identified with this tradition and hoped to build his academic career on the strength of it, developing a profoundly learned approach to poetic language and form, extending his lexical range through the study of etymology, and refining his technique by working with the great poets of the German language. In the course of his writing life he continued to explore the German language in its most elevated manifestations and sophisticated written forms. However, it was equally typical of his love of the living language that during his later life in exile, he actively sought to keep in touch with the Austro-Bavarian dialect spoken in the region he grew up in.[6] Especially during the early years of his internment, he also looked to the heritage of Expressionism with its evocative imagery and adventurous deployment of neologisms, sound repetition and form, in order to find a medium for conveying the experience of life in extremis. Instead of turning against the linguistic medium of the barbarous Nazis, Adler drew strength from his confidence in a language that had withstood the vicissitudes of territorial fragmentation, cultural division, and political strife on the scale of the Thirty Years War. Moreover, he could look to a tradition of language critique that had gained prominence in Vienna with Karl Kraus in the early decades of the century. Rather than turning his back on German, Adler dug deep into its structural resources and cultural heritage.

In defining his relationship with the German language and his motives for visiting German-speaking countries after the War, Adler elaborates on his relationship with German as follows, focusing on his emotional connection and response to it:

> Diese häufige Konfrontation mit der Sprache, mit der ich zutiefst verbunden und für die ich auch besonders empfindlich bin (fast hätte ich "allergisch" statt "empfindlich" gesagt), so daß ich mich in der Annäherung ans Deutsche und der Aneignung ihrer jüngsten Neuerungen zugleich auch davon distanzieren kann: das ist mir überaus wichtig.[7]

> [This frequent confrontation with the language, with which I am deeply involved and towards which I am also particularly sensitive (I almost said "allergic" rather than "sensitive"), so that in approaching German and assimilating its most recent developments I can simultaneously also distance myself from it: that is enormously important to me.]

What Adler describes here is a process of research with controlled engagement that has features of anthropological participant observation. It differs fundamentally from the immersion in German culture and politics practised by his younger colleague Erich Fried, a German-Jewish poet who grew up in Vienna, emigrated to London in 1938, and became a highly visible political poet, writer of love poetry and translator of Shakespeare and other English literature from the 1960s onwards.[8] Adler by contrast kept his distance, devoting much of his energy to researching and analyzing the systems and processes that underpinned and defined the mass extermination of the Jewish people. His poetry is less directly political and at no point becomes keyed into the political debates of the student movement like Fried's. He similarly writes love poetry, but it is less 'transferable' than Fried's: for example, poems written in Theresienstadt to his first wife Gertrud and compiled in the cycle 'Zuversicht' [Confidence][9] gain their communicative significance from the interplay between the specific situation of joint yet separating internment, and the spiritual closeness with the beloved addressee. The oppositional force derives entirely implicitly from the tension between the actual conditions of the two prisoners and a light-heartedly conventional style reminiscent of German 18th-century Anacreontic verse. Love imparts a confidence in values that transcend the violent constraints imposed by the regime. The mission to bear witness runs through Adler's poetry, manifesting itself in complex ways that extend from the situationally specific to the existentially abstract, and at times his verse moves in other directions that assert a spirit of independence from circumstance. Moreover, while his verse draws its energy from dialogic intensity, Adler makes no concessions to immediate impact in his modes of communication and choice of linguistic means.

The reception of Adler's verse was — and remains — limited, and he did not present it at any major public readings; readings even to large groups of friends or colleagues were rare, though he set great store by reading his poetry aloud in smaller circles. Approximately two thirds of the 1200 or so poems he deemed worthy of publication remained unpublished during his lifetime, and volumes that were published appeared with small publishers. We may speculate about the reasons for the low level of response, and the answers will coincide to a considerable extent with the explanations for the slow reception of his narrative works. We may also look to the 'modernist' quality of his poetry — not least its resistance to easy interpretation. This increases during the years in the camps, and Adler indeed comments on his aim to use technical complexity and timeless values as means of distancing his verse from the tribulations of their immediate context. He elaborates on this aim in an essay written for a PEN conference in 1980 on exile literature; the essay is entitled 'Dichtung in der Gefangenschaft als inneres Exil' [Literature during Captivity as Inner Exile].[10] He there explains that following the initial traumatic 'Einlieferungsschock' [internment shock] experienced on his arrival in Theresienstadt, he had resolved to respond to what he was experiencing in two ways, and two modes: 'Zeugnis ablegen' [to bear witness] would be the purpose of his scholarly work while his literary writing would be devoted to transforming them into works of literature, '[sie] künstlerisch [zu] gestalten' [giving them artistic form].[11] He goes on to highlight the formal techniques he used, such as complex rhyme schemes and stanza forms, and he then offers a rationale that guided his writing:

> Technisch Kompliziertes und formal Konservatives wählte ich bewußt, um mich so weit, als es erlaubt schien, von der widrigen Gegenwart zu distanzieren und durch Hingabe an zeitlose Werte meine Menschenwürde zu behaupten.[12]

> [I consciously chose technical complexity and conservative forms in order to distance myself as far as seemed permissible from the adversity of the present and assert my human dignity by devoting myself to timeless values.]

This indicates a profound tension in his verse. On the one hand the poetry responds to experienced reality. On the other hand, it counters that reality with a force of art conceived as independent of the constraints imposed by immediate reality, and independent of a rhetorical purpose. The implications of this tension may be traced in the quality of 'voice' that marks out his verse and embeds a dialogic dimension within the poem. Jeremy Adler reports that his father would regularly read his verse to himself during its composition, and would then, when a poem was finished, read it to his family and friends in order to test its aural form. Oral performance and aural reception, then, are part of the process of composition and built into the poem from its conception.

Adler developed his poetic writing from an early age, and the nine volumes of verse which he compiled and edited over the course of his life contain two volumes of poems written before his deportation, with the earliest poems having been written in 1927. He carried on writing poetry during his time in Theresienstadt, and indeed highlights that writing poetry was a popular communal activity among the prisoners:

> Tausende von Insassen in Theresienstadt schrieben Gedichte. Ihre Verfassungen gehörten zu allen Schichten der Gefangenen, Greise und Kinder dichteten. Das Verseschmieden war fast so stark wie ein beliebtes Gesellschaftsspiel.[13]

> [Thousands of inmates in Theresienstadt wrote poems. Their composition was in evidence among all the social strata of prisoners. Old men and children wrote poetry. The craft of writing verse was almost as well developed as a parlour game.]

This experience of writing, and observing others write, in the face of the Holocaust is reflected in Adler's response to Adorno's famous dictum of 1951 according to which writing poetry was now impossible because it had become a barbaric pursuit, 'nach Auschwitz ein Gedicht zu schreiben ist barbarisch' [it is barbaric to write a poem after Auschwitz].[14] In an essay on his poetics entitled 'Zur Bestimmung der Lyrik' [On the Definition of Lyric Poetry], Adler gives short shrift to Adorno's grandiose claim:

> in den letzten Jahren [wurde] öfters nach der Möglichkeit des Gedichtes [...] gefragt [...]. Der Soziologe Adorno sprach nach Auschwitz dem Gedicht sogar die Berechtigung ab. Nun, die Möglichkeit einer Kunst läßt sich theoretisch nicht dekretieren. Solche Fragen mögen nahe liegen, doch werden sie weder von Überzeugungen noch von Wünschen entschieden. Antwort erteilt die Wirklichkeit. [... Es] gibt [...] deutsch und in anderen Sprachen gute neue Gedichte. Damit ist die Frage nach der Möglichkeit der Lyrik in der Gegenwart positiv beantwortet.[15]

> [In recent years the possibility of poetry has often been called into question. The sociologist Adorno indeed denied poetry legitimacy after Auschwitz. Well, the possibility of an art form cannot be decreed theoretically. Such questions may seem obvious but they are decided neither by convictions nor by wishes. The answer is provided by reality. There are good new poems in German and in other languages. That means the question about the possibility of poetry in the present time has been answered in the affirmative.]

Reality, 'die Wirklichkeit', acts as a benchmark for what is possible in poetry and, as Adler's essay on 'Dichtung in der Gefangenschaft als inneres Exil' makes clear, the idealist poetics he develops in the essay 'Zur Bestimmung der Lyrik' is predicated on the pressure of real experience.

The aural aspect of his verse that Adler tests when reading it aloud to family and friends points to a dialogic quality that depends on voice. This voice constitutes the nexus between the poem as art, informed by the idealist precepts that Adler increasingly espoused in the face of political pressures, and the poem as an embodied response to reality. While Adler rejects a rhetorical poetics that would give the poem the significance of a message, he invests it with the rhetorical force of 'the moral character of the speaker', which Aristotle highlights in his *Rhetoric* as one of the three 'proofs furnished by the speech', alongside 'putting the hearer into a certain frame of mind' and the proof furnished by 'the speech itself, in so far as it proves or seems to prove'.[16] The moral character manifested in the poet's voice engages the reader, and provides an ongoing stimulus to pursue the pathways of interpretation it opens up, albeit often only in glimpses of meanings and arguments, images and visions. The energy of the voice expresses itself through alliteration and assonance, emphatic inversions and subtly modulated speech acts. It gains resonance from intertextual connections, and historic depth from a linguistic texture that carries its history within its etymology, and its future in the infinite morphological possibilities of the German language. The fabric of the language sets up correspondences of meaning that encourage exploration while resisting resolution. The voice engages the reader or audience in the poet's reflections or visions, and in some poems it overtly draws persuasive strength from an authorial presence that has personally witnessed what is depicted or hinted at. The reader here becomes aware of a moral compass that has gained its dependability from the real world.

Adler occasionally sketches the situation of the speaker with autobiographical details that establish the voice as living in the circumstances of the author. In 1952, five years after his arrival in London, he wrote a series of poems to which he gave the title 'Londoner Elegien' [London Elegies],[17] recalling Rilke's title *Duineser Elegien* for a cycle begun in Castle Duino. In both works, the actual place roots the poems in reality while also acting as a foil for themes that take the reader far beyond that place. Adler's group of 32 poems is more loosely composed than Rilke's cycle, and an allusion to the 'Auftrag' that is at the heart of Rilke's project in one of Adler's poems indicates that the poet's 'mission' here is more questioning and inconclusive: 'Wie aber soll da ein Auftrag ...?' [But how should a mission ...?].[18] A wide range of themes are explored with occasional concrete elements that suggest a landscape and life context far away from the British city: the cable-car that gives the poem 'Berg- und Talbahn' its title,[19] the carnival scenes in 'Aschermittwoch' [Ash Wednesday],[20] or the German nursery rhyme remembered from a childhood in a different country.[21]

The poem 'Bitte und Dank' [Request and Thanks][22] by contrast takes the reader into the immediate world of the poet and author, sketching a domestic scene in the second stanza that makes autobiographical reference to his wife and child, though as part of a scenario of gathering mourners who remain mythically indeterminate:

> Die Gäste versammeln sich, Trauerbotschaften
> Schaben die rußige Träne vom Antlitz, während
> Dein Kind in die Stube stört, ein liebes,
> Da es nicht ahnt, nur eifert hinter der Mutter.[23]

> [The guests assemble, messages of mourning
> Scrape the sooty tears from the face while
> Your child brings disturbance into the room, a dear child,
> For it has no inkling, busily following its mother.]

The theme of mourning and the elegiac tone befit the title of the 'London Elegies', as does the reflective presence of the poet and the tension between perspectives. The cheerful energy of the busy child throws the deeper knowledge of the adults into sharp relief, with the child's innocence sharpening the poignancy of lament rather than affording a glimpse of hope.

The insight into the poet's domestic life in this second stanza of the poem follows a first stanza in which the tone is more bitter and shot through with hints of satire, conveying the poet's lived experience through changing speech acts and a tension that arises from the conflict between word and thought, utterance and silence. The poet here evokes his own predicament in a strange city as he seeks elusive help from insensitive authorities. We may surmise that Adler is giving an insight into his early years in London with the daily experience of hardship and demoralising dependency following escape from a murderous regime:

> Nimm es auf, fahre die Bitte an. Dank wird schon
> Hilfe im Atem, weiser Spruch vor Behörden
> Herzlich geboten. Ach schweigen, schweigen.
> Immer schweigen müssen und sich verkriechen
> In kalte Begeisterung, kahl vor den Herren
> Im Glanz ihrer Herrscherstuben. So unbehaust
> Ist die Bitte des Volkes, fehlerhaft die Bitte
> Des Verdammten. 'Stirb!' — Und wieder schweigen
> Und wieder seinen Mörder besprechen mit Lob.
> Und wieder warten Tag um Tag, dann in fremder
> Stadt die Schritte zählen auf eisigem Grund
> Und verfremdet grübeln über lichtlose Taten.[24]

> [Take it up, approach the request. Thanks turn into
> Help in the breath, wise talk before authorities
> Warmly offered. Oh being silent, silent.
> Constantly having to be silent and retreat
> Into cold enthusiasm, bare before the gentlemen
> In the splendour of their power rooms. So homeless
> Is the plea of the people, flawed the plea
> Of the condemned one. 'Die!' — And again being silent
> And again talking about your murderer with praise.
> And again waiting day in day out, then counting
> The steps in the alien city on icy ground
> And ruminating estranged on lightless deeds.]

The vocal strength of the introductory exhortations is subtly undermined by linguistic elements that preclude easy assimilation. The introductory command 'Nimm es auf' is evidently addressed to the poet himself, suggesting a commencing project that is initially left indeterminate by the unspecific pronoun but then gradually gains shape with the noun 'Bitte' and the mention of authorities to whom the poet will address his petition. The verb 'anfahren' [to drive off, start a vehicle, or approach something in a vehicle] then introduces further nuances that slow down comprehension since the syntactic context brings different meanings into play:[25] the statement cannot be understood straightforwardly owing to the collocation with an abstract noun rather than a concrete vehicle. Once possible meanings are explored, it begins to make most sense as a neologism formed by analogy with 'angehen' [tackle]; we may then — in what is possibly an excessively literal reading — incorporate the association of traversing the city by public transport. We can here see Adler exploiting the spectrum of conventional meanings while taking the reader further into new semantic territory. While the poet is addressing himself, the reader becomes involved in a process of interpretation that replicates the difficulty of embarking on the daily grind of begging for assistance from people who speak an unfamiliar language and fail to empathise with the needs of the refugee. The significance of the autobiographical scenario is introduced in part through morphological processes: by making exceptional linguistic demands on the reader, Adler generates a spirit of exceptional thoughtfulness and imaginative engagement at the very beginning of the reading process. A further communicative nuance is then introduced through morphological irony in the word 'Herzlich', which ostensibly involves authentic expression 'from the heart' but actually highlights the hypocrisy to which the poet has to subject himself. This is then developed in the oxymoron 'kalte Begeisterung' [cold enthusiasm]. The vocal repetition of 'schweigen' [to be silent] runs counter to the meaning of the verb, making the reader aware of moving inside the poet's thoughts, trapped as they are in existentially necessary dissimulation if the poet is to survive in the public world of alien speech.

It is typical of Adler's poetry that even where we find autobiographical detail, this generates connections that take the reader far beyond the biographical. In this poem, the experience of the impoverished exile in the alien city opens out into a symbolic juxtaposition of splendid buildings housing society's rulers and the plight of their subjects, with 'homelessness' standing for the absence of human security and dignity. Experience of life in the foreign city engenders alienated rumination on the dark deeds that destroyed a world that has been left behind. At the heart of the stanza is the stark command 'Stirb!' [Die!], in which the poet's voice takes on an alien role: that of the perpetrators who drove him into exile. The transition between the rulers to whom the poet addresses his petition and the rulers that condemned him and his people to die is made only implicitly: we can infer it if we draw on biographical knowledge from beyond the poem. The reader here becomes privy to the trauma of exile, which makes homelessness into an existential condition that suffuses the psyche. The domestic scene in the following stanza briefly counteracts that alienation, but the pleasure in the young child is obliterated by the mourning symbolized in the association with London soot ['rußige Träne' — sooty tears]. The actuality of the Great Smog of 1952 here fuses with the tears of the exiles as they lament the unfathomable loss of their people.

The arc of reciprocal speech acts evoked in the title 'Bitte und Dank' is completed in the third and final stanza of the poem. Here the word 'Dank' [thanks] comes to the fore as a running motif which reciprocates that of request and petition. But the gratitude is embedded in despair as it lacks the basis of something having been granted: the final words of the poem are 'Dank, Dank, verweigerter Bitte Dank' [Thanks, thanks, thanks of/for the refused request]. The concepts of request and thanks are thus reciprocal only in words, and a dislocated relationship between them is encapsulated in the possessive genitive that connects them illogically. The power of the poetic voice, traditionally celebrated both in the ode and the elegy as a medium capable of bringing inanimate things, and the dead, before the mind's eye as living beings, here remains unable to articulate more than the ineffectiveness of communication.

In 'Bitte und Dank', the poet's voice is embodied in the figure at the centre of the poem reflecting on his predicament. As he paces the 'icy ground' of the city, the human tragedy that forms part of his life comes to the fore in glimpses as part of memories and lived experience. The incorporation of another voice in the word 'Stirb!' is here an isolated utterance, starkly effective as a command that is both disembodied and absolute. In a poem written much later, in 1979, Adler again includes the voice of a perpetrator in the poem, and it indeed provides the title: 'Vielleicht daß ich vorbeigegangen bin' [Perhaps it's that I walked past].[26] Here, the incorporated voice forms part of a dialogue scenario in which an interlocutor opens the conversation with initial questions that prompt an answer consisting of several utterances. In between the perpetrator's statements, the poet provides comments that are framed in similes and metaphors, probing significance from a perspective of ethically grounded reflection:

VIELLEICHT DASS ICH VORBEIGEGANGEN BIN

'Hast du Schuld? Fühlst du Schuld?' Die Frage
Lichtet den Vorhang. Die Antwort stockt. 'Ich
Möchte daran nicht erinnert werden, an die
Sache.' Und wie das Meer der Stimme blutschwarz

In die Stille bricht, weckt es sich hart. Da
Fügt es ungefragt hinzu: 'Ich hab abgeschaltet.
Eine Zeit hab ich so nachgedacht, wissen Sie.'
Verhallt und grimm wie Salz. Vergeßlich auch,

Denn vergeßlich ist der Tod am nächsten Tag.
'Ja, das kann ich wohl sagen. Das geht auf
Die Nerven.' Naßkälte schwemmt ein Sündenmeer
Heran. 'Na, hab ich gesagt, Mensch, die ganzen

Opfer. Was war, das brauchte nicht sein, sagen
Wir mal.' Und Schuld, Vorhalt und Schuld, gelitten
Versunken. Wir wissen nicht, wie sie versinkt
In Nacht und nicht vergeht und immer tiefer.

'Magenbeschwerden, die ich hab. Ja, auch dieses
Augenzwinkern, das ist darauf zurückzuführen.'
Zuletzt fremd: 'Das hab ich persönlich nicht
Gemacht. Vielleicht daß ich vorbeigegangen bin.'

[PERHAPS IT'S THAT I WALKED PAST

'Do you have guilt? Do you feel guilt?' The question
Raises the curtain. The answer falters. 'I
don't want to be reminded of it, of that
Issue.' And as the sea of the voice breaks into the silence,

blood black, it awakens itself hard. Then
It adds without being asked: 'I switched off.
For a while I kept on thinking, you know.'
Died away and grim as salt. Forgetful too,

For death is forgetful the very next day.
'Yes, I can certainly say that. It gets on
Your nerves.' Damp coldness washes up a sea of sin.
'Well, I said, goodness, all those

Victims. All of the stuff that happened, it really wasn't
Necessary, let's say.' And guilt, accusation and guilt, suffered,
Sunk. We do not know how it sinks
Into night and does not pass and deeper and deeper.

'Stomach trouble, I've got that. Yes, and this
Twitching eye, that's caused by it.'
Finally distant: 'I didn't personally
Do it. Perhaps it's that I walked past.']

The title of the poem 'Perhaps it's that I walked past' brings historical events into focus through the eyes of one who is being required to address the question of personal guilt, in a dialogue or perhaps interrogation. Adler here gives us utterances first-hand of the kind that are familiar from Peter Weiss's play *Die Ermittlung* [The Investigation] of 1965, which works with transcripts from the Frankfurt Auschwitz Trials of 1963–1965, or Claude Lanzmann's film *Shoah* (1985), which presents interviews with victims, witnesses and perpetrators.

The colloquial phrasing of the title sets the tone for a poem in which the choice of words and juxtaposition of registers convey different perspectives on guilt. The formal simplicity of the introductory questions with their weighty differentiation between the verbs 'haben' [have] and 'fühlen' [feel] define the terms of what is at issue: objective presence of guilt, and subjective acknowledgement of personal guilt. The questions do not specify the crime, but the answer makes clear that both dialogue partners and the poet share an understanding of the crime that is at the centre of the poem. It is thereby given a formal status that derives its communicative import from a firm basis in historical facts, a context of shared knowledge in which the reader also participates. This creates a solid foundation for interpreting communicative nuances: the reader's attention focuses not on the nature and details of the crime but on the responses of a perpetrator whose involvement is established by the poet's comment on the initial question and answer: 'Die Frage | Lichtet den Vorhang. Die Antwort stockt' [The question | Raises the curtain. The answer falters]. The metaphor of the curtain evokes the uncovering of a previously hidden scene, suggesting a process of actual revelation in which the perpetrator's inner eye participates while their conscious will blocks the process and inhibits the act of articulation. By means of an overtly poetic metaphor, the poet thereby establishes his voice as a benchmark for truth while the quoted utterances emanate from an unwillingness to access and acknowledge past actions. Rather than opening up the truth, they serve to obliterate it, using language as a means of abrogating individual responsibility in favour of collective convention that separates guilt from individual responsibility.

The perpetrator's reference to 'die Sache' [that issue] in the first stanza is so general as to convey a fundamental tendency towards evasion, which is matched by the declared unwillingness to remember. In this context, the speaker's conventionally informal mode of expression takes on special significance, for it indicates a lazy reliance on prefabricated language that precludes thoughtful, individual engagement with past actions. The effect of habitual and deliberate thoughtlessness derives from a cumulation of linguistic features typical of colloquial speech: the dropped ending in the auxiliary 'hab' (lines 7, 12, 17, 19), colloquial metaphors and idioms ('abschalten', l. 6; 'Das geht auf | Die Nerven', ll. 10–11), semantically empty conversational interjections ('wissen Sie', l. 7; 'Ja, das kann ich wohl sagen', l. 10; 'Na, habe ich gesagt, Mensch', l. 12; 'sagen | Wir mal', ll. 13–14), repetitious recapitulation for emphasis ('daran ... an die Sache', l. 3; 'dieses | Augenzwinkern, das', l. 17–18; 'ich persönlich', l. 19), colloquial syntax ('das brauchte nicht sein' instead of '...zu sein', l. 13). The speaker's banal language corresponds to their trivialising collective reference to 'die ganzen | Opfer' [ll. 12–13, all those victims] and the deliberately uncomprehending framing of the crimes as an unnecessary event (ll. 13–14). The bitter satire underlying the stereotypical linguistic routines gains additional resonance from the careful analysis of cause and effect which the perpetrator devotes to trivial personal afflictions (ll. 17–18).

By contrast with the superficiality of the perpetrator's utterances, marked out by quotation marks, the poet's interspersed comments are articulated beyond the dialogue scenario in an indeterminate space where reflection and language are at one with each other. The poet's words evoke highly individual, expressively original images, each opening up moral implications that the perpetrator seeks to close off and obliterate. The poet nowhere refers to the speaker with a personal pronoun: following the speaker's first utterance, their voice is metaphorically identified with 'das Meer' [the sea], and in the following two lines this noun becomes the reference point for the neuter pronoun 'es'. The guilt which the perpetrator seeks to hide comes to the fore in the complex metaphor of the voice as a 'blood black sea breaking into the silence', with a neologistic colour oxymoron fusing 'black' guilt with the 'blood' on the hands of the guilty. The metaphorical sea returns in the third stanza, now as an infinite 'sea of sin' associated with the simple, physical images of wetness and coldness, quite different from the meaninglessly abstract verbiage of the speaker. The perpetrator's trivializing reference to 'die ganzen | Opfer' [all those victims] is countered with weighty repetition of the word 'Schuld' [guilt] and the past participle 'gelitten', giving voice to the suffering that was ignored by the speaker.

The poet's careful choice of expressive words is evident in his use of the archaic forms 'grimm' [l. 8, grim], instead of the more usual 'grimmig', and 'der Vorhalt' [l. 14, reproach], equivalent to 'die Vorhaltung'. Adler is here working with a morphological technique commended by one of his poetic masters, F. G. Klopstock, who advocates it in order to create a poetic language that is distinct from the language of everyday prose.[27] While Klopstock is concerned above all to fashion a high style in the classical tradition that is suited to conveying metaphysical themes, the technique here serves to forge a linguistic medium that will draw strength from individual ethically grounded reflection. The poet concludes his own comments with images of sinking, depth and night, anchoring the guilt for past crimes in the human psyche, beyond the reach of knowledge. The final words are given to the perpetrator, who concludes his meandering answer with a rejection of personal guilt, followed by a tentative concession that he might have walked past — while leaving indefinite what it was that the speaker failed to acknowledge. The concession is further weakened by the introductory particle 'vielleicht' [perhaps]. As with earlier utterances, the phrasing is colloquial, and the statement hinting at potential guilt is left both indeterminate and syntactically incomplete, in stark contrast with the complete sentence rejecting personal responsibility.

The different voices in the poem provide complementary perspectives on the question of guilt, encompassing the factual introductory question, the evasive abrogation of personal responsibility that characterizes the retrospective attitude of the vast majority of perpetrators, and the poet's engagement of the moral imagination as he opens up the unfathomable implications of crimes that continue to be suppressed rather than acknowledged. Each of the three voices has a distinctive identity and a distinctive register. The features characteristic of oral speech that characterise the voice of the perpetrator serve to convey deliberate and chronic superficiality as the clichéd responses fail to connect with individual thought, personal memory or moral sensibility. By contrast, the poet's supple, colourful language with its creative use of morphology and rich metaphors is able to mediate between emotions, thought and language, relying on the imagination rather than articulated physical sound for its communicative resonance. The contrast between the different voices in the poem is here central to its meaning.

Adler's poems are mostly univocal, suggesting linguistically active reflection in a process that is shared freely with the reader or listener without explicitly involving them. The poem 'Heimat und Wandel' [Home and Transformation], written shortly after 'Vielleicht daß ich vorbeigegangen bin' in 1980, has none of that poem's rhetorical complexity. A simpler, homogeneous voice mediates between inner thought and external speech, communicating with the reader through statements and questions while evoking a poetic persona in a state of isolation:

HEIMAT UND WANDEL

Leicht führen alle Wege,
Doch wohin? Aus der Heimat?
In die Heimat? Welche Ziele
Und wie weit sind buntbleich
Sie über die Erde gestreut?
Die Schilder der Gasthäuser laden
Nicht ein ins Gemach zu Speise
Und Umtrunk. Wohin also, wohin
Sich wenden und wo das dürftig
Verhandelte Gepäck dürr gegen

Den Baum am Rande der Straße
Aufrichten, dann schlafen
Und diesen und alle Wege vergessen?
Wege führen nicht hin,
Sie führen nicht her.
Einsam behütet tasten die Füße
Stein und Staub in zeitlosem Wandel.[28]

[HOME AND TRANSFORMATION

Easily all paths lead,
But where to? Away from home?
Towards home? Which destinations
And how far are they strewn across
The earth, colourfully pale?
The inn signs do not invite you
Into the room for food and companionable
Drink. So where to go, where
To turn and where to prop up, sparsely,
The suitcase meagrely negotiated
Against the tree at the edge
Of the street, then sleep
And forget this and all paths?
Paths do not lead there,
They do not lead here.
Lonely and protected the feet feel their way
Stone and dust in timeless transformation.]

The central image of pathways opens up a space in which the speaker projects himself as exiled not only from a place of origin but from both origins and destinations. The images sketch a rudimentary inhabited landscape with a road, stones and dust, a tree, inns with signs that fail to communicate hospitality, and interiors that may provide food, drink and conviviality but are evoked only by negation. The embodiment of the speaker is conveyed directly only in the concluding image of feet, but beyond that through the activities of walking, sleeping and propping up an item of luggage. The imagery recalls the figure at the centre of the cycle *Eroberungen* [Conquests] by Adler's friend Franz Baermann Steiner: the first poem in the cycle is entitled 'Der schritt schwingt hin' [the step swings away] and this lonely figure, too, must walk without the direction and closure afforded by a destination.[29] There is no other sentient being in Adler's poem — the word 'einsam' in the penultimate line encapsulates an existence in which the individual is reliant entirely upon his own resources. The final word 'Wandel' ambiguously fuses the individual activity of walking ['wandeln'] with a universal condition of change ['Wandel' or, as a verb, 'sich wandeln']. The individual's life unfolds in a space of pathways without direction as he inhabits an existence that is 'zeitlos' [timeless]. While the first part of the poem conveys restless questioning, the final statement accepts a life without teleological purpose.

   The poet's voice plays a vital role in giving coherence and meaning to the sparse physical images, communicating an intensely reflective sensibility at the heart of the poem. It gains resonance in questions that extend through most of the poem and establish the theme of pathways, origins, and destinations. The three introductory questions are syntactically fragmentary, but integrated in a series which suggests a sustained process of searching that involves both mind and emotions, embodied in the physical activity of travel that enacts the condition of exile. The questions focused on the interrogative adverb 'wohin', twice repeated at the beginning of the long question in line 8, echo the 'wo' questions in the second stanza of Hölderlin's poem 'Hälfte des Lebens': 'Weh mir, wo nehm' ich, wenn | Es Winter ist, die Blumen, und wo | Den Sonnenschein, | Und Schatten der Erde?' [But oh, where shall I find | When winter comes, the flowers, and where | The sunshine | And shade of the earth?].[30] In both poems, the question word opens up a space that cannot be found. Hölderlin's poem projects this into the future of old age, by contrast with the statements in the first stanza of his poem, which evokes a fulfilled youth. Adler's poem by contrast offers no sense of temporal progression. The questions in his poem culminate in a statement that highlights not just the loneliness of the speaker's condition, but also the absence of direction as the feet lose momentum in a movement that is tentative ['tasten'] rather than purposeful.

The voice that sustains the poem draws subtly individual expressiveness from the lexical choices and use of syntax. The words are mostly simple and concrete: paths, inn signs, luggage, tree, feet, stone and dust. Where they hint at social life, Adler chooses words that are somewhat elevated, with a hint of the archaic that here imparts a sense of timeless human life: 'Gemach' rather than 'Raum' for the interior of an inn, 'Speise' rather than 'Essen' for food, and 'Umtrunk' conveying both drink and companionship. The morphology reveals occasional modifications of established patterns, notably in the phonetic interaction between 'dürftig' [meagrely] and 'dürr' [dryly]: they are morphologically unrelated but the sound correspondence points up a semantic similarity that allows both adverbs also to function as adjectives with an implied connection with both luggage and tree. The only striking neologism is the metaphor 'buntbleich', which confounds rational definition in a colour oxymoron fusing colourfulness ['bunt'] with paleness ['bleich']. Simultaneously affirming and negating vividness, it engages the imagination in envisioning goals that are indeterminate, and conceptualizing destinations that are randomly scattered across the earth. The alliterative neologism prompts the reader to dwell on the paradox of the human condition that palpably shapes the experience of the individual in exile.

The syntax is likewise simple, without striking inversions or subordination of multiple clauses. Throughout the poem, however, Adler creates idiosyncratic semantic and syntactic connections and eliminates expected objects, inviting the reader to explore unusual mental pathways. The theme of paths lacking a goal is established in the first line when the verb 'führen' [to lead] is initially given no direction complement to complete the first clause (the reader expects the verb to be followed by a prepositional phrase indicating the destination). Adler is here using a technique that Klopstock had introduced to enhance the expressiveness of poetic language: the unusual deployment of a verb enhances the reader's awareness of its dynamic strength. The emphatic positioning of the adverb 'leicht' at the start of the sentence thereby takes on an unexpected ambiguity: welcome effortlessness in negotiating a path becomes unsettling disorientation when the path is divested of a goal. The proposed directions from and towards home are framed as free-standing elliptic questions and negated by the preceding question 'Doch wohin?' [But where to?]. The question runs through the first half of the poem, and it is picked up in the question 'wo' in line 9, which undermines the anchoring certainty afforded to the tree by its definite article. Adler's technique of modifying the conventional syntactic connections of the verb returns in the final sentence, in the transitive use of the verb 'tasten' [feel (with the hands), grope (one's way)]. The images of stone and dust evoke a road and accord with the image of the feet, but the activity of walking is conveyed by a verb that is normally used either for an activity of the hands, or used reflexively and with a prepositional construction if it refers to an activity of the feet (e.g. 'sich an etwas entlangtasten'). The associations evoked by the unconventional use of the verb give the movement of the feet a holistic quality that involves the whole body as they tread the earth. The earth (line 5) and the road (line 11) are fused in the archetypal images of stone and dust on which the exile must travel without direction, and without meaningful past or future.

One word only in the poem hints at confidence in a dimension beyond the poet's lonely and exposed existence. No security is afforded by buildings or human company, but the participle 'behütet' intimates that the wanderer carries spiritual protection with him. The verb is central to the Priestly Blessing given to Moses for his brother Aaron and the children of Israel, 'Der Herr segne dich und behüte dich [...]' [The Lord bless thee, and keep thee], and it affords protection for the exile when Jacob is given the following promise: 'Und der Herr [...] sprach [...] Und siehe, ich bin mit dir und will dich behüten, wo du hin ziehst' [And [...] the Lord [...] said, [...] And, behold, I am with thee, and will keep thee in all places whither thou goest'].[31] The participle 'behütet' is unequivocal in giving the concluding words 'zeitloser Wandel' [timeless change] positive value. It is the word used in Luther's translation of the Old Testament — a word that might be seen as a living link between the Jewish and German people notwithstanding the cultural catastrophe that severs them. Adler's willingness to work freely with German in all its facets is testimony to the confidence he places in language to overcome cultural limitations. It is a medium that is owned as much by the individual as by the cultural group.

The concluding focus on timelessness recalls Adler's essay 'Dichtung in der Gefangenschaft als inneres Exil' where he projects a commitment to timeless values as an assertion of human dignity in the face of barbarous violence. In this late poem, the poet is engaging not with imprisonment but with life that has been divested of its cultural roots. While the long heritage of the Jewish people and the political exile of Adler's personal life may be seen as part of the poem's cultural context, the elements of the poem connect the isolated poet with the archetypal human condition. The poet uses the conventions of the German language in ways that dissolve established connections, run counter to expectations and take the reader along unexpected mental pathways. The words are in some cases conservative and the techniques are complex. But this is not the striking conservatism or overtly crafted complexity we find in some of the poetry Adler wrote in Theresienstadt.

The archetypal quality of the images is matched by simple diction and a syntax that is easy to follow. Sound effects and figures of repetition are straightforward, and the poem is relatively short and formally simple as the free verse unfolds.

The sense of live voice in Adler's poems gives them a human depth that invites ongoing engagement and exploration rather than a reading that delivers a stable meaning. The voice provides a way into the poem and a human point of reference that guides the reader to resist the unquestioning platitudes Adler satirizes in 'Vielleicht daß ich vorbeigegangen bin'. It enables the reader to accompany the poet on a journey into a realm in which the individual is on his own, and the dimensions of space and time that govern our lives cease to give it meaning. The imaginative process stimulated by the poet's voice sustains the reader on a journey in which exile gains symbolic depth, drawing moral resonance from real experience while also moving beyond historical space into realms beyond history.

More than any other part of Adler's richly diverse œuvre, his poetry draws its communicative force from the interdependence of the German language, the German poetic heritage, and the moment in German culture and time within central Europe that defined his mission as a scholar and writer. Rather than turning his back on German as a medium contaminated by barbaric speakers of the language, Adler worked with the unique semantic substance embedded within it, with its malleable morphological and syntactic structures, and its richly expressive poetic tradition. Like his scholarly works, his poems bear witness to the crimes perpetrated by the National Socialists against his own person and family, his people and humanity. But just as he refused to let internment silence the playful articulation of love, he would not allow his poetry to be limited to the cultural and political catastrophes that engulfed his people and divested him of his 'Heimat' and his people. Adler never left the themes behind that drove him into exile, but he probes them in ways that go beyond the historical event and often extend to existential questions that transcend history. The spaces of meaning Adler opens up by unconventional use of language and cryptic comment will often preclude straightforward understanding. But the poetic voice consistently engages the reader, prompting exploration and interpretation with its energy and ever-changing communicative force, its precision of expression and imaginative reach. In this way it counteracts the destructive impulses Adler witnessed so directly, embodying an indomitable spirit of humanity.

Notes to Chapter 7

1. Adler included this cycle of ten poems in the edition of collected poems which he compiled in the course of his lifetime: 'České vzpomínky / Tschechische Erinnerungen', with German translations by Eva Adler. See H. G. Adler, *Andere Wege: Gesammelte Gedichte*, ed. by Katrin Kohl and Franz Hocheneder, with Jeremy Adler. Afterword by Michael Krüger. Edition Milo 25 (Klagenfurt: Drava, 2010), pp. 946–53. This edition is hereafter abbreviated AW.

2. '"Da gäbe es noch viel mehr zu berichten ...". Interview mit H. G. Adler von Friedrich Danielis [1981]', *Zwischenwelt* 25, No. 3/4 (Dec. 2008), 19–27 (p. 20).

3. H. G. Adler, 'Zu Hause im Exil', in *H. G. Adler — Der Wahrheit verpflichtet: Interviews, Gedichte, Essays*, ed. by Jeremy Adler (Gerlingen: Bleicher, 1998), pp. 19–31 (p. 26).

4. Adler, 'Zu Hause im Exil', pp. 25–26.

5. H. G. Adler, *Die Dichtung der Prager Schule*, mit einem Vorwort von Jeremy Adler (Wuppertal: Arco, 2010). First published in 1976.

6. See Adler, 'Zu Hause im Exil', p. 25. For examples of dialect elements in his poetry see 'Es regnet am Schnürl' [It's pouring] in 'Regen am Abend' (AW, 732) and 'Sei nun stad!' [Be quiet now!] in 'Ins Ferne' (AW, p. 777). Neither is a poem in dialect: in both cases, the phrase appears in a context of standard German and without quotation marks. Rather than creating a naturalistic effect, the incorporation of dialect sensitizes the reader to the complexity of language as it stretches across registers and transcends local limitations without losing touch with its cultural lifeblood.

7. Adler, 'Zu Hause im Exil', p. 25.

8. Fried established a forum for emigré poets in London after the war. Adler and his friend Franz Baermann Steiner were part of this circle, with Adler being the only member to have experienced life in the death camps. See Jeremy Adler, 'Erich Fried, F. B. Steiner and an unknown group of exile poets in London', *Zwischenwelt 4: Literatur und Kultur des Exils in Großbritannien* (1995), 163–84.

9. AW, pp. 197–205; see also pp. 1090–91.

10. Adler, 'Dichtung in der Gefangenschaft als inneres Exil', in *Literatur des Exils: Eine Dokumentation über die PEN-Jahrestagung in Bremen vom 18–20. September 1980*, ed. by Bernt Engelmann (Munich: Goldmann, 1981), pp. 18–28.

11. Adler, 'Dichtung in der Gefangenschaft', p. 26.

12. Adler, 'Dichtung in der Gefangenschaft', pp. 26–27.

13. Adler, 'Dichtung aus Theresienstadt', in *Fruchtblätter: Freundesgabe für Alfred Kelletat*, ed. by Harald Hartung, Walter Heistermann and Peter M. Stephan (Berlin: Pädagogische Akademie Berlin, 1977), pp. 137–42 (p. 138).

14. Theodor W. Adorno, 'Kulturkritik und Gesellschaft', in Adorno, *Gesammelte Schriften*, ed. by Rolf Tiedemann (Frankfurt a/M: Suhrkamp, 1970ff.), vol. 10.1, pp. 11–30 (p. 30).

15. Adler, 'Zur Bestimmung der Lyrik' (version: 'Fassung für den Vortrag in der Münchner Akademie am 20.10.58', dated 16–18.9.1958), pp. 1–30, unpublished typescript (Deutsches Literaturarchiv Marbach, A: Adler, A II 22), p. 25.

16. Aristotle, *The 'Art' of Rhetoric*, with an English translation by John Henry Freese (Cambridge, MA: Harvard University Press, 1926), p. 17.

17. AW, pp. 444–85

18. 'Des Heiles schwache Kunst', l. 29, AW, p. 446.

19. AW, pp. 453–54.

20. 'Hoppa hoppa Reiter ...', in 'Stimmen', l. 36, AW, p. 449; 'Aschermittwoch', AW, p. 458.

21. 'Hoppa hoppa Reiter ...', in 'Stimmen', l. 36, AW, p. 449; 'Aschermittwoch', AW, p. 458.

22. AW, pp. 447–48. Adler was assiduous in documenting the dates on which he composed his poems and recorded that this poem was written on 11.2.1952 and revised on 3.2.1970. This poem and the poems below from *Andere Wege* are reproduced by kind permission of Jeremy Adler. The translations are by KK, intended to aid understanding of the original works.

23. 'Bitte und Dank', ll. 21–24, AW, p. 447.

24. 'Bitte und Dank', ll. 13–24, AW, p. 447.

25. The meaning of the verb 'anfahren' is highly nuanced, ranging from intransitive to transitive uses, as is evident from the first four meanings given under the entry for the verb in *Duden*: 1. (von Fahrzeugen) zu fahren beginnen, losfahren; 2. fahrend näher kommen; 3.a. bei einer Fahrt einen bestimmten Ort als Ziel haben; 3.b. fahrend auf etwas zusteuern; sich in seiner Fahrweise auf ein kommendes Hindernis einstellen; 4. unter Überwindung einer entgegengerichteten Kraft fahren <http://www.duden.de/rechtschreibung/anfahren>. Adler exploits this spectrum by creating a context in which none of these meanings apply literally, and the reader has to deploy interpretative thought to make sense of the statement.

26. AW, p. 832. The poem forms part of the cycle 'Nahe Entfernungen' and is dated 4.6.1979.

27. See Friedrich Gottlieb Klopstock, 'Von der Sprache der Poesie', in Klopstock, *Ausgewählte Werke*, ed. Karl August Schleiden, 2 vols, 4th edn (Munich: Hanser 1981), pp. 1016–26 (p. 1017).

See also Karl Ludwig Schneider, *Klopstock und die Erneuerung der deutschen Dichtersprache im 18. Jahrhundert* (Heidelberg: Winter, 1965), pp. 41–56 and passim.

28. AW, p. 847. The poem is dated 2.3.1980 and forms part of the cycle 'Frühes spätes Erwachen'.

29. Franz Baermann Steiner, *Eroberungen. Ein lyrischer Zyklus*, ed. by H. G. Adler (Heidelberg: L. Schneider, 1964), pp. 12–13. Like Adler, Steiner lost his family in the Holocaust, but he already spent the war years in exile in the UK. He did not complete the work, which was published only posthumously by Adler.

30. Friedrich Hölderlin, 'Hälfte des Lebens', in *Sämtliche Werke und Briefe*, ed. by Jochen Schmidt, 3 vols (Frankfurt a/M.: Deutscher Klassiker Verlag, 1992–94), vol. 1, p. 320. Translation in Friedrich Hölderlin, *Poems and Fragments*, ed. and transl. by Michael Hamburger, bilingual ed. (Cambridge: Cambridge University Press, 1980), p. 371. Adler considered the poem to be the epitome of 'das rein lyrische Gedicht' (the purely lyric poem) (Adler, 'Zur Bestimmung der Lyrik', p. 10). He quotes the beginning of the stanza in the poems 'Teile' (AW, p. 881) and 'Verschrittene Worte' (AW, p. 898), both written in 1981.

31. Num. 6, 24 and Gen. 28, 13–15. According to his son Jeremy Adler, H. G. Adler used the Bible in Luther's translation in his work (see AW, pp. 1110–11).

CHAPTER 8

❖

Irony and Black Humour in H. G. Adler's Holocaust Fiction *Eine Reise*

John J. White

Irony and black humour may seem strange features to explore in the works of a writer who preferred the term 'lyrische Ironie' [lyrical irony] for the de-familiarizing strategies he used in *Eine Reise* [*The Journey*], arguably his greatest work of Holocaust fiction. Nevertheless, H. G. Adler's deployment of them has frequently been noted and on occasions seriously debated. In the *Neue Rundschau* of 1963, for instance, Roland Wiegenstein suggested that Adler was 'a born humourist'[1] (albeit one prone to display the occasional grimace), rather than someone who resorted to black humour as a form of satire. In the *Frankfurter Rundschau* of 1999, Judith Klein questioned whether, in the case of *Eine Reise*, the irony deployed was perhaps too ironical, too satirical, or too radical.[2] But commentators rightly stress that Adler's irony should not be dismissed as merely belittling or trivializing. Jeremy Adler's Afterword to the 1999 edition of the work contains a useful account of the specific kind of 'lyrische Ironie' present in *Eine Reise*. According to him, H. G. Adler termed this the style of the book, drawing attention to the lyrical density of the language as well as the omnipresent irony. This is described as an irony which indicts, but does not wound, and which lends lightness to the terrible events that are portrayed without playing down the horror.[3]

As for the use of black humour in Adler's other works of Holocaust fiction, the approach varies from work to work and from chapter to chapter. One needs to distinguish, however, between the macro-irony usually highlighted by scholars and reviewers and the role of various other sub-genres, including gallows humour, expressed cynicism, parody, satire, black humour, sarcasm and destructive irony. All this, I should emphasize, has nothing to do with the sick humour some of us associate with certain recent deliberately shocking films, novels and provocative works of art. Whatever the individual reader's position, a decision has to be made as to whether the irony comes either from one of a work's characters or from an implied narrator or simply results from the individual reader's perspective. What is more, whereas most of us have come to terms with the various modernist connotations of irony, black humour is a more slippery concept, sitting, as it does, somewhere between gallows humour, on the one hand, and verbal demonstrations of cynicism, on the other.

This paper focuses on specific contexts and functions. However, before we turn to *Eine Reise*, it is worth bearing in mind that in 1988 H. G. Adler completed *Hausordnung: Wortlaut und Auslegung* [House Rules and Their Interpretation], a novel based on the familiar paradigm of a list of house-rules, be it of a tenement block, those of a railway company or of a particular group: the world of the Jewish detainees in Theresienstadt, for example. Adler's *Hausordnung* is a subtle work of disingenuously playful irony, verbal deconstruction and frequent passages of black humour. It suggests parallels between the Gestapo's infamous surveillance agenda during the Third Reich and more recent instances of 'inappropriately administered man', to use Adler's concept. In the case of *Hausordnung*, Adler is at his most amusing when deploying a combination of irony and black humour via the narrator's ingenious interpretations of the list of rules and regulations to be obeyed by people living in close proximity with one another, in this particular case neither in a ghetto nor in some modern European police state.

The present paper starts with close readings of three key episodes in *Eine Reise*.[4] The close readings in question focus on (i) examples of the combination of irony and black humour in the narrator's account of the enforced evacuation from Stupart (i.e. Prague); (ii) examples of the essentially black-humoured description of Dr Leopold Lustig's funeral in Ruhenthal (i.e. Theresienstadt); and (iii) a picture of the ecstatic visions of release and open-armed welcome that some of Ruhenthal's key figures, including Ida Schwarz, experience when dreaming about how the Second World War will end — in Stupart and, above all, Ruhenthal. These ironic and largely delusional visions of release and homecoming are worth comparing with some of the themes in H. G. Adler's *Die unsichtbare Wand* [*The Wall*] of 1989. What Thomas Krämer recently referred to as Adler's trilogy of autobiographical novels[5] inevitably excludes the equally important post-factual Shoah work of literature in the unique form of *Hausordnung*. Neither *Die unsichtbare Wand* nor *Hausordnung* is arguably a Holocaust novel in the received sense of the term. Hence, while I have taken examples of irony and black humour from *Eine Reise*, these features have no political equivalents in *Panorama*, *Hausordnung* or *Die unsichtbare Wand*. I will end with some considerations as to why other works treated as belonging to the main body of H. G. Adler's Holocaust fiction seldom resort to the use of either irony and black humour in the way that *Hausordnung* does.

This paper concludes with an appendix containing a series of micro-illustrations of irony and, to some extent, black humour in Adler's *Eine Reise*. The material in this inventory of seventeen examples is intended to give some sense of the sheer variety of text-types deployed and the power of irony and black humour to both amuse and revolt. As can be seen, Adler's narrative style is more protean than has been hitherto assumed. Since I shall be dealing with relatively long works of fiction, I have decided to make my main points by interpreting certain key episodes and focussing on contained sequences open to the comparative study of context and function.

(i) The Enforced Evacuation by Train from Stupart

Die Lokomotive vorne schnauft behaglich vor Freude, daß man sie aus dem Museum hervorgeholt hat. Nun wurde sie zum Dienst bestellt. Hört ihr nicht das lustige Pfeifen? Das ist nicht mehr der Schielende. Das ist die Lokomotive, oder nein, das ist der Stationsvorsteher, der die schwere Verantwortung wegpfeift. Er ist hier viel wichtiger als die Helden, die er nicht beachtet. Da ein Held auf ihn zugeht, salutiert er nachlässig. Er glaubt, das letzte Zeichen schon bald geben zu können. Die Reisenden werden es gemütlich haben. Der Zugführer sieht verläßlich aus. Noch einen Augenblick, dann rollt ihr eurem Glück entgegen. Beamte, Fürsorgeschwestern und Krankenwärter werden euer Geschick betreuen und sich um eure Bedürfnisse kümmern. Dennoch ist von euch keine Zufriedenheit zu erwarten, ihr werdet häßliche Gesichter schneiden. Es schmerzt uns, daß ihr so garstig seid wie ungezogene Kinder, denn wir sind es, die alle Verantwortung tragen, wir müssen mit unserer Unschuld für eure Schuld eintreten. Da wir euch alles abgenommen haben, sind wir eure Vormünder. In unserem Herzen sind eure Seelen, in unserem Schoß, in unserem Mund. Wir führen euch an den Händchen, damit ihr den Kampf besteht.
[...] Wir sperren die Wagentüren ab und hängen die Siegel unseres Segens daran. Jetzt könnt ihr nicht mehr entschlüpfen. Liebe Schäfchen, so fahrt denn wohl, aber singt nicht so laut und schaut nicht aus dem fahrenden Zug heraus, weil die Begleitmannschaft auf Neugierige ohne Warnung schießen wird. Ein wenig Vorsicht kann nicht schaden. Wir haben die Strecke bestimmt, bald gelangt ihr an das Ziel. (*R* 40)

[The engine up ahead gives a pleasant snort, happy that it has been pulled out of the museum. Now it's back in service. Do you hear the jolly whistle? That's not Cross-Eyes. That's the train, or wait, that's the stationmaster who blows his whistle and is in charge of everything. Here he is much more important than the mighty heroes, to whom he doesn't even pay attention. When one of the heroes comes up to him, he gives a careless salute. He believes that the last signal is about to be given. The travelers have been made comfortable. The engineers look ready. In a moment you'll be on your happy way. Officials, nurses, and orderlies will ensure your fate and attend to your every need.
But we don't expect any satisfaction from you, knowing you will just pull ugly faces. It hurts us that you are so nasty, like naughty children, because we are the ones who carry all the responsibility, for we have to pay for your guilt with our innocence. Since we have taken everything away from you, we are your guardians. Your souls are in our hearts, in our laps, in our mouths. We lead you by your little hand so that you can survive the struggle.
[...] We lock the doors of the wagons and place the seal of our blessing upon them. Now you can't get away. Pleasant journey, little sheep, but don't sing too loud and don't shout from the train, because the guards will shoot without warning at a moment's notice. A little caution couldn't hurt. We've secured the route, soon you will reach your destination. (*RE* 36)]

Although it is potentially a heartrending scene of callous mass deportation, this evacuation-by-train passage is at points remarkably humorous, while at the same time disturbing, not least because of our own hindsight into the outcome of the events in question, as well as the overarching perspective deployed by invoking a quasi-omniscient narrator. The setting is a Stupart station from which the enforced train-journey to Ruhenthal is about to set off now the deportees have been assembled. The grotesque celebratory mood of the occasion is palpable from time to time. However, thanks to an anthropomorphic twist to the early parts of the narrative, even the locomotive due to pull the train is presented as being delighted to have been liberated from its museum-prison and once more made capable of being of service to its masters, something that those assembled for the journey can now hardly claim. The officious railway personnel, for once playing a more important role than the organizing militia, are proud to be exercising their new authority, as they herd together the largely unsuspecting waiting deportees. But the guards soon undermine the atmosphere by scolding the assembled deportees, treating them like disappointingly naughty children in need of a guiding adult hand. Thus, while the train's locomotive is made to display human feelings, the passengers who believe they are going on a holiday are submitted to a quasi-mechanical form of 'administration', as set out in Adler's study of the concept.[6]

To judge by the unpredictable way in which the station officials treat the assembled Stupart deportees by calculatingly switching between blame and reassurance, the main purpose of this series of volte-face behaviour patterns would seem to be to put the deportees off their guard before their encounter with Ruhenthal ghetto-life. As the event unfolds, symbolic dark clouds begin to appear on the horizon. These reflect the patronizing way the deportees are treated as ungrateful, on the one hand, while, on the other, being continuously bombarded by rules and regulations concerning how their possessions should be prepared for transport and by rules on how 'passengers' must behave during the course of the journey. In order to reduce the deportees to mechanical compliance, the assembled crowd is both blamed for letting their guards down and specifically warned not to be afraid or get off the train at any available opportunity. There is irony *and* black humour to the guards' outrageous claim that they will have to compensate for the deportees' guilt by their own innocence and will have to lead the gullible by the hand to the waiting transport wagons. By this stage, the guards are busy locking the wagon doors shut and attaching to each wagon what they ironically refer to as the 'seal of our blessing', thus moving the mood of the scenario away from situational irony to expressional irony *on the guards' part*. Throughout the final phase of this episode, the guards' treatment of their prisoners veers towards a combination of verbal intimidation and threatening black humour. Viewed in retrospect, there is comic irony to the way the locomotive is anthropomorphized, whereas the assembled deportees continue to be berated for behaving like children, while at the same time being specifically cautioned to obey all the rules that apply to the 'journey' they are about to be sent on. Once the wagon doors are ritually closed, the people are told not to be afraid. At the same time, the latter are assured that officials, nurses and orderlies will be present to help them with their every need, an irony so positioned by the narrator as to imply that, far from being reassuring, *all assurances* are *in fact lies*, as are such declarations intended to suggest that their anticipated journey is about to begin and that they will be well taken care of on the way. That the whistle heard in the distance does not come from the locomotive joyfully emerging from its museum, but from the station-master *whistling away* his obligations, as the German has it, is a shrewd mixture of contextual irony and black humour. However, it is again essential to ascertain whether the person responsible for this explanation can be readily identified by the reader. Calling the guards 'heroes' is, of course, a crude form of irony. In fact, their uniforms give them away, while the tasks they were called upon to perform during the night-march through Stupart are anything but heroic. That the detainees' destination is presented as a happy one seems deliberately misleading, given their treatment in Stupart during the preceding hours. The ironies of their situation are ignored by those gathered on the platform. However, their predicament will be transparent to most readers, given how much knowledge he or she has accumulated concerning the enforced relocation of the alleged enemies of the 'Third Reich'.

The key question one is left with by this compact episode is whether the examples of irony and black humour emanate exclusively from the militias and other guards or are essentially the preserve of the narrator and thus, by extension, the reader? The concluding reference on the officials' part to locking the wagon doors and attaching 'the seal of our blessing' is pure context-based irony; given that the reader will be aware where such measures will lead. Moreover, the way in which the Stupart scene is evoked is closer to black humour than irony.

(ii) Dr Lustig's Funeral

> Langsam setzt sich die Trauergesellschaft in Bewegung, denn sie begibt sich auf das letzte Geleite. Die Lebenden möchten den Toten gerne weit nachfolgen. Dankbar schreiten die Lebenden aus, sobald der Wagen nur rollt, aber da die Fracht den Schlagbaum bald erreicht, werden sie an der Erfüllung ihrer Liebespflicht verhindert. Ein Zeichen belehrt den Trauerzug, daß er an seiner Endstation angelangt ist. Da bleibt er stehen. Er darf nicht folgen, doch die Handlung darf er sehen, die sich nun abspielt. Zwei Gendarmen schauen sich den Wagen an, der seine langsame Fahrt fortsetzt, und ihre Blicke fragen streng: 'Tote, habt ihr etwas zu verzollen?' Nur die Blicke fragen, keine Worte stören die Ruhe; die Gendarmen schauen aus dunkelgelben Augen und lächeln in wissender Bereitschaft. Den Toten letzte Ehre. Sie dürfen ohne Ausweis verreisen; nicht einmal abgezählt werden die Särge. Es steigt der Schlagbaum hoch, es zieht der Wagen weiter, unverzollt und vogelfrei. Die Toten haben nichts bei sich; das wird ihnen geglaubt. Auch der Tod der Toten, ihre Ehrlichkeit wird nicht bezweifelt. Niemand fährt sie an: 'öffnet eure Särge!' Die Pferde ziehen frischer an und schaukeln die abgefallene Menschenfracht von Ruhenthal auf sandgewürztem Pech und Teer. Der Schlagbaum fällt, der Abschied ist vollendet. Lustig mit purzelnden Sprüngen holpert in munterer Eile der Totenwagen dahin. (R 142)

[Slowly the funeral train begins to move as it sets off as the last escort. The living like to follow the dead as far as possible. Gratefully the living follow behind as long as the wagon continues to roll along, but when the cargo reaches the barrier they are suddenly prevented from fulfilling their responsibility. A sign informs the funeral train that it has reached its final stop. And so it stands there. It cannot follow along, though it can watch the process that then unfolds. Two policemen look at the wagon that sets off slowly, their eyes asking, 'You dead, do you have anything to declare?' Only their eyes ask this, not a word is spoken. The policemen look on with their dark brown eyes and smile in knowing readiness. The last honor of the dead. They are allowed to leave without a pass, the coffins never once being counted. The barrier lifts high, the wagon pulls ahead, duty-free and as free as a bird. The dead have nothing with them, nor does anyone question that they do. Their death, their honesty is not questioned. No one demands, 'Open all your coffins!' The horses pull more vigorously and Ruhenthal's load of human freight sways across the sand-based macadam and tar. The barrier falls, the farewell is completed. Merrily lurching ahead with sprightly speed, the funeral wagon rumbles along. (*RE* 130–31)]

The passage depicting Leopold Lustig's funeral involves contextual irony, black humour (especially on the Czech guards' part), echoes of the earlier Stupart deportation scene, as well as a sharp contrast with Zerline's death. There is an obvious layer of irony to the grotesque tarring image juxtaposed with the actual burial sequence, as if to imply that Lustig's memory will be obliterated along with the ghetto-rubbish for which he had been responsible, after being deprived of his role as a practising doctor. The passage's specific context becomes understandable, if one bears in mind that death in Theresienstadt was an anomaly for various political reasons: in particular, the ghetto's need to display a positive image of itself to the outside world (witness the infamous 1944 propaganda film *The Führer gives the Jews a City* and the International Red Cross visit). In most concentration camps, death was largely a matter of being worked to death, death by shooting or gassing and incineration, rather than a ritual funeral oration, the burial of the coffin or an open-air tribute involving a cortège of mourners.

Irony and black humour come into play at the moment when the Lustig cortège sets off. The procession comes to a complete halt upon reaching the ghetto-limits beyond which the Ruhenthaler were not permitted to go. The ghetto's so-called Wagon of Death, containing a stack of coffins, moves off followed by a bedraggled group of mourners. That the journey differs considerably from the one made by prisoners on outside working parties beyond the ghetto-walls is brought out by the way the next stage of the cortège's passage is presented. As the cortège moves on, the Czech sentries on the Ruhenthal Ghetto's main gates are symbolically transformed from being guards into customs officers. Accordingly, the ensuing discourse between Czech sentries on the gates and advancing mourners becomes more that of familiar border-crossing procedures. The consequence of this is the double image of the reification of corpses and mourners alike. The two guards ask with their eyes the statutory question 'Corpses, have you anything to declare?', after which the dead and the ghetto-prisoners both become symbols of reification. The faces of the guards, referred to ironically as 'Gendarmen' (an allusion to the militia that performed guard duties in Theresienstadt), show they are aware that nobody in Ruhenthal could possibly have 'anything to declare'. Hence, the order 'Open all your coffins' becomes redundant. The mourners are only permitted to view the cortège's progress from a distance, as are the citizens of the neighbouring town of Leitenberg, who observe the entire episode from their usual uncaring perspective. Reification, containment and denial become key leitmotifs in the novel's depiction of the relationship between Ruhenthaler and neighbouring Leitenberger, symbolizing, as they do, the victims and the callous German onlookers. The impact of this scene of ironic rules and the black humour of the border-crossing ritual differs radically from my next illustration involving dreams of peace and being welcomed back to Stupart at the end of the War. However, while one character, Ida Schwarz, is happy to believe in her vision, there is much narratorial and contextual irony to the depiction of the hopes that most Ruhenthaler still cling to.

(iii) Visions of Peace, Being Welcomed in One's Homeland and the End of All Wars

Aber nach dem Krieg. Schon bald. Überall wartet man. Von dort ist es ein bißchen weiter nachhause, aber man kann zurückfahren. Erster Klasse, wie es sich gehört. Besser als zweite ist Ida früher nicht gefahren. Aber jetzt muß man erste. Das wird wunderschön. Und wir sind die Sieger. Man holt uns ab und bringt uns im Triumph zurück. Die Lokomotiven sind geschmückt wie junge Mädchen. Es ist Hochzeit. Das Lied beginnt. Alle Waggons sind mit Geschenken vollgeladen, das sind die geretteten Menschen. Sie bekommen einen Lippenstift und Puder, damit sie sich herrichten. Sie schauen noch nicht gut genug aus. Bald werden sie wieder. Man gibt ihnen alles. Sie heiraten. Richtige Männer hat man gebracht. Jede wählt den rechten Mann. Frisches Reisig und bunte Aufschriften. WIR SIND FREI! Jeder kann uns sehen. Keine Nonnen. Die Schleier werden weggeworfen. Die Kinder spielen. WILLKOMMEN IN DER HEIMAT! Auf allen Stationen werden Erfrischungen gereicht. Freies Buffet. Die schönsten jungen Mädchen hat man ausgewählt. Niedliche Kleidchen. Die Mädchen kommen an den Zug heran und bringen Schokoladentassen mit Fruchttorte und eingepackte Liebesgaben. Ida ißt sich endlich satt.

Alle Furcht ist von der Welt verschwunden, niemand muß sich mehr verstecken, nichts muß man verstecken. Aller Schmuck wird angesteckt. Freiheit, Freiheit, in der eigenen Wohnung sitzen! Gemütlich ist der Platz beim Ofen. [...] Jetzt ist das schöne Ziel erreicht, doch von den alten Plagen spricht man nicht. Was man gestern erlitten hat, ist heute nicht mehr böse. Die Reise ist beendet, man schweigt davon. Einen ganzen Monat werden Feste gefeiert, weil wieder Frieden ist. Doch jetzt ist alles viel herrlicher als je zuvor, weil man erst heute die Freiheit richtig schätzt.

Dann wird ein Verein gegründet, Ruhenthaler Veteranen. Jede Woche setzen sie sich zusammen und spielen Karten. Jeder nimmt sich gute Kleider und erzählt. Die Mitglieder erhalten ein Abzeichen mit dem Ruhenthaler Wappen. Besichtigungsfahrten werden veranstaltet, einmal jährlich ein Wochenende in Ruhenthal! Karoline wird das leiten. Alle werden kommen. Die Eisenbahn wird Ermäßigungen gewähren. In Ruhenthal spielt die Musik, viele Reden werden gehalten. Gedichte werden geschrieben. Die Zeitungen sind voll davon. Jeder wird sagen, daß er dabei gewesen ist, als es noch traurig war und keiner an das gute Ende glaubte. (R 164–65)

[But after the war. Soon it will come. Everyone is waiting for it. From there it's just a bit farther to home, but one can still travel back. First class, which is only fitting. Though Ida has never traveled in anything higher than second class. But then it will be time for first class. That will be wonderful. For we are the victors. We are picked up and brought back in triumph. The trains are decked out like young girls. It's a celebration. The song begins. All the cars are full of gifts, namely those who have been saved. They are given lipstick and powder in order to get themselves ready. They still don't look so good. Soon they'll be better. They're given everything. They marry. Good men are brought along. Each chooses the right man. Bright banners and colorful letters. WE ARE FREE! Everyone can see us. We're not nuns. The veils have been tossed away. The children play. WELCOME HOME! At every station refreshments are laid out. Free buffet. The prettiest girls have been selected. Cute little dresses. The girls approach the train carrying cups of hot chocolate with fruit tarts and wrapped-up little gifts. Ida eats until she is finally full.

All fear has disappeared from the world, no one has to hide anymore, nothing has to be hidden. Jewelry is worn again once more. Freedom, freedom, to sit in one's own apartment! How nice to sit next to the furnace. [...] At last everything is right, and no one speaks about the old complaints. What you suffered the day before is no longer bad today. The journey is over, no one says anything about it. Parties go on for an entire month because peace has returned. Indeed, everything is much more wonderful than it has ever been, for only now is freedom truly valued.

Then the Society of Ruhenthal Veterans is founded. Every week they get together and play cards. Each dresses well and tells stories. Each member wears a badge that has the Ruhenthal coat of arms on it. Reunions are arranged, one weekend a year in Ruhenthal! Caroline will lead them. Everyone will come. The railroad will offer reduced prices. In Ruhenthal there is music and many speeches are given. Poems are written, the newspapers will cover it all. Everyone will say that he was there when it was so bleak and no one believed it would end well. (*RE* 151–52)]

There is something of the stream-of-consciousness-technique to the account of the visions of peace and being joyously received in one's homeland, especially if this is read against the backcloth of *Die unsichtbare Wand*. Given the transient nature of ghetto-life in Ruhenthal, the death-rate in the concentration camps and extermination centres to which onward transports were sent, *Eine Reise* would appear to be essentially a novel of leave-takings and loss. However, the section depicting Ida Schwarz's vision of what the end of the War will be like, being rescued, welcomed in one's homeland and reunited with old acquaintances, as well as basking in the fact that the War is over, is a mixture of schmaltz, kitsch and self-delusion (after all, Ida Schwarz is the passenger on the Stupart station described as being 'without a clue' as to where her journey would take her). But the vision some characters subsequently share with her is not confined to feelings of happiness and gratitude. Black humour looms large in various images, as in certain memories that colour the reactions of some Ruhenthaler to the fact that the War is over and they are free to go. Such sentences as 'All fear has disappeared from the world', 'No one has to hide anymore', 'Nothing has to be hidden' and 'No one can look through the window into the room' imply, *ex negativo*, that the world they are returning to is by no means what they want it to be. But the situation becomes much darker due to comments from certain characters whose reactions verge on black humour. For example: 'How nice to sit next to the furnace' ('Ofen' is the term used for the stove which it is declared pleasant to sit next to, but obviously the word's reference to furnaces has darker associations than this in the world that Ruhenthaler have until this point been sent on to). A further request ('Just feed it another shovelful') comes as close to post-concentration camp black humour as the seemingly innocuous announcement that their pet, Bunny the dog, has returned. This is news with ambiguously sinister connotations, given the later metaphor linking Zerline with the hunted rabbit. In this context, some of the above remarks appear to be more the product of authorial dark humour than the reaction of individual Ruhenthaler, or a reminder of the fact that under certain conditions even gallows humour can be a safety valve of sorts.

The emphasis on imagery based on cosmetics, implying a camouflaging of the real situation, means that the picture of a happy homecoming is about as deceptive as the feelings that the Stuparter toyed with prior to their journey to Ruhenthal. Similarly, the various slogan-bearing banners on display in Ida Schwarz's vision of her homecoming and the reception she will receive from old acquaintances and friends are about as misleading as the repeated promises made to the Stuparter, designed to take them off their guard. Added to which, the suggestion that the 'veterans' of Ruhenthal will found a weekly card-playing club where they don their finest clothes and swap memories of what life in the ghetto was like is as phony a picture of life after the War has ended as Ida Schwarz's vision of return to the homeland will prove to be. Awarding themselves medals in the shape of Ruhenthal's coat-of-arms is as false a gesture as the attempts of the ladies of Stupart to doll themselves up ready to receive the homecomers and perhaps find a suitable husband amongst their number. The irony and deflation of hopes here is achieved by an omniscient narrator who allows all participants in the façade to become the victims of their own misplaced plans. That they will go on regular visits to Ruhenthal, as if on tourist excursions, coupled with the fact that they give speeches, write poems which are printed by the local newspapers would seem like the height of self-delusion, if it were not for the fact that everyone was now proud to declare that he has 'been there when everything had been sad and none believed it would end well. The times change. No one will hide his joy.' The concluding picture is not what Ida Schwarz wants it to be. But then, neither is her vision of Ruhenthal!

Concluding Thoughts

I suggested earlier that Ida Schwarz's delusional vision is worth juxtaposing with some parts of *Die unsichtbare Wand*. The latter tends to be read as a Holocaust novel, although it is arguably also a novel about coming to terms with the experience of exile in Great Britain and not the Holocaust years. *Die unsichtbare Wand* does not display the irony and dark humour that played a major role in *Eine Reise* and parts of *Hausordnung*. This raises the question why this should be so. Those of us who met H. G. Adler and heard him recite his Holocaust poetry know him to be capable of various forms of irony and humour. To answer the above question, we have to look elsewhere.

Of the major figures encountered in Ruhenthal, Leopold Lustig is one of the few characters able to be ironic at his own expense. In the case of *Panorama*, Josef Kramer's agenda of socializing his fellow work-party comrades, forming them into close groups and preventing them from abandoning all hope is too serious a goal to lend itself to humour on his part. Moreover, the conditions in Auschwitz and Langenstein-Zwieberge were palpably not conducive to self-ironizing or any form of humour on the part of prisoners. The only remaining narrative outlets were irony and black humour *on the guards' part* (as was the case with Leopold Lustig's abortive funeral cortège) or an injection of the former on the part of either narrator or reader. The examples in my appendix suggest the irony in *Eine Reise* is enjoyed by the guards and officials at the suffering detainees' and ghettoized prisoners' expense. It would be difficult to conceive that the author of the Josef Kramer we encounter at the end of *Panorama* in Launceston Castle in Cornwall could write a Holocaust novel capable of outstripping *Eine Reise.*

(iv) Appendix: Micro-Illustrations of Irony and Black Humour

'Du sollst nicht wohnen!' (*R* 10)
[Thou shalt not dwell among us! (*RE* 8)]

'Es macht nichts, daß es keine Adresse mehr gibt. Schlimmstenfalls kommen die Bündel zu niemand zurück [...]. Da wird man feststellen, daß sie keinem mehr gehören, also gehören sie den Stellen, die herrenlose Habe durch einen einfachen Zauber wieder in Eigentum verwandeln.' (*R* 23)
[It doesn't matter that you no longer have an address. The worst that can happen is that you don't get the bundles and they are sent back. [...] That's when it dawns on them that nothing belongs to them anymore, rather it all belongs to the authorities who transform the anonymous possessions into property once again through simple magic. (*RE* 20)]

'Die Koffer und Säcke sind mit Kalkfarbe zu bemalen oder mit Zetteln zu bekleben. Es ist gut, wenn man alles bereit hat. Praktischer Sinn hat sich noch immer bewährt.' (*R* 23)
[The suitcases and bags are marked with chalk or have notes glued to them. It's good to have everything ready. Practicality always watches out for itself. (*RE* 20)]

'Was du kaufen kannst, ist dir verboten, aber du kannst nichts kaufen!' (*R* 27)
[What you can buy is forbidden, and you can't buy anything! (*RE* 24)]

'Ein bißchen Qual hat noch keinem geschadet, während man von ihrem Übermaß nichts spürt. [....] Die Fußabstreifer von gestern sind die Herren von heute.' (*R* 36–37)
[A little suffering never hurt anyone, as long as one does not feel it in the extreme. [...] The doormats of yesterday are the men of today. (*RE* 33)]

'Menschen begehen den Fehler, daß sie zu dicht beisammen leben. Darum ist es gut, vertrieben zu werden.' (*R* 37)
[People make the mistake of living too closely together. Therefore it's good to be expelled.' (*RE* 33)]

'[...] die Vorräte sind gering und werden verzehrt wie die Grüße, die man euch in die Verbannung mitgegeben hat, als man sich von euch abwandte [...].' (*R* 37)
[[...] supplies are low and as spare as the good-byes you were given when you were banished and others turned away from you [...]. (*RE* 34)]

'Kinder sind im Zug an der Leine zu halten.' (R 132)
[Children need to be kept on a leash in the train. (RE 121)]

'Teilnahme an der Reise bloß auf eigenes Risiko.' (R 132)
[You take part in the journey at your own risk. (RE 121)]

'[...], Angst ist überflüssig. Während des Aufenthaltes in Stationen nicht benützen!' (R 132)
[[...], fear is superfluous. No using the facilities when the train stops in a station! (RE 121)]

'Nein, alle Angst soll zurückbleiben, sie hätte in der letzten Station aussteigen sollen, [...].' (R 132)
[No. Let your fear fall by the wayside; it should have gotten off at the last stop, [...]. (RE 121–22)]

'Das eine wenigstens ist gut in Ruhenthal, daß die Ärzte nicht verreisen können.' (R 138)
[At least that's one thing good about Ruhenthal, the doctors can't go anywhere. (RE 127)]

'Für kranke Menschen ist eine Fahrt ins Blaue nicht gesund.' (R160)
[For sick people the journey into the wild blue yonder is not healthy. (RE 147)]

'Wer eine Geige versteckt, wird wegen Platzmangels bestraft werden, sein Lied ist aus.' (R 161)
[Whoever stows away a violin will be thrown out, the song is over. (RE 148)]

'Umgestiegen wird nicht. Das ist der Vorteil der Sonderzüge. Man steigt ein und man steigt aus, dazwischen geschieht nichts, es wird bloß gefahren. Nachher kann sich jeder ausruhen, besonders die Kranken.' (R 166)
[There's no getting off. That's the advantage of the special transport. You get on and you get off. In between nothing happens, the train just keeps going. Afterward everyone can rest, especially the sick. (RE 153)]

'Man versäumt nicht gleich den Zug. Er wartet, wenn so viele reisen.' (R 166)
[No one will miss the train. It will wait for all of those who are traveling. (RE 153)]

'Wir beehren uns [the Leitenberger Tagespost], die Leserschaft vom plötzlichen Tod eines langen Sonderzuges in Kenntnis zu setzen.' (R 174)
[We regret to inform our readership about the sudden death of a special long train. (RE 161)]

Notes to Chapter 8

1. Roland H. Wiegenstein, 'Drei KZ-Romane', *Die Neue Rundschau*, 74 (1963), 662.
2. Judith Klein, 'Zu ironisch? Zu satirisch? Zu radikal? H. G. Adlers Roman über Verfolger und Verfolgte unter dem Dritten Reich: *Eine Reise*', *Frankfurter Rundschau*, 15 May 1999.
3. H. G. Adler, *Eine Reise* (Vienna: Zsolnay, 1999), p. 313.
4. All quotations in German are taken from H. G. Adler, *Eine Reise. Roman* (Vienna: Zsolnay, 1999). The English translations are taken from H. G. Adler, *The Journey: A Novel*, translated by Peter Filkins (New York: Random House, 2008). Hereafter citations will be made in parentheses in the text, abbreviating these editions as R and RE respectively.
5. Thomas Krämer, *Die Poetik des Gedenkens: Zu den autobiographischen Romanen H. G. Adlers* (Würzburg: Königshausen & Neumann, 2012).
6. See H. G. Adler, *Der verwaltete Mensch: Studien zur Deportation der Juden aus Deutschland* (Tübingen: Mohr (Paul Siebeck), 1974).

CHAPTER 9

❖

H. G. Adler's *Panorama* and the *Bildungsroman* Tradition

Martin Swales

H. G. Adler described *Panorama* as 'einen mit Autobiographischem getränkten Roman' [a novel steeped in autobiography].[1] I am not well qualified to speak about the autobiographical aspects. For this reason — and more importantly because *Panorama,* described in its subtitle as a 'Roman in zehn Bildern' [Novel in Ten Images], is an intensely interesting and important work in its own right — I want to treat it as a novel, a novel of a quite particular kind.

Panorama opens by depicting an incident from the protagonist Josef Kramer's time as a schoolboy when he visits the panorama with his grandmother; then we learn of his life in the family in Prague. Subsequently we see him spending a year on an exchange arrangement in Umlowitz, then at a military academy, at a 'Ferienlager', and, in the fifth 'Bild' [Image] he mingles with friends and fellow students. He becomes a private tutor, a 'Hofmeister', to the Börsenrat family, before working in a 'Kulturhaus' [Cultural Institution]. In the late 1930's Czechoslovakia is occupied by the Germans and Josef finds himself doing forced labour on a railway construction project. He is then sent to a concentration camp, Lager Langenstein, and the brutality of the regime is described unsparingly. In the final, the tenth, 'Bild' he is in exile in England and visits Launceston Castle in Cornwall where Cromwell had the Quaker leader George Fox imprisoned. This too is then a site where cruelty has occurred, and the names suggest as much — Launceston echoes Langenstein, Cromwell echoes Cornwall. But it is here that Josef at last begins to find space and time to think, to reflect on his place in the world. The novel takes us then from youth to maturity, from German-speaking Europe to exile in England.

What kind of narrative does Adler put before us? Let me concentrate on the first few pages because they set the seal on everything that follows. The opening section is called 'Vorbild'; and the term denotes not an ideal model, but a prefatory image. The visit to the panorama is the first of the 'Bilder' that make up the novel; and it offers images that are both vivid, overwhelmingly urgent, but also inauthentic. And Josef registers both aspects, the glory and the falsity of the panorama:

> Dabei leuchtet alles goldig und glänzend, wie in tropisches Sonnenlicht getaucht. [...] [Josef] kann sich an der Pracht nicht sattsehen. Es ist nur schade, dass sich die Menschen, Tiere und Wagen auf den Bildern nicht bewegen. Zwar

wird das Leben der wunderschönen Bilder durch ihre Unbeweglichkeit nicht weniger herrlich, aber es scheint dadurch aus der Zeit herausgenommen.

[Everything appears lit by brilliant golden light, as if dipped in tropical sunlight. [...] [Josef] can't get enough of the splendid sights. But it's a shame that the people, animals, and wagons in the pictures don't move. Though the fact they don't move doesn't make the life depicted in the beautiful pictures any less marvellous, it does make them seem like something outside of time.][2]

The combination of vividness and unconnectedness is central to the fascination that the panorama exerts. The unreality accounts for the seductive charm of the experience, as expressed in the following reflections:

Die übrige Welt ist aufgelöst und fern. (P 10) [The daily world disappears and is gone. (PE 4)]

So ist die Welt ausgeschaltet, in der man gewöhnlich lebt. (P 11) [Thus the world you normally live in is turned off, and has in fact passed away (PE 5)]

Die andere Welt ist ein Programm, das ist wohl schön, aber mehr ist es nicht. (P 12) [The other world is a program that is immensely beautiful, but nothing more. (PE 5)]

For all its questionableness, however, the panorama remains the governing perceptual metaphor of Adler's text. One asks oneself why the novel should have 'Panorama' as its title, why should the omnipresent mode of the novel be one that conjoins vividness and insubstantiality in an energizing but disturbing dialectic? The novel is written in the third person, although Josef clearly is the central focalizing agent. It is written in the present tense throughout. And, apart from the 'Vorbild', the 'Bilder' from one to nine all end with Josef falling asleep, losing perceptual contact with the world. The final 'Bild' — number ten — is an exception, it stresses Josef's awakening. But it is not called 'Epilog'; it too is a 'Bild'. Two critics have recently made much of the questionable nature of the panorama and its 'Bilder'. Helen Finch refers to 'the sinister, objectifying function of the panorama'.[3] And John and Ann White, in a superb analysis, have suggested that the essential evil, the moral threat which Adler explores is not so much the actual cruelty and degradation which the narrative renders so powerfully but is rather the existential inadequacy inherent in the 'panorama' mode of living and perceiving, grounded in 'einer falschen Beziehung zwischen Subjekt und Objekt' [a false relationship between subject and object].[4] These are important and weighty arguments; but they still leave open one all-important question. Why should the whole novel be governed by a cognitive, perceptual, and narrative mode that enshrines a false relationship between subject and object? Were the novel in the first person, one might be able to bring a psychological perspective to bear, one that, as it were, would show Josef growing out of his inadequate relationship to worldly experience. And one could imagine that the final chapter might be exempt from the taint of being a panorama-image. But it is not; this is not how Adler's text works. So: why does it work as it does? The answer lies less in the psychology of Josef as a focalizing presence, but resides more in Adler's debate with the novel form, with particular kinds of novel narrative — and most urgently with the tradition of the German Bildungsroman.

Viewed in the simplest of terms, the Bildungsroman is a novel about growing up, about the development of a young person from youth to some kind of maturity. Now this or something like it is true of a great many European novels of psychological and social realism — one thinks, for example, of *Great Expectations* or *Le Rouge et le Noir*. But what distinguishes the German tradition from its European counterparts is that it has world enough and time to reflect on the complexity of human identity, on the gradualness and indeterminacy of the learning process. In my study of the German Bildungsroman I sought to suggest that it is sustained by a dialectic of the 'Nacheinander' [succession] of the story told, of events depicted in temporal sequence, on the one hand, and of the 'Nebeneinander' [juxtaposition] of the inner self on the other, a realm in which possibilities are esteemed as much as actualities.[5] Because potentialities matter as much as events and deeds, the genre has a reflective, thoughtful, spiritual dimension which marks it off from the realistic novel in which frequently the protagonist needs to worry about where the next meal is coming from before he or she can pursue thoughts about the complex unfolding of the self. The German Bildungsroman invokes a benign world; the world which Adler evokes is much harsher than that — and not just in the two 'Bilder', number eight (the forced labour on the railway construction project), and number nine (the unremitting hideousness of the concentration camp) which evoke a context of institutional barbarism. As John and Ann White quite rightly suggest, the threat to the individual self is present throughout *Panorama*.

Adler's novel, to repeat a point made earlier, is written in the present tense throughout; and what that temporal mode captures is the sense that Josef is consistently at the mercy of events. He is barely able to think his own thoughts, to find space for his own autonomy, to inhabit a site of reflectivity where he can get beyond the brutalizing simultaneity of his experiences and find sustained wakefulness in answer to the trancelike condition of panorama living. The trajectory of the novel echoes that of the Bildungsroman in its movement from youth to maturity. In the final analysis, *Panorama* functions as a meta-text, one that runs parallel to and debates with the Bildungsroman. It is a sustained acknowledgment and critique of the German genre, one that remains obstinately a Bilder-Roman [Image-Novel] rather than a Bildungsroman.

There are two particular ways in which Adler energizes a critical debate with the Bildungsroman. The issue of novelistic realism is salient here. One of the criticisms frequently levelled at the German Bildungsroman is that it too often softens the contours of resistant experience, of the tactile, often hurtful interaction of self and world. Adler, by contrast, writes with a magnificent feel for material reality. One could think of that moment early on, in the 'Vorbild', when Josef finds that his breath has left a layer of steam on a metal component in the panorama booth:

> Josef rutscht auf seinem Sitz, weil er dann noch besser aufmerken kann. Unterhalb der Gucklöcher ist ein Blechstück befestigt, da schlägt sich der Atem nieder. Das Blech wird feucht, und Josef streicht gern manchmal über die glatte Fläche, so dass die Fingerkuppen nass werden. Die Großmutter achtet nicht weiter auf Josef, denn sie weiß, wie sehr ihn das Panorama fesselt, wo er sich auch viel artiger aufführt als sonst. Darum bleibt die kleine Ungezogenheit mit dem Wischen der Finger unbemerkt. (*P* 11)

[Josef scoots forward on his stool in order to see better still. Beneath the peepholes a piece of tin is attached against which he breathes. The tin gathers moisture and sometimes Josef likes to run his fingers over the smooth flatness so that his fingertips feel damp. The grandmother pays no attention to Josef, for she knows how the panorama captivates him, so much so that he is better behaved than usual. That's way the little naughtiness with wiping his fingers remains ignored. (PE 5)]

This is a splendid passage, beautifully, precisely observed. And it is the kind of moment that occurs all too rarely in the German Bildungsroman tradition. It conjoins physicality and psychology as the young self explores the world of material objects in defiance of adult rules and regulations about seemliness and good behaviour. The next 'Bild', entitled 'Die Familie' (The Family), opens with a splendid invocation of those adult rules and regulations. And Adler's prose in its parataxis captures the sheer hassle of growing up in the daily deluge of adult criticism:

'Josef, kannst du denn nicht hören?' Ja, er hört, und die Stimmen laufen herum und haben lange schmutzige Spinnenbeine, und es kann doch das größte Unglück passieren. [...] Dann muss sich die Tante Gusti ärgern, aber das hilft nichts, und die Kinder machen sich schmutzig, und alles machen sie schmutzig, und trotzdem haben sie kecke Antworten, das kommt von der Unfolgsamkeit, immer wieder das alte Lied mit dem Josef, und da ruft die Tante Gusti. 'Du sollst nicht keck sein!' Das tut man nicht, sagt sie, man ist nicht vorlaut, aber lügen, das ist ganz garstig. (P 13)

['Josef, don't you hear?' Yes, he hears, and the voices run around and have long, dirty spider legs, and indeed bad things can sometimes happen. [...] Then Aunt Gusti gets mad, but that does no good, and the children get dirty, and everything gets dirty, and yet they continue to talk back, a result of disobedience, the same old song with Josef, as Aunt Gusti yells, 'Don't you talk back to me!' Don't do that, she says, don't be so smart, and don't tell lies, that's the worst of all. (PE 7)]

The breathless cascade of short clauses linked by 'und' and 'aber' captures powerfully the young person's sense of being talked at rather than talked to. The realistic mode is sustained throughout *Panorama* — and nowhere more so than in the late scenes which explore physical brutality. What starts harmlessly enough with Josef's visit with his grandmother to the panorama — that sense of being confronted with overwhelmingly vivid images without any chance of answering back — becomes the governing signature of Josef's experience. And it is at the very heart of Adler's realism and of the critical perspective it provides on the German Bildungsroman.

I suggested that one of the chief glories of the Bildungsroman is its ability to handle novelistically the 'Nebeneinander' of the life of the mind as it comes into being and develops within a young person's experience. This is one of the most enriching aspects of the German novel tradition — particularly for English readers. This dimension is present in *Panorama* — but with a crucial difference. Sometimes, within the German tradition, a certain damaging schematism can occur whereby the protagonist is allowed to develop to the point where he or she makes coherently tidy sense of his or her experience. Without wishing to be ungenerous, I feel that on occasion Hermann Hesse succumbs to this failing. Adler's protagonist Josef is a spiritually questing figure, yet we do not feel that he ever achieves definitive insight. In 'Bild' 8 we find the following description of his thought processes:

> Josef möchte es wagen, seine Beziehung zum Leben als realistisch aufzufassen, nicht sachlich, natürlich mag es sein, aber sachlich ist auch nicht natürlich, Josef meint nicht mehr und nicht weniger als ein positives Verhalten zur Wirklichkeit, zum Wirkenden also, doch möchte er keine großen Reden halten, aber wir haben noch eine Gegenwart, nämlich *die* Gegenwart [...]. (*P* 463)

> [Josef preferring to think about his relationship to life in realistic terms, not clinical, because life is not clinical, though it is natural, but clinical is not the same as natural, Josef thinking of nothing less and nothing more than a positive attitude toward reality, or the seemingly real, but he doesn't feel comfortable spinning out any grand theory, for what we can know is a present, namely *the* present (*PE* 350)]

The language here, with its sequence of short clauses each one restlessly modifying the other, enacts the toing and froing of a mind in energized and ongoing debate with itself. At such moments we eavesdrop not on definitive philosophizing, not on once-and-for-all wisdom, but rather a subjectivity looking for understanding, exploring various modes and forms of signification.

Adler's novel, ending as it does with Josef's awakening in Launceston, offers intimations of a reckoning with the past: he is fiercely critical of the panorama as a condition of entrapment from which escape is difficult, perhaps impossible:

> es ist die Panorama-Situation des Menschen, dass er auch mit seinem Willen nicht darüber hinauszukommen vermag, das Panorama ist also eine große Gefahr, vielleicht ist es bloß ein anderer Name für das Grundübel selbst, vielleicht darf man so nicht zuschauen und so sich auch nicht ansehen lassen; dann ist das Panorama eine Niederlage der Menschlichkeit, es ist unmenschlich [...]. (*P* 548)

> [it being the human equivalent of the panorama that no amount of will can allow one to escape this situation, the panorama therefore a great danger in itself, perhaps just another name for the root of all evil, it perhaps being best not to let oneself look or let oneself be seen. For then the panorama is the defeat of one's humanity, it being inhuman [...] (*PE* 416–17)]

Yet it is central to Adler's purpose, to his moral and intellectual honesty, that even this forthright insight does not herald definitive clarity and self-understanding. Even here, in the closing section of the novel, tentativeness rather than certainty prevails. Josef's visit to Launceston remains within the governing structure of the novel; it is one 'Bild' among many; it is still part of the panorama against which it inveighs. Josef awakens; but that awakening is not a once-and-for-all turning point; rather, it is a process: 'Josef erwacht und schaut mit wachen Blicken vor sich. Noch wartet er zu, das Aufwachen braucht Dauer [...]' (*P* 573) [He wakes up and looks around him with eyes wide open. Now he waits patiently, awakening takes time [...] (*PE* 435)]. Adler constantly suggests how Josef's thoughts move backwards and forwards, now this way and that. We hear him exploring philosophical issues, only to become sceptical about philosophy; perhaps philosophy too partakes of the un-connectedness of the panorama condition? Perhaps life itself takes precedence over analysis, categorization, logic:

> [...] sobald er die Philosophie in der Begrenzung gefesselt erkennt, die ihre Fragen unbeantwortbar macht, will er über Unlösbares nicht philosophieren; Josef findet die Philosophie durch das Leben widerlegt, das zwar in allen Widersprüchen besteht und durch keine Handlung von ihnen abtrennbar ist, das aber trotzdem nicht bloß in diesen Widersprüchen beruht, auch wenn er sich von ihnen nicht befreien kann. (P 573)

> [As soon as he recognizes the limits of philosophy that make such questions unanswerable, then he no longer wishes to philosophize about that which is insoluble. Josef finds that philosophy is often refuted by life, which is full of contradictions and cannot be separated from them by any approach, though it doesn't entirely rest in these contradictions, even if it cannot be freed from them. (PE 435)]

Perhaps Josef, as he takes stock of his condition then and now, comes close to that simple injunction that prefaces E. M. Forster's *Howard's End* as epigraph — 'only connect'. That, or something like it, might promise the emergence from the panorama condition.

In conclusion, it is important to remember that Adler writes this novel in exile, in England. Yet he writes in German,[6] and in debate with a particularly German mode of novel-writing. Many of the experiences undergone by Josef, his protagonist, on the soil of German-speaking Europe (and they are experiences that Josef's creator underwent too) are of surpassing, unspeakable horror. Yet the allegiance to the German language and the German literary tradition is still undiminished. That allegiance is complex, and the 'Bilder' of the *Panorama* novel generate multiple implications. At one level they debate with the notion of 'Bildung' (education/formation) — and they do so with great critical energy. The panorama model of unconnected living calls powerfully into question the Bildungsroman's propensity to create a novelistic universe in which the protagonist can have the luxury of experimenting with — rather than connecting with — the business of living. Viewed under this aspect, *Panorama* asks if the Bildungsroman is not perhaps too inward and philosophical for its own good — too much in love with the 'Nebeneinander' of teeming potentialty within the individual self and too little bothered by actuality. At yet another level the 'Bilder' acknowledge the bruising force of materiality, thereby mounting a critique of the Bildungsroman by invoking the energies of novelistic realism. So these 'Bilder', as we have already noted, have a fierce present-tense immediacy; in their hammering simultaneity they crowd in upon and threaten the individual subject. This rhetorical particularity of *Panorama* gives it a modernist feel; one is reminded of Alfred Döblin's *Berlin Alexanderplatz* or Ingeborg Bachmann's *Malina*. Such resonances challenge the Bildungroman as being too serenely humanistic and high-bourgeois to be able to speak to the fracturings and discontinuities of our world. Yet these fracturings are not allowed to prevail. In the attention paid throughout the novel to Josef's thought processes we constantly hear an urgency of ethical debate, a will to connectedness. In his invocation of the realist and modernist mode Adler offers sustained criticism of the Bildungsroman tradition. But he does so from within — and with much reluctance and heartache, one feels. He will not relinquish his hold on some kind of humanist legacy.

So what finally is left standing? Perhaps the need, against all the odds, come hell and high water, to cherish the novel's ability to give an account of what potentially or actually happens when a human self awakes to the forms and processes of its being in the world. That is, of course, a perennial theme in European literature; and it has been explored with incomparable sophistication by the German Bildugsroman, by the realistic novel, by the modernist novel. We would be infinitely poorer without such novels — and without Adler's complexly attuned engagement with all three of them by the narrative richness of his *Roman in zehn Bildern*. The writer in exile still writes in German, in the language whose culture was a threat to him and his protagonist. He still writes wonderfully well in that language. And that, surely, is no small miracle.

Notes to Chapter 9

1. H. G. Adler, 'Sonderinterview von Alfred Joachim Fischer', in *Zu Hause im Exil: Zu Werk und Person H. G. Adlers*, ed. by Heinrich Hubmann and Alfred O. Lanz (Stuttgart: Steiner, 1987), pp. 191–201 (p. 192).

2. H. G. Adler, *Panorama. Roman in zehn Bildern* (Munich: Piper, 1988), p. 10. H. G. Adler, *Panorama*, trans. by Peter Filkins (New York: Random House, 2011), p. 4. All further references to both German and English translation will be made to these editions with the abbreviations *P* and *PE* respectively.

3. Helen Finch, 'Holocaust Translation, Communication and Witness in the Work of H. G. Adler', *German Life and Letters*, 68.3 (2015), 427–43 (p. 441).

4. Ann and John J. White, '"Die Vermächtnisse von Schloß Launceston": Darstellung und Überwindung des Bösen in Hans Günther Adlers Roman *Panorama*', in *Zu Hause im Exil: Zu Werk und Person H. G. Adlers*, ed. by Heinrich Hubmann and Alfred O. Lanz (Stuttgart: Steiner, 1987), pp. 32–43 (p. 37).

5. Martin Swales, *The German 'Bildungsroman' from Wieland to Hesse* (Princeton, NJ: Princeton University Press, 1978).

6. Cf. Finch, 'Holocaust Translation'.

CHAPTER 10

❖

'To be human is to have a border, and to want to cross it through letters': Letters and Letter Writers in H. G. Adler's Novel *The Wall*[1]

Julia Menzel

Borders, barriers, and 'tabooed zones'[2] shape the inner life of Arthur Landau, the protagonist and narrator of H. G. Adler's novel *The Wall*,[3] who has survived catastrophic events. Despite the fact that these events remain a 'blind spot'[4] in the novel, as they are neither named nor explicitly described, they clearly refer to the Holocaust.[5] Even though Adler's protagonist has survived, his traumatic experiences keep separating him from 'any continuum' (*WE* 39) ['Ich habe kein Teil an einem Kontinuum' (*W* 45)]: Having lost his parents and his wife and left his hometown Prague for a 'belated exile'[6] in London after his return from the camps,[7] Landau is unable to resume his former life. Moreover, the imaginary yet impenetrable wall Landau feels himself living behind also separates him from his former self. This imaginary wall that is present throughout the novel can be read, as Sven Kramer points out, as a metaphor for 'the presence of an absence'[8] in the survivor's consciousness. The unity of Landau's self has been destroyed, since his devastating experiences 'rest behind the wall',[9] remain inaccessible to him and, thus, cannot be articulated and turned into a coherent life story: 'What lies between the time when I was me and now, when this is no longer true? This cannot be completely forgotten, but it resists being articulated, for it digs in, puts up borders that cannot be crossed.' (*WE* 47–48) ['Was liegt nun zwischen der Zeit, da ich war, und der Zeit, da dies nicht mehr zutrifft? Dies kann nicht ganz vergessen sein, aber es sträubt sich, ein Sagbares zu bilden, es verwehrt sich, setzt Grenzen, die nicht überfahren werden dürfen.' (*W* 54)] Landau also uses the complex metaphor of the wall to describe his present situation in London, where he repeatedly but unsuccessfully attempts to achieve academic and social recognition. He summarizes his sense of alienation as follows: 'I don't belong to human society. I and the wall, we are alone, we belong together; there is nothing else that I belong to' (*WE* 39) ['Da sehe ich ein, daß ich der menschlichen Gesellschaft nicht angehöre. Ich und die Wand, wir sind

allein, wir gehören zusammen; einem anderen Verband bin ich nicht angeschlossen'
(*W* 45)].

Landau's feeling of being separated from 'any continuum' (*WE* 39) corresponds to
the novel's nonlinear plot.[10] As Kirstin Gwyer points out, Adler's novel

> seek[s] to undermine causality, continuity, and teleology. [...] Time sequences
> appear jumbled and even layered, as we often cannot be sure if what we are
> reading belongs to the narrative present or the past of recollection, or if it is the
> mark of the past in the present.[11]

Landau's state of mind, which has been permanently altered by the devastating
events and experiences, also manifests itself in terrifying, Kafkaesque nightmares
and daydreams,[12] which haunt the protagonist and which are represented in the
novel 'through the connected disorder of an extended chain of thought'.[13]

Even though the traumatic experiences are not and will not be the past for
Landau, he nevertheless senses a 'new beginning' (*WE* 559) ['Neubeginn' (*W* 581)],
which he considers to be both a 'commitment and sacrifice to the future' (*WE* 559)
['die Aufgabe und das Opfer in die Zukunft' (*W* 582)] and an obligation 'to preserve
what we can preserve' (*WE* 559) ['wir wollen bewahren, was sich nur bewahren
läßt' (*W* 581)] from the past. As Kramer explains, this new beginning is, on the one
hand and most importantly, related to Landau's second wife, Johanna, and their two
children.[14] On the other hand, it is Landau's writing that allows him not only to
work through, but also to distance himself from the past.[15] As Landau puts it, 'Only
through language can we conjure, can we try to save something.' (*WE* 290) ['Nur
durch die Sprache können wir zaubern, Rettungsversuche.' (*W* 305)][16]

Several scholars have already drawn attention to the important fact that Adler's
novel is a fictitious manuscript written by its protagonist and first-person narrator.
Even if the writing of this manuscript does not allow Landau to 'restore the lost
identity', it still enables him to 'map[...] the traumatized regions of his mind and
thus [to] arrive[...] at averting the overwhelming'.[17] Yet, two other facets of Landau's
writing have not been analyzed so far: First, Adler's text not only presents Landau as
the narrator of the manuscript, it also shows him as a writer of letters, as parts of the
narrative are conveyed through one or more letters that are written by or addressed
to him. Second, Landau is also the author of a fictional text: Readers are presented
with a metadiegetic narrative entitled *The Letter Writers*, a story within the story.
Landau also reflects on what this essay will refer to as the 'mediatory property',[18]
that is, the potential and function of the letter form.[19]

My reading of *The Wall* will focus on these two different modes of the novel's
repeated 'turn to the epistolary'[20] and will examine its use of the letter form and its
emphasis on letter writing: First, Landau's attempts to represent his experiences of
surviving the Holocaust in his correspondence and to find an epistolary language
that allows him to convey to his addressees what he has lived through will be
investigated. Second, the metadiegetic narrative *The Letter Writers* will be analyzed.
Landau himself claims that this narrative says 'more about me and my thinking than
I have ever managed to express in my scholarly work' (*WE* 319) ['sie [sagt] mehr
von mir und meinem Denken aus[...], als es mir je in meinen wissenschaftlichen

Versuchen gelungen ist' (*W* 334)]. Moreover, this story within the story gives a different account of the experience of exile: The lost home that is described in *The Letter Writers* is 'much more than merely a place of habitation'.[21] By examining this particular exile experience, this article aims to illuminate one specific facet of the notion of exile in Adler's work.

Exploring the novel's depiction of the characteristics of the letter-writing situation and its use of epistolary elements, the article wishes to answer the question of why *The Wall* repeatedly refers to the letter form in order to tell the story of Arthur Landau.

'If you don't exist, write letters, so that you exist': Arthur Landau's Letters

Letters have an existential function for Landau. Having returned to his native city after the war, he recognizes that '[n]o one could know that I was alive, therefore I had to write' (*WE* 193) ['Man wisse nicht, daß ich bin, deshalb müsse ich schreiben' (*W* 203)]. In his writing, Landau uses the letter as a medium that bridges the spatial 'gap between self and other'.[22] Thus, it is well suited for the transmission of information between himself and those of his friends who, able to escape, survived in exile. The letter, however, also has many other, and perhaps more important, functions.[23] Anne Bower, for instance, argues that the letter also allows the letter writer to 'present a personal self-definition', to write or 'rewrite the self'.[24] This function is of utmost importance for Landau, whose traumatic experiences have permanently cut him off from his past and who, therefore, has the 'feeling that he is someone who has "ceased to exist [...]"'.[25] In addition, after leaving his homeland for a new beginning in the metropolis of London, Landau learns that even here, in his 'belated exile',[26] '[t]he order of the day was such that I did not exist within it' (*WE* 191) ['[d]ie Tagesordnung war hergestellt, in der ich nicht vorhanden war' (*W* 201)].[27]

Faced with the situation 'that you did not exist if you did not exist' (*WE* 191) ['daß man nicht war, wenn man auch war' (*W* 201)], Landau remembers once having read the sentence '"If you don't exist, write letters, so that you exist"' (*WE* 191) ['Wenn du nicht bist, schreib Briefe, daß du wirst' (*W* 201)]. Therefore, his letters aim to serve as self-constitutive acts. This is especially true for the first one, which is addressed to his best friend from before the war, whom he calls So-and-So. Landau's very first impulsive attempt to commit his experiences to paper results in a description of his misery: 'A portrait of my sufferings poured out of me. I suddenly said, after many long sentences, "Death."' (*WE* 195) ['[...] ein Bildnis meiner Verderbnisse entfesselte sich ungehemmt. Ich sagte kurz nach langen Sätzen: der Tod.' (*W* 205)] Even if Landau thinks that he has 'not gone too far' with this account in its 'fragmentary manner', he nevertheless is afraid that any representation might seem 'exaggerated' and 'suspect to the recipient' (*WE* 195) ['In einem Briefe behaupten, das war die unerreichbare Kunst, mich behaupten und den Angesprochenen überzeugen, daß der Brief auch wirklich von mir stammte und keine plumpe Fälschung sei, die der Empfänger mißtrauisch oder ärgerlich verwerfen würde' (*W* 205)]. Hence, he struggles to find the right words: 'How do you speak to someone when in fact you are not dead? Which words can convey the truth, such that the person believes you?' (*WE* 195) ['Wie spricht man einen Menschen an, wenn man nicht gestorben ist? Welche Worte vermitteln die Wahrheit, damit dieser Mensch einem glaubt?' (*W* 205)]. His roommate Peter offers the following simple advice: '"You write about what you experienced."' (*WE* 195) ['"Du schreibst, was du erlebt hast".' (*W* 205)] This advice makes Landau realize that he needs to turn his experiences into a narrative, that is, into 'a story with a discrete beginning, middle, and end',[28] to be understood:

> What had I experienced? There was no beginning, and thus I had not experienced anything. I had to find something, a story. [...] One had to tell it, just how it happened, first one day, then another, then. Yes, then... What happened then? [...] No matter how hard I tried, conjuring up a useful fable was not my forte. (*WE* 195–96)

> [Was hatte ich erlebt? Es gab keinen Anfang, und so hatte ich nichts erlebt. Ich hätte etwas finden müssen, eine Geschichte. [...] Man mußte das erzählen können, wie sich alles fortsetzte, wieder ein Tag, noch einer, dann. Ja, dann... Wie war das? [...] So sehr ich mich auch anstrengte, das Erfinden einer nützlichen Fabel war meine Sache nicht. (*W* 205–06)]

By writing to So-and-So, Landau forces himself 'to patch back together what had been torn apart' (*WE* 202) ['dort anzuknüpfen, wo einst abgerissen wurde' (*W* 213)].

Adler's protagonist seeks to patch together his own history, but also to write a letter that 'at least could be answered' (*WE* 202) ['was sich verantworten ließ' (*W* 213)], as he says. *The Wall* illustrates how the self-constitutive act of writing a letter is always influenced by the letter's addressee, who is present throughout the writing process.[29] Thus, in his letter to So-and-So, Landau's 'I becomes defined relative to the *you* whom he addresses':[30]

> Look, I have indeed reappeared before you — in written fashion, yes, and yet almost directly. It's my handwriting. It hasn't improved with the years but, rather, the other way round, yet you will certainly recognize it and think, indeed, it's the same old me. (*WE* 197)

> [Sieh an, ich bin da eben vor Dir aufgetaucht, nur schriftlich freilich, aber doch fast unmittelbar. Es ist meine Schrift, sie hat sich in den Jahren nicht gebessert, eher umgekehrt, doch wirst Du sie sicher erkennen und denken, beileibe, er ist der alte geblieben. (*W* 208)]

Landau's letter to his old friend is not included as one single text in the novel; instead, Adler foregrounds the writing process by interspersing the text of the letter with various asides.[31] By doing so, Adler illustrates Landau's struggle to conjure up a useful fable (see *WE* 196), that is, a story that would satisfy him and presumably his reader and that could, therefore, function as a bridge between the letter writer and his reader. Thus, the writing process is not only shaped by Landau's experiences, but also by that of his addressee. For instance, Landau starts writing to So-and-So about the death of a mutual friend not because he thinks So-and-So does not know about tragedies such as this one, but to share his grief and his distress with someone. But then he stops because he realizes So-and-So has not had the necessary experience to properly understand, remarking to himself: 'No, I can't expect So-and-So to understand such painful matters. It was smarter not to mention anything that could upset my friend. I erased the last two sentences and wrote something else.' (*WE* 199) ['Nein, solche peinlichen Dinge durfte ich Soundso nicht zumuten. Es war klüger, an nichts zu rühren, was den Freund hätte aufregen können. Ich tilgte die zwei letzten Absätze und schrieb anders weiter.' (*W* 210)]

As Helen Finch emphasizes, the seemingly tranquil and optimistic character of Landau's first letter to So-and-So should not only be regarded as a result of his wish not to burden his old friend with detailed descriptions of the horrors he has suffered, but also, and above all, as a sign or symptom of the 'evidently traumatized textuality of Landau's letter itself'.[32] This traumatized textuality manifests itself most obviously in Landau's account or, rather, lack thereof, of the death of his first wife, Franziska:[33]

> Also, Franziska is gone. But, really, no more of such sad matters. I'm taking good care of myself; I don't let myself go and have not given up on life. And so it goes on. If you could see how I'm sitting here by an open window in the almost-summer-like foliage that still looks out unchanged at the wonderful vineyard, you would smile and shake your head and say, 'That's Arthur, just like I always knew him.' (*WE* 202)

> [Auch Franziska ist gegangen. Aber nun wirklich nichts mehr von traurigen Dingen. Ich habe mich gut in der Hand, ich lasse nicht locker und habe mit meinem Leben nicht abgerechnet. So wird es auch vorangehen. Könntest Du mich sehen, wie ich hier beim offenen Fenster sitze und in das fast noch sommerliche Laubwerk der unverändert herrlichen Weinbergschanze hinausblicke, so würdest Du lächelnd den Kopf schütteln und gestehen: Das ist der Artur, wie ich ihn immer kannte. (*W* 212)]

Janet Altman argues that the letter tends 'to define itself in terms of polarities such as portrait/mask, presence/absence, bridge/barrier'.[34] These polarities also characterize the letters written by Landau: He aims to express himself to the greatest possible extent and wants his letters to build bridges. Because of the traumatic nature of the experiences he is trying to convey, however, his lines contain nothing that really speaks to his situation, and Landau senses this. (See *WE* 203) In other words, he fears that his letters may not allow him to convey what it feels like to live behind the wall and to be unable to recover his past.

Despite these problems of entering into a true dialogue in letter form, problems that are, on the one hand, inherent to the medium itself and, on the other hand, exacerbated by the very different experiences of the correspondents, the desire for an exchange remains the fundamental impulse behind Landau's writing.[35] This desire for exchange means the answers to Landau's letters are crucial to him. Altman points out that, as writing a letter is 'defin[ing] oneself in relationship to a particular you', '[i]n no other form of dialogue does the speaker await a reply so breathlessly; in no other type of verbal exchange does the mere fact of receiving a response carry such meaning'.[36] This is also true for Landau. As he puts it,

I [...] wrote [...] more and more letters to those who once knew me, people that I was looking to contact, for now I was the one who wished to find them in the hope of recognizing myself through them, of living through them. (*WE* 217)

[Auch ich habe viel geschrieben, immer mehr Briefe, an alle, die mich einst kannten, Menschen, die ich suchte, denn nun war ich es, der sie finden wollte im Wunsche, mich in ihnen anzuerkennen in ihnen zu sein [...]. (*W* 228)]

Therefore, his letters not only seek, but depend on a response:[37] ' "A letter left unanswered can be tantamount to a murder!" ' (*WE* 414) [' "Ein nicht beantworteter Brief kann manchmal fast ein Mord sein!" ' (*W* 432)]

Some of his letters remain, however, unanswered, other responses arrive late. But even when Landau receives answers, he does not feel that he is truly addressed:

[F]inally, a letter [...] arrived, which I opened hastily, yet there was nothing in it, the words empty, barely hanging together [...]. [...] I bent over the sheet and turned it every which way. Unfortunately it was true [...], [t]he letter was empty and was not a letter at all. [...] The only thing that helped was that a letter had at last arrived; this I told myself with satisfaction and plucked out individual words. I did so again and kept doing so, thinking about what they meant. [...] An answer to my letter it was not, all of it strange and dark [...]. (*WE* 192)

[Und kam dann endlich doch [...] ein Brief, den ich hastig öffnete, stand nichts darin, die Worte leer, sie hingen kaum zusammen [...]. Ich beugte mich nochmals über den Bogen und kehrte ihn nach allen Richtungen. Leider stimmte es, [...] der Brief war leer und also war es kein Brief. [...] Nun war mir doch nur wohler, ein Brief ist angekommen; das sagte ich mir zufrieden und pflückte die Worte einzeln ab. Ich tat es nochmals und wiederholt, ich dachte nach, was sie vermitteln sollten [...]. Antwort auf meine Briefe war das nicht, alles fremd und dunkel [...]. (*W* 202)]

Longing for a 'real answer' ['[d]aß ich zu einem Ziele gelange'], Landau proofreads his own letters 'almost with the pressing need of a prayer' (*WE* 193) ['fast mit der Dringlichkeit des Gebetes' (*W* 203)] to verify, with this 'switch in perspective',[38] that his lines are 'perfectly understandable' (*WE* 193) ['man mußte sie verstehen' (*W* 203)]. In other words, Landau gives his all: 'I put myself into the letters, me, in order that they be comprehensible.' (*WE* 193) ['mich gab ich in den Briefen, mich, daß es faßbar werde.' (*W* 203)] The letters that he receives, in contrast, only contain polite but meaningless phrases, such as ' "unfortunately" or "noncommittal" or "perhaps" ' (*WE* 192) [' "leider" oder "unverbindlich" und "vielleicht" ' (*W* 202)].

Even the answer from So-and-So, which is embedded as one single text in *The Wall* and, thereby, introduces a different voice into the novel,[39] does by no means meet Landau's expectations or needs. (See *WE* 208–15) Finch stresses that So-and-So 'deliberately misrecogni[zes]'[40] Landau's actual situation and state of mind. Showing neither true compassion nor offering real support, So-and-So elaborates on the difficulties he is confronted with and asks Landau to help him restore his former property. Instead of feeling addressed, Landau feels abandoned after having read the letter from his best friend from before the war. (See *WE* 216–17.)

The mediatory property of the letter could allow Landau to (re-)connect with the world; the letters that he receives only serve, however, to increase the distance and leave him even more isolated than before.[41] This sense of isolation is not only pervasive in Landau's private, but also in his professional life. Landau, who thinks of books as 'letters to the world' (*WE* 313) ['Briefe an die ganze Welt' (*W* 328)], learns that his works — especially his book project *The Sociology of Oppressed People*, which is meant to be his contribution to the debates on the Holocaust — are being rejected precisely because of his dual status as a scholar and a survivor. (See *WE* 96–98, 214)

Landau's reaction to this multi-faceted, 'insolvable conflict' ['unlösbare[r] Konflikt'] between himself, the world and the wall is to do 'something I never thought of doing before in my life. I wrote a story' (*WE* 318) ['etwas, woran ich in meinem Leben zuvor nie gedacht hatte. Ich schrieb eine Geschichte' (*W* 333)]. This story, the metadiegetic narrative *The Letter Writers*, is included in its entirety in the novel and set off from the rest of the text.[42]

Letters Addressed to the Lord: The Metadiegetic Narrative *The Letter Writers*

The Letter Writers relates the story of the breaking of the 'epistolary pact', which is expressed by the 'call for response'[43] inherent in every letter, it is a story about the absence of responses. In this story, the number of letters mailed every single day is characterized as 'astronomical' (*WE* 327) ['astronomisch[]' (*W* 341)], and yet 'no letter writer has ever received an answer back' (*WE* 320) ['noch nie hat ein Briefschreiber Antwort empfangen' (*W* 335)]. The narrator of this story within a story, however, mentions the existence of 'rumors' ['Gerüchte'] concerning 'responses found here and there' ['Antworten, die da oder dort eingetroffen seien'] and 'traces of a family tradition that says a grandfather once received a response, but which he showed to no one, though from that moment on he was supposedly happy' (*WE* 323) ['bestenfalls kommt man einer Familientradition auf die Spur, daß ein Großvater einmal Antwort empfangen, sie aber keinem gezeigt habe, doch sei er von dieser Stunde an glücklich gewesen' (*W* 337)]. The dubious character of these 'very old legends' (*WE* 323) ['sehr alte Legenden' (*W* 337)] becomes even more evident when the narrator admits that replies cannot be received for simple practical reasons: 'From whom should the responses come? In serious circles, it is surmised that among the trove of still current addresses the overwhelming majority of the names are made up or invented' (*WE* 323) ['Von wem sollten denn die Antworten stammen? Wird doch in ernsten Kreisen geschätzt, daß in dem derzeit benützten Adressenschatz die überwältigende Mehrzahl der Namen erlogen oder erfunden sei' (*W* 338)]. Consequently, the narrator indicates that 'you cannot expect that a response will ever come' (*WE* 329) ['es [ist] nicht zu erwarten, daß je eine Antwort empfangen wird' (*W* 343)]. Nevertheless and apparently against all reason, all letter writers remain hopeful and assume 'that an original response will be received' (*WE* 323) ['daß ursprünglich Antworten kamen' (*W* 337)] someday: 'It's pointless, [...] but this doesn't keep [...] humanity from waiting with determination and concentrated patience for the great miracle to occur.' (*WE* 329) ['Es ist vergeblich, [...] aber das hindert die [...] Menschheit nicht, zähe und mit geballter Geduld fortzufahren und auf das große Wunder zu harren.' (*W* 343)]

According to an 'ancient legend' (*WE* 320) ['uralte Sage' (*W* 335)] recounted in the metadiegetic narrative, the widespread custom of writing letters was invented by Adam: Adam, banished from the Garden of Eden as punishment for eating the forbidden fruit of the tree of knowledge and for hiding from the Lord, suddenly became aware of his own mortality. As he wanted the Lord to know about his struggle with finitude, he chiseled a sign of his wish into a stone and tossed that stone in the direction of the cherubim who protected the tree of life (see *WE* 321): 'Thus did Adam, according to the legend, invent the letter, and the first letter was a wish tossed toward the Paradise that had been lost.' (*WE* 322) ['So hat Adam, der Legende nach, den Brief erfunden, und der erste Brief war ein versuchter Wurf nach dem verlorenen Paradies.' (*W* 336)]

The last sentences of Landau's story point to a general truth about the situation of letter writers. They all share Adam's fate,

> [...] for they wish to live and affirm themselves, they want to survive and achieve something, they having persevered from generation to generation, which has encouraged them to think that eventually they will be saved. They sit at home in their lairs and wait to be called, dreaming of the day when they can leave behind the awareness of good and evil, and at last be able to say to the unknown familiar recipient of their letters, 'Lord, where are you?' But, as long as the Lord does not answer, each person affirms each day the truth of the ancient legends — namely, that each letter is like that first attempted toss of a stone at a lost Paradise. (*WE* 329)

> [[...] sie wollen leben und sich behaupten, sie wollen ausdauern und vollenden, sie haben ausgeharrt von Geschlecht zu Geschlecht, und das bestärkt sie, daß sie auch fernerhin sich bewahren werden. Sie sitzen zu Hause in ihren Verstecken und warten, daß man sie rufe, und träumen dabei vom Tage, an dem sie in der Erkenntnis des Guten und Bösen hinaustreten werden, den allerletzten unbekannt vertrauten Empfänger ihrer Briefe zu rufen: 'Herr, wo bist du?' Solange aber der Herr nicht antworten wird, bestätigt sich täglich jedem Menschen die Wahrheit der alten Legende, daß jeder Brief, wie schon der erste, ein versuchter Wurf nach dem verlorenen Paradies ist. (*W* 344)]

Composing the parable *The Letter Writers*, Landau explores and responds to his own post-war situation and his complex emotional state, to his hopes, difficulties and disappointments described in the previous section of this essay. His sense of isolation closely resembles the fate of the letter writers and their fruitless wait for responses.[44] Moreover, Landau repeatedly refers to himself as Adam throughout the novel.[45] By creating this alter ego, Landau not only illustrates his self-perception as 'something that is split into pieces' (*WE* 451) ['etwas Aufgespaltenes' (*W* 470)], it also, at the same time, allows him to (re-)construct his own self by mirroring it in the story of Adam. Besides, Landau's identification with Adam indicates that Adler's novel aims to examine universal questions by depicting an individual fate.[46] This becomes even more evident at the level of the metadiegetic narrative embedded into *The Wall*.

As suggested above, the parable *The Letter Writers* depicts not only Landau's life, but also a 'general fate' (*WE* 329) ['allgemeine[s] Schicksal[]' (*W* 344)]. Landau is very clear about this:

I think of the letter as a primary symbol of the person who has been excluded from something. And every person is excluded, every person reaches a border, no matter how many different ones may be drawn, some closer for some, for others farther away, [...] often not known or recognized, and yet the root of all human misery, [...] the source of our behavior and [...] of all despair and hope. To be human is to have a border, and to want to cross it through letters that will reach beyond to their goal. (*WE* 318–19)

[ich begriff den Brief als Grundsymbol des Menschen, der von etwas ausgeschlossen ist. Und jeder Mensch ist ausgeschlossen, jeder Mensch erfährt die Grenze, mag sie noch so verschieden gezogen sein, beim einen enger, beim anderen weiter, [...] oft nicht gewußt und nicht gekannt, dennoch als Wurzel alles menschlichen Leides, [...] als Quelle unseres Verhaltens [...], als Ursprung aller Verzweiflung und Hoffnung. Mensch sein, das ist eine Grenze haben und sie mit Briefen überfliegen zu wollen, daß sie jenseits davon ihr Ziel erreichen. (*W* 333–34)]

Thus, Landau suggests that his story aims to describe what it means to be human. In addition, the parable itself clearly refers to the human condition in general, as it describes Adam's fate: Adam is not only the proper name for a character in the Book of Genesis, but also a Hebrew collective noun meaning humankind.[47] This 'interplay between the individual Adam and the collective "humankind"' that characterizes 'the nature of Adam'[48] in the biblical story of the Fall is also crucial for the nature of Adam in the metadiegetic narrative *The Letter Writers*.[49] In other words, in order to capture an essential aspect of human existence, the protagonist of Adler's novel *The Wall* tells a story about letter writers.

The attempt to comprehend what it means to be human that is made in this metadiegetic narrative is, of course, complex; only three possible layers of meaning will be mentioned in the following and only one of them can be explored in greater detail. First, to be human, as suggested by *The Letter Writers*, could mean to be left without any answers, to be excluded from any true dialogue, to be thrown back upon oneself but to hold on to the idea that receiving a response is possible. Second, a 'defining aspect of human existence' might be another boundary or limit, namely that every 'human individual is *fundamentally* finite'.[50] More specifically, the supposed ancient legend of Adam as the inventor of the letter shows that it is not only 'finitude itself, but the *awareness* of finitude, [that] is constitutive of the human condition'.[51] Third and perhaps most importantly, the metadiegetic narrative describes the expulsion of Adam and Eve from the Garden of Eden and, thus, relates the 'story of the first exiles'.[52] As Steven Burr argues in his book *Finite Transcendence: Existential Exile and the Myth of Home*, Adam and Eve become 'most fully and irrevocably human'[53] by being exiled:

[T]he myth of the Fall suggests not merely that the Fall is an exile, but more precisely that exile is itself a fall into humanity. [...] Adam and Eve, as the first humans, represent not just the *origin* of the human but also the essence of what 'human' *means* — imperfect, limited, finite, banished from their original home.[54]

This experience of exile is depicted in the metadiegetic narrative embedded into

The Wall as an experience shared by Adam, the first human and inventor of the letter, and all letter writers that came after him. This experience is, thus, regarded as an 'ever-present component of human reality'.[55] As suggested by *The Letter Writers* and Landau's commentary on his own story, to be human, then, is 'to be exiled'.[56]

Burr points out, however, that '[w]hile exile invariably entails a looking back at the past and what was, it likewise implies a looking forward toward what is hoped to be again'.[57] This is also true for the exiles portrayed in Landau's story, who have not just lost their original home, but who also maintain 'a devoted hope for its restoration'.[58] More specifically, the end of the metadiegetic narrative explains that the letter writers, who share Adam's fate, long for the undoing of the Fall and, hence, for the retrieval of 'the Paradise that had been lost' (*WE* 322) ['d[as] verlorene[] Paradies' (*W* 336)]. Thus, even though the home depicted in Landau's story has been lost, there still is an 'inherent, intimate connection'[59] with it.

This story of the letter writers who have to live away from home but remain connected to it, who do not give up writing letters despite the fact that an answer will probably never be received, provides a clue for Adler's protagonist how to respond to his own situation. Landau remarks that he has learned something from his text (see *WE* 330):

> To give in but not to give up — that's what was needed. To slam into the wall as if it were not there, [...] yet to acknowledge it and not doubt such knowledge of it [...]. [...] To write letters but not to expect an answer, though not to waste one's desires by the hour writing to false idols but, rather, only to make a plea out of a continually obsessed conscience, a plea directed at someone beyond all borders. (*WE* 330)

> [Ergeben sein, aber nicht nachgeben, darauf kommt es an. Der Wand entgegenlaufen, als stünde sie nicht da, [...] doch anerkennen und nicht zu sehr über die Kenntnis verzweifeln [...]. [...] Briefe schreiben, aber auf die Antwort verzichten, doch keine Briefe an die Götzen stündlicher Wünsche verzetteln, nur das eine Gesuch im unablässig heimgesuchten Gewissen, das eine Gesuch an den einen über alle Grenzen hinweg. (*W* 344)]

Landau's thoughts indicate that he is confronted with different kinds of borders, different experiences of exile. There are primarily four kinds of exile: First, he has been displaced from his homeland. This physical separation from a particular place corresponds to the origins of the term exile.[60] And yet, as Burr emphasizes, ' "exile" cannot be limited to reference to the purely physical and immediate separation of an individual from one's home'.[61] Thus, and second, the unsurmountable wall that stands between Landau, his own past and the world is another dimension of exile depicted in *The Wall*. (See *WE* 318) Third, the metadiegetic narrative *The Letter Writers* and Landau's reflections on this story suggest that exile may also be thought of as an important if not the most important aspect of the human condition. Seen in this light, exile 'holds the key to understanding human nature'.[62] As suggested by the parable embedded into the novel, to be in exile — and this is the fourth way of understanding it in the novel — may also mean to be 'exiled from the Divine into "human" existence' or to be 'exiled from the presence of God'.[63] The last two kinds of exile represent more universal experiences than Landau's and the metaphysical[64] and 'theological ground'[65] of both narrative levels. Because of these layers of meaning and additional dimensions to the main character,[66] Adler's portrayal of the Holocaust survivor Landau is both a nuanced exploration of traumatic experiences and an investigation of the relationship between these experiences and what Adler regards as the general human condition.

The Letter as a Key Mechanism in *The Wall*

Whereas exile is portrayed as the prevailing physical, mental, emotional and spiritual condition of Arthur Landau, the protagonist and narrator of H. G. Adler's novel *The Wall*, the medium of the letter is described as having the potential ability to reconnect relations that have been ruptured or broken.[67] A letter can cross geographical borders; it allows its writer to perform a self-constitutive act and to establish a relationship with another person. Finally, letters also provide an opportunity for an encounter with the Divine if understood as prayers, as, to use Landau's images, stones tossed at a lost Paradise. (See *WE* 321–22)

On the other hand, the 'perpetual experience of absence'[68] is a fundamental characteristic of the letter writing situation.[69] Moreover, as Anne Bower points out, '[l]etters force us to perceive the distressing gap that always exists between self and other, between articulation and feeling, and between our words and the thing they "stand for"'.[70]

These paradoxical characteristics of the letter form not only correspond to, but also explicitly articulate[71] Landau's constant struggle to scale the wall, although he is aware that he is unlikely to succeed. Thus, the way Adler engages the letter form creates meaning,[72] as it foregrounds problems and questions that are essential to the novel as a whole.[73] Using epistolary elements and depicting crucial characteristics of the practice of letter writing in his novel *The Wall*, Adler explores themes such as identity, exile and belonging, addresses the question of faith and asks what it means to be human. In addition, the emphasis on the letter form allows Adler to investigate the potential and limits of language as a means of communication. As Adler's other works, *The Wall* foregrounds the promises of language and writing. As Arthur Landau, a man of letters in more than one sense of the word, puts it: 'Only through language can we conjure, can we try to save something.' (*WE* 290) ['Nur durch die Sprache können wir zaubern, Rettungsversuche.' (*W* 305)]

Notes to Chapter 10

1. I am grateful to Micha Edlich of the Leuphana University of Lüneburg, who read the manuscript more than once and offered numerous suggestions for improvements in argument and style.
2. Sven Kramer, 'Belated Exile in H. G. Adler's Novel *Die unsichtbare Wand*', in *Exile and Otherness: New Approaches to the Experience of the Nazi Refugees*, ed. by Alexander Stephan, Exile Studies: An interdisciplinary series, 11 (Oxford: Peter Lang, 2005), pp. 227–48 (p. 233).
3. H. G. Adler, *The Wall: A Novel*, trans. by Peter Filkins (New York: Modern Library, 2014). The manuscript of *The Wall* was written and revised several times between 1954 and 1961, but only published posthumously in 1989 under the German title *Die unsichtbare Wand* (H. G. Adler, *Die unsichtbare Wand: Roman*, with an afterword by Jürgen Serke (Vienna: Zsolnay, 1989)). See Ruth

Vogel-Klein, '"I Have Lost Myself": H. G. Adler's Novel *The Wall* and the Damaged Identity of the Survivor', in *H. G. Adler: Life, Literature, Legacy*, ed. by Julia Creet, Sara R. Horowitz, and Amira Bojadzija-Dan (Evanston, IL: Northwestern University Press, 2016), pp. 229–47 (p. 231). Vogel-Klein also notes that only the English title met Adler's expectation (see ibid., pp. 232–33). All further quotations from both the English and German of Adler's novel will be taken from these editions and references will be given in parentheses in the text with the abbreviations *WE* and *W.*

4. See Vogel-Klein, 'I Have Lost Myself', p. 241–43.
5. See Kramer, 'Belated Exile', pp. 233–34.
6. Ibid., p. 227.
7. Peter Filkins investigates the complex relation between the fictional and the autobiographical in Adler's novels. See Peter Filkins, 'Introduction', in *The Wall: A Novel*, by H. G. Adler, trans. from the German by Peter Filkins (New York: Modern Library, 2014), pp. XI–XIX (pp. XII–XIII) and Peter Filkins, 'The Self Positioned, The (De)posited Self, The Soul Released: The Uses of Biography in H. G. Adler's Shoah Trilogy', in *H. G. Adler: Life, Literature, Legacy*, ed. by Julia Creet, Sara R. Horowitz, and Amira Bojadzija-Dan (Evanston, IL: Northwestern University Press, 2016), pp. 47–67.
8. Kramer, 'Belated Exile', p. 234. See also Thomas Krämer, who analyzes the different layers of this metaphor in greater detail: Thomas Krämer, *Die Poetik des Gedenkens: Zu den autobiographischen Romanen H. G. Adlers* (Würzburg: Königshausen & Neumann, 2012), pp. 213–18.
9. Kramer, 'Belated Exile', p. 234.
10. See Filkins, 'Introduction', pp. XIV–XV.
11. Kirstin Gwyer, *Encrypting the Past: The German-Jewish Holocaust Novel of the First Generation* (Oxford: Oxford University Press, 2014), p. 82. Gwyer argues that Adler's novels *The Journey* and *The Wall* depict chronological time as having been 'subverted, and along with it any notion of causation, coherent space, and independently cognizant subjectivity' (ibid., p. 74; see also pp. 69–87).
12. Vogel-Klein draws attention to the intertextual connections between Adler's novel and the works of Franz Kafka. See Vogel-Klein, 'I Have Lost Myself', pp. 239–41. See also Helen Finch, 'Prague Circles: H. G. Adler's Kafkaesque Hope', in *H. G. Adler: Life, Literature, Legacy*, ed. by Julia Creet, Sara R. Horowitz, and Amira Bojadzija-Dan (Evanston, IL: Northwestern University Press, 2016), pp. 251–72, especially pp. 267–68 and Martin Modlinger, 'The Kafkaesque in H. G. Adler's and W. G. Sebald's Literary Historiographies', in *Witnessing, Memory, Poetics: H. G. Adler and W. G. Sebald*, ed. by Helen Finch and Lynn L. Wolff (Rochester, NY: Camden House, 2014), pp. 201–31.
13. Filkins, 'Introduction', p. XIV.
14. See Kramer, 'Belated Exile', pp. 240–42.
15. See ibid., pp. 243–44; Sven Kramer, 'Die Politik der Erinnerung in H. G. Adlers Roman *Die unsichtbare Wand*', *Sprache im technischen Zeitalter*, 198 (2011), 220–27 (pp. 225–26).
16. For Adler's thoughts on the importance of language for human thought and behavior especially see H. G. Adler, 'Sprache am Verstummen', in *Orthodoxie des Herzens: Ausgewählte Essays zu Literatur, Judentum und Politik*, by H. G. Adler, ed. by and with an afterword by Peter Filkins, in collaboration with and with a foreword by Jeremy Adler (Konstanz: Konstanz University Press, 2014), pp. 105–13 and Lynn L. Wolff, '"Die Grenzen des Sagbaren": Toward a Political Philology in H. G. Adler's Reflections on Language', in *H. G. Adler: Life, Literature, Legacy*, ed. by Julia Creet, Sara R. Horowitz, and Amira Bojadzija-Dan (Evanston, IL: Northwestern University Press, 2016), pp. 273–301.
17. Kramer, 'Belated Exile', p. 247; see also ibid., pp. 243–44; Kramer, 'Die Politik der Erinnerung', pp. 225–26 and Krämer, *Die Poetik des Gedenkens*, pp. 230–32.
18. Janet Gurkin Altman, *Epistolarity: Approaches to a Form* (Columbus, OH: Ohio State University Press, 1982), p. 186.
19. See ibid., p. 4.
20. Anne Bower, *Epistolary Responses: The Letter in 20th-Century American Fiction and Criticism* (Tuscaloosa, AL: University of Alabama Press, 1997), p. 10.

21. Stephen A. Burr, *Finite Transcendence: Existential Exile and the Myth of Home* (Lanham: Lexington Books, 2014), p. IX.

22. Bower, *Epistolary Responses*, p. 14.

23. See Elke-Maria Clauss, 'Brief', in *Metzler Lexikon Literatur: Begriffe und Definitionen*, ed. by Dieter Burdorf, Christoph Fasbender and Burkhard Moeninghoff (Stuttgart: Metzler, 2007), pp. 98–99 (p. 98).

24. Bower, *Epistolary Responses*, p. 14. See also Clauss, 'Brief', p. 98.

25. Filkins, 'Introduction', p. XIII.

26. Kramer, 'Belated Exile', p. 227.

27. In his essays on German-speaking exiles in Great Britain, Jeremy Adler stresses that exile has, since ancient times, often been compared to death and equated with the loss of self. See Jeremy Adler, *Das bittere Brot: H. G. Adler, Elias Canetti und Franz Baermann Steiner im Londoner Exil*, with an afterword by Michael Krüger (Göttingen: Wallstein, 2015), pp. 7–8.

28. Hayden White, 'Historical Discourse and Literary Theory: On Saul Friedländer's *Years of Extermination*', in *Den Holocaust erzählen: Historiographie zwischen wissenschaftlicher Empirie und narrativer Kreativität*, ed. by Norbert Frei and Wulf Kansteiner (Göttingen: Wallstein, 2013), pp. 51–78 (p. 53).

29. See Altman, *Epistolarity*, pp. 89–91.

30. Ibid., p. 118. Emphasis in original.

31. See ibid., p. 89.

32. Helen Finch, '*Ressentiment* beyond Nietzsche and Améry: H. G. Adler between Literary *Ressentiment* and Divine Grace', in *Re-thinking Ressentiment: On the Limits of Criticism and the Limits of its Critics*, ed. by Jeanne Riou and Mary Gallagher (Bielefeld: transcript, 2016), pp. 71–86 (p. 83).

33. Helen Finch offers a similar argument (see ibid.).

34. Altman, *Epistolarity*, p. 186.

35. See ibid., p. 89.

36. Ibid., pp. 122, 121.

37. See Bower, *Epistolary Responses*, p. 6.

38. Altman, *Epistolarity*, p. 92.

39. See Wilhelm Füger, 'Der Brief als Bau-Element des Erzählens: Zum Funktionswandel des Einlagebriefes im neueren Roman, dargelegt am Beispiel von Dostojewski, Thomas Mann, Kafka und Joyce', *Deutsche Vierteljahresschrift für Literaturwissenschaft und Geistesgeschichte*, 51 (1977), 628–58 (pp. 636–37).

40. Finch, '*Ressentiment* beyond Nietzsche and Améry', p. 83. Finch points to the similarities and differences between the fictitious correspondence of Arthur Landau with So-and-So and Adler's actual post-war correspondence with his friend Franz Baermann Steiner (see ibid., pp. 82–84). Sven Kramer emphasizes the importance of H. G. Adler's correspondence with Bettina Gross for the positive shaping of their post-war lives. See Sven Kramer, 'Shaping Survival through Writing: H. G. Adler's Correspondence with Bettina Gross, 1945–1947', in *H. G. Adler: Life, Literature, Legacy*, ed. by Julia Creet, Sara R. Horowitz, and Amira Bojadzija-Dan (Evanston, IL: Northwestern University Press, 2016), pp. 69–85 and Sven Kramer, '"Über diesem Abgrund wölben wir unsere Liebe": Die Gegenwart der Toten und der Glücksanspruch der Überlebenden in H. G. Adler's Briefwechsel mit Bettina Gross, 1945–1946', in *Literatur und Anthropologie: H. G. Adler, Elias Canetti und Franz Baermann Steiner in London*, ed. by Jeremy Adler and Gesa Dane (Göttingen: Wallstein, 2014), pp. 138–57.

41. See Altman, *Epistolarity*, p. 186.

42. Adler had already drafted the parable in August 1938 in Milan, where he was preparing his emigration to Brazil. This plan ultimately and tragically failed, and as a result he had to move back to Prague (see Franz Hocheneder, *H. G. Adler (1910–1988): Privatgelehrter und freier Schriftsteller: Eine Monographie*, with a foreword by Wendelin Schmidt-Dengler (Vienna: Böhlau, 2009), pp. 62–66). This early version of *The Letter Writers*, which is kept at the Deutsche Literaturarchiv (German Literature Archive) in Marbach am Neckar, Germany, under the signature A II 14, essentially contains almost all the main ideas and central motifs of the text

that was, two decades later, integrated into the novel *The Wall*. The conception of Adam as the inventor of the letter was, however, added later to the parable.

43. Ibid., p. 89.
44. Thomas Krämer offers a similar reading of the text. See Krämer, *Die Poetik des Gedenkens*, pp. 248–49.
45. The relationship between Adler's protagonist Landau and his alter ego Adam has not yet been thoroughly investigated. The most detailed explanations have been given by Sven Kramer: see Kramer, 'Belated exile', pp. 237–39.
46. See also Krämer, *Die Poetik des Gedenkens*, p. 253.
47. See Ronald S. Hendel, 'Adam', in *Eerdmans Dictionary of the Bible*, ed. by David Noel Freedman, Allen C. Myers, and Astrid B. Beck (Grand Rapids, MI: Eerdmans, 2000), pp. 18–19 (p. 18).
48. See ibid.
49. In his essays on Judaism, Adler repeatedly comments on the story of the Fall and the expulsion from the Garden of Eden. Especially focusing on questions of guilt and mercy, Adler refers to the idea of a 'unity of humankind in Adam' (H. G. Adler, 'Vom Ursprung der Schuld- und Gnadengemeinschaft', in *Orthodoxie des Herzens: Ausgewählte Essays zu Literatur, Judentum und Politik*, by H. G. Adler, ed. by Peter Filkins with Jeremy Adler (Konstanz: Konstanz University Press, 2014), pp. 131–42 (p. 134). Original quotation: 'Einheit des Menschengeschlechts in Adam'). See also H. G. Adler, 'Verfolger und Verfolgte nach jüdischer Lehre', in *Orthodoxie des Herzens*, pp. 117–30 (pp. 127–28).
50. Burr, *Finite Transcendence*, p. 6. Emphasis in original.
51. Ibid., p. 8. Emphasis in original.
52. Ibid., pp. 54–55. See also Adler, *Das bittere Brot*, p. 7.
53. Burr, *Finite Transcendence*, p. 55.
54. Ibid., pp. 55–56. Emphasis in original. See also Stefana Sabin, *Die Welt als Exil* (Göttingen: Wallstein, 2008), p. 7.
55. Burr, *Finite Transcendence*, p. X.
56. Ibid., p. 56.
57. Ibid. p. 82.
58. Ibid., p. X. See also Sabin, *Die Welt als Exil*, p. 10.
59. Burr, *Finite Transcendence*, p. 51.
60. See ibid., p. 54.
61. Ibid.
62. Johannes F. Evelein, *Literary Exiles from Nazi Germany: Exemplarity and the Search for Meaning* (Rochester, NY: Camden House, 2014), p. 1.
63. Burr, *Finite Transcendence*, pp. 62, 63.
64. See the chapter 'What, Then, Is Exile? Toward a Metaphysics of Exile' in Evelein, *Literary Exiles from Nazi Germany*, pp. 111–40.
65. Jeremy Adler, 'Good Against Evil? H. G. Adler, T. W. Adorno and the Representation of the Holocaust', in *The German-Jewish Dilemma: From the Enlightenment to the Shoah*, ed. by Edward Timms and Andrea Hammel, with a preface by Werner E. Mosse (Lewiston, NY: Edwin Mellen Press, 1999), pp. 255–89 (p. 285).
66. The biblical dimension of Adler's thought becomes apparent, on the one hand, in his essays on Judaism and in his study *Vorschule für eine Experimentaltheologie* ('Introduction to an Experimental Theology'), which serves, as Jeremy Adler argues, 'as a spiritual foundation of his work' (Adler, 'Good Against Evil', p. 264) and connects its different parts and writings. On the other hand, it can also be observed in his literary and his other scholarly texts. Thomas Krämer, for instance, focuses on Adler's religiously grounded concept of 'Gedenken' ('remembrance') in his analysis of three of Adler's novels. For an investigation of biblical references in the novel *The Journey* and the study *Theresienstadt 1941–1945*, see Julia Menzel, 'Between "Nothing" and "Something": Narratives of Survival in H. G. Adler's Scholarly and Literary Analysis of the Shoah', *Leo Baeck Institute Year Book*, 61.1 (2016), 119–34. The biblical dimension of Adler's thought certainly requires further critical attention.
67. See Burr, *Finite Transcendence*, p. 50.

68. Ibid., p. 81.
69. See Bower, *Epistolary Responses*, p. 6.
70. Ibid., p. 16.
71. See Altman, *Epistolarity*, p. 212.
72. See ibid., p. 4.
73. See ibid., p. 212; Füger, 'Der Brief als Bau-Element des Erzählens', pp. 643, 645–46.

PART IV

❖

Interdisciplinary Contexts and International Reception

CHAPTER 11

❖

'Order in Disorder': Understanding Nazi Law with H. G. Adler

Olivier Jouanjan

Introduction: The 'Spirit' of Nazi Law and the Semblance of Legality

Here are a few lines from a legal bill dated 1 January 1945, which was never pro-mulgated owing to the war and the situation in Germany at the time:

> Whosoever is incapable of satisfying the minimal requirements of the community of the people by reason of an unusual lack of understanding or character,
> Whosoever by his refusal to work or his dissoluteness leads an unproductive and disordered life and thus becomes a burden or danger to others and to the collectivity,
> [...]
> Whosoever by his personality and conduct demonstrates that, by his mental disposition [*Sinnesart*] he is inclined to commit grave infractions (through anti-social delinquency or delinquency by inclination),
> Shall be regarded as a stranger to the community [*gemeinschaftsfremd*].[1]

The result of being identified as a stranger to the community was simple: any stranger to the community could be automatically placed by the police in a centre of confinement or rehabilitation. The *Großdeutsche Reich* was now nothing but a vast virtual concentration camp which could, at any moment, turn into a real one for anyone whose actions or even 'mental disposition' identified him as a stranger to the community. We should note that it was not necessary to show oneself to be the *enemy* of the community, its *Feind*, only a *stranger*, a *Fremder*. To be *fremd*, in this sense, is not to be a foreigner, an *extraneus*, someone of another nationality, but someone who is different, discordant, who does not harmonise with the ideal Aryan order.

In fact, this bill of 1945 was the apogee of Nazi law. It expressed its 'inner truth'. It did not even need to be promulgated, nor even to be drafted. It had already taken effect as the 'spirit' of Nazi law. The text simply put into words what had silently become 'normal' practice in the dim obscurity of the new law already active since 30 January 1933: the *Führer* must be seen as the 'living law' of the German people:[2] thus, his investiture had meant the immediate promulgation of a new, but tacit law. The legal experts said it at the time: with the seizure of power, there was an immediate, initially implicit and silent but complete renewal — a revolution in the law.[3]

The Concentration Camps and Protective Confinement [*Schutzhaft*]

The first concentration camps appeared as early as 1933. Initially created on impulse, at the whim of some SA squadron with nothing much else to do, they rapidly became more coherently orchestrated under the authority of Goering, now the Prussian Minister of the Interior.[4] The empowering order, based on Article 48 of the Weimar Constitution, 'for the protection [*Schutz*] of the people and the State' (28 February 1933) — the famous order relating to the Reichstag fire[5] — was supposed to provide the legal basis for the practice: among other things, it formally suspended the application of Article 114 of the Weimar Constitution, which guaranteed individual liberty and, on these grounds, prohibited arbitrary arrest and detention, principally by requiring the police to bring anyone held in custody before a judge, one day at the latest after their arrest. As soon as this constitutional provision was suspended, the police no longer had their hands tied by the judicial authorities, notwithstanding the contrary provisions enshrined in the Code of Criminal Procedure, which were still formally in force.

Despite this, the semblance of a legal basis was carefully provided, to give a more solid foundation to the practice. In 1934 and 1938, two simple decrees prohibited placing someone in a camp for the purposes of criminal prosecution.[6] The distinction had to be maintained between criminal proceedings, specifically the system of remand, and the simple action of the police sending someone to a concentration camp. The latter measure was called '*Schutzhaft*', and it is particularly regrettable that French translators and historians, lacking an awareness of the niceties of legal terms, have translated this word by a phrase that seems literal but is conceptually indefensible — 'precautionary detention' [*détention preventive*]. A legally more accurate translation would be 'protective confinement' or 'secure confinement', though the latter term is used for a current institution in French law,[7] which certainly bears some similarities to *Schutzhaft* — an order of placement in a centre of confinement — but is not identical to it, particularly in light of the fact that such confinement must be authorised by judicial authority and the latter may oversee its execution, which was naturally not the case with Nazi *Schutzhaft*. In any event, it was, significantly, administrative or police *confinement*, not legal *detention*. It was decided at the — often arbitrary — discretion of police authorities and was not controlled by any judge. Exempting this confinement, as early as 1934, from the oversight of the legal processes, was a way of safeguarding the appearance of a functional separation between the police and the criminal justice and protecting the integrity of the judicial powers from police actions.

That integrity was, indeed, formally confirmed by the Law of 10 February 1936 relating to the Gestapo. Paragraph 2 of §1 specifies that 'the jurisdiction of judicial bodies is not affected [by the actions of the Gestapo]'. Nevertheless there was a blatant contradiction between this and the authority granted to the Gestapo by the application decree of the same law, in which §1 entitled the secret police, perfectly freely and independently of any judicial authority, to undertake any investigation concerning affairs of high treason, treason, the use or traffic of explosives, 'as well as any punishable attack [*strafbarer Angriff*] against the Party or the State'.[8]

In all these cases, as vaguely defined as they are, it was nowhere specified that the mission of the Gestapo was intrinsically repressive. This silence was interpreted as authorising it to act preventively. Yet, to be more precise, the German adjective '*strafbar*', translated here as 'punishable', means in German legal discourse 'punishable by a *penal* sanction'. Behind the thin veil of reaffirming the separation of police and judicial powers, the Gestapo was actually empowered to take over the role of ordinary legal mechanisms, to do this not only preventively but also repressively, entirely as it chose.

Thus, these texts can all be read as showing that the Gestapo worked within a sphere of competence, which was repressive as well as precautionary, and for this reason it was exempt on principle from the jurisdiction of a judge. The secret police was not formally encroaching on the competences of legal authority when working within its own sphere of competence; rather, it reduced those competences by excluding them. This is indeed what happened in practice.

It is obvious that the extraordinarily vague and flexible notion of a 'punishable attack against the Party or the State' really did give the Gestapo the 'competence of its competence' [*Kompetenz-Kompetenz*], the power to decide for itself the extent of its own competence. The consequences were clear: internment in a concentration camp was a purely discretionary police decision and, for all the protestations of the judiciary, it remained supremely free of the influence of judges, whether it was undertaken in a precautionary or a repressive way. The Gestapo could impose 'protective confinement' on an individual without requiring criminal proceedings or needing to defer it by bringing them 'immediately' before a judge;[9] or on an individual whom the judge had not sentenced to 'precautionary detention'; or indeed on one who had gone to trial but been given a ruling of 'non-conviction' or acquittal; or finally on someone who had been convicted but had now completed their term. The police's presumption that the person was 'a danger to the community' was a supplement, a continuation by other means, to ordinary criminal justice. Thus, it was that, in the hands of the Gestapo, protective confinement became an instrument for 'correcting' legal decisions. The binding force of the *res judicata* had no sway over the SS police.[10]

In Düsseldorf in 1938, the Public Prosecutor was still pointing out that protective confinement could never be considered by a judge to be equivalent to an arrest or remand. This was one of the last attempts to retain a minimum, a last little remnant of the 'rule of law'. But, a moment's thought reveals that it was already completely pointless: the SS could easily accept that borderline, since it was the border of a legal system already overrun on all sides by the police system, which itself had no need of criminal justice to take over the baton.[11]

Moreover, in the name of protecting the people's community [*Volksgemeinschaft*] against harmful elements, the legal *Führer*, Hans Frank, defended these police powers on the grounds that judicial procedures, however legitimate they may be, do not allow efficient enough action against the enemies of the community and this justified the 'detour' [*Umweg*] of administrative confinement.[12] The 'defendant' had to take a little side-trip to the concentration camp, with no foreseeable end-date set to their administrative confinement.

The bureaucrats of the ministry of justice published numerous circulars to clarify the problems of differentiating between judicial procedures and police procedures. For the individual and their counsel, however, the law moved in mysterious ways. Indeed, the right of a person held in protective confinement to the support of a barrister was hotly disputed. Both the Federation of German National-Socialist Lawyers [*Bund Nationalsozialistischer Deutscher Juristen*][13] and the Ministry of Justice argued for this right, which suggests, in a way, that administrative confinement was an institution *of the law*, not completely outside the sphere of justice. But the SS, in the person of Werner Best, who was known as the 'expert' in police law, argued that it was simply a question of 'expediency': this was a battle against the 'mortal enemies of the State', and having a lawyer involved would suggest a lack of trust in the State's police, and after all the enemies of (national-socialist) liberty could not be allowed to benefit from the safeguards of (national-socialist) liberty. Best's message reached the *Führer*, who communicated to Himmler, without further formalities, his decision to forbid the intrusion of lawyers into the practices of police confinement.[14]

The General Characteristics of 'Nazi Law'

The way in which legal texts — 'laws', 'decrees' or 'circulars' — organized the operation of protective confinement is typical of the everyday reality of 'Nazi law'. Firstly, they demonstrated the end of the formal hierarchy of regulatory texts. A ministerial decree or even a simple circular might carry as much or even more weight than a statute or, to be more precise, than a text described as a 'statute' (since from this point on the vast majority of 'laws' were adopted by the executive). The texts now took the form of weird loops and tangled hierarchies. As a juridical practice, Nazism is produced by and itself produces a radical 'deformalisation' of the law:[15] juridical forms always threaten to protect the enemy of the community and are just a relic of liberalism.[16] Further, the legal standing of an individual could be reversed without warning: cleared by a court of law, they could still be detained by the police. At the same time these practices, even when they were purely police matters, were the subject of 'juridical' justifications. It is in this sense, but in this sense only, that one might speak of 'Nazi law' or 'Nazi legal discourse', leaving aside the political and moral aspects of the law — it is so obvious that this 'law' perfectly rhymed with purest injustice — but observing that they raised *legal* arguments, seemingly legal at least, in order to justify the unjustifiable.

This justification relies in the first instance on the oxymoron of 'precautionary repression', cited by Werner Best to justify the exorbitant powers of the police,[17] given that the courts can only, so to speak, exercise a *repressive* repression' and are thus always, by its very principle, too late on the scene. More profoundly, it arises from a functional lack of differentiation between the police and the justice: in the Nazi community they both served the same aim — the aim of preserving and protecting the racial and moral integrity of the German people. To make this community law as effective as possible, it was right to resort to whichever method worked better in each case. As outlined above, the police is unencumbered by the protective principles under which the courts labour; thus it is the most appropriate method and often the most efficient at fulfilling the mission of a law whose whole meaning can be summed up in the adage of Hans Frank: 'The law is whatever is good for the people; injustice is whatever is harmful to it'.[18] Indeed, the people, or more exactly the concept of *community* [*Volksgemeinschaft*], was the intellectual matrix in which all these conceptual inversions took form and were justified, reversing and denaturing the traditional meanings of legal terms. By this sleight of hand, the community created a juridical Newspeak that nourished this discourse of justifying the unjustifiable.

Thus, in this discourse and this practice, both well established since 1933, the stranger to the community was by definition the enemy of the community. Even being a member of the German 'race' was no guarantee against the rigours of repression, whether precautionary or repressive. 'Equality of race' [*Artgleichheit*] did not ensure 'equality of rights' [*Gleichberechtigung*]. The only thing the aforementioned 1945 bill added was to make this point crystal clear. For anyone who had not fully taken on the meaning of the 'renewed' law, it dotted the i's and crossed the t's.

To be a 'stranger to the community' is *not to stand within* the ethical order of the community, or the concrete order of this community, in the terms of Carl Schmitt.[19] The concrete order — to be precise, the Nazi fantasy of the concrete order of Germans — was the ultimate source of Nazi normativity, a legal system more or less unanimously understood in the committed language of the lawyers as the 'vital order of the people's community'. One might think here of the idea of 'objective ethics', in Hegel's sense. Indeed the Weimar neo-Hegelian group was involved in the task of renewing the law for Nazism — with, to be sure, a tiny but terrible ideological difference: Nazi ethics was based simply on the emerging property of blood, which of course is not in Hegel. Nazi ethics is simply the moral expression of biological race.[20] Nazi law was described as a homecoming, a return to morality and ethics.[21] No one who was not of Aryan blood could ever 'come home' to the ethics of the community. But beyond this, anyone who did not conform in their behaviour or simply by their 'mental disposition' (homosexuals, mentally or physically disabled, communists, the real or supposed enemies of the regime) to the *concrete ethical order* of the Nazi community was demonstrating thereby the impurity of their blood: there was an irrefutable presumption that they could not be a pure-bred German, that they must be a 'stranger to the community'.

The 1945 bill at last announced this explicitly: the stranger to the community, whatever their blood was said to be, would be placed outside the ordinary legal system. As an 'outlaw', they were destined for the concentration camp. Those who, in virtue of their pure race, believed themselves to be protected by a sort of residual 'rule of law' merely had to *behave properly*. Otherwise, they would be demonstrating that their supposed race was not so pure. The 'We' became the be-all and end-all of the law. And there was no space outside the 'Us' other than the concentration camp or, ultimately, the non-space of destruction and extermination. This was the *juridical* logic of the renewed law.

The camp is the other side of the coin of Nazi law: it is the *logical* complement to its normality. It is not a 'law of exceptions' linked to the situation of an exception [*Ausnahme*]; rather, it is defined as a 'special' or 'specific law' [*Sonderrecht*]. This *Sonderrecht* — which refers in particular to the law applied to the Jews — will not be properly understood if one interprets it as a law of permanent exception. It is not simply a law that operates *alongside* the ordinary law belonging to the ordinary German (who conforms to the concrete order of the community) and is unconnected to that ordinary law. It is both the horizon and the justificatory cause of that ordinary law. Nazi law is *dual*.[22] Because this law, taken as a whole, is logically — and only *logically* — dual, the *Sonderrecht* announces just as logically the truth of the 'normal' law, its ontological-ethical premise: your rights depend on your being who you ought to be. The 1945 bill declares fully and explicitly this logic, in which to-be is the condition of ought-to-be, and vice versa.

The Camp, a (Miniature) Rule of Law?

The camp is thus the horizon of the whole of 'Nazi law'. The question that follows is: is there a law of the camps, a law *in* the camps, in that space outside the community? Or, to be more precise: can we speak of a 'law' of the camps?

A recent, obscene argument answers in the affirmative. Yes, hell was regulated. Starting from this statement, Nicolas Bertrand goes further: the camps were run by a certain, naturally minimal, form of the 'rule of law'.[23] It is an obscene argument in the proper sense of the word: it stages a performance that bursts open the scene of common understanding. I am not suggesting that this author is a revisionist; he does not deny the cruelty of the camps.

In the camps, there were regulations, and thus at the very least the imposition of the formal principle of a rule of law, according to which those in power submitted to their own laws (following the adage *patere legem quam ipse fecisti*), irrespective of the content of those laws. This was the very positivistic argument.

As we know, for Hans Kelsen, a legal system is only truly valid if it is, broadly speaking, effective. The thesis of the 'regulated hell' is careful — though without reference to Kelsen — to check the effectiveness of the camp regulations. Betrand concludes this effectiveness on the grounds of two or three anecdotes recounted by camp survivors in which he believes he can trace the stages of the disciplinary procedure promulgated by the SS regulations. One could not possibly dispute the validity or efficiency of the disciplinary law of the camps. Clearly, the author is untouched by the problem of induction, and there is no Popper in his library. There are many survivor stories nowadays, and one finds among them more than two or three anecdotes that falsify the thesis of effectiveness, particularly in compliance with disciplinary proceedings.

Moreover, it would have been useful if he had read the monumental work of H. G. Adler on Theresienstadt, in which a whole chapter is devoted to 'juridical relations'. He would have acquired a more accurate idea of what constituted the 'law in action' of that camp.[24]

Sham Law

Bertrand might have understood what Adler called the *Rechtskomödie*, the 'sham law' of the camps.[25] 'Normal' law is of course full of fictions, but here in the camp, law was 'fictionalizing' itself. And this legal comedy was the fiction of a real tragedy, which perhaps helped those who were putting it on and acting it out to bear it a little, or at least to *justify* it.

The title of Chapter 15 of *Theresienstadt* is *Rechtsverhältnisse* — 'Legal Relations'. This shows that, for Adler, in a *Zwangsgemeinschaft*, a coercive community, there must be something we could call a legal system. Adler begins the chapter by saying that it seems absurd to speak of the law in reference to an SS concentration camp; and yet any community, even that of a concentration camp, requires norms, a kind of legality. To acknowledge this, he specifies, one must of course set aside any definition of the law as being based on absolute values, such as dignity, liberty or equality. One must also set aside all those idealisations of the law which fail to understand 'the morphology of the social patterns and constructions (e.g., of modern states) in which a structure is developed, under the influence of various and complicated tendencies; this structure then functions within communities as actual law'.[26] In these circumstances, the law is neither the formalisation of individual desires nor the codification of ethical principles, but 'a set of rules and regulations with which those in power within a society assert and promote certain modes of behaviour and relationships'.[27]

The notion of the law invoked by Adler here is thus also purely positivistic, in the sense that it does not relate to any transcendental or transpersonal values: it is reduced to the immanence of a system of domination. We must not forget that Adler is not expounding any philosophy or theory of law; the chapter on legal relations appears in Part II of the book, which elucidates the *sociology* of the camp. Such a sociological approach to this 'law' must necessarily be based on a realistic, and thus 'positivistic' understanding of 'legal relations'. Certainly, some aspects of the definition of law that emerges coincide with certain philosophical-theoretical views of the law, such as the 'analytical jurisprudence' developed in the first half of the nineteenth century by John Austin (1790–1859). Austin argued that whatever the sovereign or legal authority imposes on a society, marking any violation as punishable by criminal penalties, is the law of that society.[28] However, we must keep in mind that Adler is not proposing any general theory of law, but simply aiming to understand in sociological terms the legal relations inside the camp of Theresienstadt, and for this purpose, he rightly makes use of his simple, 'positivistic' concept of the law. With such a simple concept of the law, he has no need to include any of the *axiological qualifications* that would be implied by the notion of the 'rule of law', understood even in the most minimal way. Adler describes the formal development of the law of the 'Ghetto' of Theresienstadt:

> At first, there was hardly any written legal foundation. This was supplied only gradually and was often amended. Initially, few lawyers were involved in its formulation — the 'legislators' were the SS and the Council of Elders. Only later were more lawyers included, in order to codify the existing law and its legal foundations. Finally, at the behest of the Council of Elders, the law was compiled for internal use and was published in mimeographed form.[29]

In this sociological sense, and only in that sense, 'the "Jewish settlement area" [*das jüdische Siedlungsgebiet*][30] was indeed a legal community [*eine Rechtsgemeinschaft*] with its own "law".[31] Adler's sociological gaze does not stop there, which is probably why he writes 'law' here in scare-quotes. For in reality, this 'law' was, to cite Adler himself, a 'sham law' [*Rechtskomödie*]. And of course there is a story within the story. Two points in particular show what brought it about.

The first is that the situation of the camp was only 'legal' from the 'point of view of the SS' — for the prisoners, obviously, it contradicted even the most minimal sense of justice. Thus it was a *horrific* law:

> the horror lies solely in the fact that acts that contradict any other legal sensibility and that, from an ethical perspective, can be viewed only as premeditated, common crimes were transformed into 'law' in a way that violated any noble sense of the concept. Therefore, individuals and the coerced community in Theresienstadt rejected this law as unjust [*Unrecht*], even if it had to be obeyed. The rejection sprang, however, not from scientifically defensible definitions but rather — happily — from *ethical* impulses.

The result of this 'law' was that 'where arbitrariness and power in and of themselves serve as law, it is possible, as here, for criminal acts to become law and vice versa'.[32] The word law had become the linguistic term for violence, nothing more. This fundamental semantic inversion, in the Nazi newspeak, expressed not only the (fake) law of the camps but also that of Nazi 'law' in its entirety.[33]

The second point that shows how this law was a sham is specific to the actual organisation of the camp at Theresienstadt. As in the Ghettos, a Jewish 'self-administration' had been set up, under the leadership of a 'Jewish elder' [*Judenälteste*] and his Council [*Ältestenrat*]. However, this was only a 'fiction'. Thus, 'two legal spheres developed, existing parallel to and permeating each other' — the law of those who held the power, which was imposed on the whole Ghetto and its subjects, and the law that the 'ghetto' provided for itself through its organs of 'self-administration', but which 'had no power of its own except as bestowed by the SS'. In these circumstances, the autonomy of the self-administration was only a front and the SS was still all-powerful: it remained in the background and reserved the right to intervene in all matters, including those pertaining in principle to the 'self-administration'. The SS management of the camp had the 'right' to cancel or modify any decision of the bodies of self-administration, particularly its law-court. 'To bring the farce full circle, every decision of the "ghetto court" had to be approved by the SS "office" [*Dienststelle*]'.[34] In the SS texts on the organisation of the camp, this *Dienststelle* was sometimes referred to as a 'supervisory authority' [*Aufsichtsbehörde*],[35] in line with the traditional rule of decentralisation that organizes the oversight of the acts of self-governing bodies (especially district councils) by a superior authority — without, however, allowing this authority to take the place of the autonomous bodies of free administration of the decentralized collective, except in duly regulated special cases. Yet, as was already the case for all the decentralized authorities of the German territories, the new regime had completely altered this concept of 'supervision' (oversight, control), transforming it into a *de facto* unlimited right by which superior authorities could *intervene* in the activities of subordinate authorities. 'Self-administration' was nothing but a word, whose normal meaning had been destroyed but which remained, like a fetish, to allow the staging of the 'sham law' — *a fortiori*, inside the camps. As we noted above, the Gestapo had given itself the right to 'correct' the rulings of the 'normal' ordinary criminal courts, that is, the criminal courts working outside the camps; it would have been strange indeed if this action, which was held to be 'legally' justified outside the camps, were not held to be equally so, *a fortiori*, inside them.

Adler specifies the meaning of this obligation of the camp's Jewish council to submit all its decisions, and especially its court rulings, to confirmation by the SS management. The juridical activity of the Ghetto Tribunal was useful to the SS by serving as a sort of 'disclosing agent'. This Tribunal only dealt with minor offences, since 'high justice', to borrow a term from medieval law, was reserved directly for the most serious crimes allocated to the SS administration. Thanks to the rulings on petty misdemeanours [*Bagatellendelikte*] made by the Jewish courts and submitted to them for sentencing, the SS administration learned of all the inherent conflicts and tensions of communal life and could correct any sentence they deemed unduly lenient: 'for the person convicted that would generally mean deportation by the next transport and probably a death sentence'.[36]

This is how the 'sham law' of the camp was staged. A truly sociological and informed gaze like that of Adler was able to bring this legal farce into the light of day. The 'regulated hell' remained a hell and never acquired the 'rule of law' — what god could have achieved such a miracle?

The 'Limits' of the Law

As we have seen, the Nazis' term for the law specific to the Jews and the law of the camps was a '*Sonderrecht*' [a special, separate law]. It was not an exceptional law but ordinary law as applied to the Jews and extended, by a sort of terrible vague analogy, to all the *Gemeinschaftsfremde*, [strangers to the community]. Thus, it is also characterized by an absolute generality, and the oxymoron of 'a general special law' is simply the expression of Nazi ideological discourse, and the way it brings together incompatible elements in order to derive from them an otherwise unimaginable justification of the unjustifiable. In any case, it is a law of juridical segregation. Here is what Georg Dahm, a famous criminal lawyer, says about it:

> The decisive point here (in relation to the *Sonderrecht*), is its attempt to separate [*trennen*] Germans and Jews and to eliminate [*ausscheiden*] Jewry [*Judentum*] from

the German population. It follows that what the Jews *lack*[37] is not only political rights but also the right to intermarry with a German and, to a great extent, the capacity to own or inherit property, to engage in legal commerce, to take part in cultural life, or any professional or commercial activities. Conversely, they are exempt from certain obligations such as mandatory military service, compulsory labour or youth service, which are incumbent on members of the people.[38]

The essential character of the *Sonderrecht*, as Dahm makes clear, is a *lack* of rights. In the voluminous collection of texts on the *Sonderrecht* compiled by Joseph Walk, one can see that the key terms of this separate law, which applies 'normally' outside the camps as well, are *Ausscheidung* and *Ausschluß*, which both mean exclusion, *Verbot*, prohibition, *Absonderung*, segregation, *Nichtzulassung*, non-admission etc.[39] One never comes across the language of '*dürfen*': permission, authorisation, entitlement, having-the-right-to, in other words, the juridical power of a subject of the law. The 'subject' of the *Sonderrecht* does not have the right to say 'I want' or 'I wish to': they do not have the right even to say 'I' — to borrow the famous formula of Hannah Arendt, they do not have 'the right to have rights'.

Some will say that the *Sonderrecht* is a specific law that leaves the normal law, the Civil Code, still in charge of relations among those of German stock. This may be so, but what the regime had been doing since 1933 and now made explicit in the 1945 bill was that, whatever your race, if you brought shame on it or were likely to bring shame on it, you instantly became *gemeinschaftsfremd*: thus, the 'specific law' was anything but. One can speak, of course, as I have suggested above, of a *dual* law in a dual State, but that would not fully explain the situation. In fact, the specific law holds the 'normal' law in the palm of its hand, for the latter was only applied on condition that its recipient was fully integrated into the community, its 'concrete order'. The *Sonderrecht* keeps the Germans, too, in their state. 'Normal law' and its application, thus, do not stand 'alongside' the special law but are dependent upon it. The duality of the law is resolved within the very unity of the community.

This can be seen especially clearly in the ways in which the new doctrine of ordinary private law was developed. The legal personality was to be replaced by the 'concrete concept' of one's 'position within the community' [*gemeinschaftliche Gliedstellung*]. Property must be understood now as a community institution, no longer as the basis of a 'subjective right' but as an 'order integrated' into the community [*gebundene Ordnung*].[40] A person's 'legal commerce' was now understood as a 'community relationship'.[41] And marriage, naturally, was no longer thought of as 'a private affair between stakeholders, but as a *duty* to conserve the racial and cultural strength of the people'.[42] 'Normal' law was thus placed in its entirety within a 'community reserve',[43] not as the *external restriction* that objective law might impose on the exercise of subjective rights, but as the determining concept that defined the very essence of 'rights', henceforth conceived as *community functions*.

This internal inversion of the concepts of legal institutions, reversing their traditional meaning, also affected private law, the law we usually think of as governing relations and exchanges between private individuals — the law that fundamentally constitutes a civil society and its autonomy in relation to the State.

Henceforth placed within the 'community reserve', in the sense described above, civil autonomy was once more under the yoke of the concrete order of 'German life'. To say 'I' presupposed that one could also speak in the name of the 'us'. But in the Ghetto of the 'strangers to the community', no one was entitled to speak in the name of the 'us'. What became then of the possibility of being a 'subject' of rights? In relation to this, the question of civil law in concentration camps is particularly instructive.

The texts reproduced by Adler show that civil law was not simply abolished within the camp.[44] Ernst Rosenthal's introduction to the General Regulations of the Jewish Self-Administration [*Allgemeine Ordnung der Jüdischen Selbstverwaltung*] provides a very useful clarification: 'It is a peculiarity of civil law in T [Theresienstadt] that legal transactions rely solely on the mutual trust of the inmates. There is no civil jurisdiction through which civil claims could be enforced.'[45] In other words, even the law-court of the Jewish self-administration could not deal with civil litigations. Individuals had to resolve their mutual relations by themselves. No one could lay claim to their rights before a tribunal *in their own name*; the civil 'rights' of strangers to the community are rights without safeguards. There was no outside body before whom one might be entitled to say 'I', even in relation to another person. Individuals are nothing but the object of criminal procedures, as described above. In relation to their fellow detainees they are in a Hobbesian state of nature: since their rights are without safeguards they are not 'rights', simply hopes that are destined to be disappointed. Such individuals are at the *limits of the law*. Is there any sense in which one could say they are within the 'law'?

Can One Speak of Nazi 'Law'?

The question whether 'Nazi law', with its distinctive structure, can be called a 'law' thus depends on one's answer to the question whether it would make sense to use this term for the *Sonderrecht*, itself the logical extension of the 'normal' Nazi law. In order to find a reasonable answer to that question, one must start with the following enquiry: Who is the recipient of this *Sonderrecht*? To whom is it addressed?

The answer is obvious: it is addressed to human beings, naturally, but to humans who have no right to say 'I' — specifically, to say 'I' to the authorities. In other words, they have no right to voice a *contradiction* in the first person *singular*. Contradiction, the basis of the adversarial system, is more than simply the guarantee of an equitable procedure: it is the *condition* of the law. In the self-administered courts of the Jewish Councils in the camps and the Ghettos, a kind of adversarial system was in use, but — as noted above — its rulings were not binding on the real authority, that of the SS.

The law of the *Sonderrecht* was pure policing, taking 'policing' in its old sense of a system for governing the lives of individuals, disciplining their bodies. This pure policing, and especially 'Nazi law', is not *at the disposal* of individuals but rather *disposes of* them. What happens between them is of concern only to them, their confidence or their disappointments. It does not affect the community, since they are no longer part of it, nor, in consequence, the judges of the community, not even those of the pseudo 'Jewish community' of the Ghetto. The police are not interested in private relations. In Germany, up to the second half of the eighteenth century, policing had nothing to do with the juridical sciences: there was a 'science of policing', and an effort to define the conditions of 'good policing' [*gute Policey*].[46] It was a science of administration and when, around 1800, it became a science of the *law* of administration, it soon had to change its name: at the beginning of the nineteenth century, it became 'administrative law'.

Nazi 'policing' was, more fundamentally still, a question of public hygiene. The aim of the 'law' was to favour whatever was good for the community (its blood) and destroy whatever harmed it. The individuals it policed were reduced to their *biologies*, in order to deprive them of their *biographies*. This is how it was expressed in legal doctrine: a trial is not there to settle a conflict of divergent and opposing interests, for the only interest protected by the law is that of the community. 'The idea of community overrides any divergence of interests', writes Karl Larenz.[47] Who are the subjects of the law who no longer have interests of their *own*? Who are the 'strangers to the community' who cannot even invoke the interest of the community for their own rights?

Indeed, there was no effective difference between the police and the judiciary: both of them were pursuing the same 'legal' goal, community hygiene. It is easy to understand, therefore, why the police had the final say: as we saw earlier, it was simply better at the job. The quintessence of this 'law' was thus revealed as simply sanitary policing. Was it not a sufficient legal definition of those strangers to the community, chief among them the Jews, to describe them as 'parasites' or 'vermin'? A rule of law for 'vermin' or 'parasites' — this is the revolutionary notion that the *regulated hell* thesis expects us to swallow, along with a preface by Stéphane Hessel, who on that day evidently forgot his indignation. A rule of law for slaves, who were nothing but *objects* of domination, mere bodies handed over to the sanitary police. A rule of law that does not govern human beings but administers them like things.

'A "State of slaves" [...]', writes Georg Jellinek (1851–1911) 'is a State in name only. There can be no juridical connection between these thousands of slaves who do not even know of each other's existence'.[48] A person who does not have the right to say 'I' equally cannot say 'you', 's/he' or 'we'. Even the 'we' of the Nazi community is not a *personal* pronoun. In his magnificent novel *A Child of our Time* [*Ein Kind unserer Zeit*, 1938], Ödön von Horváth (1901–1938), whose understanding of Nazi discourse was so acute, as though he understood it from the inside, demonstrates upon what fundamental contradiction, the source of all possible inverted meanings, totalitarian ideology depends: if the individual is nothing and the community is everything, as Nazi discourse proclaims, it follows that the community is an *everything made up of nothings*.

In order to answer the question whether one could reasonably speak of the monstrous law of Nazism as a 'law', the aforementioned great neo-Kantian, positivist jurist Georg Jellinek, offers a most productive line of argument. He died in 1911 and thus never directly confronted the problem of totalitarianisms, even on the rise. Yet his thesis that 'the law is nothing more than the *ethical minimum*' of a society[49] opens the door to a more profound examination of 'Nazi law'.

The fundamental question of the law is: how can a relation of domination be understood as and changed into a relation of rights? This does not mean that in a relation of rights there is no more domination,[50] but that this domination is exercised upon an individual *person* and, as a result, it must be limited. This is why the law is an 'ethical minimum'. In a legal system properly understood, social and state domination is not eliminated but such a system presupposes the *recognition* of the other as a subject standing face-to-face with the subject that I also am, and demanding their rights. This recognition intervenes within the relation of domination.[51] It is simplest to put this in Kantian terms: the other person must never be treated purely as an object but always also as an end in themselves — that is, as that which is capable of determining its own ends for itself, and can say 'I': a subject. This figure of the subject does not have to have any metaphysical freight: it is enough for it to be able to enter into the grammar of the law with its deep structure as a *singular pronoun*. Personhood is not an essential quality of the individual; it is purely an abstraction, a function of the juridical order,[52] and it is this function, which institutes within the legal system the person who can say I, you, s/he, we, that suffices to qualify them as a *subject of the law*.

In this concept, basically a grammatical one, we can see in action the small difference at the outer limits of the law that allows us to conceive not so much what the law *is* — law has no essence — as the conditions under which it can be *thought*. The question is, thus, not whether 'Nazi law' actually *is* a law but whether this law without subjects can be *thought of* as 'law'. And the answer to this must be negative — not because of any higher values, such as natural law or the grand ideals of humanity, but for the simple reason of the grammar of that supposed law.

Any law is, of course, only a fiction that is attached to real life and governs it. The law of the concentration camps drained its subjects. However, if law is also an 'ethical minimum', it presupposes a system of ethical relations between real-life subjects. Indeed, the system of the camps, as survivors have testified, did not only destroy the legal personality, it also — and just as violently — did away with ethical personhood. Here one must reread Part III of Adler's *Theresienstadt*, which is devoted to the psychology of individuals within the camp. He describes the fundamental psychical state of the prisoners as an 'escape from the present' [HGA/BC: 595].[53] Ethical life is always played out firstly (and not only firstly) in the here and now. The order of the camps, whether or not it could be called 'legal', instituted a 'dis-instituted' life, a bare life: 'All the legal norms which generally operate in a society and all the ethical principles we hold to be mandatory were abolished; life was lived under conditions of unlimited distress, endless terror and boundless corruption, which set all against all in a way no one could ever have imagined, so that every SS concentration camp was an experiment in evil'.[54] The camp gave form to 'the law of the jungle'.[55] This system reduced human beings to the suffering of their bodies, and relegated those bodies to what Jay Bernstein has most aptly called a state of 'existential helplessness'.[56] Anyone who can no longer hope for any existential help here and now, who is thus forced to flee the present, can no longer recognize other people or be recognized by them and is no longer really 'alive', even if they are not (yet) dead,[57] if 'to be alive is to be recognised'[58] — and, one might add, to recognize others. Without recognition, there is no hope of 'trust in the world' (*Weltvertrauen*), to quote Jean Améry.[59]

The law of the camp was not an 'ethical minimum', but, quite the contrary, it destroyed all possibility of a minimally ethical life. In his magisterial account of the history of the concentration camps, Nikolaus Wachsmann reports the following sad anecdote:

> One day toward the end of World War II, a few Dachau prisoners made a pact. Determined to show that there was an alternative to the usual strife between inmates, they would act like gentlemen; for a whole day, rough and selfish behaviour would give way to civility and compassion, as if they still lived regular lives outside. When the agreed day came, the men tried their hardest to stay true to the ideal of common decency, starting with the scramble to dress, wash, and eat in the morning. By evening, all of them failed, defeated by the harsh reality of the camp. "The beast inside humans gains the upper hand", the Belgian resistance fighter and Dachau prisoner Arthur Haulot noted in his diary on January 19, 1945, after he heard about the experiment. "One does not with impunity live so long outside the norm".[60]

Nazi 'law' placed camp inmates 'outside the norm' and destroyed relations of 'common decency' between them; but it also threatened the same consequences to anyone else who failed to comply with the concrete order of the people's community. That is why its fantasy of normality cannot be described as *normativity* — neither as juridical normativity nor as ethical normativity — because this 'law' destroyed the very possibility of an ethical life. To think about this limitation to the law one may reasonably remain 'positivistic'. One of the greatest twentieth-century positivists, Hans Kelsen, defined the law as 'a normative order of human behaviour'.[61] He simply failed to think, within that 'norm', what '*human* behaviour' might mean. In other words, to think of the law, as Jellinek did, as an 'ethical minimum'. Reading H. G. Adler's *Theresienstadt* forces us to think, and think again, about that question.

Translator's Notes

• The author distinguishes between 'détention' and 'rétention', though both terms are normally translated into English as 'detention'. To represent this distinction, I have translated 'rétention' throughout this essay as 'confinement'.

• The French 'préventif' has been translated adjectivally as 'precautionary', but in adverbial form as 'preventively'.

• All references to French editions of secondary texts originally published in other languages have been retained. However, for H. G. Adler, *Theresienstadt 1941–1945* (here rendered into French from the 2nd German edition of 1960) I have quoted from the English translation by Belinda Cooper (Cambridge, New York, Melbourne, Delhi & Singapore: CUP, 2017); page-references are in square brackets, preceded by 'HGA/BC'.

• See also addition to note 38 below.

• I am indebted to Penelope M. Lawrence for discussions of some legal terms.

Naomi Segal, Birkbeck, University of London

Notes to Chapter 11

1. Cited from Dietmut Majer, *Grundlagen des national-sozialistischen Rechtssystems* (Stuttgart: Kohlhammer, 1987), pp. 182–85.

2. On 3 November 1933, in his start-of-year address to German students in the winter semester of 1933–1934, Heidegger proclaimed: 'Your lives will be ruled from now on not by teachings or ideas. The *Führer* himself and he alone is the only reality and law of Germany' (Heidegger, *Reden und andere Zeugnisse eines Lebensweges, Gesamtausgabe*, vol 16 (Frankfurt a/M: Klostermann, 2000), p. 184). With this announcement he was reflecting the new legal doctrine which specified that 'the transmission of legislative power to the *Führer* is not simply a transfer of the competence to enact laws but imposes a completely new concept of the law': the latter is 'the embodiment of the general will of the political people', 'the implementation of the vital *völkisch* order, following the plans and decrees of the *Führer*'. Yet the will of the *Führer* is not an 'individual, subjective will'; on the contrary, 'it incarnates the general will of the people, its historic greatness' (Ernst Rudolf Huber, *Verfassungsrecht des Großdeutschen Reiches*, 2nd edn (Hamburg: Hanseatische Verlagsanstalt, 1939), pp. 240, 196). As a result, the *Führer* is 'the unwritten concrete idea of law of his people' (Karl Larenz, *Deutsche Rechtserneuerung und Rechtsphilosophie* (Tübingen: Siebeck, 1934), p. 34).

3. This legal revolution is part of the broader 'Nazi cultural revolution' (Johann Chapoutot, *La révolution culturelle nazie* (Paris: Gallimard, 2016)).

4. Karl Kroeschell, *Rechtsgeschichte Deutschlands im 20. Jahrhundert* (Göttingen: Vandenhoeck & Ruprecht, coll. UTB, 1992), p. 116.

5. This was thus a derogation justified, as the terms of Article 48 specified, by a grave threat to public safety and order. The reason — or excuse — was the *Reichstag* fire. See the text of the order in Ingo von Münch (ed.), *Gesetze des NS-Staates*, 3rd edn (Paderborn: Schöningh, 1994), p. 63.

6. Lothar Gruchmann, *Justiz im Dritten Reich: Anpassung und Unterwerfung in der Ära Gürtner*, 3rd edn (Munich: Oldenburg, 2002), p. 584.

7. The current French practice of 'rétention de sûreté' is equivalent to the German *Sicherheitsverwahrung*.

8. For the text of this law and this decree, see von Münch, *Gesetze des NS-Staates*, pp. 75–78.

9. Contrary to §114b of the Code of Criminal Procedure [*Strafprozeßordnung*] which was formally still in force at the time.

10. On 'protective confinement' and its legal regime, see Olivier Jouanjan, *Justifier l'injustifiable: L'ordre du discours juridique nazi* (Paris: PUF, 2017), pp. 148–52, plus references.

11. Thus while on one side it was backed up against the infinite extension of police jurisdiction, on the other side ordinary criminal justice was undermined by the recent institution of special repressive courts [*Sondergerichte*], of which the most emblematic was the People's Court of Justice [*Volksgerichtshof*]. Flanked on each side by these two extraordinary repressive apparatuses, 'ordinary' criminal justice had nothing left to do but deal with offences considered not to constitute any 'risk' to the life and survival of the Community or the State, and was not even able in principle to determine for itself the demarcation lines of the various jurisdictions.

12. Cited by Gruchmann, *Justiz im Dritten Reich*, p. 586.

13. In 1936, this became the *Nationalsozialistischer Rechtswahrerbund*, the National-Socialist Federation of Protectors of the Law; for more on this organisation, see Jouanjan, *Justifier l'injustifiable*, pp. 83–87.

14. Ulrich Herbert, *Werner Best: Un nazi de l'ombre (1903–1989)* (Paris: Éditions Tallandier, 2010), pp. 157ff.

15. The term 'deformalisation' is borrowed from the French translation of Max Weber, *Sociologie du droit* [Sociology of Law] (Paris: PUF, 1986), see especially p. 225.

16. Michael Stolleis, *Geschichte des öffentlichen Rechts in Deutschland*, vol. 3 (Munich: C. H. Beck, 1999), p. 318; he refers to remarks by Arnold Köttgen in 1937 and 1938 (see note 18).

17. Herbert, *Werner Best*, op. cit., p. 177.

18. Hans Frank, 'Einleitung', *Nationalsozialistisches Handbuch für Recht und Gesetzgebung* (1935), repr. in Herlinde Pauer-Studer & Julian Fink, *Rechtfertigungen des Unrechts* (Frankfurt a/M: Suhrkamp, 2014), p. 142.

19. The concept of the 'concrete order' was developed by Schmitt in his short volume of Nazi legal philosophy, *Über die drei Arten des juristischen Denkens* (Hamburg: Hanseatische Verlagsanstalt, 1934).

20. There are some terrible passages on this in the work of the 'neo-Hegelian' Larenz. For an analysis of Larenz's pseudo-Hegelian discourse, with quotations, see Jouanjan, *Justifier l'injustifiable*, pp. 262–73.

21. See, among many other examples, the text by Roland Freisler, the second chairman of the *Volksgericht*: 'Der Heimweg des Rechts in die völkische Sittenordnung', *Festschrift Franz Schlegelberger zum 60. Geburtstag* (Berlin: Franz Vahlen, 1936), p. 28. The title of this essay can be translated as 'The homecoming of the law to the *völkisch* ethical order'.

22. Here I am taking up the famous thesis of Ernst Fraenkel on the nature of the Nazi State (*The Dual State: Contribution to the Theory of Dictatorship* (New York: Oxford University Press, 1941), with an attempt to clarify its outlines. It is not true to say that there is, on the one hand, the 'legal' State and on the other, a decision-making State, since in the logic of the Nazi system pure decision-making is the condition of the ethical order of normal law. To make arbitrary decisions in relation to the 'stranger to the community' is conceived as the fundamental condition for a normal application of the law *within* the racially and ethically circumscribed circle of the community of the people, in relation to 'normal' people.

23. Nicolas Bertrand, *L'enfer réglementé: Le régime de détention dans les camps de concentration* (Paris: Perrin, 2015).

24. I am borrowing one term of the famous opposition of the American legal theorist Roscoe Pound between *law in books* and *law in action*: Roscoe Pound, 'Law in Books and Law in Action', *American Law Review*, 44.12 (1910), 12–36.

25. H. G. Adler, *Theresienstadt 1941–1945: Das Antlitz einer Zwangsgemeinschaft*, 2nd edn (1960) (Tübingen: Mohr (Paul Siebeck) chapter 15, pp. 453–92; this term p. 459 [HGA/BC: 400–36; this term 405].

26. Ibid., p. 453 [HGA/BC: 400]

27. Ibid.

28. John Austin, *The Province of Jurisprudence Determined* (1st edn 1832), ed. by W. Rumble (Cambridge: Cambridge University Press, 1995).

29. Adler, *Theresienstadt*, p. 459 [HGA/BC: 405].

30. This was the official designation of Theresienstadt from summer 1943. The camp was no longer to be called a 'Ghetto' but a 'zone of settlement', a *Siedlungsgebiet*, in which 'the Jews lived separately but happily under their own administration, an idyll in the midst of the horrors of [the] war'; typical of the *Lingua Tertii Imperii*, this was meant to show 'how well Hitler's Germany treated Jews' while 'the German civilian population, to say nothing of the fighting troops, fared much worse than the Jews under the special protection of Adolf Hitler' (ibid., p. 150) [HGA/BC: 123]. As is well known, the pre-planned visit of a Red Cross delegation in the early summer of 1944 was the occasion of a refurbishment of the camp and the making of a propaganda film (known by the title 'The Führer gives a town to the Jews'); all this was organized by SS Hans Günther and the Prague Central Commission for Jewish Emigration. What strikes one, when viewing the fifteen minutes that survive of this 'documentary on the Jewish settlement' (the film's official sub-title), is that the SS use it to represent the Jewish prisoners as living the life of a 'community of the people' on the *German* model, as conceived by the idyllic fantasy of Nazi propaganda. It was like a dreadful mirror. One can also see the sign of this specular fantasy of the SS in their organisation of the Ghetto community as though it was a German community imagined in one of the circulars of 10 March 1945, whose titles show that they are finalizing and putting together the penal regulations of the camp, and state that the 'position [of the Jewish Elder, *der Judenälteste*] in the life of the Jewish community is regulated in accordance with the *Führer* principle' (cited by Adler, ibid., p. 460) [HGA/BC: 406].

31. Ibid., p. 454 [HGA/BC: 401].

32. Ibid.

33. This is what I attempt to demonstrate in the Second Part of *Justifier l'injustifiable* (op. cit., pp. 139–209.)

34. Adler, *Theresienstadt*, p. 455 [HGA/BC: 402]. Officially *Dienststelle* meant 'the SS service under whose command the Ghetto is placed'. It came under the authority of the Central Commission for Jewish Emigration based in Prague and Berlin, as well as that of one of the offices of the RSHA (*Reichssicherheitshauptamt*), the intelligence service of the SS (ibid., p. XXXVI).
35. Ibid., p. 460. [HGA/BC: 460/406]
36. Ibid., p. 456 [HGA/BC: 456/402].
37. My emphasis.
38. Georg Dahm, *Deutsches Recht* (Hamburg: Hanseatische Verlagsanstalt, 1944), p. 348. *Translator's note: the German word* Judentum *combines the distinct meanings in English of Judaism, Jewishness and Jewry; the French* juiverie, *used by Jouanjan in this quotation, is closest to 'Jewry'.*
39. See the hundreds of documents relating to the *Sonderrecht* (laws, ministerial directives, municipal decrees, Gestapo orders, excerpts of court judgements etc.) collected in *Das Sonderrecht für die Juden im NS-Staat*, ed. by Joseph Walk, 2nd edn (Heidelberg: C. F. Müller, 1996).
40. Franz Wieacker, *Wandlungen der Eigentumsverfassung* (Hamburg: Hanseatische Verlagsanstalt, 1935), p. 70.
41. Karl Larenz, 'Gemeinschaft und Rechtstellung', *Deutsche Rechtswissenschaft* 1, (1936), 31–39 (p. 38); Heinrich Lange, *Vom alten zum neuen Schuldrecht* (Hamburg: Hanseatische Verlagsanstalt, 1934).
42. Wolfgang Seibert, 'Die Volksgemeinschaft im bürgerlichen Recht', in *Nationalsozialistisches Handbuch für Recht und Gesetzgebung*, ed. by Hans Frank, 2nd edn (Munich: Zentralverlag der NSDAP, 1935), p. 964. Also cited by Bernd Rüthers, *Die Unbegrenzte Auslegung: Zum Wandel der Privatrechtsordnung im Nationalsozialismus*, 7th edn (Tübingen: Siebeck, 2012), p. 401. In this pioneering and still uniquely useful book (1st edn 1968) one can find in detail the main amendments to the fundamental concepts of private law made in the name of the 'community of the people' (ibid., §19, pp. 322–430).
43. Jouanjan, *Justifier l'injustifiable*, p. 196.
44. Adler, *Theresienstadt*, pp. 461–64 [HGA/BC: 405–10].
45. Ibid., p. 462 [HGA/BC: 408].
46. Michael Stolleis, *Geschichte des öffentlichen Rechts in Deutschland*, vol. 1 (Munich: C. H. Beck, 1988), pp. 372–85.
47. Karl Larenz, *Rechts und Staatsphilosophie der Gegenwart*, 2nd edn (Berlin: Junker & Dünnhaupt, 1935), p. 23.
48. Georg Jellinek, *L'État moderne et son droit*, vol 2, reprint of the 1913 translation (Paris: Panthéon-Assas, 2005), p. 37.
49. Georg Jellinek, *Die sozialethische Bedeutung von Recht, Unrecht und Strafe* (Vienna: Hölder, 1878), p. 42.
50. Even in private law: the rights of the subject in private law are exercised in relation to other people and, to borrow a very classical definition, they take the form of 'a power or a domination granted by judicial order to a [person's] will', (Bernhard Windscheid, *Lehrbuch des Pandektenrechts*, vol. 1, ed. by Theodor Kipp, 9th edn (Frankfurt a/M: Rütten & Loening, 1906), p. 156).
51. For a demonstration of the importance of the theme of recognition in the work of Jellinek, see Olivier Jouanjan, 'Les droits publics subjectifs et la dialectique de la reconnaissance: Georg Jellinek et la construction juridique de l'État moderne', *Revue d'Allemagne*, 46.1 (2014), 51–62.
52. Georg Jellinek, *System der subjektiven öffentlichen Rechte* (reprint of 2nd edn, 1905) (Darmstadt: Wissenschaftliche Buchgesellschaft, 1963), pp. 28–31.
53. Adler, *Theresienstadt*, pp. 677 [HGA/BC: 595]
54. H. G. Adler, 'Selbstverwaltung und Widerstand in den Konzentrationslagern der SS', in H. G. Adler, *Nach der Befreiung: Ausgewählte Essays zur Geschichte und Soziologie*, ed. by Peter Filkins with Jeremy Adler (Konstanz: Konstanz University Press, 2013), pp. 49–70 (p. 57).
55. Ibid., p. 61.
56. Jay Bernstein, *Torture and Dignity: An Essay on Moral Injury* (Chicago: Chicago University Press, 2015), p. 13.
57. Life in the camps was one in which 'freedom concretely meant death' (Adler, *Theresienstadt*, p. 242) [HGA/BC: 205].
58. Bernstein, *Torture and Dignity*, p. 180.

59. Cited by Bernstein, ibid., p. 111.
60. Nikolaus Wachsmann, *KL: A History of the Nazi Concentration Camps*, p. 497.
61. Hans Kelsen, *Reine Rechtslehre* (2nd edn 1960, republished by Matthias Jestaedt) (Tübingen: Siebeck / Vienna: Verlag Österreich, 2017), p. 26.

CHAPTER 12

A Mystic Among the Intellectuals: H. G. Adler in Debate with Jean Améry and Hannah Arendt[1]

Jeremy Adler

The twentieth century saw the rise of the public intellectual — figures like Albert Einstein and Jean-Paul Sartre, Andrei Sakharov and Václav Havel — who by virtue of their pre-eminence, whether in the sciences or in the arts, and thanks to their overwhelming intellect and integrity, exercised a strong influence in the moral universe and thereby, also, in the political sphere. Julien Benda has given the classic definition:[2] the intellectual is the guardian of independent judgement, a thinker who owes loyalty to the truth alone. He or she is both independent and representative, both free in judgement and bound by a moral obligation. This enables, indeed compels such figures to participate in debate. The likely models for these voices were nineteenth-century originals like Heinrich Heine, who fled Germany for Paris in 1831 on political grounds, and Émile Zola, whose pamphlet, *J'accuse,* published in 1898, by disinterestedly defending a Jewish officer, laid down the parameters for every future human rights discourse as practiced by European public intellectuals. The modern term was first introduced by Maurice Barrès in the French Third Republic to denigrate the Dreyfusards as political dilettantes, but quickly took on a positive sense. Morality, then, and a crusading personality, belong to the very nature of the intellectual. Edward Said offers one of the most compelling definitions — at first sight:[3]

> Someone able to speak the truth, a [...] courageous and angry individual for whom no worldly power is too big and imposing to be criticized and pointedly taken to task. The real or true intellectual is therefore always an outsider, living in self-imposed exile, and on the margins of society. He or she speaks to, as well as for, a public, necessarily in public, and is properly on the side of the dispossessed, the unrepresented and the forgotten.

Whilst few would dissent from Said's trust in courage, anger need by no means be key, nor need the intellectual live on the margins. He or she may be as gentle as Albert Schweitzer, as gentrified as Matthew Arnold, as established as Carl Schmitt, or as supportive of the status quo as C. P. Snow; though of course, he or she may often arrive from the outside, like Václav Havel, or Edward Said himself, not to mention Jean-Paul Sartre, who insisted on own his extra-territoriality. What counts is a fine intellect that acts under an ethical imperative for the purposes of a wider good.

The modern intellectual is closely affined with the traditional philosopher, humanist, and critic, who occupied this role in earlier eras. One thinks of Cicero, Erasmus, Locke, Rousseau, Burke or Kant, all of whom directly influenced political activity. From Locke's impact on the Bill of Rights to the role of Rousseau's ideas in the French Revolution, from Burke's interventions on foreign policy or the foreshadowing of the United Nations in Kant's ideal of Universal Peace up until Einstein's letter to the General Assembly, philosophers and thinkers have helped to shape the public sphere. Mindful of these and similar interventions, post-war intellectuals sought to refashion the moral and political universe. Among the statements issued at this time, perhaps the most affecting came from Albert Einstein, whose 'Message to Intellectuals' sought a new way to think, a new way to act. Einstein pleads to abstain from warlike behaviour, proposes extending the role of the United Nations, and suggests that states concentrate on home affairs, and relinquish their foreign policy to an international body:[4]

> Mankind can only gain protection against the danger of unimaginable destruction and wanton annihilation if a supranational organization has alone the authority to produce or possess these [horrible weapons, capable of destroying in a few seconds masses of human beings]. It is unthinkable, however, that nations under existing conditions would hand over such authority to a supranational organization unless the organization would have the legal rights and duties to solve all the conflicts which in the past have led to war.

Peace is the burden of Einstein's thesis, the prime good to which he aspires, and the condition to which he subordinates all other aims. He develops his vision in similar statements, such as 'On the Abolution of the Threat of War'.[5] It is hard to measure the impact of such appeals, not least since they have not been met, but it would be hard to deny that they contributed to a climate of opinion, in which peace and supranationality located themselves as desirable values in the political arena, not least in the European Union. Einstein's proposals contain two or three key ingredients: idealism, radicality, and a will to revise, indeed sacrifice the pre-existing State. I will return to these points when I consider H. G. Adler's initial reaction to the Shoah, but will here merely note that, from today's perspective, it seems astonishing that Einstein should dwell exclusively on weapons of mass destruction, and omit any reference to the Holocaust. One searches in vain for a reference to Auschwitz in his writings. All we find are two essays on the Warsaw Ghetto, one in 1944 and the other in 1948.[6] It would almost seem as if for the world's leading intellectual, the worst atrocity of all time had never taken place. In his acceptance speech upon receiving the Nobel Prize, 'The Problem of Peace', Albert Schweitzer did not commit the same error:[7] 'Since we now know what a terrible evil war is, we must spare no effort to prevent its recurrence. To this reason must also be added an ethical one: In the course of the last two wars, we have been guilty of acts of inhumanity which make one shudder, and in any future war we would certainly be guilty of even worse. This must not happen!'

Notwithstanding his recognition of so many atrocities, Schweitzer put his efforts in service of the same cause as Einstein. Forging a unique international bond, four intellectuals, Albert Einstein, Albert Schweitzer, Bertrand Russell, and Otto Hahn, combined forces to combat nuclear testing. They sought to prevent the onset of the nuclear age. It fell to another leading intellectual to define himself by opposing the nuclear age he had helped to bring about: Andrei Sakharov.[8] This, then, provided the most pressing task for the post-war generation. In urgency, the power and imminent threat of the atomic bomb apparently overshadowed memorializing Auschwitz. That goes some way to explain why the Holocaust did not immediately arouse the outrage of the intellectuals. The enormity of the Final Solution did not become apparent at once. It took numerous testimonies, which appeared in successive waves, to demonstrate the colossal horror. A book such as Primo Levi's *Se Questo è un uomo?* of 1947 required years, during which its author lived in obscurity, before it achieved its effect,[9] and until he finally emerged as the preeminent intellectual of the Shoah. Elie Wiesel's *La nuit* did not appear until 1958, with a Christian preface by François Mauriac — a well-meaning solecism that could not have occurred ten years later.[10] Awkwardness, embarrassment, shame, and an aura of guilt surrounded the victims, created by the customary moral twist by which the onlooker blames the target. Thus the victims became the scapegoats for the dead. All this combined to prevent an acceptance of their narrative. Thirty years on, Wiesel received a Nobel Prize, and became a leading spirit on the intellectual scene. Yet it took a relative latecomer, Jean Améry, partly prompted by the Frankfurt Auschwitz Trial of 1963, to agonize about the problems of the intellectual in Auschwitz.[11] These and figures like them successfully made the transition from victim via witness to intellectual of the Shoah, and so established themselves at the very centre of debate in post-war Europe. Thus Auschwitz entered the public domain as an experience that authenticated intellectual discourse. This was also the precarious path taken by H. G. Adler, whose rather more modest career unfolded more or less in parallel to that of Primo Levi and Elie Wiesel. His views differed from both, in that he clung to a religious position. His stance was also diametrically opposed to that of Jean Améry, who believed that the intellect capitulated in the face of terror. H. G. Adler, by contrast, had buttressed his mind to confront his tormentors, and had employed the intellect to overcome suffering. In a poem he wrote in the underground factory at KL Langenstein, an outlying camp of Buchenwald, which survivors considered worse than Auschwitz, he scorned his tormentors:[12]

EINSAME WEGE

Ich habe nichts mehr zu verlieren
Und kann das kleine nicht mehr denken,
So forsch ich nach den Urgeschenken
Die einen Menschen bildend zieren.

Selbst steh ich da; die Schritte lenken
Will ich, doch nicht den wilden Tieren
Mich überlassen, die mit gieren
Gebärden meine Seele kränken.

Ich bin so alt, daß ich mit stieren
Verfolgern meinen Geist verschränken
Jetzt nicht mehr mag, mit Schmeichlern schmieren

Nun längst nicht will; nur tief mich senken
Ins Urlicht, um nicht zu erfrieren,
Dies will ich und mich selig tränken.

[LONELY WAYS

I have nothing more to lose
And can no longer think of the little things,
So I search for the original gifts
Which adorn and form a human being.

I stand here by myself; I want to direct
My steps, but not to give myself over
To the wild animals, who insult
My soul with their greedy gestures.

I have grown so old, that I no longer wish
To entangle my spirit with the fixed gaze
Of my persecutors, nor smear

With the flatterers; just lower myself deep down
Into the original light, in order not to freeze,
That is my wish and blissfully to quench.]

As a Jewish prisoner, and to bolster his identity, the speaker appropriates some of the most characteristic tenets of the German tradition. Firstly, Luther's celebrated self-defence spoken at the Reichstag in Worms of 1521: 'Hier stehe ich, ich kann nicht anders, Gott helfe mir!' [Here I stand, I cannot do otherwise, God help me.] This is here varied as 'Selbst steh ich da' [I stand here by myself.] Secondly, the title of the poem 'Urlicht' from the Romantic anthology *Des Knaben Wunderhorn* [Youth's Magic Horn (1805–1808)], edited by Achim von Arnim and Clemens Brentano, a word here used in the sense of an 'ultimate divinity'. The poem will be best known from Gustav Mahler's Second Symphony, the so-called Resurrection Symphony. It may also be assumed that this original light corresponds to the Heaven that Jacob Böhme finds in all places, notably the human heart, and that this meditative poem recalls Böhme's mystical world:[13] 'derselbe Himmel ist überall, auch in dir selber' [Heaven is everywhere, even in yourself]. By adopting these cultural icons, the speaker asserts his superiority over his tormentors, and claims his heritage as the true heir to German tradition. Thus he inverts the relationship between captor and captive, inasmuch as the guards are seen to be the prisoners, and the prisoner himself becomes free — in spirit. His refusal to tangle with his captors or to admit their power ('daß ich mit stieren / Verfolgern meinen Geist verschränken / Jetzt nicht mehr mag'; [that I no longer wish / To entangle my spirit with the fixed gaze / Of my persecutors]) further confirms his moral superiority. Even the act of 'resistance', what he calls 'Widerstand',[14] is anticipated in Böhme's theology. Thus German mysticism enables the victim to steel his intellect. Adler's position may be compared to that adopted by the members of the *Weiße Rose*. They too emphasized the importance of 'inner freedom'.[15] This whole *Weltanschauung* is in direct contradiction to Jean Améry, who claims that:[16]

> Ungeheuerlich und unüberwindlich türmte sich die Machtgestalt der SS-Staates vor dem Häftling auf, eine Wirklichkeit, die nicht umgangen werden konnte und die darum am Ende *vernünftig* erschien. Jedermann, er mochte es geistig draußen gehalten haben wie auch immer, wurde in diesem Sinne zum Hegelianer: Der SS-Staat erschien im metallischen Glanz seiner Totalität als ein Staat, in dem die Idee sich verwirklichte.

> [The power structure of the SS state towered up before the prisoner monstrously and indomitably, a reality that could not be escaped and therefore finally semed *reasonable*. No matter what his thinking may have been on the outside, in this sense he became a Hegelian: in the metallic brilliance of its totality the SS state appeared as a state in which the idea became reality.]

The problem with Améry's position is that it takes the SS-State on its own terms. His tell-tale phrase regarding its 'metallic glow' ['metallischer Glanz'] reads like naked power-worship, and concedes the enemy a victory it neither deserves nor attained. The defeat of Nazi Germany proved that its "idea" was in fact hollow. Indeed, Améry gets Hegel completely wrong. In his *Grundlinien der Philosophie des Rechts* [Foundations of the Philosophy of Right], Hegel explicitly asserts the *moral* character of the state:[17]

> Der Staat ist die Wirklichkeit der sittlichen Idee — der sittliche Geist, als der *offenbare*, sich selbst deutliche, substantielle Wille, der sich denkt und weiß und das, was er weiß und insofern er es weiß, vollführt. An der *Sitte* hat er seine unmittelbare und an dem *Selbstbewußtsein* des Einzelnen, dem Wissen und Tätigkeit desselben, seine vermittelte Existenz [...].

> [The state is the reality of the ethical idea — the ethical spirit, as that which is *manifest*, the will which is apparent to itself and substantial, which thinks itself and knows and carries out that which it knows insofar as it knows. In what is *ethical* it possesses its immediate and in the *self-consciousness* of the individual, the knowledge and activity of the same, its mediated existence [...].]

There is simply no way in which Améry's grasp of the SS-State can be reconciled with Hegel's views, albeit a case can, and has, been made for the influence of Hegel's ideas on Nazism.[18] Just as Améry's philosophical position makes little sense, in light of what Hegel actually meant, his humanism is questionable, too, since it accepts moral defeat. But whereas there is indeed little or no room for political manoeuvre in the camps, as H. G. Adler's poem agrees, no possibility to combat absolute power, although Hermann Langbein has in fact shown the possibilities for resistance,[19] it does not follow that the prisoner must renounce spiritual freedom. The path afforded by mystical contemplation, the inner way, enables the prisoner to make contact with a timeless reality — the so-called 'Urlicht', a divine archetype. Like earlier Jewish mystics, he does not envisage the *unio mystica* with God, but with a lower form.[20] The prisoner, imprisoned on account of his religious attachment, instrumentalizes religion to combat his tormentors. His putative shame becomes his badge of honour. In this regard, H. G. Adler, writing in a camp, refutes

Améry's view that the mind could not withstand Auschwitz, and acts as a free and independent intellectual. In his essay 'Geist und Grenzen des Widerstands' [The Spirit and Limits of Resistance], which appeared as early as 1978, H. G. Adler offers a morphology of resistance, and concludes that the final category lies in 'witness':[21] 'Zuletzt erfüllt sich der Widerstand in Zeugenschaft für die Nachwelt.' [In the end, resistance is fulfilled in witness for posterity.] The mere act of leaving behind a document of life in captivity, such as the messages that members of the *Sonderkommando* buried near the crematoria at Auschwitz,[22] constitutes a form of opposition. On these terms, the poems that H. G. Adler wrote in the camps, under pain of death, should be understood as resistance. In exercising his free will, like others in the camps, he asserted his independence as an intelligent being.

One of his earliest attempts to make an intervention after the war, the unpublished essay 'Nach der Befreiung — ein Wort an die Mitwelt' [After Liberation — a Message to the World], dated only a few months after the conclusion of hostilities on 12 December 1945, Adler made the same point. He recognizes the degredation imposed on the prisoners:[23] 'Das Lager also tötete jedes Gefühl und schuf aus Menschen in gröbster dumpfer Sinnlichkeit befangene stumpf funktionierende Automate.' [Thus the Camp also killed off every feeling and turned people into prejudiced, dully operating automatons in the most crude and gloomy sensuality.] Notwithstanding this predisposition of their environment to turn human beings into robots, inner freedom remained possible. What this required, though, was an effort of the will:[24]

> Seelisch ist alles auszuhalten, so lange die Seele sich nicht aufgibt, sogar wenn der Leib mißhandelt wird, und zwar bis zu den Grenzen, die die physiologisch-biologischen Voraussetzungen für die Aufrechterhaltung des Lebens nicht geradezu unmittelbar vernichten.
>
> [Spiritually it is possible to withstand everything, as long as the spirit does not renounce itself, even if the body is maltreated, namely up to the limits that do not immediately destroy the physio-biological preconditions for the maintenance of life.]

Once again, H. G. Adler's position proves to be opposed to Améry's intelligent despair. For Améry,[25] 'Der Geist in seiner Totalität erklärte sich im Lager als unzuständig.' [In the camp, the intellect in its totality declared itself to be incompetent.] H. G. Adler contradicts this position by treating the intellect as a weapon in the struggle for survival. Far from being 'incompetent', it displays a unique competence inasmuch as it can create a pristine sphere untouched by degradation. Hermann Langbein extends this insight to the entire realm of Auschwitz. At the end of his timely monograph, *Menschen in Auschwitz* [Human Beings in Auschwitz], he observes:[26] 'viele Beispiele beweisen, daß in diesem System die Stimme des Gewissens auf die Dauer nicht zu ersticken ist' [many examples demonstrate, that in the long run the voice of conscience cannot be silenced in this system]. Indeed, the very weapon that H. G. Adler employed, the ethnological method of 'participant observation' introduced by Bronislaw Malinowski in *Argonauts of the Western Pacific*,[27] confutes Améry's findings. Améry doubted the possibility to grasp society in the camps:[28]

In Auschwitz war der Geist nichts als er selber, und es bestand keine Chance, ihn an eine noch so unzulängliche, noch so verborgene soziale Struktur zu montieren [!]. Der Intellektuelle stand also allein mit seinem Geist [...].

[In Auschwitz the intellect was nothing more than itself and there was no chance to apply it to a social structure [!], no matter how concealed that may have been. Thus the intellectual was alone with his intellect [...].]

Améry's standpoint treats suffering as an absolute. The monstrous reality overpowers the mind. Pure terror defeats analysis. Judgement capitulates. For H. G. Adler, however, the attempt to grasp the social structure in every detail in the camp constituted a tool which helped him — always presupposing good luck — to survive. In turning to anthropology, H. G Adler employed one of the major disciplines that gave the twentieth century some of its chief public intellectuals, from J. G. Frazer to Malinowski himself, and on to Margaret Mead, Claude Lévi-Strauss, Mary Douglas, and Clifford Geertz. In different ways, these figures delivered generalizable truths, whether e.g. about ritual, sexuality, social structures, or symbols, that illuminated modern society as a whole. By following in the footsteps of such as Frazer and Malinowski, and by joining forces with Lévi-Strauss or Mary Douglas, who had been a pupil of his old friend, Franz Baermann Steiner, H. G. Adler brought the experience of the camps to bear on topical issues. He lit a singular light on a barbaric century. Just as Robert S. Lynd and Helen Merrell Lynd took a single town, Middletown[29] — a title which echoes George Eliot's sociological novel, *Middelmarch* (1871–72) — to epitomize America, H. G. Adler treated Theresienstadt as a case study of the Nazi system, and by extension, as a model of modernity itself.

The author has left us a record of his book's genesis in an essay he wrote in 1956, a year after its first publication, entitled 'Warum habe ich mein Buch *Theresienstadt 1941–1945* geschrieben?' [Why did I Write my Book *Theresienstadt 1941–1945*?].[30] It's worth quoting from this essay at some length, as it reveals the emergence of H. G. Adler's intellectual position. He recalls the decision to write a book on the camp a few weeks after his incarceration:[31]

Seltsam, dieser Entschluß [ein Buch zu schreiben] verlieh mir eine heilsame Kraft. Wohl dauerte es noch mehrere Monate, bevor ich so ziemlich mein seelisches Gleichgewicht wieder gewonnen hatte, aber der noch so unbestimmte Plan zu einem Buche, das ein Denkmal dieser Zeit werden sollte, veränderte wohltatig mein kümmerliches Dasein. Ich erzog mich dazu, die Dinge in einer kühlen Betrachtung zu sehen. Kühl — ja, wenn ich es bedenke, das ist das richtige Wort — aber diese Kühle mußte ständig neu erorbert werden, [ich] mußte das Feuer, den Brand, die Glut immer wieder jäh hereinstürzender grauenvoller Ereignisse über mich ergehen lassen, um geprüft, gehärtet und schließlich, als Theresienstadt mit noch viel schrecklicheren Orten vertauscht war, so unbestechlich gesichert zu werden, daß ich den Willen zur Erkenntnis der ganzen Wahrheit ertragen konnte.

[Strangely, this decision [to write a book] granted me a salutary strength. Although it still took several months before I could find my spiritual balance again, but the still vague plan to write a book that would be a monument

to this era beneficently transformed my miserable existence. I taught myself
to observe things coolly. Cool — yes, when I think of it, that's the right
word — but this coolness constantly had to be re-conquered, [I] had to let
the fire, the conflagration, the heat of horrific events that always suddenly
erupted overwhelm me, in order to become tested, hardened and finally, when
Theresienstadt had been exchanged for much more terrible places, to become
so incorruptible and certain, that I could stand the will to know the truth in
its entirety.]

H. G. Adler presents his witness as an extended process of self-education. It
resembles an apprenticeship to truth, or better: an initiation to an ordeal by fire.
The subject does not show himself as a helpless victim, battered by fortune, but as a
skilled observer, who grasps the ferocity of the events as a tool by which to sharpen
his own faculties. These doctrines, largely I think derived from the *Bhagavad
Gita*, which he had studied from the age of sixteen, and the *Spiritual Exercises* of
St. Ignatius of Loyola, which enabled him to transform adversity into a means to
knowledge. The solitude that the prisoner experiences in his isolation from the
world can be turned to good account insofar as it can be exploited to focus on
ultimate reality. As St. Ignatius puts it:[32]

> From this isolation three chief benefits, among many others, follow. The first
> is that a man, by separating himself from many friends and acquaintances,
> and likewise from many not well-ordered affairs, to serve and praise God our
> Lord, merits no little in the sight of His Divine Majesty. The second is, that
> being thus isolated, and not having his understanding divided on many things,
> but concentrating his care on one only, namely, on serving his Creator and
> benefiting his own soul, he uses with greater freedom his natural powers, in
> seeking with diligence what he so much desires. The third: the more our soul
> finds itself alone and isolated, the more apt it makes itself to approach and
> to reach its Creator and Lord, and the more it so approaches Him, the more
> it dispose itself to receive graces and gifts from His Divine Sovereignty and
> Goodness.

Spiritual practice serves a dual purpose for the initiate. It brings him closer to God.
And it enables him to harden himself in order to engage with the terrible reality
outside. As curious as it may sound, therefore, esoteric lore provides the inmate with
an wise instrument with which to attempt survival. He engages in a spiritual battle,
which mirrors the war outside, and the daily struggle with his captors. Paradoxically,
imprisonment becomes the route to self-liberation, to spiritual enrichment, and to
philosophical truth. Yet, in a daring reversal of the mystical technique, H. G. Adler
steels himself not to view God, but to know Evil. The captive instrumentalizes
mysticism in order to grasp the full horrors of physical reality. And against his
tormenters, he hurls the power of goodness, a distillation of civilization, comprising
the best of both the East and of the West. This means that for H. G. Adler, being a
homo religious enabled him to fulfil his task as an intellectual.

As has recently been argued, a major reorientation occurred in Germany after
the Second World War regarding the role of the public intellectual. This involved
politicizing culture.[33] As Johannes R. Becher, the erstwhile Expressionist and
subsequently a leading light in the emerging East Germany proclaimed in 1945:[34]

Wir haben niemals den [...] hohen Kulturleistungen gemäßen politischen
Ausdruck gefunden. Aus diesem unheilvollen Widerspruch zwischen Geist
und Macht müssen wir heraus, der uns zum schwersten Verhängnis unserer
Geschichte geworden ist und der letzten Endes jedes freies Geisteschaffen
vernichtet hat.

[We were never able to find a political expression that corresponded to [our]
high cultural achievements. We must now get beyond that unholy contradiction
between spirit and power, which has led to the worst catastrophe in our history,
and which ultimately even destroyed any free intellectual activity.]

As needs no emphasis, this reorientation deeply affected post-war German culture
on both sides of the Iron Curtain. West Germany's two Nobel laureates, Heinrich
Böll and Günter Grass, were both noted for their political interventions; and
other leading figures, notably Hans Magnus Enzensberger, perhaps owed their
reputations more to their political views than to the quality of their verse. H. G.
Adler to some extent shared their stance. He defined his position in an essay entitled
'Der Autor zwischen Dichtung und Politik' [The Writer between Literature and
Politics], first published in 1971, and originally delivered at a conference of the
Austrian PEN-Club. He argues that the writer occupies a place 'between' literature
and politics:[35]

Diese Zwischenstellung ist der Ort, der dem Autor in der Gesellschaft angewiesen ist, Kampfplatz zum Angriff und zur Verteidigung zugleich. Hier hat
der Autor auszuhalten und sich selbst zu bekennen, wofür er die Verantwortung
übernimmt und trägt. Es ist auch der Ort, in dem er seine Wirksamkeit
entfaltet [...].

[This intermediary position is the place, which is given to the author by society,
a battleground on which to attack and defend at one and the same time. The
writer has to endure here and to confess what he assumes responsibility for.
This is also the place where his work takes effect [...].]

Thus H. G. Adler largely shared the post-war German consensus that a writer
needed a political orientation. He asserts his credo not — as Enzensberger would
have it — by fusing politics and literature, but by establishing himself between these
two modes of activity.

The two chief responses to the war and its atrocities which formed the starting-
point of post-war consciousness on the international stage are Sartre's *L'Exstentialisme
est un humanisme*[36] and Heidegger's rejoinder, *Über den Humanismus*.[37] Here, too, we
miss any direct reference to the Holocaust. It seems as if the philosophers had agreed
to skirt around the Final Solution. Only gradually did a memory emerge,[38] in the
museum at Auschwitz[39] and then more widely in the western world.[40] Indeed, it
was not before 1951, in an essay written two years earlier, that 'Auschwitz' figured
prominently as a metonymy for the Shoah — namely in the writings of Theodor
Adorno.[41] Only now, arguably, did the Holocaust begin to become central to the
intellectual discourse of the age. In no small part, this must also have been thanks
to Hannah Arendt's monumental work, *The Origins of Totalitarianism*.[42] The study
of totalitarianism merged with the wider concerns of post-war Europe.

H. G. Adler's trajectory intersected with the efforts of some of the figures I have mentioned so far — Einstein, Arendt, Adorno — as he sought to effect his transition from ex-prisoner and survivor to public intellectual. Having initiated a correspondence with Hermann Broch, the latter tried to help him publish *Theresienstadt 1941–1945*, and enlisted Hannah Arendt and Albert Einstein in the attempt to find an American publisher.[43] This led nowhere. It was left to Adorno to raise the subvention to bring out the volume in Germany.[44] In coming into contact with these writers and thinkers, H. G. Adler naturally gravitated to the figures who wished to re-organize the political sphere in the immediate post-war era, and thereby aimed to restore the moral order. Whilst united in their outrage at the Holocaust, they did not dwell on retrospective analysis, but used their insight to oppose the recurrence of similar catastrophes in the future. In the camps, Rabbi Leo Baeck, the leader of the German Jewish Community, provided him with a model of the spiritual resistance he practiced throughout his life:[45]

> [...] Hingegen fühlte sich Baeck — und er sprach das auch aus — als Mittelpunkt eines sittlichen Widerstandes. Den übte und lehrte er, indem er sich so verhielt, wie seine Überzeugung nach ein Mensch sich immer und überall auch unter den widrigsten Umständen zu verhalten hat: gütig, wahrhaftig und jederzit hilfsbereit.

> [[...] But Baeck considered himself to be at the centre of a moral resistance. He practiced and inculcated this method, inasmuch as he behaved as he believed every human being should, always and everywhere, in the most hostile circumstances: kindly, truthful and ever-helpful.]

Baeck's behaviour imbued H. G. Adler with the maxims, grounded in the Talmud, by which he lived. If, however, he had one, single moment of epiphany in the camps, it was the insights garnered at Auschwitz. Firstly, in the teachings of the Sayings of the Fathers in the Talmud,[46] which he learned about from several orthodox Jews, chief among them the Slovak Jew, Max Schiff. These precepts concerning right action remained with him throughout his life. Secondly, his insight concerned how far State power can go awry: the untrammelled State may destroy the citizen. Shortly after his release, in 1946, in a short text with a title reminiscent of the anarchist tradition, entitled 'Gegen den Staat — Geharnischte Einfälle' [Against the State — Militant Thoughts], he sharpened this legacy into a radical thesis:[47] 'Was der Mensch auch Gutes schafft, der Staat ergreift es und verdirbt es.' [Whatever good a human being may do, the State will seize hold of it and destroy it.] This position, slightly tempered, remained constant. In the year before his death, we find him publishing his testament, the *Prolegomena for an Experimental Theology*. This asserts that whatever acts the State performs, however legal or well-intended, they will always constitute a form of violence against the person.[48] This view arose very much as a response to the experience of state power in Auschwitz. It cannot however be regarded as the whole story. It must be balanced by an even more powerful credo — a trust in the beneficence of the modern, humanitarian state. He hopes that the welfare state will restrain the state's more questionable tendencies:[49]

Gelingt es [dem Wohlfahrtsstaat], zur Befreiung von vermeidlichem menschlichen Elend wesentlich beizutragen, wofür die bisherigen Erfahrungen
sprechen, dann wird er vor dem Richtspruch der Geschichte als ein für seine
Zeit wertvoller Lösungsversuch gewichtiger sozialer Probleme bestehen.

[If [the welfare state] succeeds in significantly contributing to the liberation of
mankind from avoidable misery, as our experience suggests, it will go down
in the judgement of history as an invaluable attempt to resolve severe social
problems.]

Adler's questioning of state power by no means entailed an ultimate negation of the
state. On the contrary. He supports the state which supports its citizens. Besides this
positive attitude, on the balance sheet of his views, we must also place his theory
of administration layed out in *Adminstered Man*, which seeks to modify, to correct,
and to improve, but by no means to abandon the joint project of the modern state.
He subscribes to this ideal along with all right minded citizens, as the chief social
structure instituted to enable a common life acted out within the bounds of the
law.

The book with which H. G. Adler impacted the scene was his landmark study,
Theresienstadt 1941–1945: Das Antlitz einer Zwangsgemeinschaft [*Theresienstadt 1941–1945:
The Face of a Coerced Community*], first completed in 1947, but only published, in a
later version, in 1955.[50] Like Primo Levi's *If this is a Man?* it is a personal testimony;
like Eugen Kogon's *Theory and Practice of Hell,* it is a sociology; like Solzhenitsyn's
Gulag Archipelago, it is an encyclopaedia; whilst in its blend of documents, analysis,
testimony and theory, it is like no other. Hence, more than any other single text, it
laid the foundations for modern Holocaust Studies. The publication of this book in
1955 placed the author centre stage — introducing him to figures such as Buber
and Scholem in Israel, to leading intellectuals in Germany, and even providing
an entrée to the German President, Theodor Heuss. Henceforth, Adler took a
distinctive place in the intellectual debates of the Federal Republic, chiefly thanks
to his regular radio broadcasts for Westdeutscher Rundfunk [West German Radio]
and Süddeutscher Rundfunk [South German Radio].[51] For the latter, he gave talks
or series of talks on such subjects such as 'Das Auswertige Amt und die Endlösung'
[The Foreign Office and the Final Solution, 1965], 'Die Zwangslager im Dritten
Reich' [Concentration Camps in the Third Reich, 1967], and 'Das Judentum als
Religion' [Judaism as Religion, 1969]. Perhaps the high-point of his radio career
was the series he compiled with Hermann Langbein, the resistance fighter and
Auschwitz historian, 'Auschwitz: Topographie eines Vernichtungslagers', first
broadcast on 18 October 1961, and which lasted almost three hours.[52] Coming two
years before the Frankfurt Auschwitz trial, the documentary provided the first
full overview of the camp in Germany, and presumably did much to shape public
understanding. Another series, 'Die Juden in Deutschland' [The Jews in Germany]
proved so successful that it was later reprinted as a book.[53]

By now, *Theresienstadt 1941–1945* had entered the intellectual debate, most prominently in Hannah Arendt's study, *The Origins of Totalitarianism*, which borrowed
certain insights in the first edition of 1950, without acknowledgement, and before

the *Theresienstadt* book appeared, because Arendt had read it in manuscript as a referee in 1947; but then, in the next printing of 1966 of her monograph, when Adler's book was published, she acknowledges her source. The climax of the book's public effect occurred at the Eichmann trial in Jerusalem in 1961–62. On 18 May 1961, in session 45, Judge Halevi asked the State Prosecutor Bar-Or whether he had finished submitting his evidence, to which he replied that he had, though with some embarrassment he referred to what he called 'the well-known book by Dr John Adler'. He justified omitting the book from his evidence saying:[54]

> [Adler] himself was in Theresienstadt. I simply hesitate to burden the court with material. This is an excellent, authentic book. It is based on impeccable sources. It is a thick volume, and it is at the disposal of the court. I simply hesitate to admit it. Much has been written about Theresienstadt. I try to submit material which refers to the Accused, without impairing the general picture. We are faced with the difficult problem that one has somehow to compromise and select, otherwise there is no end to it.

In her reportage *Eichmann in Jerusalem*, Hannah Arendt focuses on this episode, to attack the proceedings. She claims:[55]

> The reason for the omission was clear. [Adler's book] describes in detail how the feared "transport lists" were put together by the Jewish Council of Theresienstadt after the SS had given some general directives. [...] The prosecution's case would have been weakened if it had been forced to admit that the naming of individuals who had been sent to their doom had been, with few exceptions, the job of the Jewish administration.

The opposite is true. No previous book had demonstrated with such exactitude the entire chain of command from the Führer via Himmler and Heydrich and Kaltenbrunner to Eichmann and the Jewish Elders, or had shown what Adler calls the 'almost unlimited power Eichmann exercised in the entire party system'[56] in implementing the Final Solution. In her typical preference for scandal over truth, Arendt reveals her ignorance of the most basic facts surrounding this case. Firstly, H. G. Adler's book makes crystal clear the role Eichmann played in the deportations. Far from being 'general', as Arendt claims, the 'directives' handed down to the Elders were highly specific,[57] and detailed age, country of origin, category of person, and sometimes even individuals to be deported. The book leaves no room for doubt that the responsibility for the deportations lay with the German authorities, not the Jews. Secondly, there was no such thing as a 'Jewish Council' in Theresienstadt that could have compiled the lists of deportees. Hannah Arendt presumably means the *Ältestenrat*, the so-called Council of Elders; but this body did not directly act in the matter of the deportations, which were prepared by the *Zentralevidenz* or Population Office. The actual compilation of the lists was a complex procedure, both rigorously bureaucratic and open to corruption. Yet H. G. Adler's book leaves not a shadow of a doubt that the ultimate responsibility for this activity lay with the German authorities, notably with Eichmann and the *Lagerkommandatur*,[58] i.e. the SS Camp Commander's Office. Not only that. By presenting the survival statistics of the deportees, including in some cases their zero chances, Adler demonstrates that deportations meant extermination.[59] There is no truth in Arendt's claim that Adler's book might have inculpated the Jews rather than the Nazis. Thirdly, it should be noted that Adler had in fact provided the Israeli State with an official document regarding Eichmann's role, including 19 questions for use by the State Prosecutor.[60] Adler's evidence was decisive. It helped to ensure Eichmann's conviction. As the authorities informed Adler after the trial: 'Your books and the surveys prepared by you especially for us, were used extensively in the preparation of the Eichmann-trial'.[61] And fourthly, even more remarkably, Eichmann himself read Adler's book in prison, to prepare himself for the trial — so objective were its findings. The book, then, was known to all parties, including the accused. Had they wished, and if Arendt were right, the prosecution could easily have invoked it, but there was no need. The State Prosecutor spoke the truth. Presenting a book of nearly 1,000 pages as evidence would have obscured the picture. H. G. Adler's involvement did not end with the trial. Unlike Arendt, who believed that Eichmann should hang, together with Buber and Scholem, he signed a letter to the Israeli President, to plead for Eichmann's life.

The publication of Arendt's farrago, *Eichmann in Jerusalem: A Report on the Banality of Evil* in 1963, caused an international outcry. Arendt was playing to the gallery. She derided the Jewish leader, Leo Baeck, as 'the Jewish Führer', drawing a link that is beneath contempt. She later removed the stain. But the aim is clear: to parade sensational, self-serving gossip as truthful journalism. The intellectual community was in uproar. Gershom Scholem condemned her on several occasions, beginning with a five-page private letter of 23 June 1963,[62] which accuses her of 'demagogic overstatement'. Three years later, in December 1966, Isaiah Berlin was still criticizing her in conversation with Edmund Wilson.[63] Yet her mischievous term, 'the banality of evil', with which she thought to refute Kant's concept 'radical evil', has become one of the great catch-phrases of the Shoah.

H. G. Adler, as one of the authorities she quotes, also played a role in this debate. His response,[64] 'Was weiß Hannah Arendt von Eichmann und die Endlösung?' [What does Hannah Arendt know about Eichmann and the 'Final Solution'?] was published to coincide with the German edition, in 1964. Where other intellectuals, such as Scholem, had scorned the concept of 'the banality of evil' on intuitive grounds, Adler argues as a historian, citing hard facts. The argument proceeds in several stages. I will single out just three. Firstly, he attacks her bizarre contention that the Nazis were law-abiding; secondly, he attacks her equally farcical claim that Eichmann acted in the name of a legally constituted 'State'; and finally, he attacks her concept of the 'banality of evil' on the grounds that it is based on Eichmann's weird appearance in the dock, and not on his role in the killing machine. To compress all this into one complex point: Arendt's 'banality of evil' relies on a misreading of the Nazi State, of German law, of the SS, of its operatives, and of the evidence in court. Her view, being based on the pathetic appearance of the self-righteous man in the dock, ignores the terror he instilled with his naked power, guns, dogs, henchmen, and sinister black uniform designed by Hugo Boss. His menacing aspect was anything but banal. Moreover, in blurring the line twixt perpetrator and victim, Arendt ratifies the unspeakable, normalizes evil. In contradistinction to her adjuration of 'banality', a more sober analysis reveals that the greater danger lies in the *institutionalization of evil* — a mechanism close to her own concept — and so apparent in the genocides of the post-war era, whether in Rwanda or Bosnia. If evil were truly 'banal', we wouldn't have anything to fear. But there is nothing banal about Eichmann or Pol Pot or Karadžić — when in office. These are tyrants. Masters over life and death, unbound by ethics or by law, who know how to manipulate power in order to organize their crimes on an ever-increasing scale, within a rigid social framework. The role of the public intellectual must therefore be to oppose such figures, not to justify or trivialize them, and to refute them by moral opposition. What we need, then, to limit the threat of perennial violence, is to establish, by means of political action, unequivocal and institutional limits, boundaries, and deterrents, laid down in ethics and in law, to ward off danger — as far as humanly possible.[65] In other words, arguing against Arendt and Adorno, but decidedly together with the early Sartre and the other post-war intellectuals such as Schweitzer, Einstein, and Russell, H. G. Adler advocates a return to the radical Enlightenment.

Notes to Chapter 12

1. For a study of H. G. Adler and Jean Améry, see Helen Finch, '*Ressentiment* beyond Nietzsche and Améry: H. G. Adler between Literary Ressentiment and Divine Grace', in *Re-thinking Ressentiment. On the Limits of Criticism and the Limits of its Critics*, ed. by Jeanne Riou and Mary Gallagher (Bielefeld: Transcript, 2016), pp. 71–86.
2. Julien Benda, *La Trahisons des Clercs* (1927) (Paris: Éditions Grasset, 2003).
3. Quoted after Jeremy Jennings and Anthony Kemp-Welch, eds, *Intellectuals in Politics from the Dreyfus Affair to Salman Rushdie* (London: Routledge, 1997), pp. 1–2.
4. Albert Einstein, 'A Message to Intellectuals', in Albert Einstein, *Ideas and Opinions* (New York: Wings Books, 1954), pp. 147–51 (p. 150).
5. Einstein, *Ideas and Opinions*, 1954, pp. 165–66.
6. Albert Einstein, *The Einstein Reader* (New York: Citadel Press Books, 2006), pp. 243–45.
7. Albert Schweitzer, 'The Problem of Peace', Nobel Lecture 4 November 1954.
8. Andrei D. Sakharov, *Progress, Coexistence and Intellectual Freedom*, ed. by Harrison E. Salisbury (Harmondsworth: Penguin, 1968).
9. Primo Levi, *Se questo è un uomo?* (1947) (Torino: Einaudi, 1958).
10. Elie Wiesel, *La nuit* (Paris: Les Éditions de Minuit, 1958).
11. Irene Heidelberger-Leonard, *Jean Améry: Revolte in der Resignation: Biographie* (Stuttgart: Klett-Cotta, 2004), p. 185–224.
12. H. G. Adler, 'Einsame Wege', in *Andere Wege: Gesammelte Gedichte*, ed. Katrin Kohl and Franz Hocheneder (Klagenfurt: Drava, 2010), p. 280. Unless otherwise stated, all translations by Jeremy Adler.
13. Jakob Böhme, *Aurora*, in *Sämmtliche Werke*, II, ed. by K. W. Schiebler (Leipzig: Barth, 1832), p. 288.
14. Böhme, *Aurora*, p. 289.
15. Christoph Goos, 'Würde des Menschen: Restoring Human Dignity in Postwar Germany', in *Understanding Human Dignity: Proceedings of the British Academy 192*, ed. by Christopher McCrudden (Oxford: Oxford University Press, 2013), pp. 79–93 (pp. 88–89).
16. Jean Améry, 'An den Grenzen des Geistes', in *Jenseits von Schuld und Sühne* (Stuttgart: Klett-Cotta, 1977), p. 33. 'At the Mind's Limits', in *At the Mind's Limits: Contemplations by a Survivor on Auschwitz and its Realities*, trans. by Sidney Rosenfeld and Stella P. Rosenfeld (Bloomington, IN: Indiana University Press, 1980), pp. 1–20 (p. 12).

17. G. W. F. Hegel, *Grundlinien der Philosophie des Rechts*. Berliner Ausgabe, ed. by Michael Holzinger (Berlin, 2013), § 257, p. 398.

18. Hubert Kiesewetter, *Von Hegel zu Hitler: Die politische Verwirklichung einer totalitären Machtstaatstheorie in Deutschland (1815–1945)* (Hamburg: Hoffmann und Campe, 1974).

19. Hermann Langbein, *... nicht wie die Schafe zur Schlachtbank. Widerstand in den nationalsozialistischen Konzentrationslagern* (Frankfurt a/M: Fischer, 1980).

20. Gershom Scholem, *Die jüdische Mystik in ihren Hauptströmungen* (Frankfurt a/M: Metzner, 1957), p. 132–33.

21. H. G. Adler, 'Geist und Grenzen des Widerstands', in: *H. G. Adler — Der Wahrheit verplichtet: Interviews, Gedichte, Essays*, ed. by Jeremy Adler (Gerlingen: Bleicher Verlag, 1998), pp. 163–202 (p. 199).

22. Nathan Cohen, 'Diaries of the *Sonderkommando*', in *Anatomy of the Auschwitz Death Camp*, ed. by Yisrael Gutman and Michael Berenbaum (Bloomington, IN: Indiana University Press, 1994), pp. 522–34.

23. H. G. Adler, 'Nach der Befreiung — ein Wort an die Mitwelt', in H. G. Adler, *Nach der Befreiung: Ausgewählte Essays zur Geschichte und Soziologie*, ed. by Peter Filkins with Jeremy Adler (Konstanz: Konstanz University Press, 2013), pp. 43–47 (p. 45).

24. H. G. Adler, 'Nach der Befreiung — ein Wort an die Mitwelt', note 17, p. 43.

25. Améry, 'An den Grenzen des Geistes', p. 34. 'At the Mind's Limits', p. 19.

26. Hermann Langbein, *Menschen in Auschwitz* (Vienna: Europaverlag, 1972), p. 578.

27. Bronislaw Malinowski, *Argonauts of the Western Pacific: An Account of Native Enterprise and Adventure in the Archipelagos of Melanesian New Guinea* (London: Routledge and Kegan Paul, 1922).

28. Améry, 'An den Grenzen des Geistes', p. 20. 'At the Mind's Limits', p. 6.

29. Robert S. Lynd and Helen Merryl Lynd, *Middletown: A Study in American Culture* (London: Constable, 1929).

30. H. G. Adler, 'Warum habe ich mein Buch *Theresienstadt 1941–1945* geschrieben?', in *H. G. Adler — Der Wahrheit verpflichtet: Interviews, Gedichte, Essays*, ed. Jeremy Adler (Gerlingen: Bleicher, 1998), p. 111–14.

31. H. G. Adler, 'Warum habe ich mein Buch *Theresienstadt 1941–1945* geschrieben?', p. 112.

32. St. Ignatius of Loyola, *The Spiritual Exercises*, trans. by Father Elder Mullan (New York: Kennedy, 1914), p. 16.

33. Stephen Brockmann, 'Establishing Cultural Fronts in East and West Germany', *Comparative Critical Studies*, 13.2 (2016), 149–72.

34. Johannes R. Becher, 'Auferstehen', *Gesammelte Werke*, XVI, *Publizistik II 1939–1945* (Berlin: Aufbau, 1978), pp. 454–62 (p. 461).

35. H. G. Adler, 'Der Autor zwischen Literatur und Politik', in *Orthodoxie des Herzens: Ausgewählte Essays zu Literatur, Judentum und Politik*, ed. by Peter Filkins with Jeremy Adler (Konstanz: Konstanz University Press, 2014), pp. 13–25 (p. 24–25).

36. Jean-Paul Sartre, *L'Existentialisme et un humanisme* (Paris: Nagel, 1946).

37. Martin Heidegger, *Über den Humanismus* (Frankfurt a/M: Klostermann, 1949).

38. Aleida Assmann and Geoffrey Hartman, *Die Zukunft der Erinnerung und der Holocaust* (Konstanz: Konstanz University Press, 2012).

39. Jonathan Huener, *Auschwitz, Poland, and the Politics of Commemoration, 1945–1979* (Athens, OH: Ohio University Press, 2003).

40. James E. Young, *Writing and Rewriting the Holocaust: Narrative and the Consequences of Interpretation* (Bloomington, IN: Indiana University Press, 1988).

41. Theodor Adorno, 'Kulturkritik und Gesellschaft' (1949/1951), in *Prismen* (Frankfurt a/M: Suhrkamp, 1955).

42. Hannah Arendt, *The Origins of Totalitarianism* (New York: Harcourt Brace, 1951).

43. H. G. Adler und Hermann Broch, *Zwei Schriftsteller im Exil: Briefwechsel*, ed. by Ronald Speirs and John White (Göttingen: Wallstein, 2004).

44. H. G. Adler, *Theresienstadt 1941–1945: Das Antlitz einer Zwangsgemeinschaft*, 2nd edn (1960). Mit einem Nachwort von Jeremy Adler. (Göttingen: Wallstein, 2005), p. 914.

45. H. G. Adler, 'Botschaft in dunkler Zeit — Leo Baeck und sein Werk', in *Orthodoxie des Herzens*, ed. by Filkins with Adler, pp. 169–88 (p. 180).

46. *Sayings of the Fathers: Pirke Aboth*, the Hebrew Text with English translation and commentary by Joseph H. Hertz (1945) (New Jersey: Behrman House, 1986).

47. H. G. Adler, 'Gegen den Staat — Geharnischte Einfälle'. 7 April 1946. Typescript 3pp. Estate of H. G. Adler. Schiller-Nationalmuseum, Deutsches Literaturarchiv, Marbach am Neckar.

48. H. G. Adler, *Vorschule für eine Experimentaltheologie: Betrachtungen über Wirklichkeit und Sein* (Stuttgart: Steiner, 1987), p. 30.

49. H. G. Adler, 'Der Weg zum Wohlfahrtsstaat', in *Die Erfahrung der Ohnmacht: Beiträge zur Sozologie unserer Zeit* (Frankfurt a/M: Europaische Verlaganstalt, 1964), pp. 163–68 (p. 168).

50. H. G. Adler, *Theresienstadt 1941–1945: Das Antlitz einer Zwangsgemeinschaft* 2nd edn (Tübingen: Mohr (Siebeck), 1960). Reprint with an Afterword by Jeremy Adler (Göttingen: Wallstein, 2005).

51. The SDR preserves a list of the talks H. G. Adler delivered between 1957 and 1969, from which the following details are taken. I am grateful to Peter Filkins for a copy.

52. This broadcast has recently been issued on CD. See H. G. Adler and Hermann Langbein, *Auschwitz: Topographie eines Vernichtungslagers* (Berlin: Der >Audio< Verlag, 2015).

53. H. G. Adler, *Die Juden in Deutschland: Von der Aufklärung bis zum Nationalsozialismus* (Munich: Kösel, 1960). See the article by Michael Schaich in this volume.

54. Shofar FTP Archive File: Archive/File:people/e/eichmann.adolf/transcripts/Sessions/ Session-045–02. Last-Modified: 1999/06/02

55. Hannah Arendt, *Eichmann in Jerusalem: A Report on the Banality of Evil* (1963) with an Introduction by Amos Elon (London: Penguin Books, 2006), p. 120.

56. H. G. Adler, *Theresienstadt 1941–1945*, pp. 5–6.

57. H. G. Adler, *Theresienstadt 1941–1945*, p. 286.

58. H. G. Adler, *Theresienstadt 1941–1945*, pp. 292–93.

59. H. G. Adler, *Theresienstadt 1941–1945*, pp. 37–59.

60. Marcel Atze, *'Ortlose Botschaft': Der Freundeskreis H. G. Adler, Elias Canetti und Franz Baermann Steiner im englischen Exil* (Marbacher Magazin 84) (Marbach am Neckar: Deutsche Schillergesellschaft, 1998), pp. 146–47.

61. Atze, *'Ortlose Botschaft'*, p. 147.

62. Gershom Scholem, *Briefe* II. 1948–1970, ed. by Thomas Sparr (Munich: C. H. Beck, 1995), pp. 95–100.

63. Amos Elon, 'Introduction', Hannah Arendt, *Eichmann in Jerusalem* (2006), pp. vi–xxiii (p. vii).

64. H. G. Adler, 'Was weiß Hannah Arendt von Eichmann und der Endlösung?', *Allgemeine Wochenzeitung der Juden* 19 (20 November 1964), 8–9.

65. On the need to avoid danger in society, see Franz Baermann Steiner, *Taboo*, in *Taboo, Truth, and Religion: Selected Writings*, vol. II, ed. by Jeremy Adler and Richard Fardon (Oxford: Berghahn, 1999), pp. 103–214 (pp. 209–14).

CHAPTER 13

❖

The Jews in Germany:
H. G. Adler as a Public Historian

Michael Schaich

H. G. Adler's career as a writer has often been described in terms of a division between the (marginalized) literary author and the (successful) historian, however much these two sides were connected in reality. In an unpublished autobiographical text from 1964–65 Adler split the personae which he had to assume during his life time even further. Alongside his research on the Holocaust published in academic articles and monumental books, he recognized an obligation to enlighten a wider audience about the history of the Third Reich through public lectures and talks: 'Ähnlich bemühte er sich, durch öffentliche Vorträge und bei Tagungen [...] dem Unglauben den Glauben, dem Wahn die Erkenntnis gegenüberzustellen'.[1] Indeed, Adler was a prominent figure in discourses about the recent German past in the early decades of the Federal Republic. During the 1960s, in particular, he regularly spoke at institutions of adult education, lectured in universities, and appeared on panels organized by the newly founded academies of the Catholic and Protestant Churches. He also became a frequent contributor to the network of public broadcasting corporations in Germany making a name for himself as a distinct voice on the destruction of German Jewry during the Third Reich. A comprehensive picture of Adler's role as a public intellectual has yet to be assembled,[2] but his book *Die Juden in Deutschland: Von der Aufklärung bis zum Nationalsozialismus* illustrates some of the central aspects of this side of his calling.

Die Juden in Deutschland is in many respects an unusual piece in Adler's vast body of work. Biographical sketches often mention it in the same breath with *Theresienstadt* and *Der verwaltete Mensch* as one of the major scholarly books he wrote. Today, however, it is the least known (and read) of the three, notable in its absence from the burgeoning secondary literature on Adler. Published in 1960, five years after the first edition of *Theresienstadt* and fourteen years before the appearance of *Der verwaltete Mensch*, it falls chronologically between these two other books. As a slim volume of roughly 180 pages it lacks the monumentality that is so characteristic of Adler's writing including his novels. It also dispenses with the heavy baggage of densely referenced research in the primary sources that usually underpins Adler's scholarship. Equally, it does not zoom in on a relatively compressed time span as do the two Holocaust studies but rather provides a wide-angle sketch of one and half centuries of German-Jewish history.

It is tempting, therefore, to write off *Die Juden in Deutschland* as a small volume in an œuvre of otherwise big books, but this would not do justice to the text. For a start *Die Juden in Deutschland* was arguably one of Adler's most successful works. In contrast to the 'difficult publishing history'[3] of his other writings, both literary and scholarly, *Die Juden in Deutschland* was swiftly accepted by a publisher, went through several editions, and was the only one of Adler's historical books to be translated into English during his lifetime.[4] It thus qualifies to a certain extent the assumption underlying much research on Adler that, with the possible exception of his book on *Theresienstadt*, he struggled throughout his life to make his voice heard. Even more importantly, what Adler had to say in *Die Juden in Deutschland* addressed momentous questions in post-war Germany and among the Jewish community more widely: How should one explain the rise of antisemitism in German history that led to the Third Reich? And: What should be the verdict about almost two centuries of a shared German-Jewish history? For these issues alone Adler's book, which he himself still thought 'unsurpassed' at the beginning of the 1970s,[5] merits closer attention.

The present chapter locates *Die Juden in Deutschland* in the historical context in which it was written and published during the late 1950s and early 1960s. Proceeding in three steps, it first elucidates the cultural environment in which the text saw the light of day. I then reconstruct the publishing history of the book and Adler's relationship with his publisher which for a few years held the promise of becoming one of the more fruitful and lasting literary partnerships in Adler's life. The final section turns to the main arguments of the book and relates them to discourses about antisemitism and Jewish emancipation in the post-war period. This three-pronged approach may help to throw Adler's career as a public historian into sharper relief.

I

The origins of *Die Juden in Deutschland* were closely bound up with the West German broadcasting system as it developed after 1945. One of its striking features was the emergence, under the benevolent tutelage of the Allied occupation powers, of intellectually stimulating programmes for the educated elite in the immediate post-war period.[6] Inspired by the BBC's Third Programme the newly established German radio stations introduced the famous 'Nachtstudios', programmes that were usually broadcast in the two hours before midnight and addressed a wide range of literary, artistic, and political issues. As a rule the programmes were written and often also presented by literary writers, critics, and academics many of whom went on to form the crème de la crème of cultural life in the early Federal Republic. For some, the generous honoraria that publicly funded broadcasting corporations could offer became the main source of income allowing them to pursue livelihoods as independent authors. Within a few years of its inception the 'Nachtstudio' had thus become a byword for intellectual rigour and serious engagement with the Zeitgeist satisfying a demand for cultural re-orientation after the Nazi period.

The heyday of the 'Nachtstudio' lasted for only about ten years until the middle of the 1950s, but its elitist approach and insistence on in-depth analysis informed the 'Bildungsprogramme' that all regional broadcasters began to establish from the second half of the 1950s onwards. The new programmes were on air for much longer than the original 'Nachtstudios' but still catered to the needs of an educated minority. They presented a mixture of spoken text and avant-garde or Jazz music and were usually broadcast in the evening when the majority of the public was more and more tuning in to television. Despite their intellectual high-mindedness, however, they were not meant to be academic ivory towers. They may have reached only 1–4% of the total number of listeners, but in the case of large broadcasting stations such as the Bayerischer Rundfunk and the Westdeutscher Rundfunk this still amounted to more than 100.000 people, numbers that few other cultural outlets could boast of in the early years of the Federal Republic. To an even larger extent than the 'Nachtstudios', the extended programmes also turned to reflection on and analysis of topical themes. Their aim was to provide a sense of direction in a whole variety of topics of contemporary concern among which the history of National Socialism increasingly came to the fore. Recent research has shown that the end of the 1950s saw the beginning of what was to be called the coming to terms with the past in German society.[7] Since 1957 a series of widely reported scandals about the involvement of members of the political and social elites of the Federal Republic in the Third Reich and a number of high-profile trials against Holocaust perpetrators, most significantly the Ulmer Einsatzgruppenprozess (1958), the Eichmann trial (1961), and the Auschwitz trials (1963–65), inaugurated a critical reassessment of the years from 1933–45. At the same time, the growing demand for enlightenment about the recent past invariably created an opening for writers and journalists who were able to explain what had happened during this period.

This was certainly true for H. G. Adler who, from the 1950s to the 1970s, became a regular contributor to various regional public service broadcasters in Germany.[8] As with so many other advances in his life, it was the book on Theresienstadt that launched him on this path. Although he had written manuscripts for the radio on a few occasions before 1955,[9] the appearance of the volume suddenly gave him a much wider cachet. In January 1956, Gerhard Szczesny, the well-known editor-in-chief of the 'Nachtstudio' at the Bayerischer Rundfunk in Munich, invited him to both pen and present an hour long programme based on Theresienstadt, 'die dem deutschen Hörpublikum die Ungeheuerlichkeit des 3. Reiches wieder in Erinnerung ruft und ihm deutlich macht, aus welcher jüngsten Vergangenheit sich die so glanzvolle deutsche Gegenwart herleitet'.[10] Combining Adler's detached description of the concentration camp with the voice of the survivor struck Szczesny as an effective way of unsettling what he regarded as the self-congratulatory and neglectful political climate of the Adenauer years. Adler, for his part, sensed a growing interest in his work among the editors of culture programmes at the various radio stations and decided to exploit it. Encouraged by Theodor W. Adorno, he approached another prominent and highly influential figure on the 'Nachtstudio' circuit, Alfred Andersch at the Süddeutscher Rundfunk in Stuttgart, even before the programme on Theresienstadt had been aired by the Bayerischer Rundfunk in September 1956 and suggested a re-transmission.[11] Initially, Andersch hesitated because he had already commissioned a review of *Theresienstadt* by the historian Eugen Kogon which, under the editorial auspices of Hans Magnus Enzensberger, Andersch's assistant, was to be broadcast on 11 September 1956. But after a personal meeting of the two men at the end of January 1957 he agreed to a newly written text which went on air as part of Andersch's famous series 'Radio-Essay' on 22 July 1957.

After this promising start Adler's radio career took off rapidly. For almost twenty years he wrote manuscripts for all West German broadcasting stations although in a few cases, like the Saarländischer Rundfunk, the Norddeutscher Rundfunk, and RIAS Berlin he supplied only a couple of texts respectively. Altogether Adler produced more than a hundred programmes some lasting for only 10–15 minutes, many, however, for 45 or 60 minutes.[12] Especially close relationships developed with the radio stations in Munich, Stuttgart, and Cologne. The Westdeutscher Rundfunk (WDR), in particular, became a regular outlet for Adler's essays and features. In contrast to his work for other broadcasting stations, however, it was the political department that made use of Adler as a historian of the Third Reich while the cultural editors commissioned him to write on Jewish history and literary topics. August Hoppe and later on Ulrich Gembardt, two of the leading political journalists at the WDR during the 1960s and 1970s, had a keen interest in 'Vergangenheitsbewältigung' and employed Adler again and again to write about various aspects of the Holocaust, including a famous three hour long programme on Auschwitz in October 1961 which Adler composed together with Hermann Langbein, another survivor of the death camp.[13] As Ronald Wiegenstein, then a literary editor at WDR, later reminisced, Adler was highly esteemed in Cologne 'als Verfasser zeitgeschichtlicher Studien, als einen der Aufrechten, die versuchten Klarheit zu gewinnen über das ganze Ausmaß der Verbrechen, die Deutsche über "tausend Jahre" begangen hatten' ['as author of studies on contemporary history, as one of the righteous who tried to gain clarity about the whole extent of the crimes which Germans had committed during a "thousand years"'].[14]

If his work for the radio provided Adler with a platform to teach a wide audience about the recent past, on a more mundane level it enabled him to make ends meet. Well into the 1970s, the fees that he was paid by the various radio stations were his most reliable and extensive source of income. It is probably no coincidence that Adler began to step up his efforts to get a foothold in the German broadcasting system at exactly the same time in the late 1950s when the grants paid for his scholarly work began to peter out and hopes for a permanent position at a university were dashed.[15] Like many German authors at the time, Adler began to rely for a living on his earnings from writing manuscripts for the radio — and presenting them personally on the airwaves. Remunerations could almost double if texts were read by the author himself, which is why Adler usually offered either to travel to Germany for a recording or to record the text in the studios of the BBC in London. The logistics of carefully planning his journeys around dates for recordings and meetings with editors to discuss new projects must have taken up a significant portion of his time and they can clearly be seen from his extensive correspondence. In the end, however, this was time well spent. During the early 1960s in particular, Adler earned up to 19–20,000 DM a year from the WDR alone.[16] In total, the WDR paid Adler almost 189.000 DM for his manuscripts during the years 1953–74. When Adler's active career came to an end, his editor, Ulrich Gembardt, tried to secure him a pension in addition to the rather meagre annuity that the network of German broadcasting stations (ARD) granted Adler as part of a scheme for former free-lance contributors. For a transitional period of two and a half years the WDR indeed paid a monthly subsidy of 500 DM. A proper pension, however, was never forthcoming. Despite Gembardt's best efforts he only managed to convince the broadcasting corporation to award Adler an annual donation of 2,000 DM from 1978. Although he repeatedly highlighted Adler's long-standing relationship with the WDR and hailed him as someone who, in a spirit of reconciliation, had helped to build bridges between Germany and the rest of the world after the Holocaust ['zu den Deutschen eine Brücke geschlagen hat'[17]] his pleas fell on deaf ears. The administration blocked all his requests on the grounds that Adler's other income was too high. Still, regularly contributing to the cultural and political programmes of the German broadcasting system supplied Adler with his most regular financial support and helped him deal with 'the at times almost unbearable insecurity' ['[d]ie oft schwer zu ertragende (...) Unsicherheit'] that came with being a free-lance author and private scholar.[18]

II

To a certain extent, Adler's work for the radio also shaped his intellectual œuvre. Many of the articles which, later on, were published in journals or in collections of essays originated in manuscripts written for broadcasting. One of Adler's early appearances on the WDR proved to be of particular consequence in this respect. In March 1959, during the annual *Woche der Brüderlichkeit*, a weeklong series of events organized since 1952 to champion dialogue between Christians and Jews, Adler recorded two three-hour long programmes on 'Deutschlands Juden im Zeitalter der Emanzipation (1780–1930)'.[19] Despite the comprehensive title this was not a general survey of Jewish history from the Enlightenment to the end of the Weimar Republic. Adler gave little information about the social and economic conditions of Jews in Germany or about the cultural and intellectual achievements of Jewish writers and artists. Rather, he presented an extended essay on the ultimately futile attempts at Jewish emancipation and the concomitant rise of antisemitism in German society. Quoting extensively from contemporary letters, memoirs, speeches, and pamphlets he chronicled the history of German Jews between the two extremes of civic enfranchisement and social assimilation on the one hand and the rising tide of antisemitic utterances, physical assaults, and marginalisation on the other. Intricately interweaving both strands Adler's narrative resulted in a political history of German Jewry that was marked by missed opportunities and ended tragically in the Third Reich.[20]

The topic had initially been suggested by August Hoppe who also strongly advised to see the text into print.[21] Undeterred by his earlier experiences with *Theresienstadt*, Adler complied and, within weeks of the broadcast, broached the matter with Kösel Verlag, a publisher in Munich.[22] At first glance, this choice seems rather odd. Dating from the late sixteenth century, Kösel was one of Germany's oldest publishing and printing firms but had made its name primarily as a Catholic outlet by issuing liturgical texts, theological tracts, and, in particular, the journal *Hochland*, arguably Catholic Germany's foremost intellectual mouthpiece during the twentieth century.[23] After 1945, under the leadership of the new owner, Heinrich Wild, however, Kösel had widened its appeal and begun to produce books on philosophy and contemporary history as well as literary works by Jewish and Protestant writers. Among its authors were such diverse figures as Karl Kraus, Gertrud Kolmar, Else Lasker-Schüler, Simone Weil, Eric Voegelin, and Romano Guardini. It is not entirely clear why Adler chose Kösel as his first point of call but one of the editors at the publishing house seems to have struck up a correspondence with Adler, perhaps to secure his expert advice on submitted manuscripts. In any case, Adler seized the opportunity and at the beginning of April 1959 proffered his text. Unusual for his dealings with publishers, he enjoyed almost instant success.

Heinrich Wild promised to consider the manuscript for publication and by the end of May received a glowing review from one of his external readers.[24] Heinz Robert Schlette, a young Catholic theologian and philosopher from Freiburg, recommended publication without any revisions to the text. Full of praise for Adler's thorough treatment of the topic he stressed the historical lesson to be learned from the book: antisemitism was not the reserve of the Third Reich but an intrinsic feature of German history and psyche. No one who had read Adler's book would in future be able to blame 'all guilt in this issue which has gained renewed currency' ['in dieser heute wieder aktuellen Frage alle Schuld'] on National Socialism and then walk away to pronounce a new, seemingly more justified form of antisemitism instead. Given this unequivocal stance, it is hard to believe that Schlette himself ended his review on a rather disconcerting note. Scarcely six years before *Nostra Aetate*, the Second Vatican Council's declaration on the relation of the Catholic Church to the Jews, he commented on what he saw as a hardly visible tendency in Adler's text to treat all Jews as 'candid, conspicuously candid people, who are always unjustly persecuted' ['lautere, auffallend lautere Menschen, die stets ungerechterweise verfolgt werden']. Drawing on traditional Catholic teaching that the Jews had to be redeemed for their crimes, he concluded by saying, that 'this constant persecution of the Jews must then have a religious sense' ['dieses ständige verfolgtwerden [!] der Juden doch wohl einen religiösen Sinn haben müsse'].

It is to Wild's credit that he ignored Schlette's recommendation that Adler include a sentence to this effect in the foreword.[25] Over the summer he negotiated a contract with Adler which was signed by both parties in early autumn.[26] Originally, a print run of 3,000 to 4,000 copies was envisaged, a figure that was later revised to 5,000, with Adler receiving ten per cent of the sales' price of the paperback edition of 6,80 DM. The deadline for submission of the final manuscript was set for the end of 1959. Although ill health held Adler back from work for almost three months in the autumn and winter of that year, he still managed to finish the various parts of the manuscript, including even the blurb for the sleeves of the dust jacket, by the middle of January 1960.[27] During the ensuing production process Adler proved to be as exacting as he had been diligent in the previous months.[28] He reminded his publisher, rather unnecessarily, that the book needed a contents page and insisted, less obviously, on an index. Eager to establish a trusting relationship with his author, Wild personally dealt with all these requests acquiescing in everything that was demanded of him. On 14 September 1960 he could finally report to a clearly anxious Adler that *Die Juden in Deutschland: Von der Aufklärung bis zum Nationalsozialismus*, as the title now ran, had come off the press, just in time for the Frankfurt book fair.[29] In his response Adler acknowledged gratefully 'that the book in its printing, formatting, paper and binding appears very dignified' ['daß sich das Buch in Druck, Satz, Papier und Einband sehr würdig ausnimmt'].[30]

He was less gratified with some of the responses which the volume elicited, although it has to be said that, on the whole, *Die Juden in Deutschland* met with a favourable reception. The reviews in the daily press were almost universally positive, albeit neither 'intelligent' ('klug') nor 'interesting' ('interessant') as Adler opined.[31] The cultural and literary journals seem to have done a better job. Their critical assessments of the book, according to Adler, were at least partly 'not only excellent, but really intelligent' ('nicht nur vorzüglich, sondern auch wirklich klug').[32] A passionately written review in the *Deutsche Rundschau* which reiterated many of the arguments put forward in the book found particular favour with him.[33] Academic periodicals, on the other hand, by and large took no notice of the volume. This should come as no surprise, though, since neither the publisher, nor the author himself specifically targeted the book at a scholarly audience. A list of more than twenty potential reviewers drawn up by Adler contained public intellectuals and literary figures such as Günter Eich and Heinrich Böll but, with very few exceptions, no professional historian or academic publication.[34] As a consequence the major German historical journals which in the past had written about Adler's other books did not print a review of *Die Juden in Deutschland*.[35]

By contrast, due to Kösel's reputation as a Catholic publishing house, some theological periodicals did pay attention to Adler's book, although some of them played a rather ignominious role in the reception of the volume. Two Austrian journals published what can only be described as antisemitic reviews. In one case, an anonymous reviewer in the journal of the theological faculty of Innsbruck University attributed the rise of antisemitism to the alleged economic oppression of Christians by Jews and the 'pernicious influence' of liberal Jews on Austria's cultural and political life during the nineteenth and early twentieth century.[36] In another, one Anton M. Pichler used the *Christlich-Pädagogische Blätter* to take Adler to task for his portrayal of the mayor of Vienna, Karl Lueger, and other events in Austrian history as antisemitic closing his review for good measure with a hint at Jewish profiteers from the First World War, 'a good antisemitic blow of the best old school type' ['ein braver antisemitischer Hieb aus der besten alten Schule'], as Adler commented. While he seems to have been unaware of the first assault, he brought the second to the attention of his publisher and urged Wild to publicly refute views that he regarded, after the experience of the death camps, as entirely unacceptable and the sole reserve of 'nazi-friendly papers' ['philonazistischen Blättern'].[37] For once, however, Wild did not oblige and counselled restraint.[38] The Pichlers of this world, he claimed, would not be swayed and rather feel emboldened if challenged in public. Adler was clearly disappointed and invoked the example of Britain where publishers defended their authors as a matter of course, but there the case rested.[39]

Against this background it is deeply ironic that the initial commercial success of Adler's book was probably also owing to a rise of antisemitic incidents in the Federal Republic in the late 1950s. The publication of the volume coincided with a heated debate about the possible revival of National Socialist feelings among the German population.[40] This debate had been triggered by a growing number of reported insults against Jews, the proliferation of antisemitic texts, and a wave of desecrations of Jewish cemeteries and religious sites which culminated in the winter of 1959–60, with the defilement of Cologne's synagogue on Christmas Eve being the most notorious of these incidents.[41] Over the coming months the debate reached the German parliament and led to the passing of a law against the incitement of hatred. Measures were also taken to remedy the unsatisfactory state of school education on National Socialism and antisemitism. In this climate Adler's book was a timely intervention giving historical depth to a conversation that was conducted mainly on political terms as Wild recognized early on. Only two weeks after the event in Cologne he told Adler: 'The recent incidents in Germany, and also in other European countries as I have been told only lately, are proof of how important books enlightening readers about this topic [i.e., antisemitism] are.' ['Wie wichtig Aufklärungsschriften über dieses Thema sind, zeigen die jüngsten Vorkommnisse in Deutschland und, wie ich erst kürzlich hörte, auch in anderen Ländern Europas.'][42]

If this remark was meant to predict demand from readers, it certainly came true when the volume hit the bookshops in the autumn of 1960. Well before the publicity generated by Kösel could have any effect, interest among booksellers was strong.[43] Only half a year after the release, the sales figures were so promising that Adler started thinking about a second edition.[44] Initially, Wild prevaricated,[45] but his delay tactics were quickly overtaken by events. In March 1961, the Hessian ministry of culture made a bulk order for 700 copies of *Die Juden in Deutschland*,[46] provoked in all likelihood by the public debate about the need to give the Third Reich more prominence in school curricula and to better equip school libraries with books on its history.[47] All of a sudden, Kösel had to start preparing a second edition.[48] Adler submitted half a dozen factual corrections to his text, supplied a new foreword, and on 1 August 1961 another 5.000 copies left the printing press. Unexpectedly, however, the sale of the second edition never fulfilled the high hopes that Adler and Wild had harboured and slackened fairly soon after the new release. Characteristically, this downward trend coincided with more general developments in the German public. After 1961 the debate about antisemitism quickly abated. Antisemitic incidents were still reported, but they did not cause the same sensation that they had done only a few months earlier. With great bitterness, Adler lamented in 1963 the unsatisfactory sale of his book: 'Da reden die Menschen von "moralischer Wiedergutmachung", und wenn man ihnen sachliche Aufklärung auch für wenig Geld anbietet, kümmern sie sich nicht darum.'[49] In 1966 only 137 copies were sold,[50] a figure that fell to between 50 and 100 copies per annum over the next few years.[51]

The initial success of *Die Juden in Deutschland*, however, had established a close relationship between Adler and Wild that gave rise to a number of further publishing projects. Over the next six or seven years both men constantly conferred at personal meetings or in their extensive correspondence about ideas for books, with varying outcomes. Significantly, Adler was more adept at promoting texts written by others than his own. Acting as an 'honorary literary agent' ['literarischer Agent h.c.'] as he jokingly referred to himself for writers that he considered neglected, he persuaded Wild to take on the collected works of Alfred Mombert which finally appeared in three volumes in 1963–64.[52] His suggestion to translate the American jurist and historian Jacob Robinson's harsh critique of Hannah Arendt's book on Eichmann which chimed well with his own verdict about Arendt's 'chaotic and dilettante' treatment of the topic was also pursued by Wild and fell through only at the last minute probably because of the refusal of the American publisher to grant Kösel the translation rights.[53] By contrast, Adler's attempts to champion the cause of the philosopher Erich Unger, whom he had known since the 1930s, remained unsuccessful from the start.[54] Wild clearly could not relate to Unger's philosophical style.

The same, unfortunately, was true of Adler's own literary texts. Kösel was among the numerous publishers that Adler approached about his novel *Die Reise*. As all his predecessors, however, Wild rejected the manuscript after much foot-dragging in March 1961, in his case on the grounds of form rather than content. Adler's literary style remained alien to him, as he confessed. In addition, he saw no audience for such a piece of avant-garde literature among Kösel readers. With *Die Reise* he also declined to publish Adler's philosophical novel *Raoul Feuerstein*, which remains unpublished to this day.[55] The rejection of Adler's novels, however, is less surprising than the ultimate failure to come to an agreement over two other projects which Wild was keen to secure for Kösel. In 1961 and 1962 the two men discussed a collection of Adler's essays on 'Jewry, persecution, hatred, inhumanity, and the death penalty' ['Judentum, Verfolgung, Hass, Unmenschlichkeit, Todesstrafe'].[56] Adler had submitted 25 pieces, from full-blown essays and book reviews to marginalia and aphorisms, not all of which the publisher wanted to include in the volume. In an internal memorandum an anonymous reviewer, probably one of the in-house editors, dismissed the more philosophical and literary pieces as stylistically 'weak', 'now and then a mixture of artificiality and clumsiness' ['schwach', 'bisweilen eine Mischung von Manieriertheit und Unbeholfenheit']. The historical and sociological texts, on the other hand, among them such well known essays as 'Gedanken zu einer Soziologie des Konzentrationslagers'[57] and 'Selbstverwaltung und Widerstand in den Konzentrationslagern der SS',[58] and the now lost 'Zur

Soziologie des jüdischen Volkes',[59] passed muster. Adler was at his best, the verdict ran, 'when he stayed close to a concrete subject' ['wo er am konkreten Gegenstand bleibt']. Rehearsing a recurring motif in Adler's biography, the reviewer preferred the historian to the literary writer, with the only difference that in this instance even the historian came away empty-handed. Wild had pitched the collected essays to the newly founded Deutscher Taschenbuchverlag, since he deemed a hard cover edition with Kösel too risky. Deutscher Taschenbuchverlag, however, rejected the proposal as commercially not viable, and when Wild then recommended trying Fischer Verlag, another paperback publisher, Adler pulled the plug on the project. He had already started thinking about a new idea which was to become his essay collection *Die Erfahrung der Ohnmacht: Beiträge zur Soziologie unserer Zeit* (1964), to be realized, however, with a different publisher.

For a short while, there was also talk about a selection of Adler's article on Jewishness which again was to contain the 1949 essay 'Zur Soziologie des jüdischen Volkes'.[60] This article was clearly dear to Adler, although he was ashamed of the style in which it had been written in 1949 and reserved the right to rework the text completely. In the end, the project was dropped tacitly, superseded in 1965–67 by a much larger undertaking, an abridged version of *Theresienstadt*. Undoubtedly the most ambitious of Adler's and Wild's plans, it had the potential to transform Adler's standing as a public historian. A shorter, more compact, and reasonably prized edition would have put the text in the reach of a wide, non-academic audience and, together with his appearances on the radio, could have propelled Adler into the first rank of public commentators on the Third Reich in the 1960s. Indeed, the start to the project was promising.[61] Initial disagreement about the shape of the volume was quickly overcome. Rather than selecting only the third, 'psychological' part of *Theresienstadt* and publishing it on its own as Wild had originally suggested, Adler prevailed with his insistence on a complete overhaul of the text which would result in a much shorter book of roughly 300 pages, about a third of the original length. The new version should consist mainly of parts I and III, while the middle section with its focus on sociological issues was to be compressed most. The appendix and the glossary also had to go. The whole project seemed feasible because Wild was willing to pay Adler a stipend that would allow him to work on the manuscript undistracted for several months. Adler, in turn, made concessions with regard to his writer's fee so that the abridged version could have been brought on the market for about 20 DM. There was one obstacle, however, neither Wild nor Adler had reckoned with. Hans G. Siebeck, the original publisher of *Theresienstadt*, wanted to be in on the deal, too. When asked for his permission to an abridged version, he demanded a licence fee from Kösel since, according to him, the first two editions of *Theresienstadt* and the subsequent volume *Verheimlichte Wahrheit* had run up a deficit of 20.000 DM by the end of 1963. If this had not been bad enough, the situation got worse when the two publishers settled the dispute at what Adler could only interpret as his own cost. Wild and Siebeck agreed on a split of the royalties for the new edition with only three quarters going to the author and the rest to the original publisher. Incensed at this arrangement, Adler effectively called the deal off. He suggested a complex compromise arrangement that Wild, however, could never endorse. Unwilling to go back on his agreement with Siebeck, he asked Adler to negotiate a solution of his own, an idea which Adler, in turn, loath to compromise his relationship with Siebeck and angry about the latter's perceived greediness, rebuffed. After a silence of almost nine months, in February 1967, Wild finally told his author in a terse letter that he had no intention of pursuing the project further. What had been a productive and stimulating relationship between author and publisher from now on became a sober business affair.

This was clearly evident, when in 1967 the opportunity for an English-language translation of *Die Juden in Deutschland* presented itself.[62] Emily M. Schossberger, the director of Notre Dame Press, one of the leading American university presses, had taken a personal interest in the book and tried to gain the translation rights from Kösel. Both companies were part of an informal network of Catholic publishing houses that spanned the Atlantic and also included the London-based firm Sheed and Ward. While their cooperation progressed rapidly and soon resulted in an agreement that also envisaged a parallel English edition with Sheed and Ward, which for unknown reasons never materialized, Adler became increasingly dissatisfied with his American contacts. The crux of the matter was a translation that he judged entirely unsatisfactory. His demands for changes, however, were firmly rejected by Wild who was clearly unwilling to compromise his partnership with Schossberger. The translation, he argued, was the sole responsibility of the interpreter, not the author, any criticism by reviewers would be directed to the former, not the latter. Stopped in his tracks, Adler still complained about 'irresponsible sloppiness' ['unverantwortliche Schlampereien'] but reluctantly signed off on the translation.[63] The success of the American edition once it had been published, however, mollified him to some extent. He still spoke sarcastically of 'the forceful and energetic manner of Madam Schossberger' ['der so forsch und temperamentvoll auftretenden Madame Schossberger'],[64] but acknowledged that the 'awful translation' ['miserable Übersetzung'] was reviewed favourably and sold rather well.[65]

The same could not be said of the German original, though. In the early 1970s few copies were sold and the proceeds did not even cover the cost for storage. In the spring of 1975, with 2,700 volumes still sitting in the warehouse, Kösel decided to pulp all but 500 copies of the remaining print run giving the author no advance notice.[66] Adler's angry complaint and Wild's conciliatory, but unapologetic reply were among the last exchanges between the two men who for eight years, from 1959 to 1967, had discussed and, in a few instances, also realized a number of important publishing projects. *Die Juden in Deutschland*, however, gained a new lease of life when Piper Verlag, which in 1988 also published a paperback edition of *Panorama*, reprinted the volume twice in 1987 and 1988 producing 7,000 more copies of what was, despite prolonged periods of neglect, Adler's most popular text during his lifetime.

III

Even more importantly, however, *Die Juden in Deutschland* constitutes a distinct contibution to the intellectual history of post-war Germany. It engaged in a number of debates about German-Jewish history that were current at the time, adding the voice of both the survivor of the death camps and the émigré to the conversation. Invariably, Adler took strong positions of his own, expressing his thoughts in ways that made them intelligible to a wider audience.

Most prominent among these debates was the discourse about German anti-semitism which was still in its infancy when Adler wrote *Die Juden in Deutschland*. Modern research on antisemitism started only in the 1940s with methodologies informed by psychoanalysis and social psychology being at the forefront of discussion.[67] None of this, however, seems to have cut any ice with Adler. *Die Juden in Deutschland* contains no allusion to Adorno's concept of the Authoritarian Personality.[68] References to the seminal collection of essays *Anti-Semitism — A Social Disease*, edited by Ernst Simmel in 1946, are nowhere to be found either. More traditionally historical works on antisemitism that had appeared in the wake of the Third Reich are also conspicuous by their absence or did not have a profound impact on Adler's argument. The first major study of the antecedents of National Socialist antisemitism by the German émigré Paul Massing, for example, was missing from the bibliography. And while both Eva Reichmann's *Hostages of Civilisation* (1950) and Eleanore Sterling's *Er ist wie Du* (1956) were listed,[69] Adler may have mined them for historical examples but did not subscribe to their central tenets. Neither Sterling's identification of the religious roots of antisemitism in the early nineteenth century nor Reichmann's insistence on the 'inner insecurity behind a particularly bold front' of German nationalist ideology which compensated its own perceived weaknesses by excluding the Jews, is much in evidence in Adler's book.[70] Peter Pulzer's ground-breaking work *The Rise of Political Anti-Semitism in Germany and Austria*, on the other hand, was only to appear four years after *Die Juden in Deutschland*.[71]

The one study Adler came closest to was arguably Hannah Arendt's *The Origins of Totalitarianism* (1951). Like Arendt, Adler put the nation state as it developed after the French Revolution and, in particular, its claim on cultural centralism at the centre of his analysis. Built on the idea of a uniform populace, as Adler repeatedly pointed out, modern states did not recognize the rights of minorities but bestowed privileges and liberties exclusively on individual citizens.[72] The principle was most famously expressed by Count Stanislas de Clermont-Tonnere in December 1789, when he stated: 'als Nation muß man den Juden alles verweigern, als Individuen muß man ihnen alles zubilligen'.[73] Applied to the German lands, this meant that individual Jews might achieve civil equality, while the group as such never stood the chance of becoming an integral part of the society in which it was living. On the contrary, in order to be fully integrated into the body politic, Jews had to assimilate into the dominant culture and renounce any group cohesion. The loss of a distinct Jewish identity became the price to be paid for emancipation. Benevolent as it may have seemed in the beginning, under the conditions of the modern nation state the civic improvement of the Jews could only lead to calls for ever closer integration and self-dissolution. Capturing the process with the evocative term 'Ungeduld' ['imaptience'],[74] Adler described in great historical detail the almost dialectical mechanism by which Jews aspired to become German citizens while the majority society constantly raised the stakes, never satisfied with the steps taken so far towards assimilation. The ultimate sacrifice demanded of the Jews was the renunciation of their religion.[75] Everything that fell short of this final goal inevitably resulted in recriminations and ever growing antisemitism until the whole project of emancipation was brutally cut short with the advent of National Socialism.[76] In an almost Foucauldian vein, Adler identified the modern state with its own intrinsic logic as the driving force behind the rise of antisemitism in German history.[77] This was not an entirely novel argument to make,[78] but here, as in his other scholarly works, Adler provided further proof for his reading of the modern world as dominated by what he called 'mechanischer Materialismus'.

While the inquiry into the roots of antisemitism was at the heart of *Die Juden in Deutschland*, on a second, more concealed level, Adler also joined in the controversy about Jewish emancipation and assimilation which had been raging since the latter part of the nineteenth century and had only gained in poignancy after the Holocaust.[79] The dispute moved between the two extremes of outright condemnation and whole-hearted defence of emancipation. The latter position was clearly in the minority after 1945, although such a prominent figure as the historian Selma Stern in her history of the Jews in Prussia still insisted on the beneficial effects of emancipation and described it as an attempt at modernizing Jewish communities.[80] Whereas Stern denied any causal link between emancipation and the destruction of German Jewry and insisted on the openess of German history before 1933, at the other end of the spectrum, critics of emancipation denounced the naïve hopes of successful integration into German society as a loss of Jewish spiritual identity and an illusion that, ultimately, contributed to the annihilation of the Jews during the Third Reich.

Adler positioned himself somewhere in between these two opposites. Writing still before the major shift in research on emancipation that came about since the mid-1960s with the ascent of social history and the arrival of the concept of acculturation, he is, to start with, inherently critical of the historical process as might be expected from what has been said above. His narrative hardly dwells on the positive consequences of emancipation, such as the increase in economic wealth or legal security. Instead he repeatedly passes judgement on instances where German Jews had gone too far in their efforts to assimilate. His text is littered with critical remarks about individuals who behaved in an undignified manner ['würdelos', 'unwürdig'] while trying to curry favour with their Gentile environment.[81] Occasionally he talks of 'a process of national self-dissolution' ['nationaler Auflösungsprozeß'] or even of 'far-reaching national as well as ethnic self-destruction' ['weitreichenden nationalen wie ethnischen Selbstvernichtung'], caused by inter-marriage, conversion, emigration, and religious indifference among Jews in general,[82] sometimes backing this up with detailed statistical evidence about the steady decline in the proportion of Jews among the German population.[83] Small wonder, then, that for Adler, emancipation as a historical phenomenon amounted to 'the dissolution or destruction of all Jewish peculiarity and feeling of unity' ['eine Auflösung oder Zerstörung aller jüdischen Eigenart und Zusammengehörigkeit'].[84]

Significantly, this story of loss and even self-denial resonated not only with an inner-Jewish dialogue but worked as a critique of a self-congratulatory description of German history in the 1950s and 1960s. Adler undermined an all too facile desire to distance the new (West) German state from the Third Reich by idealising the history of Jewish emancipation and, in particular, its flipside, the so-called 'German-Jewish symbiosis'.[85] Expressly declining to recite the usual roll-call of great German-Jewish artists and scholars which to his mind gave any narrative invariably an 'apologetic' inflection, he reminded his readers that it was the 'Geistigkeit der Gruppe' and not the individual achievement which had been the basis of any German-Jewish symbiosis.[86] It was, of course, exactly this recognition of the Jewish community on its own terms that too often had not been forthcoming from German society. Against all attempts at portraying the Jewish contribution to German culture in a rosy light, therefore, Adler's text served as a salutary reminder of the more than ambivalent nature of the German-Jewish past. Throughout the book which by no coincidence was called *Die Juden in Deutschland* rather than *Die deutschen Juden*, Adler pointed to the missed opportunities and the 'tragedy'[87] ['Tragik'] that more than anything else accompanied the deeply flawed process of assimilation as it came to pass during the nineteenth and early twentieth century.

And yet, Adler did not condemn emancipation as such. He welcomed it as a departure from the narrow, almost medieval state of mind German Jews were living in before the later eighteenth century and expressed great respect for Moses Mendelssohn and Christian Wilhelm Dohm who advocated civic improvement while allowing Jews to retain their religion.[88] It was only the rise of the nation state after 1789 that derailed the historical process. Adler even claimed that despite the catastrophic end a revival of the German-Jewish symbosis which had made considerable progress before 1933 was still possible,[89] if only the lessons from history were learned. In his concluding remarks Adler sketched a vision of the future that rested to a large extent on Jewish self-assertiveness. Following in the tradition of 'thinkers of religio-national sensibility, like Franz Rosenzweig and Martin Buber',[90] he advocated a spiritual rebirth of German Jewry. Referring to a text by Buber from 1936, Adler claimed the right of German Jews to be different from but not alien to their environment ['wesensverschieden, aber nicht wesensfremd'].[91] Only such an understanding of the role of Jews in Germany, based on 'self-awareness' ['Selbstbestimmung'] and 'self-respect' ['Selbstachtung'],[92] held the promise of a new German-Jewish symbiosis which would grow equally out of 'dem tiefsten Geiste des Judentums und des Deutschtums'.[93]

If this was a measured response to radical condemnations of Jewish emancipation and assimilation, Adler's conclusion also reminded German society of its historic obligation to finally accept the Jewish minority on its own terms. At a time when the history of National Socialism was slowly becoming a topic of debate, Adler held a mirror up to the German public in which it could reflect on its own past and present. In *Die Juden in Deutschland* and in many of the broadcasts which he produced during the long 1960s Adler, acting as a public historian, insisted on remembering and explaining 'was doch verdrängt werden wollte' ['what wanted to be denied'].[94]

Notes to Chapter 13

1. Quoted from Franz Hocheneder, *H. G. Adler (1910–1988): Privatgelehrter und freier Schriftsteller* (Vienna: Böhlau, 2009), p. 205.
2. See Jeremy Adler's contribution to this volume.
3. Helen Finch and Lynn L. Wolff, 'Introduction: The Adler-Sebald Intertextual Relationship as Paradigm for Intergenerational Literary Testimony', in *Witnessing, Memory, Poetics: H. G. Adler and W. G. Sebald*, ed. by eid. (Rochester, NY: Camden House, 2014), pp. 1–21 (p. 4).
4. For Adler's English publications see Jeremy Adler, 'H. G. Adler: A Prague Writer in London', in *Keine Klage über England? Deutsche und österreichische Exilerfahrungen in Großbritannien 1933–1945*, ed. by Charmian Brinson et al. (Munich: Iudicium, 1998), pp. 13–30 (p. 27).
5. Eichstätt University Library, Verlagsarchiv Kösel (VA I), Autorenkorrespondenz H. G. Adler [henceforth EUL, Verlagsarchiv Kösel], H. G. Adler to J. Wild, 1.4.1972.
6. Konrad Dussel, *Deutsche Rundfunkgeschichte: Eine Einführung* (Konstanz: UVK Medien, 1999), pp. 208–13; Axel Schildt, *Zwischen Abendland und Amerika: Studien zur westdeutschen Ideenlandschaft der 50er Jahre* (Munich: Oldenbourg, 1999), pp. 83–119; Monika Boll, 'Das Kulturradio nach 1945', in *Radiotage, Fernsehjahre: Studien zur Rundfunkgeschichte nach 1945*, ed. by Markus Behmer (Münster: Lit, 2006), pp. 151–62; Monika Boll, 'Verehrte Hörerinnen und Hörer! Radiogebildet — Zur Geschichte des Nachtstudios 1948–1970', in *Nachtstudio: Radioessays*, ed. by Barbara Schäfer and Antonio Pellegrino (Munich: Belleville, 2008), pp. 13–41.
7. For a summary of the vast body of literature: Axel Schildt and Detlef Siegfried, *Deutsche Kulturgeschichte: Die Bundesrepublik: 1945 bis zur Gegenwart* (Munich: Hanser, 2009), pp. 208–11, for the media in particular: Christina von Hodenberg, *Konsens und Krise: Eine Geschichte der westdeutschen Medienöffentlichkeit 1945–1973* (Göttingen: Wallstein, 2006).
8. Little has been written on Adler's broadcasting career, see Marcel Atze, 'Ortlose Botschaft': Der Freundeskreis H. G. Adler, Elias Canetti und Franz Baermann Steiner im englischen Exil (Marbach am Neckar: Deutsche Schillergesellschaft, 1998), pp. 141–42; Hocheneder, *H. G. Adler*, p. 204; Helmut Göbel, 'Eine lange und schwierige Freundschaft: H. G. Adler und Elias Canetti', in *H. G. Adler* (Munich: text + kritik, 2004), pp. 71–85 (p. 78); Frank Finlay, ' "Der verwerfliche Literaturbetrieb unserer Epoche": H. G. Adler and the Postwar West German Literary Field', in *Witnessing, Memory, Poetics*, ed. by Finch and Wolff, pp. 254–74 (p. 262 and 270).
9. Archive of Westdeutscher Rundfunk, Cologne, 2177: H. G. Adler to W. Honig, 11.1.1955.
10. Historisches Archiv des Bayerischen Rundfunks, Munich, HF / 6197.1: G. Szczesny to H. G. Adler, 20.1.1956 (quote), 5.6.1956, Adler to Szczesny, 26.1.1956, 26.4.1956.
11. Historisches Archiv des Südwestrundfunks, Stuttgart, H. G. Adler to A. Andersch, 17.8.1956, 18.12.1956, Andersch to Adler, 5.9.1956, 2.1.1957; *Radio-Essay 1955–1981: Verzeichnis der Manuskripte und Tondokumente* (Stuttgart: Süddeutscher Rundfunk, 1996), p. 67 and 88; Atze, 'Ortlose Botschaft', 141.
12. This estimate is based on an analysis of the following sources: *Radio-Essay 1955–1981*; Deutsches Rundfunkarchiv, Frankfurt a.M., entry on Adler in 'ARD Hörfunkdatenbank'; the finding aids on the 'Nachtstudio' of the Bayerischer Rundfunk made available online <http://www.br.de/unternehmen/inhalt/geschichte-des-br/uebersicht-findbuecher-hoerfunk100.html>; and lists of Adler's broadcasts for the Westdeutscher Rundfunk, Norddeutscher Rundfunk, Hessischer Rundfunk and Saarländischer Runfunk, provided by the archives of the respective broadcasting stations.

13. This program is now avaible in a set of three CDs: H. G. Adler and Hermann Langbein, 'Auschwitz: Topographie eines Vernichtungslagers. Überlebende berichten', (Berlin: Der Audio Verlag, 2015).

14. Ronald H. Wiegenstein, 'Radio-Reminiszenzen', in *Zu Hause im Exil: Zu Werk und Person H. G. Adlers*, ed. by Heinrich Hubmann and Alfred O. Lanz (Stuttgart: Steiner, 1987), pp. 165–67 (p. 165). Translations of German quotations have been provided by Lynn L. Wolff.

15. Nicolas Berg, *Der Holocaust und die westdeutschen Historiker: Erforschung und Erinnerung* (Göttingen: Walstein, 2004), pp. 307–11.

16. For the following see Historisches Archiv des WDR, Cologne, no. 15890.

17. U. Gembardt to K. v. Bismarck, 20.3.1976, Historisches Archiv des WDR, Cologne, no. 15890.

18. H. G. Adler, 'Nachruf bei Lebzeiten', *H. G. Adler — Der Wahrheit verpflichtet: Interviews, Gedichte, Essays*, ed. by Jeremy Adler (Gerlingen: Bleicher, 1998), pp. 7–16 (p. 12).

19. EUL, Verlagsarchiv Kösel, H. G. Adler to H. M. Jürgensmeyer, 4.4.1959.

20. The emotive term 'Tragik' recurs repeatedly in Adler's narrative, see, for example, Adler, *Die Juden in Deutschland*, pp. 68, 122.

21. Adler, *Die Juden in Deutschland*, pp. 11–12.

22. EUL, Verlagsarchiv Kösel, Adler to Jürgensmeyer, 4.4.1959.

23. *400 Jahre Kösel-Verlag: 1593–1993* (Munich: Kösel, 1993).

24. EUL, Verlagsarchiv Kösel, Jürgensmeyer to Adler, 15.4.1959 and report by H[einz] R[obert] Schlette, Freiburg 21.5.59.

25. Ibid., Wild to Adler, 12.6.1959.

26. Ibid., Wild to Adler, 4.9.1959, 28.9.1959, 2.10.1959, 14.9.1960; Adler to Wild, 7.9.1959, 30.9.1959; publisher's contract, Munich 2.10.1959 and London 30.0.1959.

27. Ibid., B. Adler to Wild, 17.10.59, Wild to B. Adler, 22.10.1959; Wild to Adler, 16.12.1959, 4.1.1960, 14.1.1960, 29.1.1960; Adler to Wild, 22.12.1959, 7.1.1960, 19.1.1960.

28. Ibid., Adler to Wild, 7.1.1960, 12.7.1960. For an example from after the publication of the volume see ibid., Adler to Wild, 24.10.1960 and Kösel Verlag to Adler, 28.10.1960.

29. Ibid., Adler to Wild, 5.9.1960, Wild to Adler, 12.9.1960, 14.9.1960.

30. Ibid., Adler to Wild, 10.10.1960.

31. Ibid., Adler to Wild, 29.3.1961. One review which Adler might have had in mind was by Paul Arnsberg in *Frankfurter Allgemeine Zeitung*, 23 March 1961, p. 2 (Literaturbeilage).

32. Ibid., Adler to Wild, 4.5.1961.

33. Hans Kühner, 'Hitlers antisemitische Vorläufer', *Deutsche Rundschau* 87 (1961), 375–78.

34. EUL, Verlagsarchiv Kösel, Adler to Wild, 19.1.1960, 12.7.1960, 16.9.1960. The exceptions were *Neue Politische Literatur*, a review journal that counted Adler among its regular contributors, and the Bulletin of the Wiener Library in London.

35. See, for example, the flagship journal of the German historical profession, *Historische Zeitschrift*. It had reviewed several texts by Adler (183 (1957), 642–43: *Theresienstadt*; 190 (1960), 725–26: *Verheimlichte Wahrheit*; 194 (1962), 243: *Der Führer ins Nichts*, containing Adler's essay 'Hitler als Persönlichkeit'), but disregarded *Die Juden in Deutschland*. Adler's house journal *Neue Politische Literatur* equally abstained from giving its opinion of the book.

36. M., *Zeitschrift für katholische Theologie* 85 (1963), 103–04.

37. EUL, Verlagsarchiv Kösel, Adler to Wild, 29.3.1961.

38. Ibid., Wild to Adler, 17.4.1961.

39. Ibid., Adler to Wild, 26.4.1961.

40. Werner Bergmann, *Antisemitismus in öffentlichen Konflikten: Kollektives Lernen in der politischen Kultur der Bundesrepublik 1949–1989* (Frankfurt a/M: Campus, 1997), pp. 187–277.

41. This act of vandalism led to the foundation of Germania Judaica in Cologne. Through Heinrich Böll's good offices Adler attended one of the first meetings to set up the organization, see Finlay, 'Der verwerfliche Literaturbetrieb', pp. 262–63.

42. EUL, Verlagsarchiv Kösel, Wild to Adler, 4.1.1960.

43. Ibid., Wild to Adler, 14.9.1960, 28.10.1960.

44. Ibid., Adler to Wild, 21.3.1961.

45. Ibid., Wild to Adler, 27.3.1961.
46. Ibid., Wild to Adler, 27.3.1961.
47. See Bergmann, *Antisemitismus*, pp. 262–63.
48. EUL, Verlagsarchiv Kösel, Adler to Wild, 22.4.1961, 4.5.1961, Wild to Adler, 26.4.1961, 1.8.1961.
49. Ibid., Adler to Wild, 29.4.1963.
50. Ibid., Adler to Wild, 6.3.1967.
51. Ibid., Adler to Wild, 11.4.1974, Wild to Adler 30.5.1974.
52. Ibid., Adler to Wild, 21.4.1960 (quote), 8.5.1960, 12.7.1960, 10.10.1960, 21.3.1961, 11.11.1963, 16.3.1964, 30.7.1964, 14.3.1965, Wild to Adler, 19.12.1960, 15.3.1961, 27.3.1961, 25.3.1964, 8.3.1965.
53. Jacob Robinson, *And the Crooked Shall Be Made Straight: The Eichmann Trial, The Jewish Catastrophe, and Hannah Arendt's Narrative* (New York: Macmillan, 1965). EUL, Verlagsarchiv Kösel, Adler to Wild, 14.3.1965 (quote), Wild to Adler, 14.4.1965.
54. Ibid., Adler to Wild, 27.6.1961, 20.7.1961, 9.6.1962, Wild to Adler, 4.7.1961, 24.5.63. About Adler's relationship to Unger see Manfred Voigts, *Jüdische Geistesarbeit und andere Aufsätze über Jacob Franck bis H. G. Adler* (Würzburg: Königshausen & Neumann, 2016), pp. 381–403.
55. EUL, Verlagsarchiv Kösel, Adler to Wild, 13.6.1960, 5.9.1960, 23.12.1960, 28.2.1961, 21.3.1961, Wild to Adler, 12.9.1960, 15.3.1961. Wild returned the manuscript of *Die Reise* while he passed 'Raoul Feuerstein' at Adler's request on to Graf Christoph von Schwerin who was working in Frankfurt for Fischer at the time. For Adler's attempts to find a publisher for *Die Reise* see Finlay, ' "Der verwerfliche Literaturbetrieb" ', pp. 267–71 as well as Ruth Vogel-Klein's contribution to this volume.
56. EUL, Verlagsarchiv Kösel, Adler to Wild, 27.6.1961, 9.6.1962, Wild to Adler, 4.7.1961, 2.3.1962, 10.5.1962, referee's report on Adler, Essays, n.d. [summer 1961], all the following quotes are from this report.
57. See the reprint in *H. G. Adler — Der Wahrheit verpflichtet: Interviews, Gedichte, Essays*, ed. by Jeremy Adler (Gerlingen: Bleicher Verlag, 1998), pp. 142–62.
58. Now easily accessible in H. G. Adler, *Nach der Befreiung: Ausgewählte Essays zur Geschichte und Soziologie*, ed. by Peter Filkins (Konstanz: Konstanz University Press, 2013), pp. 49–70.
59. 'Nachweise', in ibid., pp. 259–60.
60. EUL, Verlagsarchiv Kösel, Adler to Wild, 30.7.1964, 28.11.1964, 14.2.1965, Wild to Adler, 21.12.1964.
61. Ibid., Adler to Wild, 2.7.1965, 8.8.1965, 19.9.1965 (with draft letter to H. G. Siebeck, dated 20.9.1965), 23.9.1965 (with letter to Siebeck, dated 30.9.1965), 6.12.1965, 26.4.1966, 3.5.1966, Wild to Adler, 20.7.1965, 12.8.1965, 17.9.1965, 30.9.1965, 30.11.1965, 7.4.1966, 28.4.1966, 28.2.1967; Siebeck to Adler, 8.10.1965, Adler to Siebeck, 10.10.1965.
62. Ibid., F. Pfäfflin to Adler, 23.3.1967, 5.5.1967, 23.5.1967, 7.6.1967, Adler to Pfäfflin, 25.3.1967, 8.5.1967, Adler to Wild, 28.8.1967, 30.11.1968, 25.6.1969, Wild to Adler, 7.9.1967, 26.11.1968, 11.12.1968. The archives of the University of Notre Dame contain no records of Adler's book; communication by Kevin Cawley to the author, 31 October 2016. An inquiry to University of Notre Dame Press did not receive a reply.
63. EUL, Verlagsarchiv Kösel, Adler to Wild, 30.11.1968.
64. Ibid., Adler to Wild, 25.6.1969.
65. Ibid., Adler to Wild, 1.4.1972.
66. Ibid., Adler to Wild, 11.4.1975, Wild to Adler 30.5.1975.
67. Peter G. J. Pulzer, *Die Entstehung des politischen Antisemitismus in Deutschland und Österreich 1867 bis 1914: Mit einem Forschungsbericht des Autors* (Göttingen: Vandenhoeck & Ruprecht, 2004), pp. 7–11; Klaus Holz, 'Theorien des Antisemitismus', in *Handbuch des Antisemitismus: Judenfeindschaft in Geschichte und Gegenwart*, vol. 3, ed. by Wolfgang Benz (Berlin: De Gruyter, 2010), pp. 316–28; Hans-Joachim Hahn and Olaf Kistenmacher (eds.), *Beschreibungsversuche der Judenfeindschaft: Die Geschichte der Antisemitismusforschung vor 1944* (Berlin: De Gruyter, 2015).
68. He discussed it, though, in his first letter to Adorno from April 1950; Jeremy Adler, ' "Die Macht des Guten im Rachen des Bösen": H. G. Adler, T. W. Adorno und die Darstellung der Shoah', *Merkur* 54 (2000), 475–86, at 482.

69. *Hostages of Civilization: The Social Sources of National Socialist Anti-Semitism* (London: Gollancz, 1950); *Er ist wie Du: Aus der Frühgeschichte des Antisemitismus in Deutschland (1815–1850)* (Munich: Chr. Kaiser, 1956).
70. Reichmann, *Hostages of Civilization*, pp. 150–64, the quote at 151.
71. Peter Pulzer, *The Rise of Political Anti-Semitism in Germany and Austria* (New York: Wiley, 1964).
72. Adler, *Juden in Deutschland*, pp. 15–16, 20, 40, 91, 103, 139, 156.
73. Ibid., p. 15.
74. Ibid., p. 11, 16.
75. Ibid., p. 39–40.
76. Ibid., p. 11, 19.
77. I want to thank Jeremy Adler for discussion of this point.
78. See for example the almost identical explanation in Robert Weltsch, 'Einleitung', in *Deutsches Judentum: Aufstieg und Krise: Gestalten, Ideen, Werke* (Stuttgart: Deutsche Verlags-Anstalt, 1963), pp. 7–24 (p. 9–10).
79. David Sorkin, 'Emancipation and Assimilation: Two Concepts and their Application to German-Jewish History', *Leo Baeck Institute Year Book*, 35 (1990), 17–33; Till van Rahden, 'Treason, Fate, or Blessing: Narratives of Assimilation in the Historiography of German-Speaking Jewry since the 1950s', in *Preserving the Legacy of German Jewry: A History of the Leo Baeck Institute 1955–2005*, ed. by Christhard Hoffmann (Tübingen: Siebeck, 2005), pp. 349–73; Nils Roemer, 'The Making of a New Discipline: The London LBI and the Writing of the German-Jewish Past', in ibid., pp. 173–99 (pp. 179, 180, 184, 189–90, 195); Christhard Hoffmann, 'Historicizing Emancipation: Jewish Historical Culture and *Wissenschaft* in Germany, 1912–1938', in *Modern Judaism and Historical Consciousness: Identities, Encounters, Perspectives*, ed. by Christian Wiese (Leiden: Brill, 2007), pp. 329–55.
80. Christhard Hoffmann, 'Zerstörte Geschichte: Zum Werk der jüdischen Historikerin Selma Stern', *Exilforschung* 11 (1993), 165–73.
81. Adler, *Juden in Deutschland*, pp. 17, 45, 65, 76, 125.
82. Ibid., pp. 45, 17, similarly 16, 59, 83.
83. Ibid., pp. 17, 59, 124, 145.
84. Ibid., pp. 11.
85. Christhard Hoffmann, 'German-Jewish Encounter and German Historical Culture', *Leo Baeck Institute Year Book*, 41 (1996), 277–90, at 281–84.
86. Adler, *Juden in Deutschland*, pp. 160, 161.
87. Ibid., p. 68.
88. Ibid., pp. 30–42.
89. Ibid., pp. 130–36, esp. 134, 156–63.
90. Moshe Schwarz quoted in van Rahden, 'Treason', p. 363.
91. Adler, *Juden in Deutschland*, p. 159.
92. Ibid., p. 116.
93. Ibid., p. 160.
94. Wiegenstein, 'Radio-Reminiszenzen', p. 165.

❖

CHAPTER 14

The Reception of H. G. Adler's
Eine Reise in the
Federal Republic of Germany

Ruth Vogel-Klein[1]

The history of the reception of H. G. Adler's novel,[2] *Eine Reise* [*The Journey*],[3] is revealing in several ways, allowing for a detailed exploration of the various interpretations of this exceptional book. This exploration is intimately imbricated with what Maurice Halbwachs terms 'cadres sociaux de la mémoire', frameworks for collective memory, in West Germany. According to Halbwachs, a society's dominant ideas influence, and even determine the memories of its individual members.[4] The following therefore not only presents the different stages of *The Journey*'s reception, but also situates these stages in their respective contemporary context in the West-German scope of memory and the attendant literary landscape. The book's reception is outlined in three stages here: first, the early phase of looking for a publishing house, between 1951 and 1962; then, the phase of reviews for the first, 1962 edition; and lastly, the reception of the new, 1999 edition 37 years later.

Adler's Correspondence with Publishers — 1951–1962

The first phase of reception began in 1951. Adler made countless attempts to find a publisher for *Eine Reise* in an historical context that was blind to the recent past. Within the framework of collective memory in 1950s West Germany, there was no place for the Holocaust. Except for Eugen Kogon's book on Buchenwald, practically no historical studies existed at this time,[5] the German Nazi Trials had not taken place yet, and the general discourse on victimhood concerned mainly the displaced Germans from the Eastern Territories and the victims of the war.[6] Until 1955 on the literary scene, the most popular bestsellers were war books[7] that recounted soldierly virtues, such as Kurt Hohoff's *Woina, Woina*[8] from 1951 (10 000 copies were sold in one year) or Ernst Jünger's War-Diary *Strahlungen*[9] [Reflections] from 1949 (20,000 copies sold in one year) and radical right-wing Ernst von Salomon's *Der Fragebogen*[10] [The Questionnaire] (1951) which portrayed Denazification as an unacceptable injustice,[11] and sold 200,000 copies in two years.[12] Heinrich Böll's critical novel *Der Engel schwieg* [The Silence of the Angel] (1950) was refused by publishers.[13] Most of the remaining literature in 1950 and 1951 retreated from history, politics, and social critique, instead turning inward or to religiosity and a sacralisation of nature.[14] On the other hand, 'kitsch' films, *Heimatfilme*, had an immense success. Finding a publisher for *Eine Reise*, whose original title 'Die Reise' was already protected under copyright,[15] was therefore very difficult in this context. In addition, there were other hurdles, too.

Living in London, far from the German-speaking world, the survivor of Auschwitz and three other concentration camps, H. G. Adler was impoverished and experienced a degree of social isolation. At this point he had already expended a considerable amount of energy to write a large number of works, only to see them all be rejected by publishers: *Panorama*,[16] *Die Wand* [The Wall],[17] *Theresienstadt 1941–1945*,[18] *Die Ansiedlung* [The Settlement, unpublished], *Raoul Feuerstein* [unpublished], collections of novellas, and poetry.[19] The string of rejections weighed on Adler's latest book, *The Journey,* since he wrote necessarily to the same publishing houses. Then a new problem arose from 1955 onwards, when Adler gained instant recognition as major scholar of the Holocaust with the publication of his *Theresienstadt 1941–1945: Das Antlitz einer Zwangsgemeinschaft* [Theresienstadt 1941–1945: The Face of a Coerced Community],[20] a development that overshadowed Adler's literary writing. Thus, in sending Adler ecstatic praise of his Theresienstadt book in 1958, the publisher Claassen also sent criticism of *The Journey*: 'Maybe it was the conflict between science and art that tripped you up in writing your ballad *THE JOURNEY*'.[21] Several other publishers had concerns about the modernism of Adler's style and the construction of the novel.[22] The other replies Adler received were non-committal or polite letters of rejection. Most presses said that the book was a poor fit either for their publishing strategy or for their readership.[23] As for the publishing house Suhrkamp, Jeremy Adler reports that Peter Suhrkamp verbally and violently rejected *The Journey* in the 1950s with the words: 'As long as I live, this book will not be published in Germany.' ['Solange ich lebe, wird das Buch in Deutschland nicht gedruckt.'][24] The fact that a great literary expert and opponent to the Nazis made such a polemical statement on a book of such literary importance as *The Journey* requires further explanation. One plausible explanation can be found in Carl Zuckmayer's memoirs.[25] Peter Suhrkamp told Zuckmayer in 1946 about his own ordeal in the concentration camp and the awful things he had been forced to witness. However, he urgently warned against written descriptions of such atrocities, saying that, rather than deterring the readers, they would stimulate their unconscious drive to cruelty.[26] Suhrkamp's ban on representation was based on the fear that the 'demons [might] be stirred and called forth again' ['die bösen Geister [könnten] so wieder aufgerührt und neu gerufen werden'].[27]

Yet it is uncertain whether Peter Suhrkamp (who died in 1959) passed his strict prohibition on to his colleagues. When Adler sent his novel to the publishing house in 1955, editors Friedrich Podszus and Siegfried Unseld were very positive towards him in their letters. But, was it all just a front? Unseld told Adler of his various attempts to place the book with other publishers, since he did not want to have *The Journey* printed himself. Venting his disappointment to Unseld in 1956, Adler wrote:

Any other writer in my situation, especially as a Theresienstadt and Auschwitz survivor, would have long since lost his sense of humour, would be bitter and say: All these protestations of "reparation" and all those other catchphrases are nothing but lies and hot air as soon as you move beyond kitsch and sentimentality and into the sphere of art. I know that it is not your fault and I am grateful to you for your efforts.

[Jeder andere Dichter in meiner Lage, gerade als Überlebender von Theresienstadt und Auschwitz wäre längst weniger zu Humor geneigt, sondern verbittert und würde sagen: Alles Beteuern von "Wiedergutmachung" und wie die Schlagworte noch heißen, ist verlogenes Geschwätz, sobald es sich, jenseits von Kitsch und Sentimentalität, um den Bereich der Kunst handelt. Dafür können Sie nichts, ich weiß, ich bin Ihnen dankbar für Ihre Bemühungen.][28]

Adler found a publishing house in 1962. By this time, the *Einsatzgruppen* trial in Ulm (1958) and the Eichmann trial in Jerusalem (1961) had taken place. Adler himself had published different books on Jewish history and the Holocaust and conducted a successful radio broadcast on Auschwitz with Hermann Langbein. Germany continued to repress its Nazi past, however, using five different mechanisms identified by Aleida Assmann: setting suffering against suffering, externalization of guilt, ignoring the past, silence, and falsification of the facts.[29] Even *The Diary of Anne Frank*, which was published in 1950, sold 750,000 copies by 1960, and was adapted as a highly popular play in 1956, contributed to this situation. Depicting the Germans as not directly responsible, and censoring some critical passages, these representations left the young girl's deportation, her time in the camps, and her death invisible.[30]

The Christian publisher Knut Erichson could see from the start that *The Journey* was hardly going to be a commercial success in his 'bibliotheca christiana'. Sending the first copies, he wrote Adler in 1962:[31]

I personally published your book in memory of all my father's friends, who, like you, were persecuted, and whose fate leaves me no peace. Even if 'A JOURNEY' does not become a 'success', I, as a publisher, who is also responsible for the commercial part of the company, am convinced that this book had to be published.

[Ich persönlich habe das Buch zum Andenken an alle die Freunde meines Vaters herausgebracht, die wie Sie verfolgt wurden, und deren Schicksal mich nie hat zur Ruhe kommen lassen. Selbst wenn 'EINE REISE' kein 'Erfolg' wird, bin ich als Verleger und damit auch als für den wirtschaftlichen Teil unseres Unternehmens Verantwortlicher davon überzeugt, daß dieses Buch erscheinen mußte].

When negotiations with several foreign publishing houses failed a few months later,[32] Erichson wrote:

We're going to have to reconcile ourselves to the fact that your books are going to be read only by a small number of people, amid many other books. Its high literary quality and content make your book, like many others, uncomfortable reading.

[Wir werden uns damit abfinden müssen, daß Ihre Bücher neben vielen andern

Autoren nur von einer kleinen Zahl von Menschen gelesen werden. Sowohl Ihre, wie auch viele andere Bücher, sind im Grunde der literarischen Qualität wie dem Inhalt nach unbequem für den Leser.]

Needless to say, the many years of rejection or silence from publishers were a very bitter experience for Adler. The sales figures were also discouraging: in December 1963, only 1,300 copies had been sold, and there was no second print run.

Adler's many letters to publishers, contained in his estate housed in the Archive of German Literature in Marbach, are themselves palimpsests. Many of these letters are typed on thin copy paper, the reverse side of which shows through, revealing his texts on Theresienstadt. This chance overlap testifies not only to the fact that Adler had to save paper, but also to the material visibility of his double status as a historian and a writer, showing how he used multiple perspectives to put one and the same personal and historical experience into writing.

The Reviews in 1962 and the Relationship between Text and Paratexts

Once *The Journey* finally appeared in 1962, it met with a remarkable and unanimously positive reception in the media. Of decisive influence were the zones between text and paratext, according to the categories established by Genette. In his book *Seuils* [Thresholds], Genette distinguishes between the editorial paratexts: dustjacket, commentaries, etc. and the author's paratexts: dedication, foreword and title.[33] In his foreword to Genette's book, Philippe Lejeune speaks of a fringe of the printed text, which in reality controls one's whole reading of the text.[34] I want to stress particularly five paratextual and peritextual elements, which had a decisive influence on the reception. First, the 'Vorzeichen', 'Augury', a dense philosophical and non-narrative text, which Adler inserted before the beginning of the novel itself, stressed the novel's reflexive and general elements. In addition to this, the jacket blurb mentions H. G. Adler's previous historical works, since other literary works had not yet been published, which privileged Adler the historian at the expense of Adler the writer. Mainly, however, reviewers referred to the comments on the dust jacket and the jacket blurb. They show two long, very positive reviews from the journalist Benno Reifenberg and the editors as well as lavish praise from Elias Canetti, quoted from a personal letter to his friend Adler. Adler had dedicated the book to Canetti and his wife.[35] Many elements of these comments resurfaced in the later reviews, often textually.

In the letter cited, Canetti enthusiastically welcomed the 'beautiful, pure prose' ['die schöne, reine Prosa'] of a 'masterpiece' ['Meisterwerk'], Benno Reifenberg lauded its 'quiet, almost ethereal voice' ['leise, fast zarte Stimmgebung'] and the publisher's comment praised Adler for having succeeded in recounting the 'ballad of his journey' ['die Ballade seiner Reise'] 'in the swaying rhythm of the old heroic songs'.[36] We find more or less the same terms in a range of the later reviews.[37] Most reviewers agree on Adler's accomplishment of having found an appropriate language.[38]

But what was the theme of this 'masterpiece'? The three paratextual commentaries did not clearly name what stands at the heart of *The Journey*, namely the Holocaust.

In a general, dehistoricizing movement and a conspicuous difficulty to find the right term, characteristic for these years, the paratexts, followed by most reviewers, referred to the Holocaust as the 'horror of this journey into the void' ['Grauen dieser Reise ins Nichts' (publisher)], the 'atrocity' ['das Entsetzliche'], the 'devastation' ['die Verwüstung'(Canetti)], the 'outrage' ['das Ungeheuerliche'] that 'is hardly depicted' ['kaum beschrieben' (Reifenberg)], or via a mythologizing poetic evocation:

> There was a time when messengers went around, entering the houses [...] with deadly messages. There was a time when people were singled out for their origins: those who were considered permissible were separated out from those who were not. [...] They were taken out of everything that belonged to them and sent on a journey. The only purpose of the stations in this journey was to unload the dead.][39]

> [Es gab eine Zeit, da gingen Boten umher, kamen in die Häuser [...], um tödliche Botschaften zu überbringen. Es gab eine Zeit, in der man die Menschen nach ihrer Herkunft aussonderte: solche, die sein durften, von solchen, die nicht sein durften [...]. Man nahm sie fort aus allem, was ihnen gehörte und schickte sie auf die Reise. Die Stationen dieser Reise dienten nur dazu, die Toten auszuladen.]

Although this is an oft-quoted paragraph, the fact is that many reviewers chose not to present their own view of the contents of a novel that did not employ historical terms. Furthermore, they also followed the relative terminological vagueness concerning the Holocaust[40] that was still common practice in the Western German mainstream in 1962.

The three paratexts by Reifenberg, Canetti, and the publisher all made a point of remarking that the novel was stylistically convincing in 'vanquishing' ['bezwingen'] and 'overcoming' ['bewältigen'] the terrible past [das Entsetzliche], describing its literary representation as 'floating, gentle, and conquerable' ['schwebend, zart und verwindlich'].[41] Canetti, evidently also thinking of his friend Adler the man, wrote that the novel was 'above resentment and bitterness', and an 'expression of an essential reformation' ['jenseits von Groll und Bitterkeit, Ausdruck einer essentiellen Läuterung']. The comforting, conciliatory tone of these comments created a widespread pattern for the reception of *The Journey*.[42] These early comments picked up the term *Bewältigung* [overcoming] in particular, in line with a wider tendency in the fifties and sixties, when the notion of *Vergangenheitsbewältigung* [overcoming the past] was a widely used, albeit problematic concept.

These conciliatory interpretations of *The Journey* were based on a specific cultural context in the late forties and fifties of the twentieth century.[43] Jost Hermand has noted that what 'the bourgeois middle class' ['die bürgerliche Mitte'] in Western Germany longed for most in those years was to be consoled, saved, healed, and uplifted, even to be provided with catharsis. Literature in the post-war era was therefore seen as having a 'therapeutic' function ['Lebenshilfe'].[44] The *topos* of a past supposedly overcome was matched by the astonishing claim, formulated especially by Canetti and quoted by most of the later reviewers, that *The Journey* did not contain any form of accusation. This claim seems highly doubtful: even if the novel does not formulate any direct accusations, the persistent, implicitly accusatory, bitter tone of caustic irony, or biting sarcasm can be heard loudly and clearly.[45] Two voices among the critics who had a particular echo were Heimito von Doderer and Heinrich Böll.

Contemporary Critics

Emphasizing Adler's formal and stylistic achievement in two detailed articles, Heimito von Doderer, too, assumed that the 'horror' ['Entsetzen'] had been overcome by art: Adler had made a song of a whole mountain of terror. Even if Doderer, the famous writer, was one of the few to recognize Adler's literary accomplishment — to Adler's delight — , his praise seems dubious: Doderer describes Adler's novel as 'quiet' ['still'], even 'silent' ['lautlos'], 'despite the object of the narrative, about which there is so much noisy ado' ['trotz des Gegenstandes der Erzählung, um welchen doch wahrlich viel Lärmens herrscht'].[46]

Doderer, a former member of the Nazi party NSdAP, was not the only reviewer to combine praise of Adler's novel with a dig at other Holocaust narratives.[47] He made another, even more disconcerting comment when he claimed that Adler had 'discovered a great secret that no one had really become aware of, namely the fact that all this awfulness took place with permission from high up, so to speak!' ['großes Geheimnis entdeckt, das bisher noch niemand recht zu Bewußtsein gekommen ist: daß nämlich all dieses Gräßliche gewissermaßen mit [...] höherer Zulassung geschah'].[48] By 'all this awfulness' ['all dieses Gräßliche'], von Doderer presumably meant the Holocaust.

A very different viewpoint emerged from Heinrich Böll's writing, one of the most prominent authors of the time. In his acclaimed Frankfurt Lectures on Poetics in 1964, Böll put forward some ideas on 'Writing after Auschwitz' and cited *The Journey* as an example of what he termed an 'aesthetic of the humane', acknowledging his friend H. G. Adler's literary accomplishment in long quotes and comments. Unfortunately, Böll's favourable representation of the novel mostly dispensed with references to the Holocaust. In addition to this omission, Böll's discussion of *The Journey* in his Frankfurt Lectures lost focus and became rather misleading due to his attempt to establish the commonalities between Jewish and Non-Jewish Germans, and to reconcile to the two groups as if there were a common denominator for their experience. Böll's comparisons between the fate of German speaking Jews in *The Journey* with that of Non-Jewish Germans during the war and in the immediate post-war period departed from terms such as *Heimat* ['home country'], *Heimatverlust* ['loss of the home country'], *Vertreibung* ['displacement from the Eastern territories'], *zerstörte Nachbarschaft* ['destroyed neighbourhoods'], *Reise* ['journey']. Böll thus created what was objectively a distorted understanding of the novel and the experiences of Jewish German survivors.[49]

Christian Media, Jewish Media, and Warnings About the Book's Difficulty

The Christian media produced a large number of reviews of *The Journey*, possibly because the novel had been placed with a Christian publisher. The Christian Church (both Catholic and Protestant) was hugely influential at the time, a fact to which Böll's novels testify. Most of these reviews approached Adler's novel from a theological angle, focusing on questions such as good and evil, mercy,[50] God, conscience, which was an exception in comparison to other critics.[51] While the novel testified to Adler's determination to create a literary representation of the persecution of the Jews, to unmask perpetrators and bystanders through their own discourses, and to commemorate the Jewish victims, these reviewers read the work as a confirmation of Christian doctrine, as if Jewish religion did not exist.

The reception of *The Journey* by two Jewish newspapers (*Germania Judaica, Allgemeine Zeitung der Juden in Deutschland*)[52] offers specific examples of the ways in which the memory and worldview of Jewish and Non-Jewish Germans diverged in the post-war period, as shown in *Die andere Erinnerung* de Stefan Braese.[53] The reviews in these two Jewish publications presented the testimony of a Jewish survivor as the book's most essential dimension. This viewpoint was nowhere to be found in the other media sources. The Jewish newspapers accurately situated *The Journey* within historical events, contextualizing it within a persecution of the Jews that had been taking place 'since the dawn of times' ['seit Urzeiten']. These commentaries took note of the horror at the heart of the novel and spoke of 'terror, suffering, and pain' ['Schrecken, Leiden und Leid'] and how the novel drives 'a thorn' ['Stachel'] into the reader's 'side'. The optimistic dénouement was interpreted as a weakness by one Jewish review (*Germania Judaica*), while the other review considered it specifically Jewish as an example of the Jewish individual's inextinguishable hope (*Allgemeine Zeitung der Juden in Deutschland.*)

Repeatedly, reviewers warned the reader that the book was difficult, and very, even excessively demanding.[54] Doderer's review for instance stressed that this was a very difficult book, which was nevertheless worth the effort. Another review presupposed that only few readers would be up to the challenge of reading this demanding book.[55] Questioning the reader's ability to understand the book, these warnings did little to boost sales. Such warnings were nowhere to be found with the new 1999 edition, even if the novel does contain difficulties.

The 1999 Reedition and the Framework for Collective Memory

When the Austrian publishing house Zsolnay brought out a new edition of Adler's novel *Eine Reise*,[56] critics were not just unanimous in their praise — they positively raved. In contrast to 1962, even major national German-language newspapers were now publishing positive reviews. The jacket included short excerpts from two peritexts written in 1962, the publisher's commentary and the letter from Canetti (who in the meantime had won the Nobel Prize in 1981), but their sense was deeply changed by the precise information related to Adler's fate in the concentration camps and the loss of his family. Another peritext, Jeremy Adler's afterword, combined historical and biographical details with a penetrating analysis of the literary aspects and influences, as well as the reception of *The Journey*, which would all have an incisive influence on the 1999 reception.

At this point, the framework for collective memory in Germany had fundamentally changed compared to what it had been in 1962. While this shift cannot be reconstructed in detail here, it is worth noting some milestones in this development: the Auschwitz trials, which took place between 1963 and 1965[57] and which H. G. Adler had actively helped prepare; the *Verjährungsdebatten*, the parliamentary debates on the limitation on murder, in 1965, 1969, and 1979; the television series *Holocaust*, which was broadcast in 1975; Richard von Weizsäcker's speech on 8 May 1985. In the literary arena, the great success of the works of Paul Celan,[58] Nelly Sachs[59] and Peter Weiss, author of *Die Ermittlung*[60] [*The Investigation*], reveal how central the Holocaust had become to German cultural memory. Ruth Klüger's *weiter leben*[61] [*Still alive*],[62] on her childhood in concentration camps and published in 1992, sold 200,000 copies.

With regard to the literary movements at the time, authors who — like Adler — were influenced by Joyce, including Arno Schmidt, Uwe Johnson, and Wolfgang Koeppen, had been recognized for the modernism of their writing.[63] This cultural context framed the later reception of *Eine Reise*. The modernist literary model had now achieved general acceptance and reviews concentrated on *how* the historical events of the Holocaust were represented.

Aesthetic Questions, Comparisons, Style

The question of how to represent the Shoah and the literary devices Adler deployed stand at the heart of these discussions. The reviews agreed that *The Journey* was absolutely outstanding, an exemplary instance of how to deal with the difficulty of representing mass murder, killing centres, camps, and deportations.

Gone were the misreadings of 1962, which had downplayed the horror at the heart of the novel and had claimed that Adler's narrative made no accusations. Reviewers now generally highlighted that Adler had traced an exemplary picture of the ultimately terrifying, which Adler had put into writing 'with immense rage' ['voll Furor'].[64]

Several reviewers cited H. G. Adler's Holocaust literature in the same breath as Paul Celan. But, unlike Celan, whose writing navigated the limits of silence,[65] Adler's style, reviewers claimed, was epically expansive, reminiscent of poetic rhythm.[66] Commentators also expressed their appreciation for Adler's prose by comparing it to that of Primo Levi and Aharon Appelfeld.[67] Imre Kertész's 1975 *Sorstalanság* [*Fateless*[68]], which was published in German in 1990 as *Mensch ohne Schicksal*[69] and 1996 as *Roman eines Schicksallosen*,[70] was cited as a comparison for the delayed reception of a remarkable book on the Holocaust.[71] Reviewers anticipated in 1999 that the reception pattern for *The Journey* would be similar, but this did not occur.

All reviewers underlined Adler's stylistic accomplishment, reading the blend of a poetic, flowing, virtuoso language[72] with the technical and cool instructions and orders as a means to disconcert and terrify the reader. They also counted Adler's irony and sarcasm among these disturbing elements, highlighting their subversive function. Critics also saw a new dimension in the representation of the Holocaust offered by Adler's use of *stream of consciousness*, a fragmentary and kaleidoscopically diffracted world, and a collage of unfamiliar elements.[73] Hermann Broch, James Joyce, and Virginia Woolf were cited as models of Adler's prose.[74] Writing in the *Frankfurter Rundschau*, literary scholar Judith Klein assigned *The Journey* a paradigmatic role.

> Adler overcomes an apparently unresolvable conflict between aesthetic modernism and the claim to bearing witness. While literary modernism maintained the autonomy of a form of writing that was supposed to eternally serve no truth but its own, the survivors wanted to bear witness to reality. *The Journey* offers a unique combination of testimony and modernist aesthetics.
>
> [Adler überwindet im übrigen den unlösbar scheinenden Widerspruch zwischen der ästhetischen Moderne und dem Anspruch des Bezeugens. Während die literarische Moderne die Autonomie der Schrift behauptete, die endlos für sich und im Dienste keiner Wahrheit stehen sollte, wollten die Überlebenden Wirklichkeit bezeugen. In *Eine Reise* sind Zeugenschaft und Ästhetik der Moderne eine einzigartige Verbindung eingegangen.][75]

Despite all this praise, Adler's book never achieved great commercial success: Zsolnay sold only 3,000 copies, while Aufbau-Taschenbuch has sold only 500 copies since 2002. More recently, the novel has gone out of print. It is hoped, however, that its success in the English-speaking world will provide the impetus for a successful new edition in German.

Notes to Chapter 14

1. Thanks to Susannah Ellis for translating this chapter from French into English. I also thank the Deutsches Literaturarchiv Marbach and its efficient staff. I thank Jeremy Adler, who authorized citations from the unpublished letters.
2. Adler himself argued for 'Erzählung' [tale]. This did become the subtitle to the first edition, but for reasons related to the book's length and structure, it was eventually replaced by 'Roman' [novel].
3. This is the title of the English translation. H. G. Adler, *The Journey*, trans. by Peter Filkins (New York: Random House, 2009).
4. Maurice Halbwachs, *Les cadres sociaux de la mémoire* (Paris: Albin Michel 1994).
5. Eugen Kogon, *Der SS-Staat* (Frankfurt a/M: Verlag der Frankfurter Hefte, 1946).
6. Peter Reichel, *Vergangenheitsbewältigung in Deutschland: Die Auseinandersetzung mit der NS-Diktatur von 1945 bis heute* (Munich: C. H. Beck, 2001), p. 68. On the place of the Shoah in the public perception in the Federal Republic of Germany prior to the Auschwitz trials, see Ruth Vogel-Klein, 'Einleitung', in *Die ersten Stimmen: Deutschsprachige Texte zur Shoah 1945–1963*, ed. by Ruth Vogel-Klein (Würzburg: Königshausen & Neumann 2010), pp. 7–21.
7. Volker Wehdeking, *Anfänge westdeutscher Nachkriegsliteratur, Aufsätze, Interviews, Materialien* (Aachen: Alano, 1989), p. 39.
8. Kurt Hohoff, *Woina, Woina — Russisches Tagebuch* (Düsseldorf: Diederichs, 1951).
9. Ernst Jünger, *Strahlungen* (Tübingen: Heliopolis Verlag, 1949).
10. Ernst von Salomon, *Der Fragebogen* (Hamburg: Rowohlt, 1951).
11. Published in the United Kingdom as *The Answers of Ernst von Salomon to the 131 Questions in the Allied Military Government 'Fragebogen'* (London: Putman, 1954); and in the United States

as *Fragebogen: The Questionnaire* (Garden City, NY: Doubleday, 1955). Both editions trans. by Constantine Fitzgibbon.

12. First edition issued on 20 March 1951. By 1952, 200,000 copies had been sold. Ralf Heyer, *Verfolgte Zeugen der Wahrheit: Das literarische Schaffen und das politische Wirken konservativer Autoren nach 1945 am Beispiel von Friedrich Georg Jünger, Ernst Jünger, Ernst von Salomon, Stefan Andres und Reinhold Schneider* (Dresden: Thelem, 2008).

13. Published after Böll's death. Heinrich Böll, *Der Engel schwieg* (Cologne: Kiepenheuer & Witsch, 1992).

14. Walter Delabar, 'Zwischen Dichtung und Kahlschlag: Zwei Exkursionen in die bundesdeutsche Nachkriegsliteratur', *Juni: Magazin für Literatur und Politik* 23 (1995), 97–116 (p. 98). Stephan Hermlin, returning after emigration, wrote in 1947 that contemporary German poetry reminded him of 'the poetry of cavemen' ['Dichtung von Höhlenbewohnern']: 'In terms of form, this results in a tendency towards the conservative, the static, the retrograde. In terms of its intellectual content, this brand of poetry avoids direct and concrete expression, retreating as it does into the metaphysical and preferring to call the killers demons.' ['Daraus ergibt sich formal der Zug zum Konservativen, zum Statischen, zum Rückwärtsgewandten. Was den geistigen Gehalt angeht, scheut man das Direkte, das Konkrete, man flüchtet in die Metaphysik und nennt die Totschläger am liebsten Dämonen'], in *Die andere deutsche Frage: Kultur und Gesellschaft der Bundesrepublik Deutschland nach 30 Jahren*, ed. by Walter Scheel (Stuttgart: Klett, 1981), p. 139. According to Ralf Schnell, post-war literature presented a 'penchant for a metaphysical or religious vision of the world' ['Neigung zur metaphysischen oder religiösen Weltdeutung'] and made up a '*mixtum compositum* of inwardness, religiosity, spiritual elitism, and a yearning to commune with nature, at a safe distance from, even attacking, the crude reality of everyday life'. ['Mixtum compositum aus Innerlichkeit und Religiosität, Geistesaristokratie und Naturinnigkeit, das, fern der kruden Alltagsrealität, dieser den Prozess macht']. Ralf Schnell, 'Traditionalistische Konzepte', in *Literatur in der Bundesrepublik Deutschland bis 1967*, ed. by Ludwig Fischer (Munich: dtv, 1986), pp. 214–29, (p. 215). Horst Ohde: 'Die Magie des Heilen: Naturlyrik nach 1945', in Ludwig Fischer (ed.), *Literatur in der Bundesrepublik Deutschland bis 1967*, pp. 349–56.

15. Adler spent a long time looking for a title. He first wanted to call the novel 'Die Reise: Eine Ballade' [The Journey: A Ballad], which his publisher did not agree to. On 27 May 1962, Adler suggested 'Die Reise: Eine Sage' [The Journey: A Legend] to his publisher. They finally agreed on *Die Reise: Eine Erzählung* [The Journey: A Tale], only to find that the title had already been taken and could not be used. After some initial protestations, Adler then suggested *Die Auflösung — Eine Erzählung* [The Dissolution — A Tale], arguing that this title conveyed several meanings, the decomposition and the *solutio* of the dénouement (9 October 1962). Adler rejected the editor's suggestion to call the novel *Die gewaltsame Reise* [The Forcible Journey], stating that this title would falsify the intention of the novel, since the element of force was only one aspect of this journey, as shown, for example, by the last sentence in the novel. 'He thinks they are waving him off on a good journey, because the waste has been overcome' ['Er glaubt, sie winken ihm zu einer guten Reise, weil der Abfall überwunden ist' (9 October 1962). All parties finally came to an agreement: *Eine Reise: Eine Erzählung* [A Journey: A Tale].

16. H. G. Adler, *Panorama* (Olten: Walter Verlag, 1968). Published in English as *Panorama: A Novel*, trans. by Peter Filkins (New York: Random House, 2011).

17. H. G. Adler, *Die unsichtbare Wand* (Vienna: Zsolnay, 1989). Published in English as *The Wall*, trans. by Peter Filkins (New York: Random House, 2014). Since Marlen Haushofer had published a novel entitled *Die Wand* [The Wall] in 1963, copyright protection on the German title meant that when Adler's novel came out in 1989, it had to be called *Die unsichtbare Wand* [The Invisible Wall]. Haushofer's novel has since been published in France as *Le mur invisible* [The Invisible Wall] (Arles: Actes Sud, 1985).

18. *Theresienstadt 1941–1945: The Face of a Coerced Community*, trans. by Belinda Cooper (Cambridge: Cambridge University Press, 2017).

19. H. G. Adler was also trying to help his friend Franz Baermann Steiner publish his work. He did succeed in helping Steiner publish a collection of poems with Lambert Schneider in 1954,

a publishing house where he would have liked to place *The Journey*. Franz Baermann Steiner, *Unruhe ohne Uhr* (Heidelberg: Lambert Schneider, 1954).

20. H. G. Adler, *Theresienstadt 1941–1945: Antlitz einer Zwangsgemeinschaft* (Tübingen: Mohr (Paul Siebeck), 1955).

21. Dr. Franz Schönauer of Claassen publishing to H. G. Adler, 30 April 1958. (Adler's estate is housed in the Deutsches Literaturarchiv Marbach, quoted as DLA.) DLA, Adler: AII 80. Schönauer writes of *The Journey* that 'the reader has nothing to hold on to and loses all means of finding direction' ['hat gar nichts, woran er sich festhalten kann und verliert jede Orientierungsmöglichkeit']. *Panorama* had long since been turned down by Inge Claassen for financial reasons, on 3 May 1949: 'I am especially and truly sorry about this in your case, given that you suffered so badly under the Third Reich.' A more detailed rejection of *Panorama* and a very negative report on the manuscript was sent on 9 March 1950. H. G. Adler enquired with Claassen publishing about five different works: *Panorama*, *Theresienstadt 1941–1945*, *The Journey*, *Erzählungen* [Short Stories], and *The Wall*. Despite various promises and a decade-long correspondence, the publisher kept backing out and, in the end, printed none of these books. DLA, Adler: AII 80.

22. Alexandra von Miquel (Kiepenheuer & Witsch) to H. G. Adler, 23 November 1953. She was sorry to have to decline his proposal for financial reasons, especially 'since your book makes for extraordinarily impressive reading and we believe that the difficult topic of your work has found a sophisticated, poetic form which should be made available to German literature, and especially to the German public'. ['weil uns die Lektüre ungewöhnlich beeindruckt hat und weil wir glauben, daß das schwierige Thema Ihres Werkes eine souveräne und dichterische Darstellung gefunden hat, die der deutschen Literatur, vor allem aber dem deutschen Publikum zugänglich gemacht werden müßte'.] DLA, Adler: AII 81.

23. Publisher Langen-Müller also took such a long time to send a response to the manuscript that Adler sent an embittered reminder on 3 November 1952. On 12 December 1952, however, he noted that he had received an outstanding report from the publisher, along with a friendly letter from the director of the publishing house. The book was not sent to print, however.

24. Jeremy Adler, 'Nachwort: Nur wer die Reise wagt, findet nach Hause', in H. G. Adler, *Eine Reise*, Roman (Vienna: Zsolnay, 1999), pp. 307–15 (p. 310).

25. 20 October 1956.

26. Carl Zuckmayer, *Als wär's ein Stück von mir. Erinnerungen* (Frankfurt a/M: Fischer, 1969), pp. 464–65.

27. Ibid.

28. Letter Adler to Unseld, 20 October 1956. DLA: Adler AII 81.

29. The German terms are: Aufrechnen, Externalisieren der Schuld, Ausblenden, Schweigen und Umfälschen. Aleida Assmann, *Der lange Schatten der Vergangenheit, Erinnerungskultur und Geschichtspolitik*. (Munich: C. H. Beck, 2006), pp. 169–72.

30. Hanno Loewy, 'Das gerettete Kind: Die "Universalisierung" der Anne Frank', in *Deutsche Nachkriegsliteratur und der Holocaust*, ed. by Stephan Braese, Holger Gehle, Doron Kiesel, and Hanno Loewy (Frankfurt a/M: Campus, 1998), pp. 19–41; Sander L. Gilman, *Jüdischer Selbsthaß: Antisemitismus und die verborgene Sprache der Juden*, (Frankfurt a/M: Jüdischer Verlag, 1993), p. 314; Stephan Braese: 'Deutschland — ein Krieg gegen das Erinnern: Zum Ende der Nachkriegszeit', *Diskussion Deutsch*, 119 (1991), pp. 240–44.

31. 23 November 1962.

32. 21 February 1963.

33. Gérard Genette, *Seuils* (Paris: Éditions du Seuil, 1987).

34. Philippe Lejeune, *Le Pacte Autobiographique* (Paris: Éditions du Seuil, 1975), p. 45, quoted by Genette.

35. Jeremy Adler, 'Nachwort', p. 312. Personal aspects of the somewhat uneasy history of Adler's and Canetti's friendship also play out in this letter. On the relationship between H. G. Adler and Elias Canetti, see Jeremy Adler, *Das bittere Brot: H. G. Adler, Elias Canetti und Franz Baermann Steiner im Londoner Exil* (Göttingen: Wallstein, 2015).

36. As mentioned above, the term 'ballad' was one of Adler's suggestions for the book's subtitle.

37. *Seele*, Regensburg (November-December, 1962). This and the following references to reviews of first editions of H. G. Adler's works are taken from the materials in Adler's archive held at the DLA. The excerpted reviews from newspapers were most likely compiled by his publishers; some were transcribed with only cursory references, and some of these newspaper clippings do not include the page numbers.

38. 'Superior literary qualities' ['Hochstehende literarische Qualitäten'], *Gottesfreud*, Köln (February 1963). 'Even only from a stylistic perspective, it is a masterpiece. Adler has not only recounted the fate his friends met with, but also had the strength to shape it.' *Seele*, Regensburg (November-December 1962); 'Controlled, disciplined style' ['Beherrschte und zuchtvolle Sprache']. *Konradsblatt*, Karlsruhe (23 December 1963); 'A style [...] noticeably resonating with the rhythm of the verse of old heroic songs.' [Sprache [...] in der spürbar der Versrhythmus alter Heldenlieder mitschwingt.'] *Das Neue Buch* (2 January 1963); 'The book searches for a language that could still express the atrocious events. In this, the author succeeds.' ['Das Buch sucht nach einer adäquaten Sprache, das grausame Geschehen noch auszudrücken. Das gelingt dem Verfasser.'] *Priester und Arbeiter*, Cologne (March-April 1963); 'Hohe Kunst des Erzählers' [The High Art of the Narrator], *Südkurier* (8 July 1964); 'He crafts a convincing language for the journey into extermination' ['So gewinnt er für die Reise in die Vernichtung eine überzeugende Sprache'], *Rheinische Post*, Düsseldorf (8 June 1963).

39. This text from the publisher was quoted verbatim in *Kölnische Rundschau* (27 April 1963).

40. 'A truly timeless representation makes visible the horror which, emanating from human beings, can strike other human beings.' ['In wahrhaft überzeitlicher Darstellung wird das Grauen sichtbar, das, vom Menschen ausgehend, den Menschen treffen kann.'] *Wiener Bücherbriefe* (May 1964).

41. Elias Canetti, jacket blurb.

42. 'This book provides many encouraging insights, as the horrors are overcome in a way that is, ultimately, comforting.' ['Dieses Buch gibt viele ermutigende Hinweise, weil hier in einer letzlich tröstlichen Weise das Grauen überwunden ist.']. This article, however, does name 'the horrors'. *Evangelisches Sonntagsblatt* (2 April 1963). Another article speaks of a 'comforting perspective' ['tröstlichen Ausblick'] and a 'conciliatory mood' ['versöhnliche Stimmung']. *Evangelische Verantwortung*, Bonn (June 1964).

43. Maren Jäger, *Die Joyce-Rezeption der deutschsprachigen Erzählliteratur nach 1945* (Tübingen: Niemeyer, 2009), p. 413.

44. Jost Hermand, *Kultur im Wiederaufbau: Die Bundesrepublik Deutschland 1945–1965* (Frankfurt a/M: Ullstein, 1989), p. 157.

45. Ruth Vogel-Klein, 'Keine Anklage? Der Deportationsroman *Eine Reise* (1951–1962): Publikation und Rezeption', in *Die ersten Stimmen. Deutschsprachige Texte zur Shoah 1945–1963*, ed. by Ruth Vogel-Klein (Würzburg: Königshausen & Neumann, 2010), pp. 79–111. See also John White's contribution to the present volume.

46. Heimito von Doderer, *Welt am Sonntag*, 29 December 1963. 'The unjustly forgotten. Writers answer a survey. National newspaper 'Die Welt am Sonntag' carried out an end-of-year survey with a number of German (sic!) writers, asking them about non-sellers of their choice, i.e. books unjustly forgotten in their opinion.' ['Zu Unrecht sind sie vergessen. Schriftsteller antworten auf eine Umfrage. Zum Jahresende fragte die 'Welt am Sonntag' eine Reihe prominenter deutscher (sic!) Schriftsteller nach den 'Nonsellern' ihrer Wahl, nach den Büchern, die ihrer Meinung nach zu Unrecht vergessen wurden.'].

47. According to another review, not only the henchmen lost their dignity, but the victims did, too, 'when they sputter with talk of revenge' ['wenn sie vor Rache schnauben'] and 'allow themselves to be mentally humiliated' ['sich innerlich erniedrigen lassen.'] Alfons Bungert, *Deutsche Tageszeitung* (28 June 1963).

48. Heimito von Doderer, *Welt am Sonntag* (29 December 1963).

49. The analysis takes another direction in one of Böll's newspaper articles, where he uses more concrete details and remains closer to the text. But here, too, Böll makes a problematic generalization. The Germans' Nazi past and the damage it had wreaked in their home country had given them a thirst for travel, a fact, Böll tells us, that meant that the Germans, too, had a

share in the narrative of the 'journey'. Heinrich Böll, 'Wir Deutsche, Ein fahrendes Volk', *Der Tagesspiegel*, Berlin (22 September 1963), 37.

50. *Evangelische Verantwortung*, Bonn (June 1964).

51. 'Through Adler, we feel the spirit of God, which shakes us to the core, only to leave us strengthened.' ['In Adler spüren wir den Geist Gottes, der erschüttert, um zu befestigen.']. *Deutsche Tageszeitung* (28 June 1963).

52. The third Jewish newspaper, *Die Tribüne*, did not publish a review.

53. Stephan Braese, *Die andere Erinnerung: Jüdische Autoren in der westdeutschen Nachkriegsliteratur* (Vienna: Philo, 2001).

54. *Kirchenzeitung*, Cologne (17 January 1963); *Konradsblatt* (23 December 1963); 'not an easy read' ['keine leichte Lektüre'] in *Stimmen der Zeit* (September 1963).

55. *Kirchenzeitung*, Cologne (17 January 1963).

56. H. G. Adler, *The Journey*, trans. by Peter Filkins (New York: Random House, 2009).

57. See Ruth Vogel-Klein, 'Einleitung', in *Die ersten Stimmen. Deutschsprachige Texte zur Shoah 1945–1963*, ed. Ruth Vogel-Klein, (Würzburg: Königshausen & Neumann, 2010), pp. 7–21.

58. For the history and the reception of Celan's 'Todesfuge' see Thomas Sparr, 'Todesfuge' in *Enzyklopädie jüdischer Geschichte und Kultur*, vol. 6, ed. by Dan Diner, (Stuttgart: Metzler, 2015), pp.119–24.

59. The poems of Nelly Sachs became immediately very successful. First edition: Nelly Sachs, *In den Wohnungen des Todes* (Berlin: Aufbau, 1947). Sachs won the Nobel Prize in 1966.

60. Peter Weiss, *Die Ermittlung, Oratorium in 11 Gesängen* (Frankfurt a/M: Suhrkamp 1965). *The Investigation: A Play*, transl. by Jon Swan and Ulu Grosbard, (London: Pocket Books, 1967).

61. Ruth Klüger, *weiter leben* (Göttingen: Wallstein 1992).

62. Ruth Klüger, *Still Alive: A Holocaust Childhood Remembered* (New York: The Feminist Press, 2001).

63. Maren Jäger, *Die Joyce-Rezeption der deutschsprachigen Erzählliteratur nach 1945* (Tübingen: Niemeyer, 2009), pp. 422–24.

64. Anonymous, 'Zwangsreise', *Stuttgarter Zeitung* (11 April 2003), 32; Marion Löhndorf, 'Buch der Verwüstung', *Neue Zürcher Zeitung* (30 November 1999), 35.

65. Lothar Müller, 'Das Böse ist nicht banal: H. G. Adlers Buch *Eine Reise*', *Frankfurter Allgemeine Zeitung* (27 November 1999), 9.

66. Ibid.

67. *Stuttgarter Zeitung*, 'Zwangsreise'.

68. Transl. by Christopher C. Wilson and Katharina M. Wilson (Evanston, IL: Northwestern University Press, 1992). New English translation *Fatelessness*, transl. by Tim Wilkinson (New York: Vintage International, 2004).

69. Transl. by Jörg Buschmann (Berlin: Rütten und Loening, 1990).

70. New translation by Christina Viragh (Berlin: Rowohlt, 1996).

71. Iris Buchheim, 'Leben nach dem Überleben', *Falter* (28 May 1999), 66.

72. Buchheim, 'Leben nach dem Überleben'; Löhndorf, 'Buch der Verwüstung'.

73. Jörg Plath, 'Wir sind Überlebende', *Tagesspiegel* (25 July 1999), 105.

74. Adler, 'Nachwort', p. 311.

75. *Frankfurter Rundschau* (15 May 1999), 4.

CHAPTER 15

❖

H. G. Adler as Modernist
Historiographer in North America

Julia Creet

H. G. Adler's reception in North America has been a story of starts and stops, of cameo appearances, complete neglect and, finally, belated recognition.[1] Here, I will trace Adler's uneven reception in North America through three somewhat overlapping stages, the first and longest from 1948 to 2009, what I am calling 'A German among Germanists', a stage of intermittent acknowledgement limited mostly by the difficulty of translating his major works; the second, from 2009 to 2011, 'The Novels Arrive', the period of Peter Filkins' translations of Adler's trilogy, *The Journey, Panorama*, and *The Wall* and the immediate critical response; and, the third, 'The Scholars Follow', which came quite quickly on the heels of the translations and is certainly just gaining momentum.

Through these three stages, Adler emerges as a historian who comes to be recognized as such through his novels, making them, as Hayden White will observe works of modernist historiography. White argues that historical representations of the Holocaust in particular, but 'all other events even vaguely resembling it' require technically and ethically, 'modernist techniques of literary writing', because they provide 'both a perspective on "history" and a mode of presenting the complex relationships between past and present in modern culture'.[2]

A German among Germanists

A frequent observation about the reception of H. G. Adler's writing in general is that his commitment to writing in German and the absence of translation confined him to a German-reading public and primarily a German-Jewish audience, one deeply ambivalent about the German language itself and, of course, enormously reduced by the Holocaust. As Peter Demetz writes in *After the Fires,* 'We asked ourselves whether it would not be nobler to be inarticulate in another language rather than articulate in German [...] and [there were] those like H. G. Adler who rarely wavered in their allegiance to the German classical heritage before or after Auschwitz'.[3] And, as Demetz writes similarly in his afterward to Peter Filkins's English translation of *Panorama,* 'Like many of his background, at certain moments he may have doubted that German could still be used to write and speak, and yet he decided that what he wanted to say and write had to be done in German, which was also the language of the murderers, be it those at their writing desks or those at the barbed wire'.[4]

And yet, H. G. Adler knew very well that English readers and an American publisher would have brought his work — beginning with *Theresienstadt 1941–1945* — to a much wider audience. In April 1948 Adler's friend Veza Canetti, the wife of Elias Canetti, wrote to Hermann Broch, an Austrian writer in exile, precariously employed at Yale, asking that Broch might help find an American publisher for Adler's Theresienstadt study, which he had completed in manuscript earlier in the year.[5] Broch replies encouragingly to Adler, but also realistically, that publishers 'take fright at massive works like this, especially as the public would prefer to read friendly stories' ['vor so ausgedehnten Werken zurückschrecken, besonders da ja das Publikum lieber freundliche Geschichten liest'].[6] Broch suggests that a subvention grant for translation costs would also be necessary (a sum that was later calculated as a not-inconsiderable $5,000, something close to $50,000 in contemporary value). Broch, recognizing that it would become the standard work on the subject, and that Adler's 'cool and precise method not only grasps all the essential details but manages further to indicate the extent of the horror in an extremely vivid form',[7] advocated on the book's behalf, enlisting Hannah Arendt and her publishing contacts in the effort. Broch wrote to Adler in March of 1949,

> As I mentioned before, Elliot E. Cohen, the publisher of *Commentary*, is to take the matter in hand. This plan of campaign was drawn up by Dr. Hannah Arendt. As you do not know *Commentary*, you will also be unfamiliar with her, for she is one of the main figures working for the journal; she is a philosopher, has turned to politics, [...] she commits herself with great seriousness and passion to everything that seems truly important to her, and she wants to do precisely that for your work. She now wants a few people with some reputation to draw attention to the necessity of publishing the work — in Princeton these are to be, in the first instance, Erich Kahler, Dean Gauss (from the University here) and myself, and in N. Y. she will persuade a series of others to do the same — in order thereby to support Cohen's approach to publishers. Could you, for the same reason, *get Leo Baeck to write to Cohen along these lines?* — or to declare his willingness *to supply and introduction to the book?*

> [Wie ich Ihnen bereits schrieb, soll Elliot E. Cohen, der Herausgeber des *Commentary*, die Sache in die Hand nehmen. Dieser Feldzugsplan wurde von Dr. Hannah Arendt entworfen. Da Sie *Commentary* nicht kennen, so wird auch sie, die dort eine der Hauptmitarbeiterinnen ist, unbekannt sein: sie ist Philosophin, hat sich der Politik zugewandt, [...] setzt mit großem Ernst und großer Leidenschaft sich für alles ein, was ihr wahrhaft wichtig erscheint, und will eben genau das für Ihr Werk tun. Sie will nun, dass ein paar Leute von einigem Namen — in Princeton sollen es fürs erste Erich Kahler, Dean Gauss (von der hiesigen Universität) sowie ich sein, während sie in N.Y. auch noch eine Reihe hierzu bringen wird — auf die Publizierungs-Notwendigkeit hinweisen, um solcherart den Schritt Cohens bei den Verlegern zu unterstützen. Könnten Sie aus dem gleichen Grund *Leo Baeck veranlassen, dass er Cohen in diesem Sinne schreibe?* resp. sich bereit erkläre, *das Buch mit seiner Einleitung zu versehen?*][8]

This flurry of activity marks the highpoint of Broch and Arendt's enthusiasm for the project. At the same time, Broch, whose health was failing, and whose mother had died in Theresienstadt, soon found the book too painful. Hannah Arendt took over as the main advocate of the publication, but, as Broch conveys to Adler in a letter in May 1950, they met with frustrating indifference, in no small part because the 'bestseller system is becoming more and more of an insurmountable barrier' ['das bestseller-System wird mehr und mehr zur unübersteigbaren Barrikade'].[9] By this point, Broch and Adler had become embroiled in a protracted discussion about Adler's novel 'The Settlement' [*Die Ansiedlung*], which he had sent to Broch in the hopes that it too might find an American publisher. Broch reacted badly to the manuscript, finding it a baffling modernist allegory, presaging German reactions to *Eine Reise*. 'I have a feeling that you are aiming at an abstraction analogous to that of modern painting, but this has presented you with insuperable obstacles' ['Ich habe das Empfinden, dass Sie eine der modernen Malerei analoge Abstraktheit anstreben, dass sie Ihnen aber unübersteigbare Hindernisse entgegengesetzt hat'].[10] Broch is quite sure that no American publisher can be found for the 'task' of translating and publishing the novel.[11] Adler defends his work in turn: 'The "Settlement" has no limits because it is the world, or at least it became the world — that is an empirical fact which I used my right as a writer to put in a more pointed way, and I did so for the sake of salvation, for the sake of a metaphysical disposition which alone ought to preserve and separate the work from the abstraction of "modern" painting and other experiments' ['Die "Ansiedlung" hat keine Grenzen, weil sie die Welt ist, wenigstens zu ihr wurde — das ist ein empirisches Faktum, das ich mit dem Rechte des Dichters pointiert habe, und zwar um des Heiles willen, um der Möglichkeit einer metaphysischen Anlage willen, die allein von der Abstraktion "moderner" Malerei und anderer Experimente bewahren und auch trennen sollte'].[12] Broch, overwhelmed with trying to finish his own work under his impending sense that death was near, nonetheless takes the time to reread the manuscript and a long philosophical exchange between them ends in Broch claiming their common ground. Arendt's efforts come to naught and the Theresienstadt book would remain untranslated until 2017 and then in England and not the United States in spite of the vast North American academic and popular interest in the history of the Holocaust.

Nonetheless, the Theresienstadt book does become the vehicle through which H. G. Adler first comes to American readers, in second-hand fashion, figuring obliquely in Hannah Arendt's *Eichmann in Jerusalem* (1964) and in Jacob Robinson's blistering retort to Arendt (sentence by sentence it seems) *And the Crooked Shall Be Made Straight* (1965). Robinson, slightly softening his attack through three editions, argued strenuously that Arendt had minimized Eichmann's monstrosity and thus his responsibility for the absolute and knowing evil he had wrought in Europe. Moreover, Robinson was incensed by the blame Arendt placed on the complicity of the *Judenrat*.[13]

Adler's book was placed at the disposal of the court and Adler, through Yaakov Bar-Or, one of the prosecutors, submitted an affidavit at Eichmann's trial. Eichmann requested, through his own lawyer, a copy of Adler's *Theresienstadt* three months before his trial. Eichmann read it, but the book itself was never submitted as evidence. Controversially, Arendt uses the prosecution's unwillingness to introduce it at trial as evidence about the complicitous role of the *Judenrat* in the camp, verifying the ambiguously moral environment in which Eichmann operated.[14] According to Robinson, however, legally the book could have not been submitted as long as there were living witnesses who would testify to the reality of Theresienstadt.[15] Arguing that Arendt had misread and misused Adler (and projected her thoughts and emotions onto Eichmann), Robinson uses Adler in exactly the opposite fashion to refute much of Arendt's representation of the conditions and Jewish complicity at Theresienstadt[16] Adler remained somewhat of a footnote to this prolonged battle, though Arendt might have drawn more from his book than she acknowledged. Nonetheless, without any direct English access to his work, the potential importance of *Theresienstadt* as one of the first and most extensive documents of camp life faded from American view.

Discussing the failure of his efforts to find enough support for a translation, H. G. Adler lamented the necessity of writing in German,

> When I came to settle in London ..., I had distanced myself in practical terms, as far as my career plans were concerned, as well as psychologically from all things German, to such a degree that I wished to turn my back on my mother tongue and to publish in English (with the exception of my poetry, which of course had to remain in German). I completely failed in my plan to publish in English. ...My first lengthy literary project [...], was my monograph about the coercive Jewish ghetto of Theresienstadt...which I finished in 1954. The material it treated and the conditions it depicted were unpleasant and linguistically so bound up with the German language, often on the most trivial of planes, that a German version was inevitable, especially given my limited command of English. I thought that once I had my text together in a rough draft, English and American as well as Jewish and Christian public opinion could be won over to support my book's publication and would at the same time be prepared to support an English version. Such expectations were misguided'.[17]

The first translation that does appear in the United States is an essay in 1958, 'Ideas Towards A Sociology of the Concentration Camp', in the *American Journal of Sociology*, but the essay does little to advance Adler as a familiar name in the nascent field of Holocaust studies as it garners few citations until nearly fifty years later.

In 1967, H. G. Adler visits the United States for the first time delivering a talk to the YIVO conference in NYC, 'The "Autonomous" Jewish Administration of Terezin (Theresienstadt)'.[18] He also travels with Ilse Aichinger to Lorton, VA on the same trip (though we do not know any further details) and gives a talk at the Union Theological Institute. Three years later, the first and only of Adler's historical books to be translated into English appeared; *The Jews in Germany: From the Enlightenment to National Socialism* was published by the University of Notre Dame Press in 1970.[19] The book had been immediately successful in Germany when it was originally published in 1960, but sales had floundered after the first two years.[20] *The Jews in Germany* had been published by Kösel, a publisher known as a Catholic house. Michael Schaich's essay on the German publishing history of

The Jews in Germany in this volume, gives the following account derived primarily from Adler's correspondence:

> Emily M. Schossberger, the director of Notre Dame Press, one of the leading American university presses, had taken a personal interest in the book and tried to gain the translation rights from Kösel. Both companies were part of an informal network of Catholic publishing houses that spanned the Atlantic and also included the London-based firm Sheed and Ward. While their cooperation progressed rapidly and soon resulted in an agreement that also envisaged a parallel English edition with Sheed and Ward, which for unknown reasons never materialized, Adler became increasingly dissatisfied with his American contacts. The crux of the matter was a translation that he judged entirely unsatisfactory. His demands for changes, however, were firmly rejected by Wild who was clearly unwilling to compromise his partnership with Schossberger. The translation, he argued, was the sole responsibility of the interpreter, not the author, any criticism by reviewers would be directed to the former, not the latter.[21]

Adler finally agreed to the translation, but 'still complained about "irresponsible sloppiness" [unverantwortliche Schlampereien]'. Tantalizingly, Schaich finds evidence that the success of the American edition mollified Adler to some extent, but we have no publishing history.

One review of the book was published in The *Journal of Church and State* in 1971. It's author, Franklin H. Littell, uses the review to write a pointed attack on the American *Christian Century*, 'the leading journal of Liberal Protestantism', and says almost nothing about Adler's book except:

> When one reads Adler's book on the blindness of the humanists pre-Hitler Germany, he is struck to the heart by the parallels to the blindness of the intellectuals and liberal churchmen in America.[22]

The publication of *The Jews in Germany* with a Catholic Publishing House and this review in *Church and State*, suggests that Adler garnered attention from Christian readers; evidence of the book's reception by Jewish readers is scant and I can find no evidence that it immediately became a reference work. Most citations of the book come much later; however, according to Worldcat.org, the book is held in a not-inconsiderable 431 libraries across the United States and Canada, and judging by the well-marked copy in my library, and the old due-date leaves that cling to its frontispiece, it was a frequently-consulted source in student essays throughout the 1980s and 90s and well into the 2000s, which may, in the end, indicate a quite sizable readership. But, as we have seen so far, references to Adler in North America from 1948 to the 1980s are exclusively in relation to his historical and sociological work; we find no mention at all of his fiction or poetry other than Broch's adverse reaction to 'The Settlement'.

As a literary figure, H. G. Adler is acknowledged for the first time by Peter Demetz in his survey *After the Fires: Recent Writing in the Germanies, Austria and Switzerland* (1986). Demetz had known Adler in Prague after the war, one of a group of young men and women who gathered weekly at Adler's studio apartment to talk poetry and literature and listen to Adler read from his. Demetz often visited

Adler again in London, seeing him for the last time in 1978. Demetz chooses Adler as his first example of Holocaust writing in German in part because of Adler's authenticity as a witness, but, also, because Adler, as a sociologist, philosopher, writer, and secular Jew understood the in-between place of the German Jews. As Demetz will put it later, 'H. G. Adler was always reluctant to easily attach himself to any group, class, or nation, preferring instead to think of himself as a "single unique individual", in the radical spirit of the Enlightenment'.[23] Demetz renders his own complicit experience as a 'Mischling ersten Grades' in 'On Auschwitz, and on writing in German: A Letter to a student'. Demetz was a 'bastard first-class', a category of the Nuremberg laws, half-Aryan, half-Jewish, who helped his mother pack her rucksack for Auschwitz.[24]

By the time Demetz writes about Adler, Adler had been living in London for twenty years. The fact of Adler's exile was characteristic of the body of German Jewish writing as a whole, not aberrant, but almost a condition. Demetz provides summary readings of *Eine Reise* and *Panorama* and this oft-quoted assessment: 'It is one of the great intellectual scandals of our time that his most important books, both the personal ones and those in search of historical truth, have yet to be translated into English'.[25] Demetz offered an introduction to Adler as a critical literary figure writing in German; unfortunately, summaries can only go so far without accompanying translations, for, as Sara Horowitz points out in her 'Recovered Gems: Neglect and Recovery of Holocaust Fiction', 'his name did not receive any mention in the influential studies of Holocaust literature spanning several decades.'[26]

After the 1970 translation of *The Jews in Germany*, the next translation of Adler's work in North America was not drawn from his fiction nor his poetry, nor even his monumental *Theresienstadt*, but from a case study taken from his *Der verwaltete Mensch: Studien zur Deportation der Juden aus Deutschland* [*The Administered Man: A Study of the Deportation of the Jews from Germany*]. The translation appears in a collection of essays *Displacements: Cultural Identities in Question* (1994) edited by Angelika Bammer. Interestingly, Adler himself is not a figure of displacement, but, rather, his study of the inexorable process of one man's exclusion from the German polity. Jamie Owen Daniel, the translator and commentator, observes that the work exemplified Adler's approach, '15 years of meticulous archival research' — and 'a *Trauerarbeit*, a labor of mourning undertaken as a testament to both the millions who were murdered and to Adler's own experience'. The 1,000 page book maintains this 'double movement' between its broader context and the personal details of the case studies. Daniel translates the case study of Ernst Brüll. Adler describes Brüll's situation:

> The battle waged by Ernst Brüll — the co-proprietor of the Plutzar & Brüll textile manufacturing company from Nikelsdorf near Bielitz [Poland] who, as a half-Jew, steadfastly demanded that he be recognized as a German citizen — came to a bitter end. His case merits description in some detail.[27]

Perhaps not surprisingly, Brüll, dedicated to his German heritage and language, became, much like Adler, an outcast whose attachment to German did not save him, but made him suspect in Poland, as Adler was in post-war Prague, and, one might assume, later in London.

Adler's proper literary introduction to North American scholars does not really come until 1997, almost ten years after Adler's death, with Jeremy Adler's entry on his father in Sander Gilman and Jack Zipes' *Yale Companion to Jewish Writing and Thought in German Culture, 1096–1996*. The *Companion* is ingeniously devised as a chronology of events, events that launched a literary or intellectual legacy, a self-consciously fragmented approach that nonetheless presents 'the moment's human face'.[28] Adler's entry is thus titled: '**February 8, 1942** H. G. Adler is deported to Theresienstadt and begins his life's work writing a scholarly testimony to his experience'.[29] Adler's entry comes between '**1941** A four-year debate on child psychoanalysis begins between Anna Freud and Melanie Klein within the British Psychoanalytical Society' and the entry that follows Adler's, somewhat ironically: '**1944** Hannah Arendt writes "The Jew as Pariah: A Hidden Tradition", in which she describes the forgotten tradition of Jewish "conscious pariahs"'. One might argue that Adler, in Arendt's terms, had, by way of Theresienstadt, shifted, like so many German Jews, from parvenu to pariah, by the end fully aware and carefully guarding his status as the uncomfortable outsider warning against the delusions of assimilation.

Sander Gilman knew Adler's Theresienstadt book and 'deeply admired it'.[30] He had met Adler in London in the 1970s through a mutual acquaintance at the Leo Baeck Institute. When Zipes and Gilman were conceiving the *Yale Companion* they wanted to make sure that 'both the Holocaust but also "exile literature" were well represented'. Adler's son, Jeremy Adler, a Germanist at the University of King's College, London, whom Gilman had never met, was the obvious choice to write on his father's work given that few others knew H. G. Adler's contributions in as much depth or breadth. Gilman's respect for H. G. and Jeremy Adler made Gilman one of the rare cognisanti in North America and, having read the early novels in German, Gilman would also prove very supportive about the eventual prospect of their translation. He recognized their potential as part of 'a rediscovery of such exile texts in French and German with a rather successful resonance in the Anglophone world'.[31] As Gilman observed, 'a wide range of texts written in the late 40s and 50s had completely vanished, while later texts took their place. This was, I am sure, because of a desire to repress the Holocaust on virtually everyone's part who had had active memory of the period but also on a substantial shift of generational interest by the 1970s'.[32] Jeremy Adler blends an intimate portrait of his father, his history and his personality, with his mysticism, his political insights and his prose, discussing the one-hundred poems written in Theresienstadt, the logic of *Theresienstadt* itself, an unsparing description of Auschwitz from *Panorama*, and the trilogy as a whole. The entry gives a brilliant introduction to Adler, but does not obviously promote further interest in his work.

'It's hard to calibrate the impact of the Yale accession of its HGA collection in 1998' as Jeremy Adler remarked to me.[33] Purchased from Bernard Quaritch, Ltd. by the Beinecke German Literature Collection Fund, the fonds contain various items from the estate of H. G. Adler, including, as listed in the Beinecke Rare Book and Manuscript Library: an annotated typescript draft of his *Vorschule für eine Experimentaltheologie*; typescript draft of 'Neun Gedichte aus Theresienstadt' (with a note by Adler's son, Jeremy); a copy of Alfred Otto Lanz's dissertation on Adler; a typescript of Rüdiger Görner's article on Adler for *Literatur und Kritik*; typescripts of two uncredited poems, several pieces of correspondence received by Adler's widow, Bettina, after his death; and a death notice for Bettina Adler, 1993. According to Jeremy Adler, the Yale fonds at the Beinecke have the largest holdings of Adler's works anywhere in North America, including rare items, otherwise only at Marbach or KCL, holding an almost complete collection of works published in his lifetime and the critical works that have followed.

At the very end of this period of Adler's early reception, primarily as a historian, comes an intriguing reference that presages his literary reception. Historiographer Hayden White begins his essay, 'Historical Truth, Estrangement and Disbelief', with an epigraph from H. G. Adler's *Eine Reise* that White translates as:

> Blissful is the nonbeliever who hides the future's misfortune beneath the protective covering of the present moment, for now everything is obscured by darkness. No one seeks protection when hope and silence alone mark the passing of time and make it believable.[34]

The quote suggests that the blissful innocence of the present is a dangerous disavowal, the opening salvo in an essay that continues his twenty-year-old debate with Saul Friedländer about the literary devices of history. In a previous essay, 'The Modernist Event', White argued that 'anti-narrative non-stories produced by literary modernism offers the only prospect for adequate representations of the kind of "unnatural" events — including the Holocaust — that mark our era and distinguish it from all of the "history" that has come before it'.[35] Saul Friedlander (also a German speaking Jew from Prague and a survivor), ever vigilant about the implications of narrative relativism that would undermine the historical facts of the Holocaust, argued strenuously against White.[36] White's invocation of *Eine Reise* as an exemplar becomes clearer in its second reference, a footnote that comes in the middle of this paragraph.

> In his [Friedlander's] response to my suggestion that artistic images might be more effective than statements or numbers for presenting the shock of events like those of the Holocaust,★ Friedlander said that "the only solution...for keeping to the strictest historical practice and nonetheless giving expression to those moments of shock, amazement, or denial, was to turn to the reactions of the victims as they were confronted by the events as expressed mainly in diaries and letters, ... in memoirs, etc".[37]

White's footnote reads:

> I had suggested as a model of what I had in mind H. G. Adler's *Eine Reise*, which, in my view, could be considered a veritable lexicon of figures and tropes for representing the Holocaust with all of the "facts" left out. Professor Friedlander and I disagree over whether Adler's book is to be considered a "fiction". I consider it to be a deconstruction of the fact-fiction dichotomy when it comes to the problem of representing the Holocaust. It is neither factual nor fictional but metafictional, in Linda Hutcheon's and Amy Elias's sense of the term. It shows how the contract between fictional and factual presentations

of an event like the Holocaust cannot do justice to all of the ghostly aspects of that event, the ways in which the facts seem grotesque and the fictions more truthful to them that any simple chronicle or history of them might be.[38]

White's observation and its context introduce the manner in which H. G. Adler's trilogy, which was on the horizon in North America, would be read as modernist historiography, as complex allegory, a literary, philosophical, and historical *Trauerarbeit*. Adler the witness and historian is never far from the story, but *The Journey*, in particular, an anti-narrative non-story of literary modernism deconstructs, as White observes, the 'fact/fiction dichotomy'. Ironically, through Adler's literary modernism, he would finally make his mark as a historian, writ large through Adler's life history and the fairy-tale quality of how the books came to be translated in the United States. The novels, while arguably metafictional, would be read back into testimony and forward into a literary discovery, eschewing to some extent the literary difficulty of the texts themselves.

The Novels Arrive

The further we delve into the history of Adler's reception in North America, the more we see that the integration of the biographical, the historical, and the literary becomes not just a question of the genre of a work (is the trilogy fictive or grounded in the historical?) but a quality of its history of publication and reception. The circuits of history, literature, and belated discovery are, in Adler's case, hardwired into our reading practices and thus into the meaning of the works themselves.

We have arrived at the moment of Peter Filkins' discovery of Adler. Filkins makes no reference to his discovery of *Eine Reise* in his introduction to *The Journey*, nor Jeremy in his afterward, both of which otherwise offer vital paratextual information about how to read the novel in the context of Adler's life, its historical fugues, and as a work of modernist fiction. Filkins, browsing through Schoenhof's Foreign Books in Cambridge in November 2002, came across *Eine Reise*. After reading a few pages, Filkins knew on the spot that he had to translate the book. 'The attraction was not that it was a novel about the Holocaust, but rather the dense musicality of the language and the voice propelling the sentences', as Filkins put it to me. At the time, Filkins had no idea who H. G. Adler was. The book had been reissued in a handsome edition in 1999 so Filkins assumed Adler was fairly well known and that it would not be that hard to find a publisher for a translation. He was wrong. The motivating force behind the reissue was Jeremy Adler who had been working tirelessly to create a receptive climate in Germany in which it would be possible to revive his father's works. As Jeremy remarked to me, 'the fire was already alight in Germany'; nonetheless, the flame was hard to kindle across the Atlantic.[39] Over the next six years, Filkins proposed the translation of *Eine Reise* [*The Journey*] to some 40 different publishers without a bite. *The Journey* was finally begun again when Paul Taunton, an editor at Random House in New York, recognized that it was a 'lost gem', as Sara Horowitz describes it: 'there was something instantly arresting and vital about it', Taunton recalled. 'Eventually you start to realize what's going on even without the benefit of the back story, but the realization of how long ago it was actually written (and how prescient it was) is very powerful'.

Sander Gilman's support manifested as attestation on the cover of *The Journey* (along with Harold Bloom, Peter Constantine and Bernice Eisenstein):

> H. G. Adler's *The Journey*, published first in 1962, captures the anguished cry of a survivor of the Holocaust as his world becomes reduced to his family and the family is murdered one by one. One of a slim handful of novels written in German by survivors of Hitler's murder of European Jewry, Adler's personal and intimate tale allows us to observe the slow-motion destruction of a society and of a family. As important a find as Irène Némirovsky's *Suite Française*, and as well translated into English, it is indeed, as Veza Canetti wrote to the author in 1962, "*too beautiful* for words and too sad".

Harold Bloom's blurb is somewhat more ambivalent, but still celebrates Adler's work as exceptional. 'The Journey is a tribute to the survival of art and a poignant teaching in the art of survival. I tend to shy away from Holocaust fiction, but this book helps redeem an all–but–impossible genre'.

Many reviews of the three books in the trilogy in translation, *The Journey, Panorama*, and *The Wall*, mostly glowing, if sometimes bewildered, begin with some biographical notes about Adler's life, a necessary intervention given that Adler was virtually unknown in North America prior to the translations. In one of the most influential reviews of *The Journey* in 2009, Richard Lourie, writing in the *New York Times Book Review* calls it a work of 'Holocaust modernism, an improbable formulation if ever there was one'.[40] The segue into the next paragraph is telling, for the immediate shift from the generic improbable to the historic. 'H. G. Adler's fate was as unusual as his art'.[41] We are it seems quickly in territory where art and life, though not mimetic, are indistinguishable. The leap is one that we all make. Describing the action of the novel, Lourie writes, 'The novel follows the members of a family, the Lustigs, something like Adler's, as they journey through the Holocaust to a place something like Theresienstadt'.[42] Those of us who have studied *The Journey* carefully know that Adler never uses the word Holocaust and never refers to Prague or the Germans or Theresienstadt in any direct way. He perhaps assumes that we will provide the historical context or that we will read the book as an allegory for memory, as he suggests we might in the 'Augury',[43] as much as for its descriptions of the absurd and grotesque processes of dehumanization. We, as readers, supply the facts, for, to repeat Hayden White, the novel is 'a veritable lexicon of figures and tropes for representing the Holocaust with all of the "facts", left out'.

Similarly, a short review under the rubric of 'Discoveries' by Susan Salter Reynolds in the *Los Angeles Times* begins with the revivification of Adler's figure in W. G. Sebald's *Austerlitz*. 'It seems unpardonable to me today, [...] that it is now too late for me to seek out Adler...'.[44] We may certainly pardon Sebald now, (treating *Austerlitz* as the metahistorical work that it is) because Adler's revival has had much to do with Sebald's atonement. The backstory of how *The Journey* came to be published in English has everything to do with Sebald's missed encounter, for Paul Taunton, on whose desk Peter Filkins's prospectus finally landed, who, in 2006, already a Sebald fan recognized Adler as the figure of Austerlitz's lament. Thus, Adler is resurrected as a historical author through his figuration in a fiction. Indeed, Filkins begins his introduction to *The Journey* with that famous Sebald passage as epigraph, framing both the history of Adler and the novel to come. We, as the editors of the *H. G. Adler: Life, Literature, Legacy* could not help but invoke the same quote, and Lynn Wolff and Helen Finch took up the Sebald/Adler filament in their volume *Witnessing, Memory, Poetics* published on this side of the Atlantic, fully suturing these now-inseparable figures of history and literature.[45]

These various backstories then become vital to the reception of *The Journey*, and consequently *Panorama* and *The Wall*. Tellingly, both *The Journey* and *Panorama* were Editor's Choices of the Historical Novel Society in their respective years of publication. (As well as many other accolades, that included both books as Editor's choices in the *New York Times Books Review* and *Paper Back Row*.) As Filkins himself writes in the introduction to *Panorama*, Adler's 'dovetailing of fact and fiction' tries 'to both scientifically and imaginatively encompass his experience'.[46] But not everyone saw the dovetailing of Adler's fictions, his history and his rediscovery as illuminating. In perhaps the most aggravated review of *The Journey*, Mike Peed writing in the *Washington Post* attacks those backstories themselves as elevating a 'disorientating' book to a modern masterpiece:

> The book's overarching problem is less Adler's approach to literature than contemporary society's relationship to art. "The Journey", like a Spielberg flick timed for Oscar season, incorporates, however unwittingly, all the touchstones of a modern "masterpiece" (the word, in fact, is used in two of the book's dust jacket blurbs): written decades ago by an obscure self-styled philosopher poet; chanced upon by Filkins among the dusty stacks of a Harvard bookshop; and wrestling, ever obliquely, with the great stain of the 20th century. But art demands more than a romantic back story and a potent starting point, and while Adler can hardly be faulted, it appears that writing the book served as more of a catharsis for him than an epiphany for us.[47]

Peed's grouchy review refuses a kind of reverence for the 'difficulty' of reading Adler as a necessary exercise that embodies the difficulty of the history itself. Adjectives of struggle are frequent in reviews: 'never an easy writer; inventive, challenging style; the appeal of Adler's novel depends on your tolerance for experimentation' (Mandle in *The New Criterion*); 'difficult, neglected, unconventional, unusual, oblique, extraordinarily ambitious attempt to articulate the unspeakable' (*Kirkus Reviews*).[48] Perhaps the harshest review and one that again refuses the difficulty of Adler's prose and the problems of translation is by Nan Goldberg who called the translation of *Panorama* 'virtually unreadable'. Writing in the *Boston Globe* in 2011, Goldberg acknowledged the difficulty of the task of translating Adler, but that did not change the fact, in her eyes, that 'the result is a tangle of clumsy, uncoordinated sentences, painful to read...'[49] And yet Jonathan Kirsch, reviewing exactly the same book for the *Los Angeles Times* calls it 'expertly and elegantly translated', arguing that 'the convoluted syntax of the original German text compels us to parse the words and phrases for sense and meaning'.[50]

The ability to read Adler's work in the context of modernist literature depends on one's familiarity with German, British and Irish modernism, and postmodernism, invoked in many of the literary reviews. But, in contrast, I think Hayden White's modernist historiographical reading, including rereading history back into the allegorical and rebuking the death of the author are the approaches that dominate North American literary reception. These readings are not literal readings, but certainly historical. Reviewing *The Wall* in the *New York Times*, Cynthia Ozick provides no better example of this:

> [...] on occasion there emerges a tale that refuses to let go of its teller, that is unwilling, even in the name of art, to break fee; or cannot. This is less a question of autobiographical influence or persuasion than of an uncanny attachment: call it haunting, the relentlessly obsessive permeation of a book by its author. Or imagine a man condemned for the rest of his days to carry, and care for, and inconsolably preserve his own umbilical cord.

Ozick continues:

> In this way "The Wall", the final novel of an exilic trilogy by H. G. Adler, is inseparable from the lacerating fortunes of the writer's life; the chronicle he gave birth to continues to claim him.[51]

Though I cannot say that the extended metaphor of Adler birthing his books is all that compelling for me, even drawing as it does on the bloody grotesque, the suturing of history and story makes Adler's novels into strong testimony. We may eschew Friedlander's contention that one drop of the imaginative undermines historical truth, and struggle with the demand, as Ruth Franklin put it in her review of *Panorama* and *The Journey* in *The New Yorker*, that 'the idea of a Holocaust writer who fails to confine himself to the facts of his experience has always been difficult to accept. We expect our survivors to be witnesses and chroniclers, not artists'.[52] Nonetheless, North American readers were coming to appreciate Adler's novels in the in-between zone, claiming them for the nonfictive as well as the literary, and placing them squarely into Hayden White's definition of the modernist historiography that grants the same ontological order to real and imaginary renditions of events.

The Scholars Follow

Not surprisingly, Peter Filkins' translations of the trilogy and the critical attention the translations received were the key to generating wider scholarly interest in North America. When *The Journey* came out Paul Taunton and Filkins spoke together at the Austrian Cultural Forum, as Filkins did again with Ruth Franklin when *Panorama* was published.[53] Filkins gave talks about the Adler novels at Colgate, Cornell, Kelly Writers House at the University of Pennsylvannia, Williams, Wisconsin-Madison, Wisconsin-Milwaukee, Beloit, Columbia, Simon's Rock, and several other north American colleges and universities. In 2011, Filkins was invited, along with Michel Govrin from Israel to participate on a panel on translation at the International Author's Festival in Toronto, Canada. From there a small panel at York University led to the idea that a symposium dedicated to Adler was timely and important. Convened by Sara Horowitz, Julia Creet, and Amira Dan, the 'H. G. Adler: Life,

Literature, Legacy', symposium, held over two days in November of 2012, dedicated singly to Adler, was the first of its kind in North America, gathering together the foremost Adler scholars working in English along with new critics invited by the conveners as a way to enlarge scholarly interest.[54] The symposium led to the publication of a volume by the same title by Northwestern University Press in 2016, making it the first volume in English dedicated to Adler research.[55] With essays on Adler's life, letters, novels, poetry and philology, the contributions to the volume reflected the new breadth of Adler's reception, now a fully literary writer whose historical and sociological work had become background.

Attention to Adler is now growing, mostly spearheaded by Filkins, including (but not exhaustively) a performance and discussion in February 2014 with Larry Wallach at Simon's Rock on two settings of Adler poems by Viktor Ullmann; the first MLA Conference roundtable discussion devoted to Adler, 'H. G. Adler's Shoah Trilogy' in January 2015 in Vancouver;[56] a panel interview on *The Wall* at Deutsches Haus NYC in January 2015 with Eric Banks and George Prochnik; a talk on H. G. Adler's Shoah Trilogy to the New York Institute for the Humanities at NYU in February 2015; a symposium held at Bard College in May of 2015, 'Translating the Holocaust: H. G. Adler as Writer and Scholar';[57] and a panel exploring the Adler's legacy at the Jewish Museum in New York in May of 2105.[58]

With the translation of *Theresienstadt 1941–45* on the horizon as well as Peter Filkins' biography of Adler, the next few years should see the scholarly integration of Adler's historical contributions and his literary works on a scale that will, at last, make Adler a modernist historiographer in North America.

Notes to Chapter 15

1. *H. G. Adler: Life, Literature, Legacy*, ed. by Julia Creet, Sara R. Horowitz, and Amira Bojadzija-Dan, Cultural Expressions of World War II (Evanston, IL: Northwestern University Press, 2016). For an exploration of this belated reception see 'Introduction: Encountering H. G. Adler', pp. 3–20 and Sara R. Horowitz, 'Recovered Gems: Neglect and Recovery of Holocaust Fiction', pp. 89–118.

2. Hayden White, 'Historical Truth, Estrangement, and Disbelief', in *Confronting the Burden of History: Literary Representations of the Past*, ed. by Izabela Curyllo-Klag and Bozena Kucala (Krakow, Poland: Universitas, 2013), pp. 15–42 (p. 16).

3. Peter Demetz, *After the Fires: Recent Writing in the Germanies, Austria, and Switzerland* (San Diego: Harcourt Brace Jovanovich, 1986), p. 20.

4. H. G. Adler and Peter Demetz, *Panorama: A Novel*, trans. by Peter Filkins (New York: Random House, 2011), p. 441.

5. Ronald Speirs and John J. White, 'Hermann Broch and H. G. Adler: The Correspondence of Two Writers in Exile. Translated by Ronald Speirs. Edited with an Introduction by John J. White and Ronald Speirs', *Comparative Criticism: Myth and Mythologies*, 21 (2000), 131–200 (p. 185, Letter 1, Note 1). The correspondence was originally published in German, and the German quotes are to be found in the edition: H. G. Adler und Hermann Broch, *Zwei Schriftsteller im Exil*, Briefwechsel ed. and commented by Ronald Speirs and John White (Göttingen: Wallstein, 2004). The subsequent translation offers an excellent overview of the context and tenor of their exchange. As Speirs and White observe, 'The dialogue with H. G. Adler must have involved Broch in reading, mainly from his hospital bed, some 1,800 quarto pages of manuscript material [...]. All this Broch did for a reasonably young unknown (Adler had just turned thirty-eight when he received the first letter from Broch), with no publications to his name, someone who

had been liberated from a concentration camp by the US Army little more than two years earlier, and whose main calling card consisted of the recommendation of Elias Canetti and Leo Baeck' (p. 133). Speirs and White suggest that Broch might have suffered a very similar fate to Adler had Broch not managed to go into exile in 1938, and that his mother had died in Theresienstadt, perhaps motivating factors for Broch's generous support.

6. Speirs and White, 'Hermann Broch and H. G. Adler', p. 145 / p. 5.
7. Speirs and White, 'Hermann Broch and H. G. Adler', p. 158 / p. 25.
8. Speirs and White, 'Hermann Broch and H. G. Adler', p. 151 / p. 16.
9. Speirs and White, 'Hermann Broch and H. G. Adler', p. 177 / p. 50.
10. Speirs and White, 'Hermann Broch and H. G. Adler', p. 164 / p. 33.
11. Speirs and White, 'Hermann Broch and H. G. Adler', p. 157 / p. 23.
12. Speirs and White, 'Hermann Broch and H. G. Adler', p. 165 / pp. 35–36.
13. Jacob Robinson, *And the Crooked Shall Be Made Straight: The Eichmann Trial, the Jewish Catastrophe, and Hannah Arendt's Narrative* (New York: Macmillan, 1965), p. 143 (See note 37).
14. Hannah Arendt, *Eichmann in Jerusalem: A Report on the Banality of Evil* (Penguin, 1977), pp. 119–20. See also Jeremy Adler's contribution to the present volume.
15. Robinson, *And the Crooked Shall Be Made Straight*, p. 114.
16. Though they never met nor corresponded, Adler, after the publication of *Eichmann in Jerusalem* grew to dislike Arendt. The H. G. Adler collection at King's College London includes Adler's heavily annotated copy of Arendt's book and an early typescript of Robinson's response in which Adler records his rather scathing criticisms of Arendt. According to Peter Filkins, Adler 'thought her book was riddled with errors, and that she had made ample use of his work without real acknowledgment'. (Personal email 5 October 2016). Adler wrote a newspaper article titled 'Was weiß Hannah Arendt über die Shoah?' ('What does Hannah Arendt know about the Shoah?'), also delivering a radio essay outlining her many failings. See Jeremy Adler's contribution to the present volume.
17. Quoted in Speirs and White, p. 189–90, note 3. (*Zu Hause im Exil*, p. 248).
18. H. G. Adler, 'The "Autonomous" Jewish Administration of Terezin (Theresienstadt)', in *Imposed Jewish Governing Bodies under Nazi Rule. YIVO Colloquium, December 2–5, 1967.* (New York: Yivo Institute for Jewish Research, 1972), pp. 70–82.
19. H. G. Adler, *Jews in Germany: From the Enlightenment to National Socialism* (University of Notre Dame Press, 1970). Translator unknown. See Michael Schaich's contribution to the present volume.
20. Michael Schaich, '*The Jews in Germany:* H. G. Adler as a Public Historian', in this volume.
21. Schaich, '*The Jews in Germany:* H. G. Adler as a Public Historian', p. 179.
22. Franklin H. Littell, review of *Review of The Jews in Germany: From the Enlightenment to National Socialism*, by H. G. Adler, *Journal of Church and State*, 13.3 (1971), 539–41.
23. Peter Demetz, 'Afterword', in H. G. Adler, *Panorama*, trans. by Peter Filkins (New York: Random House, 2011), pp. 441–50.
24. Demetz, *After the Fires*, p. 19.
25. Demetz, *After the Fires*, p. 34.
26. Creet, Horowitz, and Bojadzija-Dan, *H. G. Adler: Life, Literature, Legacy*, p. 91. Adler's absence in Holocaust literature is not only a matter of his works not being translated into English. Adler's difficult publication history and lack of attention in the German-speaking world is detailed in Ruth Vogel-Klein's article in *Monatshefte*, Lynn Wolff and Helen Finch's Introduction to *Witnessing, Memory, Poetics: H. G. Adler and W. G. Sebald*, ed. by Helen Finch and Lynn L. Wolff (Rochester, NY: Camden House, 2014), and Kirstin Gwyer's chapter on Adler in *Encrypting the Past* ('Writing of Broken Time(s): H. G. Adler, Eine Reise, Die unsichtbare Wand', in Kirstin Gwyer, *Encrypting the Past: The German-Jewish Holocaust Novel of the First* (Oxford: Oxford University Press, 2014), pp. 57–89).
27. Angelika Bammer, *Displacements: Cultural Identities in Question* (Bloomington, IN: Indiana University Press, 1994), p. 207.
28. *Yale Companion to Jewish Writing and Thought in German Culture, 1096–1996*, ed. by Sander L. Gilman and Jack Zipes (New Haven: Yale University Press, 1997), p. xvii.

29. Ibid., p. 599.
30. Personal email, 18 September 2016
31. Ibid.
32. Ibid.
33. Personal email, 30 May 2016.
34. Hayden White, 'Historical Truth, Estrangement, and Disbelief', in *Confronting the Burden of History: Literary Representations of the Past*, ed. by Izabela Curyllo-Klag and Bozena Kucala (Krakow, Poland: Universitas, 2013), pp. 15–42 (p. 17).
35. Hayden White, 'The Modernist Event', in *The Persistence of History: Cinema, Television, and the Modern Event*, ed. by Vivian Carol Sobchack (New York: Routledge, 1996), pp. 17–32.
36. Saul Friedländer, *Probing the Limits of Representation: Nazism and The 'final Solution'* (Cambridge, MA: Harvard University Press, 1992).
37. White, 'Historical Truth', p. 30, note 17.
38. Ibid.
39. See Ruth Vogel-Klein's contribution to the present volume.
40. Richard Lourie, 'Book Review | The Journey, by H. G. Adler. Translated by Peter Filkins', *The New York Times*, 9 January 2009 <http://www.nytimes.com/2009/01/11/books/review/Lourie-t.html> [accessed 28 April 2016].
41. Ibid.
42. Ibid.
43. Creet, Horowitz, and Bojadzija-Dan. See Creet's essay in this volume for a discussion of the allegory of memory in 'The Augury'.
44. Susan Salter Reynolds, 'Discoveries', *Los Angeles Times*, 9 November 2008 <http://articles.latimes.com/2008/nov/09/entertainment/ca-discoveries9> [accessed 28 April 2016].
45. *Witnessing, Memory, Poetics*, ed. by Finch and Wolff.
46. H. G. Adler, *The Journey*, trans. by Peter Filkins (New York: Random House, 2008), p. 7.
47. Mike Peed, 'The Going Gets Tough', *Washingtonpost.com*, 12 January 2009 <http://www.washingtonpost.com/wp-dyn/content/article/2009/01/12/AR2009011203146.html> [accessed 28 April 2016].
48. Dara Mandle, 'The Long Journey: A Review of The Journey by H. G. Adler', *The New Criterion*, 27.6 (2009), 77; 'THE JOURNEY by H. G. Adler, Peter Filkins | Kirkus Reviews', *Kirkusreviews.com*, n.d. <https:// www.kirkusreviews.com/book-reviews/hg-adler/the-journey/> [accessed 28 April 2016].
49. Nan Goldberg, 'Story of Survival in "Panorama" Gets Lost in Translation', *Boston.com*, 29 January 2011 <http://www.boston.com/ae/books/articles/2011/01/29/story_of_survival_in_panorama_gets_lost_in_translation/> [accessed 15 December 2016].
50. Jonathan Kirsch, 'Book Review: "Panorama"', *Los Angeles Times*, 10 April 2011 <http://www.latimes.com/books/la-ca-hg-adler-20110410-story.html> [accessed 28 April 2016].
51. Cynthia Ozick, '"The Wall," by H. G. Adler', *The New York Times*, 17 December 2014 <http://www.nytimes.com/2014/12/21/books/review/the-wall-by-h-g-adler.html> [accessed 15 March 2016].
52. Ruth Franklin, 'The Long View', *Newyorker.com*, 2011 <www.newyorker.com/magazine/2011/01/31/the-long-view> [accessed 15 March 2016].
53. See <https://peterfilkins.com/links/>. Filkins and Franklin also spoke together at the Center for Jewish Studies at the UMass.
54. Helen Finch and Lynn Wolff organized a comparative H. G. Adler and W.G. Sebald symposium, 'Witnessing, Memory, Poetics', held at the Austrian Cultural Forum, London and Institute of Germanic & Romance Studies in October of 2012.
55. Symposium participants were: Jeremy Adler, Peter Filkins, Sven Kramer, Sara R. Horowitz, Omer Bartov, Lawrence L. Langer, Amira Bojadzija Dan, Emily Budick, Julia Creet, Ruth Vogel-Klein, Helen Finch, Lynn L. Wolff, Katrin Kohl, Deborah P. Britzman, Dorota Glowacka, Leslie Morris, and John J. White. All but White, who had fallen quite ill, contributed essays to the published volume. His contribution is published in the present volume.
56. Participants were Peter Filkins, Jeremy Adler, Christopher Browning, Lynn L. Wolff, Katrin Kohl, and Sara Horowitz.

57. Participants were Peter Filkins, Jeremy Adler, Roger Berkowitz, Amy Lowenhaar, Belinda Cooper, Lawrence Wallach, Wyatt Mason and Cecile Kuznitz, including a Performance of Two Viktor Ullmann/Adler Songs by Rufus Müller and Bill T. Jones on his own rendering of a Holocaust experience.
58. 'The Jewish Museum' <http://thejewishmuseum.org/press/press-release/hg-adler-release> [accessed 15 December 2016].

H. G. ADLER:
A CHRONOLOGY

❖

Compiled by Lynn L. Wolff

H. G. Adler in Lauterbrunnental, Switzerland, late August 1977, taken by Manfred Sundermann. Copyright © Manfred Sundermann.

Soll man überhaupt Gedenktage halten? Oft zweifle ich. Aber ich muss doch gedenken. Mein feines Empfinden für Zeit und Zahlen nötigt mich fast dazu. Nein, wir wollen nicht die Ungunst der Verhältnisse triumphieren lassen.

[Should one observe days of remembrance at all? I often doubt it. But I must remember. My keen feeling for time and numbers practically forces me to. No, we do not want to let the unfavourable circumstances triumph.]

— H. G. Adler in a letter to Bettina Gross, 10 April 1946, after recalling his last days in the Langenstein forced labour camp, liberation, and arrival in Halberstadt, and in response to the obstacles they face in securing his visa for Britain

Er hatte ein Zahlengedächtnis. Denkwürdige Tage waren ihm stets bewusst indem er schweigend die Jahre überdachte. Manchmal sprach er die Jahrestage aus, ohne Emotion. Er sagte z. B. 'Heute vor 25 Jahren kam ich nach Auschwitz'. Das war alles.

[He had a memory for numbers. He remained ever aware of memorable days, silently thinking about the years. Sometimes he pronounced these anniversaries, without emotion. He would say, for instance, 'Twenty-five years ago today, I arrived in Auschwitz'. That was all.]

Erinnern war ihm Lebensstrategie.

[Remembering was a life strategy for him.]

— Jeremy Adler, 'Vermischte Erinnerungen' [Miscellaneous Memories]

★   ★   ★   ★   ★

The following chronology has been compiled using numerous sources, most notably H. G. Adler's 'Nachruf bei Lebzeiten' [Obituary in One's Lifetime], Franz Hocheneder's 2009 biography *H. G. Adler (1910–1988): Privatgelehrter und freier Schriftsteller*, the 2004 *Text + Kritik* volume dedicated to H. G. Adler, and '*Ortlose Botschaft': Der Freundeskreis H. G. Adler, Elias Canetti, and Franz Baermann Steiner*, based on the 1998–1999 exhibition at the Schiller-National Museum in Marbach which also traveled to Berlin, Vienna, and Prague. The second epigraph is taken from '*Ortlose Botschaft*'. The materials held in Adler's estate at the Deutsches Literaturarchiv Marbach also proved invaluable. This overview is intended as a brief orientation into Adler's life and work, and it can be supplemented by Peter Filkins' authoritative biography *H. G. Adler: A Life in Many Worlds* (Oxford University Press, 2019).

1910

2 July 1910: born in Prague-Karlín (Karolinenthal) to Emil Alfred and Alice Adler and raised in a German-speaking, non-practicing Jewish family.

1910–1920

Receives private lessons in Czech throughout childhood; friendship with Franz Baermann Steiner (1909–1952).

1920–1921

Sent to a village in Bohemia for two years because of his mother's illness; attends elementary school in the small city of Deutsch-Beneschau.

1921–1923

Attends the Realschule am Freimaurerinstitut, a boarding school in Dresden-Striesen.

1923–1925

Attends the Deutsches Staatsrealgymnasium in the small town of Moravská Třebová [Mährisch-Trübau].

1925–1927

Attends the Deutsches Staatsrealgymnasium Prag III Malá Strana (Kleinseite), participates in the scouting movement, makes first attempts at literary writing, most notable is his activity in a literary circle with Franz Baermann Steiner (who goes to London in 1936 to study with Bronislaw Malinowski and remains there from 1938 on).

1927

Leaves school to prepare for the 'Matura' on his own.

1928–1935

Member of the mystic circle of photographer František Drtikol (1883–1961); through Steiner, makes the acquaintance of author Emanuel Lešehrad (1877–1955); is a member of a small group of writers including Steiner, Peter Brömse (1912–2004), and Helmut Spiesmayr (1911–1945).

1930

Receives Matura from the Deutsches Staatsrealgymnasium Prag II.

1930–1935

Student of musicology, literary studies, and philosophy at the German University of Prague and plans to pursue a professorship in Germanistik at a German university.

Around 1931: Friendship with the Gross family, who holds a regular salon, and makes the acquaintance of his future wife Bettina Gross (1913–1993).

1931

First literary publication: *Meer und Gebirge* (Radolfzell am Bodensee: Heim-Verlag).

1932

Begins friendship with artist and sculptor Bernard Reder (1897–1963).

1933

January to April: while conducting research in Berlin, sees Hitler come to power and his chances for an academic career dashed.

1935

22 June: completes studies and receives his doctorate (Dr. phil.) with a dissertation on 'Klopstock und die Musik' under Prof. Dr. Gustav Becking.

1935–1938

December 1935 to July 1938: employed as secretary and instructor at the Urania, a pedagogical institute in Prague and also works for the German-speaking programming of the Czechoslovakian Radio.

1936

7 October: first public reading of poems in Prague.

1937

Begins friendship with Hermann Grab (1903–1949).

21 May: invites Elias Canetti (1905–1994) to give a reading from his novel *Die Blendung* at the Urania in Prague.

1938

July to December: in Milan, Italy, attempting to secure emigration to Brazil, which ultimately fails; birth of his idea of an experimental theology [Experimentaltheologie].

31 December: meets Gertrud Klepetar, a doctor and chemist, whom he later marries.

Continues to make further attempts to escape Prague.

1939–1941

Lives in occupied Prague and works for his father's book binding shop until it is taken over by a trustee [Treuhänder] in November 1940.

1941

Mid-August to Mid-December: forced labour on railway construction in the Jewish work camp Sázava-Velká Losenice (near the border between Bohemia and Moravia).

October: father is deported (after the war, he notes that he last saw his father on 17 August 1941).

30 October: marries Gertrud Klepetar.

Mid-December: part of the group forced to 'liquidate' Prague's Jewish cultural community [Kultusgemeinde] (after the war, he recalls how the books from Franz Kafka's library passed through his hands).

1942

6/7 February: arrested and on 8 February deported to Theresienstadt together with his wife Gertrud and her parents.

9 February: arrival in Theresienstadt, where he is to some extent shielded, due to his wife's position overseeing the camp's medical laboratory; during

his time in Theresienstadt, Adler is intentional in performing duties that are outside of the Jewish administration, such as working as a mason and in the camp's library [Zentralbücherei].

March: begins collecting materials in Theresienstadt with the intention of writing a scholarly monograph of the camp.

2 July: Adler's mother arrives in Theresienstadt.

Despite difficult and dangerous conditions, Adler manages to write poetry and prose (*Theresienstädter Bilderbogen* and short texts that are later published in 1964 as *Der Fürst des Segens: Parabeln — Betrachtungen — Gleichnisse*, and an initial version of the novel *Raoul Feuerstein*, which is still unpublished).

Adler's father and mother die in Chełmno (Kulmhof) and Maly Trostinets extermination camps.

1943

April: death of Adler's father-in-law.

Gives lectures and readings in the camp, including a lecture on 'Juden in der deutschen Dichtkunst' [Jews in German Literature] and one on Franz Kafka on the occasion of the author's 60th birthday and in the presence of Kafka's sister Ottilie.

1944

Adler takes part in the action to beautify Theresienstadt [Verschönerungsaktion] in preparation of the International Red Cross's inspection of the camp.

12 October: deported from Theresienstadt.

14 October: arrives in Auschwitz together with his wife Gertrud and her mother, but they are separated during the process of 'selection', and she chooses to go with her mother to the bad side.

28 October: transported to Niederorschel im Eichsfeld, a satellite camp of Buchenwald, part of a forced labor detail that makes airplane wings; mentors two young boys, including Ivan Ivanji (b. 1929 in Zrenjanin, Yugoslavia, today Serbia), who would later become an author of literary works and translations.

1945

16 February: further transport to Langenstein-Zwieberge, a camp near Halberstadt, continued forced labor in an underground factory, building airplanes under dire conditions, until being promoted to a secretarial position [Hallenschreiber].

11/12 April 1945: the US army liberates Langenstein, and Adler sets out for Halberstadt on 12 April, where he stays for two months, due to severe illness.

20 June 1945: after repatriation by the Americans, Adler returns to Prague with hardly any belongings and learns that eighteen members of his family as well as many friends have perished; deprived of his Czechoslovakian citizenship, because his native language is German.

End of June: returns to Theresienstadt to meet Rabbi Dr. Leo Baeck (1873–1956), who gives him the briefcase of documents, notes, and literary works that Adler entrusted to him upon transport to Auschwitz.

Summer to Fall 1945: works in an institution run by Přemysl Pitter (1895–1976) for orphaned children who had survived the war; devotes particular attention to Jehuda Bacon (b. 1929), serves as a mentor and helps mediate Bacon's study at Bezalel Academy of Arts and Design in Jerusalem.

November: reconnects with Bettina Gross, a sculptor and friend from his early years in Prague who managed to flee to Great Britain in December 1938; reaches out to his other pre-war contacts, like Steiner and Canetti.

1945–1947

October 1945 to January 1947: works to rebuild the Jewish Museum of Prague and begins intensive work on the Theresienstadt book, continuing to build up an archive that documents both the years of persecution and the Theresienstadt camp.

1 October 1946: the Jewish Community of Prague informs Adler and Bettina Gross that they will be unable to marry in Czechoslovakia, since they no longer have citizenship, and it is recommended that they marry in England.

11 February 1947: flees Czechoslovakia, arrives in Great Britain, exile begins.

16 February 1947: marries Bettina Gross; the couple moves to London and later they have a son.

June to December 1947: gives lectures to German prisoners of war in England.

Unsuccessful attempts to secure a job as a librarian or teacher and refuses to move to Germany to work on behalf of the British.

Adler publishes exclusively with his initials 'H. G.' to avoid any connection to the SS-Sturmbahnführer Hans Günther, who from 1939–1945 was Adolf Eichmann's deputy in charge of deportations from the Protectorate of Bohemia and Moravia.

Reconnects with Franz Baermann Steiner and Elias Canetti, meets Grete Fischer (1893–1977), develops friendships with Ilse Aichinger (1921–2016), Ingeborg Bachmann (1926–1973), Michael Hamburger (1924–2007), Wilhelm Unger (1904–1985), and Franz Wurm (1926–2010).

Begins correspondence with Theodor W. Adorno (1903–1969).

Active in a literary circle of German-language exile authors around Erich Fried (1921–1988) that also includes Steiner.

1948

Completes first draft of the Theresienstadt book, which he continues to revise until it appears in 1955; Hermann Broch advocates on behalf of Adler to secure a publisher.

Writes autobiographical novel *Panorama*, which does not appear until 1968.

1949

Works on novel *Die Ansiedlung*, which remains unpublished, and makes first plans to travel to Germany to present his research on Theresienstadt (among others at the university in Cologne).

1950–1951

Revises Theresienstadt book, works on his novel-length story *Die Reise*, which is published in 1962 as *Eine Reise*; does unpaid work to establish a German library, which opens in London in June 1951.

September to November: first trip to Germany after the war, gives lectures and makes radio appearances.

1952

Finishes *Die Prüfung*, a novella which remains unpublished.

Franz Baermann Steiner dies and Adler becomes the executor of Steiner's estate.

1953

Becomes a member of the PEN-Zentrum of German-speaking authors abroad.

1954

Edits a collection of Steiner's poems *Unruhe ohne Uhr*.

Begins friendship with Heinrich Böll (1917–1985).

1954–1961

Works on a novel under the title *Die Wand* that is published posthumously in 1989 as *Die unsichtbare Wand*.

1955

Theresienstadt 1941–1945: Das Antlitz einer Zwangsgemeinschaft is published and recognized as a pioneering work, bringing many invitations to give lectures and make radio appearances in the Federal Republic of Germany; after this he becomes known as 'Theresienstadt Adler'; Theodor W. Adorno helped secure the publication subvention.

1956

31 July: receives British citizenship.

1957

Begins friendship with Heimito von Doderer (1896–1966).

1958

Receives the Leo Baeck Prize for his contribution to research on Theresiensadt.

Publishes *Die verheimlichte Wahrheit: Theresienstädter Dokumente*, a companion piece to the Theresienstadt book, and *Der Kampf gegen die 'Endlösung der Judenfrage'*, a publication funded by the 'Bundeszentrale für Heimatdienst' in Bonn.

1958–1973

Conducts research at the Institute of Contemporary History in Munich for a major study of the deportations, published in 1974 as *Der verwaltete Mensch*.

1959

Hermann Langbein (1912–1995) invites Adler to become a member of the International Auschwitz Committee, and this marks the beginning of their scholarly collaboration.

1960

Publication of *Die Juden in Deutschland: Von der Aufklärung bis zum Nationalsozialismus* (appears in English translation in 1969 as *The Jews in Germany: From the Enlightenment to National Socialism*), and a second, revised, and expanded edition of the Theresienstadt book appears.

1961

Makes his literary debut with *Unser Georg und andere Geschichten*.

Adler's research on Theresienstadt plays an important role in the Eichmann Trial.

'Auschwitz: Topographie eines Vernichtungslagers', a three-hour feature, written by Adler and Langbein, is broadcast on West German Radio (WDR); this is one of the earliest major presentations of Auschwitz in Germany prior to the Auschwitz Trials (1963–1965).

1962

Publications include: *Eine Reise* and *Auschwitz: Zeugnisse und Berichte*, a collaborative work with Hermann Langbein and Ella Lingens-Reiner (1908–2002).

1964

Publications include: *Erfahrung der Ohnmacht: Beiträge zur Soziologie unserer Zeit* and *Der Fürst des Segens: Parabeln — Betrachtungen — Gleichnisse*.

Edits *Eroberungen*, Franz Baermann Steiner's cycle of poems.

1965

Sodoms Untergang: Bagatellen appears.

1968

Panorama: Roman in zehn Bildern appears.

1969

Receives Charles Veillon Prize for *Panorama*.

Publications include: *Ereignisse: Kleine Erzählungen und Novellen*, a collection of short stories, *Kontraste und Variationen*, a collection of essays and photographs, and the English translation *The Jews in Germany*.

1973–1985

Active as president of the PEN-Zentrum for German-speaking authors abroad.

1974

Publication of *Der verwaltete Mensch: Studien zur Deportation der Juden aus Deutschland*, for which he receives the Buber Rosenzweig Medal (the book appears on 8 February, the anniversary of his deportation to Theresienstadt).

Collection of poems *Fenster: Sechs Gedichte* appears.

1975

Collection of poems *Viele Jahreszeiten* appears.

H. G. Adler: Buch der Freunde, a *Festschrift* for Adler's 65th birthday edited by Willehad P. Eckert and Wilhelm Unger, appears.

1976

Collection of essays *Die Freiheit des Menschen: Aufsätze zur Soziologie und Geschichte* appears.

1977

Receives the title of Professor, bestowed by the Austrian president.

Becomes the executor of Grete Fischer's literary estate.

1978

Publications include: *Spuren und Pfeiler: Gedichtzyklus* and *Transubstantiations Mixed and Fixed: Konkrete Lautgedichte*.

1979

Publications include: *Blicke: Gedichte 1947–1951, Zeiten auf der Spur: Zwei Gedichtzyklen*, and a second, revised edition of *Auschwitz: Zeugnisse und Berichte*.

Becomes corresponding member of the Bavarian Academy of Arts.

1980

Stimme und Zuruf: Gedichte appears.

Pädagogische Hochschule of Berlin bestows honorary doctorate upon Adler.

1981–1985

Works on his *Vorschule für eine Experimentaltheologie*, which is published in 1987.

1984

November: Official trip to Germany upon invitation by the West German government.

1985

Receives the Federal Cross of Merit from the Federal Republic of Germany and the Austrian Cross of Honour for Science and Art.

Publication of English translation of *Windows*.

1986

Television special on Adler is broadcast in the series 'Zeugen des Jahrhunderts' (ZDF).

1987

Vorschule für eine Experimentaltheologie appears.

Zu Hause im Exil, a *Festschrift* for Adler's 75th birthday edited by Heinrich Hubmann and Alfred O. Lanz, appears.

1988

Hausordnung: Wortlaut und Auslegung appears.

21 **August**: H. G. Adler dies in London.

1989

The novel *Die unsichtbare Wand* appears.

BIBLIOGRAPHY

❖

I. Unpublished Sources

Archival Collections

A: H. G. Adler, Deutsches Literaturarchiv Marbach

Eichstätt University Library, Verlagsarchiv Kösel (VA 1), Autorenkorrespondenz H. G. Adler.

Historisches Archiv des Bayerischen Rundfunks, Munich, HF / 6197.1, Autorenkorrespondenz H. G. Adler.

Historisches Archiv des Südwestrundfunks, Stuttgart, Autorenkorrespondenz H. G. Adler.

Historisches Archiv des Westdeutschen Rundfunks, Cologne, no. 15890, Autorenkorrespondenz H. G. Adler.

Unpublished Letters

ADLER, H. G., Letter to Wolfgang Burghart, 17 October 1947. A: H. G. Adler, Deutsches Literaturarchiv Marbach.

——Letter to W. Honig, 11 January 1955. Archive of Westdeutscher Rundfunk, Cologne, 2177.

——Letter to Hans Reichmann, 10 September 1961. A: H. G. Adler, Deutsches Literaturarchiv Marbach.

——Letter to Theodor Sapper, 21 January 1974. A: H. G. Adler, Deutsches Literaturarchiv Marbach.

——Letter to Wilhelm Unger, 10 May 1950. A: H. G. Adler, Deutsches Literaturarchiv Marbach.

——Letter to Sigfried Unseld, 20 October 1956. A: H. G. Adler, Deutsches Literaturarchiv Marbach, AII 81.

——Letter to Hans Winterfeldt, 22 October 1964. A: H. G. Adler, Deutsches Literaturarchiv Marbach, A I 63.

REICHMANN, HANS, Letter to H. G. Adler, 18 August 1961. A: H. G. Adler, Deutsches Literaturarchiv Marbach.

SCHÖNAUER DR. FRANZ (Claassen), Letter to H. G. Adler, 30 April 1958. A: H. G. Adler, Deutsches Literaturarchiv Marbach, A II 80.

MIQUEL, ALEXANDRA VON (Kiepenheuer & Witsch), Letter to H. G. Adler, 23 November 1953. A: H. G. Adler, Deutsches Literaturarchiv Marbach, A II 81.

Unpublished Manuscripts

ADLER, H. G., *England: Eindrücke eines Ahnungslosen*. Typescript. King's College London Archives; A: H. G. Adler, Deutsches Literaturarchiv Marbach, A II 2, Mappe 5.

——'Gegen den Staat: Geharnischte Einfälle'. 7 April 1946. Typescript 3pp. A: H. G. Adler, Deutsches Literaturarchiv Marbach.

——'Literarische Selbsteinsicht'. Typescript. A: H. G. Adler, Deutsches Literaturarchiv Marbach.

——'Nicht mit den Wölfen heulen: Menschlichkeit gegen Unmenschlichkeit', WDR (Hauptabteilung Politik), program of 20 August 1961. A: H. G. Adler, Deutsches Literaturarchiv Marbach.

——'Warum habe ich mein Buch "Theresienstadt 1941–1945" geschrieben?' 12 April 1956. Typescript 5 pp. A: H. G. Adler, Deutsches Literaturarchiv Marbach, A II 26: Folder 'Theresienstadt / Kleine Arbeiten'.

——'Wissenschaftler oder Gelehrter?' 9 February 1962. Typescript 8 pp. A: H. G. Adler, Deutsches Literaturarchiv Marbach, A II 25.

——'Zur Bestimmung der Lyrik' (version: 'Fassung für den Vortrag in der Münchner Akademie am 20.10.58', dated 16–18.9.1958). Typescript 30pp. Deutsches Literaturarchiv Marbach, A: Adler, A II 22.

KOGON, EUGEN, 'Ein Buch und eine Meinung: Eugen Kogon spricht über das Buch Theresienstadt von H.G. Adler'. A: H. G. Adler, Deutsches Literaturarchiv Marbach, A II 64.

PETERSEN, J., 'H. G. Adler: Theresienstadt', Das Buch der Woche, Hessischer Rundfunk, Frankfurt am Main, 25 March 1956. A: H. G. Adler, Deutsches Literaturarchiv Marbach, A II 64.

II. Published Works by H. G. Adler

ADLER, GÜNTHER, Meer und Gebirge (Radolfzell am Bodensee: Heim-Verlag Adolf Dessler, 1931).

ADLER, H. G., Andere Wege: Gesammelte Gedichte, ed. by Katrin Kohl and Franz Hocheneder, with the collaboration of Jeremy Adler and with an afterword by Michael Krüger (Klagenfurt: Drava, 2010).

——'Arnold Schönberg: Eine Botschaft an die Nachwelt', Literatur und Kritik, 103 (1976), 129–39.

——'The "Autonomous" Jewish Administration of Terezin (Theresienstadt)', in Imposed Jewish Governing Bodies under Nazi Rule, YIVO Colloquium, December 2–5, 1967 (New York: Yivo Institute for Jewish Research, 1972), pp. 70–82.

——'Der Autor zwischen Literatur und Politik', in H. G. Adler, Orthodoxie des Herzens: Ausgewählte Essays zu Literatur, Judentum und Politik, ed. by Peter Filkins with Jeremy Adler (Konstanz: Konstanz University Press, 2014), pp. 13–25.

——Blicke: Gedichte 1947–1951 (Berlin: Europäische Ideen, 1979).

——'Botschaft in dunkler Zeit: Leo Baeck und sein Werk', in H. G. Adler, Orthodoxie des Herzens: Ausgewählte Essays zu Literatur, Judentum und Politik, ed. by Peter Filkins with Jeremy Adler (Konstanz: Konstanz University Press, 2014), pp. 169–88.

——'"Da gäbe es noch viel mehr zu berichten ...". Interview mit H. G. Adler von Friedrich Danielis [1981]', Zwischenwelt 25, No. 3/4 (2008), 19–27.

——Die Dichtung der Prager Schule: Mit einem Vorwort von Jeremy Adler (Wuppertal: Arco, 2010) [First published in 1976].

——'Dichtung in der Gefangenschaft als inneres Exil', in: Literatur des Exils: Eine Dokumentation über die PEN-Jahrestagung in Bremen vom 18–20. September 1980, ed. by Bernt Engelmann (Munich: Goldmann, 1981), pp. 18–28.

——'Dichtung aus Theresienstadt', in Fruchtblätter: Freundesgabe für Alfred Kelletat, ed. by Harald Hartung, Walter Heistermann, and Peter M. Stephan (Berlin: Pädagogische Akademie Berlin, 1977), pp. 137–42.

——'Einladung zu meinem *Panorama*: H. G. Adler über seinen neuen Roman', in *Literarium* 16 (Olten/Freiburg im Breisgau: Walter Verlag, 1968) p. 3.

——*Ereignisse: Kleine Erzählungen und Novellen* (Olten/Freiburg im Breisgau: Walter, 1969).

——*Die Erfahrung der Ohnmacht: Beiträge zur Soziologie unserer Zeit* (Frankfurt a/M: Europäische Verlagsanstalt, 1964).

——'"Es gäbe viel Merkwürdiges zu berichten": Interview mit Hans Christoph Knebusch', in *H. G. Adler — Der Wahrheit verpflichtet: Interviews, Gedichte, Essays*, ed. by Jeremy Adler (Gerlingen: Bleicher Verlag, 1998), pp. 32–55.

——*Fenster: Sechs Gedichte* (London: Alphabox Press, 1974).

——*Die Freiheit des Menschen: Aufsätze zur Soziologie und Geschichte* (Tübingen: J. C. B. Mohr (Paul Siebeck), 1976).

——*Der Fürst des Segens: Parabeln — Betrachtungen — Gleichnisse* (Bonn: Bibliotheca Christiana, 1964).

——'Gedanken zu einer Soziologie des Konzentrationslagers', in *H. G. Adler — Der Wahrheit verpflichtet: Interviews, Gedichte, Essays*, ed. by Jeremy Adler (Gerlingen: Bleicher Verlag, 1998), pp. 142–62.

——'Geist und Grenzen des Widerstands', in *H. G. Adler — Der Wahrheit verpflichtet: Interviews, Gedichte, Essays*, ed. by Jeremy Adler (Gerlingen: Bleicher Verlag, 1998), pp. 163–202.

——'The Great Tragedy' [Review of Léon Poliakov's *Harvest of Hate* [Transl. by Albert J. George from the French *Bréviaire de la Haine*] (London: Elek Books, 1956)], *The Jewish Quarterly*, 4.3 (1956/1957), 41–42.

——*Hausordnung: Wortlaut und Auslegung* (Vienna: Wiener Journal, 1988).

——*The Jews in Germany: From the Enlightenment to National Socialism* (Notre Dame, IN: University of Notre Dame Press, 1970) [Translator unknown].

——*The Journey*, trans. by Peter Filkins (New York: Modern Library, 2009).

——*Die Juden in Deutschland: Von der Aufklärung bis zum Nationalsozialismus* (Munich: Kösel, 1960).

——*Der Kampf gegen die 'Endlösung der Judenfrage'* (Bonn: Bundeszentrale für Heimatdienst, 1958).

——*Kontraste und Variationen* (Würzburg: Echter, 1969).

——Letter to Jehuda Bacon on 15 February 1953, in *Jehuda Bacon: Malerei und Grafik*, ed. by Michael Koller and Jürgen Lenssen, trans. by Sarah Polewski; Jens Oertel (Würzburg: Stiftung Kunstsammlung der Diözese Würzburg, 2015), p. 62.

——'Nach der Befreiung — ein Wort an die Mitwelt', in H. G. Adler, *Nach der Befreiung: Ausgewählte Essays zur Geschichte und Soziologie*, ed. by Peter Filkins with Jeremy Adler (Konstanz: Konstanz University Press, 2013), pp. 43–47.

——*Nach der Befreiung: Ausgewählte Essays zur Geschichte und Soziologie*, ed. by Peter Filkins with Jeremy Adler (Konstanz: Konstanz University Press, 2013).

——'Nachruf bei Lebzeiten', in *H. G. Adler — Der Wahrheit verpflichtet: Interviews, Gedichte, Essays*, ed. by Jeremy Adler (Gerlingen: Bleicher, 1998), pp. 7–16.

——*Orthodoxie des Herzens: Ausgewählte Essays zu Literatur, Judentum und Politik*, ed. by Peter Filkins with Jeremy Adler (Konstanz: Konstanz University Press, 2014).

——*Panorama: Roman in zehn Bildern* (Munich: Piper, 1988).

——*Panorama: A Novel*, trans. by Peter Filkins (New York: Modern Library, 2012).

——*Eine Reise* (Vienna: Zsolnay, 1999).

——Review of *Persecution and Resistance under the Nazis*, ed. by Ilse R. Wolff (London: Vallentine Mitchell, 1960) in *Neue politische Literatur*, 5.12 (1960), columns 1113–16.

——'The Scholar and the Catastrophe: A Guide to Research', *The Wiener Library Bulletin*, 15.2 (1961), 23.

——*Schuldig und Unschuldig: Symphonische Miniaturen*, ed. by Franz Hocheneder, with a foreword by Jeremy Adler, *Gesammelte Erzählungen* Vol. 4 (Vienna: Löcker, 2016).

——'Selbstverwaltung und Widerstand in den Konzentrationslagern der SS', in H. G. Adler, *Nach der Befreiung: Ausgewählte Essays zur Geschichte und Soziologie*, ed. by Peter Filkins with Jeremy Adler (Konstanz: Konstanz University Press, 2013), pp. 49–70.

——*Sodoms Untergang: Bagatellen* (Bonn: Bibliotheca Christiana, 1965).

——'Sonderinterview von Alfred Joachim Fischer', in *Zu Hause im Exil: Zu Werk und Person H. G. Adlers*, ed. by Heinrich Hubmann and Alfred O. Lanz (Stuttgart: Steiner Verlag, 1987), pp. 191–201.

——'Sprache am Verstummen', in H. G. Adler, *Orthodoxie des Herzens: Ausgewählte Essays zu Literatur, Judentum und Politik*, ed. by Peter Filkins with Jeremy Adler (Konstanz: Konstanz University Press, 2014), pp. 105–13.

——'Die Sprache der Gewalt und ihre Wörter', in *Abhandlungen aus der Pädagogischen Hochschule Berlin*, vol. 7 of *Spätlese aus Forschung und Lehre einer aufgelösten Hochschule*, ed. by Walter Heistermann (Berlin: Colloquium Verlag / Otto H. Hess, 1980), pp. 179–217.

——*Spuren und Pfeiler: Gedichte von H. G. Adler mit Zeichnungen von Friedrich Danielis* (London: Alphabox Press, 1978).

——*Stimme und Zuruf: Gedichte* mit einem Nachwort von Manfred Bieler (Hamburg: Knaus, 1980).

——*Theresienstadt 1941–1945: Das Antlitz einer Zwangsgemeinschaft* (Tübingen: J. C. B. Mohr (Paul Siebeck), 1955, and second revised edition 1960).

——*Theresienstadt 1941–1945: Das Antlitz einer Zwangsgemeinschaft* (Göttingen: Wallstein, 2005).

——*Theresienstadt 1941–1945: The Face of a Coerced Community*, trans. by Belinda Cooper (New York: Cambridge University Press, 2017).

——*Transubstantiations Mixed and Fixed: Konkrete Lautgedichte* (London: Writers Forum, 1978).

——*Unser Georg und andere Geschichten* (Vienna: Bergland, 1961).

——*Die unsichtbare Wand* (Vienna: Zsolnay, 1989).

——'Verfolger und Verfolgte nach jüdischer Lehre', in H. G. Adler, *Orthodoxie des Herzens: Ausgewählte Essays zu Literatur, Judentum und Politik*, ed. by Peter Filkins with Jeremy Adler (Konstanz: Konstanz University Press, 2014), pp. 117–30.

——*Die verheimlichte Wahrheit: Theresienstädter Dokumente* (Tübingen: J. C. B. Mohr (Paul Siebeck), 1958).

——*Der verwaltete Mensch: Studien zur Deportation der Juden aus Deutschland* (Tübingen: J. C. B. Mohr (Paul Siebeck), 1974).

——*Viele Jahreszeiten: Gedichte* (Vienna and Munich: Albrecht Dürer, 1975).

——'Vom Ursprung der Schuld- und Gnadengemeinschaft', in H. G. Adler, *Orthodoxie des Herzens: Ausgewählte Essays zu Literatur, Judentum und Politik*, ed. by Peter Filkins with Jeremy Adler (Konstanz: Konstanz University Press, 2014), pp. 131–42.

——*Vorschule für eine Experimentaltheologie: Betrachtungen über Wirklichkeit und Sein* (Stuttgart: Franz Steiner Verlag, 1987).

——*The Wall: A Novel*, trans. by Peter Filkins (New York: Random House, 2015).

——'Warum habe ich mein Buch *Theresienstadt 1941–1945* geschrieben?', in *H. G. Adler — Der Wahrheit verpflichtet: Interviews, Gedichte, Essays*, ed. by Jeremy Adler (Gerlingen: Bleicher Verlag, 1998), pp. 111–14.

——'Was weiß Hannah Arendt von Eichmann und der "Endlösung"?', *Allgemeine Wochenzeitung der Juden*, 19.34 (20 November 1964), 8–9.

——'Der Weg zum Wohlfahrtsstaat', in *Die Erfahrung der Ohnmacht: Beiträge zur Soziologie unserer Zeit* (Frankfurt a/M: Europäische Verlagsanstalt, 1964), pp. 163–68.

—— *Windows / Fenster*, trans. by Jeremy Adler with illustrations by Bob Cobbing (London: Writers Forum, 1985).

—— *Zeiten auf der Spur: Zwei Gedichtzyklen* (Aachen: Fachhochschule Aachen — Fachbereich Design, 1978).

—— 'Zu Hause im Exil', in *H. G. Adler — Der Wahrheit verpflichtet: Interviews, Gedichte, Essays*, ed. by Jeremy Adler (Gerlingen: Bleicher, 1998), pp. 19–31.

ADLER H. G. and HERMANN BROCH, *Zwei Schriftsteller im Exil: Briefwechsel*, ed. by Ronald Speirs and John White (Göttingen: Wallstein, 2004).

ADLER, H. G. and HERMANN LANGBEIN, *Auschwitz: Topographie eines Vernichtungslagers. Überlebende berichten* (Berlin: Der Audio Verlag, 2015).

ADLER, H. G., HERMANN LANGBEIN, and ELLA LINGENS-REINER, *Auschwitz: Zeugnisse und Berichte* (Cologne: Europäische Verlagsanstalt, 1962).

III. Other Works

400 Jahre Kösel-Verlag: 1593–1993 (Munich: Kösel, 1993).

ADLER, JEREMY, 'Afterword', trans. by Jeremiah Riemer, in H. G. Adler, *Theresienstadt 1941–1945: The Face of a Coerced Community*, trans. by Belinda Cooper (New York: Cambridge University Press, 2017), pp. 803–28.

—— *Das bittere Brot: H. G. Adler, Elias Canetti und Franz Baermann Steiner im Londoner Exil* (Göttingen: Wallstein, 2015).

—— 'Erich Fried, F. B. Steiner and an Unknown Group of Exile Poets in London', *Zwischenwelt 4: Literatur und Kultur des Exils in Großbritannien* (1995), 163–84.

—— 'Good against Evil? H. G. Adler, T. W. Adorno and the Representation of the Holocaust', in *The German-Jewish Dilemma: From the Enlightenment to the Shoah*, ed. by Edward Timms and Andrea Hammel (Lewiston, NY: Mellen, 1999), pp. 255–89.

—— 'Good against Evil? H. G. Adler, T. W. Adorno and the Representation of the Holocaust', in *Studies in Social and Political Thought 2: Social Theory after the Holocaust*, ed. by Robert Fine and Charles Turner (Liverpool: Liverpool UP, 2000), pp. 71–100.

—— 'H. G. Adler. A Prague Writer in London', in *Keine Klage über England? Deutsche und österreichische Exilerfahrungen in Großbritannien 1933–1945*, ed. by Charmian Brinson (München: Iudicium, 1998), pp. 13–30.

—— '"Die Macht des Guten im Rachen des Bösen": H. G. Adler, T. W. Adorno und die Darstellung der Shoah', in *Merkur*, 54 (June 2000), 475–86.

—— *The Magus of Portobello Road* (London: Alphabox Press, 2015).

—— 'Nachwort', in H. G. Adler, *Theresienstadt 1941–1945: Das Antlitz einer Zwangsgemeinschaft* (Göttingen: Wallstein, 2005), pp. 895–926.

—— 'Vorwort', in H. G. Adler, *Schuldig und Unschuldig: Symphonische Miniaturen*, ed. by Franz Hocheneder, *Gesammelte Erzählungen* Vol. 4. (Vienna: Löcker, 2016), pp. 9–10.

—— 'The World of My Father's Memory Writing: The *Gesamtkunstwerk* of H. G. Adler', in *H. G. Adler: Life, Literature, Legacy*, ed. by Julia Creet, Sara R. Horowitz, and Amira Bojadzija-Dan (Evanston, IL: Northwestern University Press, 2016), pp. 23–46.

ADORNO, THEODOR W., 'Cultural Criticism and Society' [1951], in Theodor W. Adorno, *Prisms*, trans. by Samuel and Shierry Weber (Cambridge, MA: The MIT Press, 1983), pp. 17–34.

—— 'Kulturkritik und Gesellschaft', in Adorno, *Gesammelte Schriften*, ed. by Rolf Tiedemann (Frankfurt a/M: Suhrkamp, 1970ff.), vol. 10.1, pp. 11–30.

Als der Holocaust noch keinen Namen hatte — Before the Holocaust Had Its Name, ed. by Regina Fritz, Éva Kovács, and Béla Rásky (Vienna: New Academic Press, 2016).

ALTMAN, JANET GURKIN, *Epistolarity: Approaches to a Form* (Columbus, OH: Ohio State University Press, 1982).

AMÉRY, JEAN, 'An den Grenzen des Geistes', in *Jenseits von Schuld und Sühne* (Stuttgart: Klett-Cotta, 1977), pp. 23–54.

—— 'At the Mind's Limits', in *At the Mind's Limits: Contemplations by a Survivor on Auschwitz and its Realities*, transl. by Sidney Rosenfeld and Stella P. Rosenfeld (Bloomington, IN: Indiana University Press, 1980), pp. 1–20.

Die andere deutsche Frage: Kultur und Gesellschaft der Bundesrepublik Deutschland nach 30 Jahren, ed. by Walter Scheel (Stuttgart: Klett, 1981).

ANON., '*The Journey* by H. G. Adler, Peter Filkins | Kirkus Reviews', Kirkusreviews. com, n.d., <https://www.kirkusreviews.com/book-reviews/hg-adler/the-journey/> [accessed 28 April 2016].

ANON., 'Zwangsreise', *Stuttgarter Zeitung* (11 April 2003), 32.

The Answers of Ernst von Salomon to the 131 Questions in the Allied Military Government 'Fragebogen', transl. by Constantine Fitzgibbon (London: Putman, 1954).

ARENDT, HANNAH, *Eichmann in Jerusalem: A Report on the Banality of Evil* (1963), with an Introduction by Amos Elon. (London and New York: Penguin Books, 2006).

—— *The Origins of Totalitarianism* (New York: Harcourt Brace, 1951).

ARISTOTLE, *The 'Art' of Rhetoric*, with an English translation by John Henry Freese (Cambridge, MA: Harvard University Press, 1926).

ARNSBERG PAUL, Review of H. G. Adler, *Die Juden in Deutschland*, in *Frankfurter Allgemeine Zeitung* (23 March 1961), 2 (Literaturbeilage).

ASSMANN, ALEIDA, *Der lange Schatten der Vergangenheit: Erinnerungskulturen und Geschichtspolitik* (Munich: C. H. Beck, 2006).

ASSMANN, ALEIDA and GEOFFREY HARTMANN, *Die Zukunft der Erinnerung und der Holocaust* (Konstanz: Konstanz University Press, 2012).

Auschwitz: Zeugnisse und Berichte, ed. by H. G. Adler, Hermann Langbein, and Ella Lingens-Reiner, with an introduction to the 6th edition by Katharina Stengel (Hamburg: Europäische Verlagsanstalt, 2014).

AUSTIN, JOHN, *The Province of Jurisprudence Determined* (1st edn 1832), ed. by W. Rumble (Cambridge: Cambridge University Press, 1995).

BAMMER, ANGELIKA, *Displacements: Cultural Identities in Question* (Bloomington, IN: Indiana University Press, 1994).

BARKOW, BEN, 'A Heroic Work of Extraordinary Scholarship: On the New Translated Edition of H. G. Adler's *Theresienstadt* of 1960', *German Historical Institute London Bulletin*, 40.1 (2018), 86–98.

BAUMANN, ZYGMUNT, *Modernity and the Holocaust* (Ithaca, NY: Cornell University Press, 2000).

BECHER, JOHANNES R., 'Auferstehen', in *Gesammelte Werke*, XVI, *Publizistik II 1939–1945* (Berlin: Aufbau, 1978), pp. 454–62.

BENDA, JULIEN, *La Trahisons des Clercs* (1927) (Paris: Éditions Grasset, 2003).

BENZ, WOLFGANG, *Theresienstadt: Eine Geschichte von Täuschung und Vernichtung* (Munich: C. H. Beck, 2013).

BERG, NICOLAS, *Der Holocaust und die westdeutschen Historiker: Erforschung und Erinnerung* (Göttingen: Wallstein, 2004).

BERGMANN, WERNER, *Antisemitismus in öffentlichen Konflikten: Kollektives Lernen in der politischen Kultur der Bundesrepublik 1949–1989* (Frankfurt a/M: Campus, 1997), pp. 187–277.

BERNSTEIN, JAY, *Torture and Dignity: An Essay on Moral Injury* (Chicago and London: Chicago University Press, 2015).

BERTRAND, NICOLAS, *L'enfer réglementé: Le régime de détention dans les camps de concentration* (Paris: Perrin, 2015).

Beschreibungsversuche der Judenfeindschaft: Die Geschichte der Antisemitismusforschung vor 1944, ed. by Hans-Joachim Hahn and Olfa Kistenmacher (Berlin: De Gruyter, 2015).

BEST, OTTO F., 'Panorama und Topographie: Anmerkungen zu Alfred Döblin, Peter Weiss, H. G. Adler und anderen', *Deutsche Exilliteratur, Literatur der Nachkriegszeit: Akten des III. Exilliteratur-Symposiums der University of South Carolina*, ed. by Wolfgang Elfe, James Hardin, and Günther Holst (Bern: Peter Lang, 1981), pp. 96–102.

BETTELHEIM, BRUNO, 'Individual and Mass Behavior in Extreme Situations', in *Readings in Social Psychology* ed. by Eleanor E. Maccoby, Theodore M. Newcomb, and Eugene C. Hartley (New York: Holt, Rinehart & Winston, Inc., 1958), pp. 300–10.

BÖHME, JAKOB, *Aurora*, in *Sämmtliche Werke*, II, ed. by K. W. Schiebler (Leipzig: Johann Ambrosius Barth, 1832).

BÖLL, HEINRICH, *Der Engel schwieg* (Cologne: Kiepenheuer & Witsch, 1992).

—— 'Wir Deutsche, Ein fahrendes Volk', *Der Tagesspiegel*, Berlin, (22 September 1963), 37.

BOLL, MONIKA, 'Das Kulturradio nach 1945', in *Radiotage, Fernsehjahre: Studien zur Rundfunkgeschichte nach 1945*, ed. by Markus Behmer (Münster: LIT, 2006), pp. 151–62.

—— 'Verehrte Hörerinnen und Hörer! Radiogebildet — Zur Geschichte des Nachtstudios 1948–1970', in *Nachtstudio: Radioessays*, ed. by Barbara Schäfer and Antonio Pellegrino (Munich: Belleville, 2008), pp. 13–41.

BOWER, ANNE, *Epistolary Responses: The Letter in 20th-Century American Fiction and Criticism* (Tuscaloosa, AL: University of Alabama Press, 1997).

BRAESE, STEPHAN, *Die andere Erinnerung: Jüdische Autoren in der westdeutschen Nachkriegsliteratur* (Vienna: Philo, 2001).

—— 'Deutschland — ein Krieg gegen das Erinnern: Zum Ende der Nachkriegszeit', *Diskussion Deutsch*, 119 (1991), 240–44.

BROCH, HERMANN, 'H. G. Adler: Theresienstadt (1949)', in Hermann Broch, *Schriften zur Literatur I: Kritik*, Kommentierte Werkausgabe 9/1, ed. by Paul Michael Lützeler (Frankfurt a/M: Suhrkamp, 1976), pp. 404–05.

BROCKMANN, STEPHEN, 'Establishing Cultural Fronts in East and West Germany', *Comparative Critical Studies*, 13.2 (2016), 149–72.

BUCHHEIM, IRIS, 'Leben nach dem Überleben', *Falter* (28 May 1999), 66.

BUNGERT, ALFONS, *Deutsche Tageszeitung* (28 June 1963).

BURR, STEPHEN A., *Finite Transcendence: Existential Exile and the Myth of Home* (Lanham: Lexington Books, 2014).

CASTONIER, ELISABETH, *Mill Farm und ihre zwei- und vierbeinigen Originale* (Munich: Heimeran, 1959).

CHANG, JUN, *Wild Swans: Three Daughters of China* (New York: Simon & Schuster, 1991).

CHAPOUTOT, JOHANN, *La révolution culturelle nazie* (Paris: Gallimard, 2016).

CHESTERTON, G. K., *The Napoleon of Notting Hill* (London: John Lane, 1904).

CLAUSS, ELKE-MARIA, 'Brief', in *Metzler Lexikon Literatur: Begriffe und Definitionen*, ed. by Dieter Burdorf, Christoph Fasbender, and Burkhard Moeninghoff (Stuttgart: Metzler, 2007), pp. 98–99.

COHEN, ELIE, *Human Behaviour in the Concentration Camp* (London: Jonathan Cape, 1954).

COHEN, NATHAN, 'Diaries of the *Sonderkommando*', in *Anatomy of the Auschwitz Death Camp*, ed. by Yisrael Gutman and Michael Berenbaum (Bloomington, IN: Indiana University Press, 1994), pp. 522–34.

CREET, JULIA, 'A Dialectic of the Deictic: Pronouns and Persons in H. G. Adler's *The Journey*', in *H. G. Adler: Life, Literature, Legacy*, ed. by Creet, Horowitz, and Bojadzija-Dan (Evanston, IL: Northwestern University Press, 2016), pp. 205–27.

CREET, JULIA, SARA R. HOROWITZ, and AMIRA BOJADZIJA-DAN, 'Introduction: Encountering

H. G. Adler', in *H. G. Adler: Life, Literature, Legacy*, ed. by Julia Creet, Sara R. Horowitz, and Amira Bojadzija-Dan (Evanston, IL: Northwestern University Press, 2016), pp. 3–20.

DAHM, GEORG, *Deutsches Recht* (Hamburg: Hanseatische Verlagsanstalt, 1944).

DANE, GESA, 'Einleitung', in *Literatur und Anthropologie: H. G. Adler, Elias Canetti und Franz Baermann Steiner in London*, ed. by Jeremy Adler and Gesa Dane (Göttingen: Wallstein, 2014), pp. 7–15.

DELABAR, WALTER, 'Zwischen Dichtung und Kahlschlag: Zwei Exkursionen in die bundesdeutsche Nachkriegsliteratur', *Juni: Magazin für Literatur und Politik*, 23 (1995), 97–116.

DEMETZ, PETER, *After the Fires: Recent Writing in the Germanies, Austria, and Switzerland* (San Diego: Harcourt Brace Jovanovich, 1986).

DODERER, HEIMITO VON, *Welt am Sonntag* (29 December 1963).

DUSSEL, KONRAD, *Deutsche Rundfunkgeschichte: Eine Einführung* (Konstanz: UVK Medien, 1999).

Düsteres Idyll: Trost der deutschen Romantik, Fotografien von H. G. Adler mit einem Essay von Péter Nádas (Marbach am Neckar: Deutsche Schillergesellschaft, 2015 [Marbacher Magazin 149]).

EINSTEIN, ALBERT, *The Einstein Reader* (New York: Citadel Press Books, 2006).

——'A Message to Intellectuals', in Albert Einstein, *Ideas and Opinions* (New York: Wings Books, 1954), pp. 147–51.

EVELEIN, JOHANNES F., *Literary Exiles from Nazi Germany: Exemplarity and the Search for Meaning* (Rochester, NY: Camden House, 2014).

FILKINS, PETER, 'Both Sides of the Wall: Theresienstadt in H. G. Adler's Scholarship and Fiction', in *Literatur und Anthropologie: H. G. Adler, Elias Canetti und Franz Baermann Steiner in London*, ed. by Jeremy Adler and Gesa Dane (Göttingen: Wallstein: 2014), pp. 82–96.

——*H. G. Adler: A Life in Many Worlds* (New York: Oxford University Press, 2019).

——'Introduction', in *The Wall: A Novel*, by H. G. Adler, trans. Peter Filkins (New York: Modern Library, 2014), pp. XI–XIX.

——'The Self Positioned, The (De)posited Self, The Soul Released: The Uses of Biography in H. G. Adler's Shoah Trilogy', in *H. G. Adler: Life, Literature, Legacy*, ed. by Julia Creet, Sara R. Horowitz, and Amira Bojadzija-Dan (Evanston, IL: Northwestern University Press, 2016), pp. 47–67.

FINCH, HELEN, 'Holocaust Translation, Communication and Witness in the Work of H. G. Adler' *German Life and Letters*, 68.3 (2015), 427–43.

——'Prague Circles: H. G. Adler's Kafkaesque Hope', in *H. G. Adler: Life, Literature, Legacy*, ed. by Julia Creet, Sara R. Horowitz, and Amira Bojadzija-Dan (Evanston, IL: Northwestern University Press, 2016), pp. 251–72.

——'*Ressentiment* beyond Nietzsche and Améry: H. G. Adler between Literary *Ressentiment* and Divine Grace', in *Re-thinking Ressentiment: On the Limits of Criticism and the Limits of its Critics*, ed. by Jeanne Riou and Mary Gallagher (Bielefeld: transcript, 2016), pp. 71–86.

FINCH HELEN and LYNN L. WOLFF, 'Introduction: The Adler-Sebald Intertextual Relationship as Paradigm for Intergenerational Literary Testimony', in *Witnessing, Memory, Poetics: H. G. Adler and W. G. Sebald*, ed. by Helen Finch and Lynn L. Wolff (Rochester, NY: Camden House, 2014), pp. 1–21.

FINLAY, FRANK, ' "Der verwerfliche Literaturbetrieb unserer Epoche": H. G. Adler and the Postwar West German "Literary Field" ', in *Witnessing, Memory, Poetics: H. G. Adler and W. G. Sebald*, ed. by Helen Finch and Lynn L. Wolff (Rochester, NY: Camden House, 2014), pp. 254–74.

FRAENKEL, ERNST, *The Dual State: Contribution to the Theory of Dictatorship* (New York: Oxford University Press, 1941).

Fragebogen: The Questionnaire, transl. by Constantine Fitzgibbon (Garden City, N.Y.: Doubleday, 1955).

FRANK, HANS, 'Einleitung', *Nationalsozialistisches Handbuch für Recht und Gesetzgebung* (1935), repr. in Herlinde Pauer-Studer & Julian Fink, *Rechtfertigungen des Unrechts* (Frankfurt a/M: Suhrkamp, 2014).

FRANKLIN, RUTH, 'The Long View', *Newyorker.com*, 2011 <www.newyorker.com/magazine/2011/01/31/the-long-view>[accessed 15 March 2016].

FREISLER, ROLAND, 'Der Heimweg des Rechts in die völkische Sittenordnung', in *Beiträge zum Recht des neuen Deutschland: Festschrift Franz Schlegelberger zum 60. Geburtstag*, ed. by Erwin Bumke, J. Wilhelm Hedemann, and Gustav Wilke (Berlin: Vahlen, 1936), pp. 28–44.

FRIEDLÄNDER, SAUL, *Probing the Limits of Representation: Nazism and the 'Final Solution'* (Cambridge, MA: Harvard University Press, 1992).

FRITZ, REGINA, ÉVA KOVÁCS, and BÉLA RÁSKY, 'Der NS-Massenmord an den Juden: Perspektiven und Fragen der frühen Aufarbeitung', in *Als der Holocaust noch keinen Namen hatte — Before the Holocaust Had Its Name,* ed. by Regina Fritz, Éva Kovács, and Béla Rásky (Vienna: New Academic Press, 2016), pp. 7–19.

FÜGER, WILHELM, 'Der Brief als Bau-Element des Erzählens: Zum Funktionswandel des Einlagebriefes im neueren Roman, dargelegt am Beispiel von Dostojewski, Thomas Mann, Kafka und Joyce', *Deutsche Vierteljahrsschrift für Literaturwissenschaft und Geistesgeschichte*, 51 (1977), 628–58.

GENETTE, GÉRARD, *Seuils* (Paris: Éditions du Seuil, 1987).

Gesetze des NS-Staates, ed. by Ingo von Münch, 3rd edn (Paderborn: Schöningh, 1994).

GILMAN, SANDER L. *Jüdischer Selbsthaß: Antisemitismus und die verborgene Sprache der Juden* (Frankfurt a/M: Jüdischer Verlag, 1993).

GLENN, JERRY, Review of H. G. Adler, *Stimme und Zuruf* [c1980, 94 pages], *World Literature Today: A Literary Quarterly of the University of Oklahoma*, 55 (1981), 464–65.

GÖBEL, HELMUT, 'Eine lange und schwierige Freundschaft: H. G. Adler und Elias Canetti', in *H. G. Adler* (Munich: text+kritik, 2004), pp. 71–85.

GOLDBERG, NAN, 'Story of Survival in "Panorama" Gets Lost in Translation', Boston.com, 29 January 2011 <http://www.boston.com/ae/books/articles/2011/01/29/story_of_survival_in_panorama_gets_lost_in_translation/> [accessed 15 December 2016].

GOOS, CHRISTOPH, 'Würde des Menschen: Restoring Human Dignity in Postwar Germany', in *Understanding Human Dignity: Proceedings of the British Academy 192*, ed. by Christopher McCrudden (Oxford: Oxford University Press, 2013), pp. 79–93.

GRENVILLE, ANTHONY, *Encounters with Albion: Britain and the British in Texts by Jewish Refugees from Nazism* (Cambridge: Legenda, 2018).

——*Jewish Refugees from Germany and Austria in Britain, 1933–1970: Their Image in 'AJR Information'* (London: Mitchell, 2010).

GRUCHMANN, LOTHAR, *Justiz im Dritten Reich: Anpassung und Unterwerfung in der Ära Gürtner*, 3rd edn (Munich: Oldenburg, 2002).

GWYER, KIRSTIN, *Encrypting the Past: The German-Jewish Holocaust Novel of the First Generation* (Oxford: Oxford University Press, 2014).

HAUSHOFER, MARLEN, *Die Wand* (Gütersloh: S. Mohn, 1963).

——*Le mur invisible* (Arles: Actes Sud, 1985).

'H. G. Adler im Gespräch mit Hans Christoph Knebusch: Aufzeichnung der Gespräche im Januar 1986. Erstsendung 11.11.1986', in *Jüdische Lebenswege — Nahum Goldmann, Simon Wiesenthal, H. G. Adler*, ed. by Karl B. Schnelting (Frankfurt a/M: Fischer, 1987), pp. 157–86.

H. G. Adler: Buch der Freunde: Stimmen über den Dichter und Gelehrten mit unveröffentlichter Lyrik, ed. by Willehad P. Eckert and Wilhelm Unger (Cologne: Wienand, 1975).

H. G. Adler: Life, Literature, Legacy, ed. by Julia Creet, Sara R. Horowitz, and Amira Bojadzija-Dan (Evanston, IL: Northwestern University Press, 2016).

H. G. Adler (Text + Kritik 163), ed. by Heinz-Ludwig Arnold (Munich: text+kritik, 2004).

HALBWACHS, MAURICE, *Les cadres sociaux de la mémoire* (Paris: Albin Michel 1994).

HAMBURGER, MICHAEL, 'The Face of Force', *The Jewish Quarterly*, 4.3 (1956/1957), 42.

HAMILTON, PATRICK, *Hangover Square* (London: Constable, 1941).

Handbuch der deutschsprachigen Exilliteratur, ed. by Bettina Bannasch and Gerhild Rochus (Berlin: De Gruyter, 2013).

HEGEL, G. W. F., *Grundlinien der Philosophie des Rechts*, ed. by Michael Holzinger, Berliner Ausgabe, 2013.

HEIDEGGER, MARTIN, *Reden und andere Zeugnisse eines Lebensweges, Gesamtausgabe*, vol. 16 (Frankfurt a/M: Klostermann, 2000).

——*Über den Humanismus* (Frankfurt a/M: Klostermann, 1949).

HEIDELBERGER-LEONARD, IRENE, *Jean Améry: Revolte in der Resignation: Biographie* (Stuttgart: Klett-Cotta, 2004).

HENDEL, RONALD S., 'Adam', in *Eerdmans Dictionary of the Bible*, ed. by David Noel Freedman, Allen C. Myers, and Astrid B. Beck (Grand Rapids, MI: Eerdmans, 2000), pp. 18–19.

HERBERT, ULRICH, *Werner Best: Un nazi de l'ombre (1903–1989)* (Paris: Éditions Tallandier, 2010).

HERMAND, JOST, *Kultur im Wiederaufbau: Die Bundesrepublik Deutschland 1945–1965* (Frankfurt a/M: Ullstein, 1989).

HEYER, RALF, *Verfolgte Zeugen der Wahrheit: Das literarische Schaffen und das politische Wirken konservativer Autoren nach 1945 am Beispiel von Friedrich Georg Jünger, Ernst Jünger, Ernst von Salomon, Stefan Andres und Reinhold Schneider* (Dresden: Thelem, 2008).

HOCHENEDER, FRANZ, *H. G. Adler (1910–1988): Privatgelehrter und freier Schriftsteller* (Vienna: Böhlau, 2009).

VON HODENBERG, CHRISTINA, *Konsens und Krise: Eine Geschichte der westdeutschen Medienöffentlichkeit 1945–1973* (Göttingen: Wallstein, 2006).

HÖLDERLIN, FRIEDRICH, 'Hälfte des Lebens', in *Sämtliche Werke und Briefe*, ed. by Jochen Schmidt (Frankfurt a/M: Deutscher Klassiker Verlag, 1992–94), vol. 1, p. 320.

——'The Middle of Life', in Friedrich Hölderlin, *Poems and Fragments*, ed. and transl. by Michael Hamburger, bilingual edition (Cambridge: Cambridge University Press, 1980), p. 371.

HOFFMANN, CHRISTHARD, 'German-Jewish Encounter and German Historical Culture', *Leo Baeck Institute Year Book*, 41 (1996), 277–90.

——'Historicizing Emancipation: Jewish Historical Culture and *Wissenschaft* in Germany, 1912–1938', in *Modern Judaism and Historical Consciousness: Identities, Encounters, Perspectives*, ed. by Christian Wiese (Leiden: Brill, 2007), pp. 329–55.

——'Zerstörte Geschichte: Zum Werk der jüdischen Historikerin Selma Stern', *Exilforschung*, 11 (1993), 165–73.

HOHOFF, KURT, *Woina, Woina — Russisches Tagebuch* (Düsseldorf: Diederichs, 1951).

HOLZ, KLAUS, 'Theorien des Antisemitismus', in *Handbuch des Antisemitismus: Judenfeindschaft in Geschichte und Gegenwart*, vol. 3, ed. by Wolfgang Benz (Berlin: De Gruyter, 2010), pp. 316–28.

HOROWITZ, SARA R., 'Recovered Gems: Neglect and Recovery of Holocaust Fiction', in *H. G. Adler: Life, Literature, Legacy*, ed. by Julia Creet, Sara R. Horowitz, and Amira Bojadzija-Dan (Evanston, IL: Northwestern University Press, 2016), pp. 89–118.

HUBER, ERNST RUDOLF, *Verfassungsrecht des Großdeutschen Reiches*, 2nd edn (Hamburg: Hanseatische Verlagsanstalt, 1939).

HUENER, JONATHAN, *Auschwitz, Poland, and the Politics of Commemoration, 1945–1979* (Athens, OH: Ohio University Press, 2003).

Intellectuals in Politics from the Dreyfus Affair to Salman Rushdie, ed. by Jeremy Jennings and Anthony Kemp-Welch (Routledge: London, 1997).

JÄGER, MAREN, *Die Joyce-Rezeption der deutschsprachigen Erzählliteratur nach 1945* (Tübingen: Niemeyer, 2009).

JELLINEK, GEORG, *L'État moderne et son droit*, vol. 2 (reprint of the 1913 translation) (Paris: Panthéon-Assas, 2005).

——*Die sozialethische Bedeutung von Recht, Unrecht und Strafe* (Vienna: Hölder, 1878).

——*System der subjektiven öffentlichen Rechte* (reprint of the 2nd edn 1905) (Darmstadt: Wissenschaftliche Buchgesellschaft, 1963).

JOCKUSCH, LAURA, *Collect and Record! Jewish Holocaust Documentation in Early Postwar Europe* (New York: Oxford University Press, 2012).

JOUANJAN, OLIVIER, 'Les droits publics subjectifs et la dialectique de la reconnaissance: Georg Jellinek et la construction juridique de l'État moderne', *Revue d'Allemagne* 46.1, (2014), 51–62.

——*Justifier l'injustifiable: L'ordre du discours juridique nazi* (Paris: PUF, 2017).

JÜNGER, ERNST, *Strahlungen* (Tübingen: Heliopolis Verlag, 1949).

KELSEN, HANS, *Reine Rechtslehre* (2nd edn, 1960, republished by Matthias Jestaedt) (Tübingen: Mohr Siebeck / Vienna: Verlag Österreich, 2017).

KERTÉSZ IMRE, *Fateless*, transl. by Christopher C. Wilson and Katharina M. Wilson (Evanston, IL: Northwestern University Press, 1992).

——*Fatelessness*, transl. by Tim Wilkinson (New York: Vintage International, 2004).

——*Mensch ohne Schicksal*, transl. by Jörg Buschmann (Berlin: Rütten und Loening, 1990).

——*Roman eines Schicksallosen*, transl. by Christina Viragh (Berlin: Rowohlt, 1996).

KIESEWETTER, HUBERT, *Von Hegel zu Hitler: Die politische Verwirklichung einer totalitären Machtstaatstheorie in Deutschland (1815–1945)* (Hamburg: Hoffmann und Campe, 1974).

KIRSCH, JONATHAN, 'Book Review: "Panorama"', *Los Angeles Times*, 10 April 2011 <http://www.latimes.com/books/la-ca-hg-adler-20110410-story.html>[accessed 28 April 2016].

KLEIN, JUDITH, 'Zu ironisch? Zu satirisch? Zu radikal? H. G. Adlers Roman über Verfolger und Verfolgte unter dem Dritten Reich: *Eine Reise*', *Frankfurter Rundschau* (15 May 1999), 4.

KLOPSTOCK, FRIEDRICH GOTTLIEB, 'Von der Sprache der Poesie', in Klopstock, *Ausgewählte Werke*, ed. by Karl August Schleiden, 2 vols, 4th edn (Munich: Hanser 1981), pp. 1016–26.

KLÜGER, RUTH, *Still Alive: A Holocaust Childhood Remembered* (New York: The Feminist Press, 2001).

——*weiter leben* (Göttingen: Wallstein 1992).

KOGON, EUGEN, *Der SS-Staat* (Frankfurt a/M: Verlag der Frankfurter Hefte, 1946).

——*Der SS-Staat: Das System der deutschen Konzentrationslager* (Munich: K. Alber, 1946).

——*The Theory and Practice of Hell: The German Concentration Camps and the Theory behind them* (London: Secker & Warburg, 1950).

KONRÁD, GYÖRGY, 'A Speech at the Opening of the Holocaust Exhibition in Berlin's Historisches Museum', *Kultur Chronik*, 20/2 (2002), 19–21.

KRÄMER, THOMAS, *Die Poetik des Gedenkens: Zu den autobiographischen Romanen H. G. Adlers* (Würzburg: Königshausen & Neumann, 2012).

KRAMER, SVEN, 'Belated Exile in H. G. Adler's Novel *Die unsichtbare Wand*', in *Exile and Otherness: New Approaches to the Experience of the Nazi Refugees*, ed. by Alexander Stephan, Exile Studies: An interdisciplinary series, 11 (Oxford: Lang, 2005), pp. 227–48.

——'Die Politik der Erinnerung in H. G. Adlers Roman *Die unsichtbare Wand*', *Sprache im technischen Zeitalter*, 198 (2011), 220–27.

——'Shaping Survival through Writing: H. G. Adler's Correspondence with Bettina Gross, 1945–1947', in *H. G. Adler: Life, Literature, Legacy*, ed. by Julia Creet, Sara R. Horowitz, and Amira Bojadzija-Dan (Evanston, IL: Northwestern University Press, 2016), pp. 69–85.

——'"Über diesem Abgrund wölben wir unsere Liebe": Die Gegenwart der Toten und der Glückanspruch der Überlebenden in H. G. Adlers Briefwechsel mit Bettina Gross 1945–1946', in *Literatur und Anthropologie: H. G. Adler, Elias Canetti und Franz Baermann Steiner in London*, ed. by Jeremy Adler and Gesa Dane (Göttingen: Wallstein, 2014), pp. 138–57.

KROESCHELL, KARL, *Rechtsgeschichte Deutschlands im 20. Jahrhundert* (Göttingen: Vandenhoeck & Ruprecht, UTB, 1992).

KÜHNER, HANS, 'Hitlers antisemitische Vorläufer', *Deutsche Rundschau* 87 (1961), 375–78.

LaCAPRA, DOMINICK, *Writing History, Writing Trauma* (Baltimore: The Johns Hopkins University Press, 2001).

LANGBEIN, HERMANN, *Menschen in Auschwitz* (Vienna: Europaverlag, 1972).

——*...nicht wie die Schafe zur Schlachtbank: Widerstand in den nationalsozialistischen Konzentrationslagern* (Frankfurt a/M: Fischer, 1980).

LANGE, HEINRICH, *Vom alten zum neuen Schuldrecht* (Hamburg: Hanseatische Verlagsanstalt, 1934).

LANGER, LAWRENCE, 'Holocaust Fact and Holocaust Fiction: The Dual Vision of H. G. Adler', in *H. G. Adler: Life, Literature, Legacy*, ed. by Julia Creet, Sara R. Horowitz, and Amira Bojadzija-Dan (Evanston, IL: Northwestern University Press, 2016), pp. 139–59.

——*Holocaust Testimonies: The Ruins of Memory* (New Haven: Yale University Press, 1991).

LARENZ, KARL, *Deutsche Rechtserneuerung und Rechtsphilosophie* (Tübingen: Mohr Siebeck, 1934).

——'Gemeinschaft und Rechtstellung', *Deutsche Rechtswissenschaft*, I (1936), 31–39.

——*Rechts und Staatsphilosophie der Gegenwart*, 2nd edn (Berlin: Junker & Dünnhaupt, 1935).

LEJEUNE, PHILIPPE, *Le Pacte Autobiographique* (Paris: Éditions du Seuil, 1975).

LEVI, PRIMO, *If this is a Man*, trans. by Stuart Woolf (London: Abacus, 1979).

——'Nickel', in Primo Levi, *The Periodic Table* (London: Abacus, 1985) pp. 61–78.

——*Se questo è un uomo?* [1947] (Torino: Einaudi, 1958).

LEVIN, YUVAL, 'Burke, Paine and the Great Law of Change', <https://thepointmag.com/2011/politics/burke-paine-and-the-great-law-of-change> [accessed 8 March 2016].

LITTELL, FRANKLIN H., 'Review of *The Jews in Germany: From the Enlightenment to National Socialism*, by H. G. Adler', *Journal of Church and State*, 13.3 (1971), 539–41.

LÖHNDORF, MARION, 'Buch der Verwüstung', *Neue Zürcher Zeitung* (30 November 1999), 35.

LOEWY, HANNO, 'Das gerettete Kind: Die 'Universalisierung' der Anne Frank', in *Deutsche Nachkriegsliteratur und der Holocaust*, ed. by Stephan Braese, Holger Gehle, Doron Kiesel, and Hanno Loewy (Frankfurt a/M: Campus, 1998), pp. 19–41.

LOURIE, RICHARD, 'Book Review of "The Journey", by H. G. Adler. Translated by Peter Filkins', *The New York Times*, 9 January 2009 <http://www.nytimes.com/2009/01/11/books/review/Lourie-t.html> [accessed 28 April 2016].

ST. IGNATIUS OF LOYOLA, *The Spiritual Exercises*, transl. by Father Elder Mullan (New York: Kennedy, 1914).

LYND, ROBERT S. and HELEN MERRYL LYND, *Middletown: A Study in American Culture* (London: Constable, 1929).

M., *Zeitschrift für katholische Theologie*, 85 (1963), 103–04.

MAJER, DIETMUT, *Grundlagen des national-sozialistischen Rechtssystems* (Stuttgart: Kohlhammer, 1987).

MALINOWSKI, BRONISLAW, *Argonauts of the Western Pacific: An Account of Native Enterprise and Adventure in the Archipelagos of Melanesian New Guinea* (London: Routledge and Kegan Paul, 1922).

MANDLE, DARA, 'The Long Journey: A Review of The Journey by H. G. Adler', *The New Criterion*, 27.6 (2009), 77.

MENZEL, JULIA, 'Between "Nothing" and "Something": Narratives of Survival in H. G. Adler's Scholarly and Literary Analysis of the Shoah', *Leo Baeck Institute Year Book*, 61.1 (2016), 119–34.

MICHMAN, DAN, 'Shoah, Churbn, Cataclysm, Judeocide, Holocaust, Genocide (and more): On Terminology and Interpretation', 23 October 2014 <https://www.youtube.com/watch?v=vfScF7cxjCs> [accessed 1 April 2018].

MODLINGER, MARTIN, 'The Kafkaesque in H. G. Adler's and W. G. Sebald's Literary Historiographies', in *Witnessing, Memory, Poetics: H. G. Adler and W. G. Sebald*, ed. by Helen Finch and Lynn L. Wolff (Rochester, NY: Camden House, 2014), pp. 201–31.

MÜLLER, LOTHAR, 'Die böse ist nicht banal: H. G. Adlers Buch *Eine Reise*', *Frankfurter Allgemeine Zeitung* (27 November 1999), 9.

Das Nürnberger Gespräch: Haltungen und Fehlhaltungen in Deutschland: Ein Tagungsbericht, ed. by Hermann Glaser (Freiburg: Rombach, 1965), pp. 107–19.

OHDE, HORST, 'Die Magie des Heilen: Naturlyrik nach 1945', in *Literatur in der Bundesrepublik Deutschland bis 1967*, ed. by Ludwig Fischer (Munich: dtv, 1986), pp. 349–56.

Opfer als Akteure: Interventionen ehemaliger NS-Verfolgter in der Nachkriegszeit, edited on behalf of the Fritz Bauer Institute by Katharina Stengel and Werner Konitzer (Frankfurt a/M: Campus Verlag, 2008).

'Ortlose Botschaft': Der Freundeskreis H. G. Adler, Elias Canetti und Franz Baermann Steiner im englischen Exil, ed. by Marcel Atze, Marbacher Magazin 84 (Marbach am Neckar: Deutsche Schillergesellschaft, 1998).

OTTMANN, FRANÇOIS, 'H. G. Adlers *Theresienstadt 1941–1945: Das Antlitz einer Zwangsgemeinschaft*: Ein gattungsübergreifendes Manifest für den Menschen', in *Die ersten Stimmen: Deutschsprachige Texte zur Shoah 1945–1963 / Les premières voix: Écrits sur la Shoah en langue allemande 1945–1963*, ed. by Ruth Vogel-Klein (Würzburg: Königshausen & Neumann, 2010), pp. 113–26.

OZICK, CYNTHIA, '"The Wall," by H. G. Adler', *The New York Times*, 17 December 2014 <http://www.nytimes.com/2014/12/21/books/review/the-wall-by-h-g-adler.html> [accessed 15 March 2016].

PEED, MIKE, 'The Going Gets Tough', Washingtonpost.com, 12 January 2009 <http://www.washingtonpost.com/wp-dyn/content/article/2009/01/12/AR2009011203146.html> [accessed 28 April 2016].

PLATH, JÖRG, 'Wir sind Überlebende', *Tagesspiegel* (25 July 1999), 105.

POUND, ROSCOE, 'Law in Books and Law in Action', *American Law Review*, 44.12 (1910), 12–36.

PULZER, PETER G. J., *Die Entstehung des politischen Antisemitismus in Deutschland und Österreich 1867 bis 1914: Mit einem Forschungsbericht des Autors* (Göttingen: Vandenhoeck & Ruprecht, 2004).

——— *The Rise of Political Anti-Semitism in Germany and Austria* (New York: Wiley, 1964).

Radio-Essay 1955–1981: Verzeichnis der Manuskripte und Tondokumente (Stuttgart: Süddeutscher Rundfunk, 1996).

RAHDEN, TILL VAN, 'Treason, Fate, or Blessing: Narratives of Assimilation in the Histo-riography of German-Speaking Jewry since the 1950s', in *Preserving the Legacy of*

German Jewry: A History of the Leo Baeck Institute 1955–2005, ed. by Christhard Hoffmann (Tübingen: Mohr Siebeck, 2005), pp. 349–73.

REICHEL, PETER, *Vergangenheitsbewältigung in Deutschland: Die Auseinandersetzung mit der NS-Diktatur von 1945 bis heute* (Munich: C. H. Beck, 2001).

REICHMANN, EVA G., *Hostages of Civilization: The Social Sources of National Socialist Anti-Semitism* (London: Gollancz, 1950).

Reisen: Fotos von unterwegs, ed. by Heike Gfrereis (Marbach am Neckar: Deutsche Schillergesellschaft, 2014 [Marbacher Katalog 67]).

REYNOLDS, SUSAN SALTER, 'Discoveries', *Los Angeles Times*, 9 November 2008 <http://articles.latimes.com/2008/nov/09/entertainment/ca-discoveries9> [accessed 28 April 2016].

RICHTER, SANDRA, *Eine Weltgeschichte der deutschsprachigen Literatur* (Munich: Bertelsmann, 2017).

ROBINSON, JACOB, *And the Crooked Shall Be Made Straight: The Eichmann Trial, The Jewish Catastrophe, and Hannah Arendt's Narrative* (New York: Macmillan, 1965).

ROEMER, NILS, 'The Making of a New Discipline: The London LBI and the Writing of the German-Jewish Past', in *Preserving the Legacy of German Jewry: A History of the Leo Baeck Institute 1955–2005*, ed. by Christhard Hoffmann (Tübingen: Mohr Siebeck, 2005), pp. 173–99.

ROSEN, STEVEN M., *Dimensions of Apeiron: A Topological Phenomenology of Space, Time, and Individuation* (Amsterdam: Rodopi, 2004).

ROUSSET, DAVID, *L'Univers concentrationnaire* (Paris: Éditions de Pavois, 1946).

—— *L'Univers concentrationnaire* [1965], préface d'Émile Copfermann, (Paris: Éditions de Minuit, 1993).

—— *A World Apart*, trans. by Yvonne Moyse and Roger Senhouse (London: Secker and Warburg, 1951).

RÜTHERS, BERND, *Die unbegrenzte Auslegung: Zum Wandel der Privatrechtsordnung im Nationalsozialismus*, 7th edn (Tübingen: Mohr Siebeck, 2012).

SABIN, STEFANA, *Die Welt als Exil* (Göttingen: Wallstein, 2008).

SACHS, NELLY, *In den Wohnungen des Todes* (Berlin: Aufbau, 1947).

SAKHAROV, ANDREI D., *Progress, Coexistence and Intellectual Freedom*, ed. by Harrison E. Salisbury (Harmondsworth: Penguin, 1968).

SALOMON, ERNST VON, *Der Fragebogen* (Hamburg: Rowohlt, 1951).

SARTRE, Jean-Paul, *L'Existentialisme et un humanisme* (Paris: Nagel, 1946).

Sayings of the Fathers: Pirke Aboth, the Hebrew Text with English Translation and Commentary by Joseph H. Hertz [1945] (New Jersey: Behrman House, 1986).

SCHILDT, AXEL, *Zwischen Abendland und Amerika: Studien zur westdeutschen Ideenlandschaft der 50er Jahre* (Munich: Oldenbourg, 1999).

SCHILDT, AXEL and DETLEF SIEGFRIED, *Deutsche Kulturgeschichte: Die Bundesrepublik: 1945 bis zur Gegenwart* (Munich: Hanser, 2009).

SCHMITT, CARL, *Über die drei Arten des juristischen Denkens* (Hamburg: Hanseatische Verlagsanstalt, 1934).

SCHNEIDER, KARL LUDWIG, *Klopstock und die Erneuerung der deutschen Dichtersprache im 18. Jahrhundert* (Heidelberg: Winter, 1965).

SCHNELL, RALF, 'Traditionalistische Konzepte', in *Literatur in der Bundesrepublik Deutschland bis 1967*, ed. by Ludwig Fischer (Munich: dtv, 1986), pp. 214–29.

SCHOLEM, GERSHOM, *Briefe* II, 1948–1970, ed. by Thomas Sparr (Munich: C. H. Beck, 1995).

—— *Die jüdische Mystik in ihren Hauptströmungen* (Frankfurt a/M: Alfred Metzner, 1957).

SCHÜTTPELZ, ERHARD, 'Der Auszug aus Ägypten: Zum Vergleich der sozialtheoretischen Schriften von H. G. Adler, Elias Canetti und Franz Baermann Steiner', in *Literatur und*

Anthropologie: H. G. Adler, Elias Canetti und Franz Baermann Steiner, ed. by Jeremy Adler and Gesa Dane (Göttingen: Wallstein, 2014), pp. 158–75.

SCHWEITZER, ALBERT, 'The Problem of Peace', Nobel Lecture, 4 November 1954.

SEIBERT, WOLFGANG, 'Die Volksgemeinschaft im bürgerlichen Recht', in *Nationalsozialistisches Handbuch für Recht und Gesetzgebung*, ed. by Hans Frank, 2nd edn (Munich: Zentralverlag der NSDAP, 1935).

SERKE, JÜRGEN, *Böhmische Dörfer: Wanderungen durch eine verlassene literarische Landschaft* (Vienna: Zsolnay, 1987).

SHEPPARD, RICHARD, 'Book Review: Helen Finch and Lynn L. Wolff (eds), *Witnessing, Memory, Poetics: H. G. Adler and W. G. Sebald'*, *Journal of European Studies*, 45 (2015), 275–77.

SIJE, DAI, *Balzac and the Little Chinese Seamstress* (London: Vintage, 2002).

Das Sonderrecht für die Juden im NS-Staat, ed. by Joseph Walk, 2nd edn (Heidelberg: C. F. Müller, 1996).

SORKIN, DAVID, 'Emancipation and Assimilation: Two Concepts and their Application to German-Jewish History', *Leo Baeck Institute Year Book*, 35 (1990), 17–33.

SPARR, THOMAS, 'Todesfuge', in *Enzyklopädie jüdischer Geschichte und Kultur*, vol. 6, ed. by Dan Diner (Stuttgart: Metzler, 2015), pp. 119–24.

SPEIRS, RONALD and JOHN J. WHITE, 'Hermann Broch and H. G. Adler: The Correspondence of Two Writers in Exile. Translated by Ronald Speirs. Edited with an Introduction by John J. White and Ronald Speirs', *Comparative Criticism: Myth and Mythologies*, 21 (2000), 131–200.

STEINER, FRANZ BAERMANN, *Eroberungen: Ein lyrischer Zyklus*, ed. by H. G. Adler (Heidelberg: L. Schneider, 1964).

——'Taboo', in *Taboo, Truth, and Religion. Selected Writings*, vol. II, ed. by Jeremy Adler and Richard Fardon (Oxford: Berghahn, 1999), pp. 103–214.

——*Unruhe ohne Uhr* (Heidelberg: Lambert Schneider, 1954).

STERLING, ELEONORE, *Er ist wie Du: Aus der Frühgeschichte des Antisemitismus in Deutschland (1815–1850)* (Munich: Chr. Kaiser, 1956).

STOLLEIS, MICHAEL, *Geschichte des öffentlichen Rechts in Deutschland*, vol. 1 (Munich: C. H. Beck, 1988).

——*Geschichte des öffentlichen Rechts in Deutschland*, vol. 3 (Munich: C. H. Beck, 1999).

SWALES, MARTIN, *The German 'Bildungsroman' from Wieland to Hesse* (Princeton, NJ: Princeton University Press, 1978).

THOMAS, GINA, 'Zeuge des Grauens', in *Frankfurter Allgemeine Zeitung*, Nr. 131, (8 June 2016), N3.

UNGER, WILHELM, 'Das andere Deutschland', in *H. G. Adler: Buch der Freunde*, ed. by Willehad P. Eckert and Wilhelm Unger (Cologne: Wienand Verlag, 1975), pp. 14–18.

VOGEL-KLEIN, RUTH, 'Einleitung', *Die ersten Stimmen: Deutschsprachige Texte zur Shoah 1945–1963 / Les premières voix: Écrits sur la Shoah en langue allemande 1945–1963*, ed. by Ruth Vogel-Klein (Würzburg: Königshausen & Neumann, 2010), pp. 7–30.

——'H. G. Adler: Zeugenschaft als Engagement', in Special Issue: H. G. Adler, ed. by Rüdiger Görner and Klaus L. Berghahn, *Monatshefte*, 103.2 (2011), 185–212.

——'"I Have Lost Myself": H. G. Adler's Novel *The Wall* and the Damaged Identity of the Survivor', in *H. G. Adler: Life, Literature, Legacy*, ed. by Julia Creet, Sara R. Horowitz, and Amira Bojadzija-Dan (Evanston, IL: Northwestern University Press, 2016), pp. 229–47.

——'Keine Anklage? Der Deportationsroman 'Eine Reise' (1951–1962): Publikation und Rezeption', in *Die ersten Stimmen. Deutschsprachige Texte zur Shoah 1945–1963*, ed. by Ruth Vogel-Klein (Würzburg: Königshausen & Neumann, 2010), pp. 79–111

VOIGTS, MANFRED, *Jüdische Geistesarbeit und andere Aufsätze über Jacob Franck bis H. G. Adler* (Würzburg: Königshausen & Neumann, 2016).

WACHSMANN, NIKOLAUS, *KL: A History of the Nazi Concentration Camps* (New York: Farrar, Straus and Giroux, 2015).

WEBER, MAX, *Sociologie du droit* (Paris: PUF, 1986).

WEHDEKING, VOLKER, *Anfänge westdeutscher Nachkriegsliteratur, Aufsätze, Interviews, Materialien* (Aachen: Alano, 1989).

WEISS, PETER, *Die Ermittlung: Oratorium in 11 Gesängen* (Frankfurt a/M: Suhrkamp, 1965).

——*The Investigation: A Play*, transl. by Jon Swan and Ulu Grosbard (London: Pocket Books, 1967).

WELTSCH, ROBERT, 'Einleitung', in *Deutsches Judentum: Aufstieg und Krise: Gestalten, Ideen, Werke* (Stuttgart: Deutsche Verlags-Anstalt, 1963), pp. 7–24.

WHITE, HAYDEN, 'Historical Discourse and Literary Theory: On Saul Friedländer's *Years of Extermination*', in *Den Holocaust erzählen: Historiographie zwischen wissenschaftlicher Empirie und narrativer Kreativität*, ed. by Norbert Frei and Wulf Kansteiner (Göttingen: Wallstein, 2013), pp. 51–78.

——'Historical Truth, Estrangement, and Disbelief', in *Confronting the Burden of History: Literary Representations of the Past*, ed. by Izabela Curyllo-Klag and Bozena Kucala (Krakow, Poland: Universitas, 2013), pp. 15–42.

——'The Modernist Event', in *The Persistence of History: Cinema, Television, and the Modern Event*, ed. by Vivian Carol Sobchack (New York: Routledge, 1996), pp. 17–32.

WHITE, ANN and JOHN J., ' "Die Vermächtnisse von Schloß Launceston": Darstellung und Überwindung des Bösen in Hans Günther Adlers Roman *Panorama*', in *Zu Hause im Exil: Zu Werk und Person H. G. Adlers*, ed. by Heinrich Hubmann and Alfred O. Lanz (Stuttgart: Steiner, 1987), pp. 32–43.

WHITE, JOHN J., ' "Zum Humoristen Geboren": Irony and Black Humour in H. G. Adler's Novel *Eine Reise*', in *Mnemosyne Träume: Festschrift zum 80. Geburtstag von Joseph P. Strelka*, ed. by Ilona Slawinski (Tübingen: Francke, 2007), pp. 511–27.

WIEACKER, FRANZ, *Wandlungen der Eigentumsverfassung* (Hamburg: Hanseatische Verlags-anstalt, 1935).

WIEGENSTEIN, ROLAND H., 'Drei KZ-Romane', *Die Neue Rundschau*, 74 (1963), 662.

——'Radio-Reminiszenzen', in *Zu Hause im Exil: Zu Werk und Person H. G. Adlers*, ed. by Heinrich Hubmann and Alfred O. Lanz (Stuttgart: Steiner, 1987), pp. 165–67.

WIESEL ELIE, *La nuit* (Paris: Les Éditions de Minuit, 1958).

WINDSCHEID, BERNHARD, *Lehrbuch des Pandektenrechts*, vol. 1, 9th edn, ed. by Theodor Kipp (Frankfurt a/M: Rütten & Loening, 1906).

Witnessing, Memory, Poetics: H. G. Adler and W. G. Sebald, ed. by Helen Finch and Lynn L. Wolff (Rochester, NY: Camden House, 2014).

WOLFF, LYNN L., ' "Die Grenzen des Sagbaren": Toward a Political Philology in H. G. Adler's Reflections on Language', in *H. G. Adler: Life, Literature, Legacy*, ed. by Creet, Horowitz, and Bojadzija-Dan (Evanston, IL: Northwestern University Press, 2016), pp. 273–301.

——'H. G. Adler and W. G. Sebald: From History and Literature to Literary Historiography', Special Issue: H. G. Adler, ed. by Rüdiger Görner and Klaus L. Berghahn, *Monatshefte*, 103.2 (2011), 257–75.

Yale Companion to Jewish Writing and Thought in German Culture, 1096–1996, ed. by Sander L. Gilman and Jack Zipes (New Haven: Yale University Press, 1997).

YOUNG, JAMES E., *Writing and Rewriting the Holocaust: Narrative and the Consequences of Interpretation* (Bloomington, IN: Indiana University Press, 1988).

Zeugen der Vergangenheit: H. G. Adler — Franz Baermann Steiner, Briefwechsel 1936–1952, ed. by Carol Tully (Munich: Iudicium, 2011).

Zivilisationsbruch: Denken nach Auschwitz, ed. by Dan Diner, trans. by Susanne Hoppmann-Löwenthal (Frankfurt a/M: Fischer, 1988).

Zu Hause im Exil: Zu Werk und Person H. G. Adlers, ed. by Heinrich Hubmann and Alfred
O. Lanz (Stuttgart: Steiner Verlag, 1987).

ZUCKMAYER, CARL, *Als wär's ein Stück von mir: Erinnerungen* (Frankfurt a/M: Fischer,
1969).

INDEX OF NAMES

❖

INDEX OF SUBJECTS

❖

www.ingramcontent.com/pod-product-compliance
Lightning Source LLC
Chambersburg PA
CBHW080541090426
42734CB00016B/3172